TELLING A GO

TELLING
A GOOD ONE

The Process of a Native American
Collaborative Biography

By Theodore Rios
and Kathleen Mullen Sands

·

University of Nebraska Press
Lincoln and London

© 2000 by the University of Nebraska Press
All rights reserved. Manufactured in the United States of America
Library of Congress Cataloging in Publication Data
Rios, Theodore.
Telling a good one: the process of a Native American collaborative biography /
Theodore Rios and Kathleen Mullen Sands.
p. cm. Includes bibliographical references and index.
ISBN 0-8032-4265-4 (cloth : alk. paper) – ISBN 0-8032-9281-3 (pbk. : alk. paper)
1. Autobiography – Authorship 2. Biography as a literary form. 3. Authorship –
Collaboration. 4. Rios, Theodore. 5. Sands, Kathleen M., 1954–6.
6. Tohono O'Odham Indians – Biography. 7. Arizona – Biography.
I. Sands, Kathleen M., 1954– II. Title.
CT25 .R56 2000 808'.06692–dc21
00-029920

In memory of THEODORE RIOS
For Nina Marlene
and Johannes Raymond

.

CONTENTS

ILLUSTRATIONS

ૐ

PREFACE

This volume is a quarter century overdue. And it may well be a quarter century premature, though I believe there are reasons that make this the right time to present Theodore Rios's life story in book form. *Telling a Good One* is an experiment that makes no claim to solve the complex problems of presenting a collaborative Native American life story. Rather, its intention is to focus on the very problematic nature of that paradoxical concept of what is currently called collaborative autobiography. This study examines the process of collaboration and the engagement of Native American narrator and non-Native collector-editor in the production of a life story. Thus the co-authorship of this volume. While the making of this book in its present form is my work, there would be no book, would never have been a narrative text, had Theodore Rios not recorded his life in his own words. It is Ted's narrative and his life experiences and style of telling that are central to this study. His name as co-author is not a courtesy or an honorific but simply his due as an essential partner in the project. And in some measure I hope the co-authorship of this volume is a corrective to the scores of Native American collaborative autobiographies that bear the name of the collector-editor as sole author.

This book testifies to a non–Native American collaborator's fallibility. By fallibility I mean that what follows is a record of a project that I did not, and in many ways could not, complete as the conventional personal narrative of a Native American that Ted and I envisioned when we began our work together. It has been a project that over time has made me increasingly and uncomfortably aware of the difficulty and ethical ambiguity of undertaking to represent the life of another human being. By using the term fallibility, I do not mean to offer some sort of a solipsistic *mea culpa* for the literary colonization of Native American peoples' lives. The colonial nature of the collaborative Native American autobiography has already been well documented. I wish, in fact, to argue against the interpretation of the collaborative effort as necessarily a mode of dominance or victimization of the Native collaborator. In the case of Ted Rios, it would be naive to think that I was the first non-Indian with whom he had interacted. His range of experience with the dominant society and individuals in it was wide and varied, as is evidenced in his narrative. And while many aspects of his life demonstrate the oppressive nature of the dominant society on his life, he was more than capable of negotiating literary collaboration for his own purposes, as parts of this volume will show. In fact, he was already experienced in collaborative life story before we began our work together.

What I hope this volume presents is an honest, in fact intimate and vulnerable disclosure of the interactions, words, emotional and intellectual decisions, and the political realities that shape the bringing to publication of a particular Native American life. Every step in the process is treacherous both intellectually and ethically. Each interaction with the narrator and subsequent handling of the words he or she produces presents a chance for error in representation and interpretation. Yet without the collaboration between Native American narrator and (usually) non-Native collector-editor, a life story remains private even where there is a desire on the part of the narrator to reach an audience both within and outside the Native American community. So collaborators have taken and continue to take the risks entailed in telling "a good one," hoping fallibility will not outweigh good intentions and skills.

There are multiple layers of narration and interpretation in the following chapters that I hope demonstrate the provisional nature of meaning in a life — or lives — constructed of language. What follows incorporates numerous and various narrative and analytical sources and strategies that I hope engage one another and, by creating highly discomforting levels of self-consciousness — not Ted Rios's but mine and yours as reader — heighten our understanding of the process that transforms Native American oral narration into an inscribed text. Above all, I hope this study helps to reveal to us why we find this form of inscription intellectually and ethically disturbing — and inadequate.

The project that is described and analyzed in this book has absorbed and haunted me in varying degrees over the past twenty-five years. Initially, Ted and I intended to produce a conventional "as told to" narrative of his life as a Tohono O'odham man born in the first quarter of the twentieth century and coming to maturity in a culture and time intensely influenced by assimilation policies and the pervasiveness of dominant American culture. Ted did his part to fulfill that purpose in responding to my questions by narrating the incidents of his life that he remembered and thought would provide the stuff of a life story. And I attempted to fulfill my part of our intention by editing his narrative and putting it in the chronological order conventional in previously published Native American autobiographies. My attempt was a failure. Ted's style of narration thwarted my notions of a comprehensive and linear autobiography. Did he consciously resist conventional Euro-American conventions of autobiography? I don't think so. He simply told his life in response to my rather ineptly framed questions in a way that suited his idea of his own experience. What I thought at the time of our interview sessions in 1974 was a collaborative effort was, in retrospect, an act of narrative resistance on the part of Ted. Not an active form of resistance but simply a way of conceiving and narrating experience on Ted's part that had little to do with the generic concept of autobiography I brought to the project and everything to do with his cultural idea of life story. The cross-cultural collaboration so naively conceived by me when we undertook the project was, in fact, far more complex that I could begin to understand when I began trying to force his narrative into my preconceived notions of Native American autobiography.

Frustrated, I set the transcripts of his narrative — including the clip-

pings of anecdotes I had grouped under various conventional chronological headings—aside, thinking that there really wasn't enough sustained substance in his style of narration to produce a fully fleshed-out
autobiography. Maybe I could make it work, I thought, by doing more
interviews with Ted, by interviewing people who knew him, by incorporating biographical data gleaned from tribal records. But I didn't
do further interviews or research. Though I picked up the "Rios files"
time after time, tinkered with them, even made an outline that would
allow me to fill in gaps and clarify ambiguities, I lost faith in the idea of
producing the book we had mutually agreed upon. I simply couldn't
work with Ted's narrative on its own terms. Equally importantly, the
more I read of and about Native American autobiographies, the more
paralyzed I became about the ethics of even presuming to produce a
collaborative book. At the same time, I knew I was letting Ted down;
he was counting on me to hold up my end of our agreement. The dilemma was both intellectual and emotional. On one hand, I doubted
the ethics of producing a conventional Native American autobiography—and still do for that matter. On the other, I had a moral responsibility to Ted to do just that.

If this sounds like a weak *apologia* for my delay in addressing Ted's
narrative, I suppose it is. I'd really like to place the blame for my failure to produce a timely book anywhere but on myself or, failing that,
make it into a strictly intellectual issue. I can't, and I recognize that
very keenly. But the confessional form has its limits. To make something of value from the project Ted and I began together, perhaps the
best I can do is offer some analysis of the factors that in hindsight
I think contributed to my delay in producing a book from Ted's life
story. One is that it has taken me literally two decades to achieve a
level of scholarly maturity that I did not even know existed when we
began the project. Whatever competency this volume exhibits is primarily the result of access to a significantly higher level of sophistica-
tion in the scholarship produced by critics of autobiography and particularly Native American autobiography that began in the 1980s and

exploded in the 1990s with the application of postmodern, postcolonial, and ethnographic theories. Of equal or perhaps more importance has been the crisis in ethnographic theory that has opened up new forms of inscription of field research.

For the project as Ted and I conceived it, the mid-1970s were out of joint. Our project was too late to fit into the "personality and culture" form of personal narrative of the previous four decades and too early to find a form that would accommodate his style of telling. Perhaps now the time is right for a volume that presents a collage of Ted's personal narratives—he narrated his life several times to me and to other immediate audiences—against a background of my recollections of our collaboration and in the context of other Tohono O'odham and Native American life stories as well as current literary and anthropological theory.

My deepest regret is that this book comes too late for Ted, who did not live to see its completion. I believe Ted genuinely enjoyed remembering and narrating his life. He liked to talk, enjoyed attention, and through his role as narrator achieved some recognition both in his own community and in the local academic community. He would have liked to have held this book in his hand and to have shown it to people. It's easy to be sentimental about Ted. In fact, it's a convention of the genre to wax nostalgic about the Native American partner in a collaborative autobiography. It's much harder to admit that I failed him in a very personal way. This book cannot compensate for that specific failure, but I do hope that it honors Ted. He deserved and deserves more and better.

The ensuing study might best be described as a series of interconnected essays focused on Ted Rios's narrative from multiple angles and in various voices. Consistent throughout is Ted's voice. It is his language and experience that give the following chapters their authority, though it is my voice that dominates throughout much of this book. Ted is the central character in his own life. We are both characters in the description and analysis of our collaboration. Mine is the dominant voice in the self-reflexive narratives and interpretations. And in some instances the voice is impersonal and disembodied, a counterpoint to the narrative selves of the collaboration. The claim to authority for any voice is, of course, dubious, and in the case of collaboration undesirable. Instead, I hope the interaction of voices — and silences where memory and words fail — disperses authority and creates a dialogue in which the reader is an active participant in attempting to comprehend the interactions that produce a cross-cultural collaborative personal narrative.

What follows is a book about the process of collaborative "autobiography." However, it is not simply a case study. It addresses not only Ted's narrative but many Native American collaborative autobiographies in the hope that some general principles of critical methodology can be derived from examining a range of ways of inscribing Native American lives. The methodology of the book itself is self-reflexive, using mixed forms that might best be described as somewhere between literary criticism and narrative ethnography. It began with a prospectus, but the actual writing is experimental. The book in fact begins here, with the preface. Not that I won't come back to tinker with and revise this piece; no book, least of all a scholarly study, is genuinely spontaneous. That is one of the major themes of the chapters that follow. But I want the reader to know that the shaping of this book begins at the beginning and intends to reveal its methodology as it progresses. So here goes.

ACKNOWLEDGMENTS

For Theodore Rios telling "a good one" was easy. As he says at the end of a videotaped interview in 1975, "I could go on talking all day." For me, telling "a good one" about the collaboration between Ted and I has not been easy. The process of the transformation from oral interviews to this book could not have come about without the support of a great many people who helped me initiate it and work through it.

I owe a great deal to anthropologist Dr. Bernard Fontana, who, when I was a doctoral student in literary studies, accommodated my interest in Native American life stories by directing me to the Doris Duke Collection at the University of Arizona. When I expressed particular interest in a series of interviews with O'odham men and women housed in the collection, and especially in the transcripts of a series of interviews conducted with Theodore Rios, he immediately encouraged me to work directly with Ted and took me to meet him. Fontana set me off on my first experience of fieldwork, a method of research that has served me well. This book honors his kindness to and faith in me when there was little to warrant it.

To Larry Evers I owe a debt for his encouragement of this project from inception to publication, and for making Ted the subject of a trial run for his fine video series, *Words and Place*. The tape has provided me not only with variants of stories Ted told on audiotape but gave Ted a great deal of pleasure and a modicum of recognition. Ted was also very pleased that his story "The Magic Egg," taken from our audiotaped interviews, was published in *The South Corner of Time*, which Evers edited in 1981.

Several institutions also deserve recognition. To the Newberry

Library, I am grateful for a 1997 summer fellowship for research on Tohono O'odham culture and for the opportunity to present the history and intention of this project in a seminar there. To the participants of the conference on "Theories of Representation in American Indian Literatures," sponsored by the University of California at Santa Barbara and held at Château de la Bretesche, France, in 1997, my thanks for encouragement and suggestions for completing this book.

To the Arizona State University College of Liberal Arts and Sciences, my gratitude for a summer travel grant to complete library research, and to the English Department, which granted me travel funds to complete field research. Without the support of my departmental colleagues and the college, I would not have been able to take the sabbatical leave that has allowed me to complete this project.

The Arizona Historical Society and the staff of its Tucson library deserve thanks for making the Peter Blaine transcripts and audiotapes available for my use and for permission to use photographs from their archives. Photo permissions from the Arizona Historical Foundation are also appreciated.

A number of other individuals also merit recognition. Thanks to Timothy Dunnigan for permission to quote from transcripts of his interviews with Ted and for his interest in the project.

To Margaret Blackman and Julie Cruikshank, whom I admire greatly for the quality of their contributions to the field of Native American life story, appreciation for such careful consideration of my book proposal and for suggestions that have strengthened this work.

To John Purdy, who read drafts of the manuscript, made helpful suggestions, and gave encouragement when my confidence and resolve flagged, my appreciation. To Don Bahr, who helped me work through ideas and challenged me to face difficult decisions head on, many thanks. And to LaVonne Ruoff who has been a generous listener and advisor along the way, many thanks.

A very sincere thanks to Consuela Mendoza, archivist at Mission

San Xavier del Bac, for her help in verifying Rios family marriage, baptismal, and funeral data.

And, ultimately, my friends and family deserve recognition for their patience and support, and my granddaughter, Nina, and my grandson, Johannes, for keeping me grounded.

TELLING A GOOD ONE

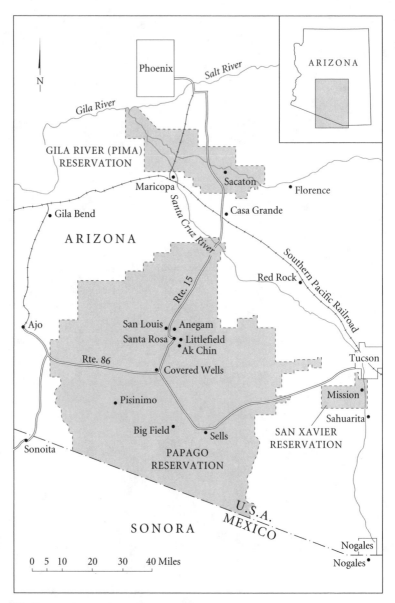

The Papago Reservation and surrounding area

INTRODUCTION

Theodore Rios, a member of the Tohono O'odham[1] nation and resident of the San Xavier del Bac District southwest of Tucson, Arizona, expected his autobiography to begin:

> I was born October first, 1915. Jose Rios was my grandfather, and I think he was from San Xavier. No idea where he was born. 'Course, I was just a little tot when he died, as far as I can remember — little. Oh, he farms, and then he represents San Xavier. He went to Washington. He was tribal chairman.[2] 'Course at that time they don't have many officers. Just maybe one or two for the whole reservation, San Xavier. So he's got to go to Washington. You know, he went once. They settle disputes for the lands and all that. I don't think he was educated. Maybe he understands English, but he speaks Spanish. Tucson was hardly settled at the time, you know. My grandmother was younger, so I saw her more. Her name was Agnes. She looked just like an ordinary old lady. They call my mother's father Arnito Williams.[3] He's from Santa Rosa, but he moved from there and settled down at San Xavier. Moved around a lot before that. He was in cattle business, a rancher. I lived with him sometimes. He was close by, close. I was pretty old — about eight or something — when he died. My grandmother was called Martina. She was from Santa Rosa too. She died not too long ago; I don't know when, but she claims she's real close to ninety. She lived at San Xavier, so I saw her all the time because I was around most of the time.
>
> My father was Frank Rios. He was pretty old, about seventy-two, I think, when he died. He's a farmer, rancher. He went to school at Santa Fe. He went to Washington too. He represented most of the tribe, the whole reservation and San Xavier. My

mother's name was Anselma. She had one brother, I know, my Uncle William. He's her younger brother. He died. My father had a sister and a brother, Sally and Juan, both younger. Both are dead now. Sally had children, but they're all dead too. Josephina was my stepmother. She died after the war. She and my father have children — Rosanna, Jacob, and Wilfred. He died. I have brothers and sisters from my mother too, but only one living, Lena. We're the only ones. She lives at San Xavier too, widowed. I had brothers and a sister, but they're all gone — Juan, George, Marciana.

I was prematurely born at home at San Xavier. They didn't think I'd live at the time, they say. I was baptized very young. Just one name was given to me at the church.

Most often I used to spend time with my grandfather up at the ranch, my mother's father. Usually we worked the cattle, milking cows and making cheese and all that. The house was mud, adobe, an adobe house. [See photo 1.] One was used for the kitchen and of course, they had two or three for the barn. They keep everything there like saddles, and there was an ocotillo[4] fence around where they keep the wagons, buggies, and even chickens. 'Course it was quite a ways from San Xavier, southwest of it about twelve miles, at the foot of a hill. Sierra Blanca they call it. Well, they take me out there — wagon or horseback. Summer days I stayed there because there was always day school other times. I like both places.

The food we're eating, it's mostly like the Mexicans', cooking the same thing — chile, beans, whatever. Of course, at the time, the older people they know much more about these fruits you get out of that cactus, the prickly pear and the saguaros. They could gather them when they're ripe, mix it so, make jam out of it. 'Course there's a certain time when they come out, a certain season. And they gather it. The saguaros, they had up in the mountains. They camp up there and when they get enough syrups and jams, well, they make all kinds. Of course, at the time, that olden people know how. Now they don't. (edited tape 1: 1–3)

Ted did not begin telling his life story as it appears above.[5] This excerpt from Ted's narration is edited. Though the material comes from the first taped interview we did, the format has been changed.[6] Questions have been removed, some sentences reordered, and deletions of repetitions have been made. This version reads like the beginning of a conventional autobiography because the dialogic nature of the collaborative methodology has been suppressed. But this is, in fact, what Ted expected to go into print—a continuous narrative that I would order and edit from the interviews we did.

What's disturbing about this assumption is not that it is Ted's but that it is what readers of personal narrative expect because that is how the genre is defined—a comprehensive and continuous narrative in chronological order. We expect a personal narrative "to present a unified life through anecdotes that reveal this unity while, at the same time, demonstrating change and growth." As L. L. Langness and Geyla Frank explain, "Westerners make a story out of a life, telling it chronologically from early childhood on, ferreting out the subject's own feelings and interpretations of events, and centering it around a moral paradigm of cause and effect" (1981: 101). But genres are institutional designations for literary forms as constituted by Euro-Americans. Despite that fact, they have dominated the construction of Native American literature as well. Unfortunately, the genre of autobiography has not served the inscribing or study of Native American collaborative autobiography at all well. Precisely because of the collaborative nature of Native American orally narrated life story, forcing it into a Euro-American literary genre wrests the narrative out of the cross-cultural process from which it has been generated. Process, not genre, characterizes Native American collaborative auto-bio-graphy. As Geyla Frank notes, it is a process "that blends together the consciousness of the investigator and the subject, perhaps to the point where it is not possible to disentangle them" (1979: 85). Native American collaborative personal narrative is neither written nor autonomously produced. What's left of the term auto-bio-graphy, then is "bio." It does present a life story, but its methods are antithetical to the Euro-American understanding of autobiography, even if many of the Native life stories in print take the form of the literary genre as it is generally understood in the dominant society. A more accurate term for the process of collaboration between Native narrator and the collector-editor would be collaborative biography. Analysis of the Rios-Sands methodology and intentions supports the use of this term rather than autobiography.

In the course of this volume I intend to demonstrate that preserving and exposing the process of collaborative work that goes into the recording and publication of Native American life story offers the possibility of developing a critical methodology better suited to understanding the inscribing of Native American voices talking about their lives than even the most rigorous application of theories of Euro-American autobiography. The opportunity to examine the process of collaboration and text-making that comes of it is unfortunately seldom available. Even rarer are publications of field projects which fail. As Hein Streefkerk notes, "Research that fails is seldom worthy of publication and such reports are therefore unlikely to come to the reader's attention" (1993: 16). But a record of the collaboration Ted and I engaged in — by institutional standards a failure in field research and literary inscription — does exist, albeit a bit frayed and dimmed by the passage of time. Nonetheless, between fieldnotes, tapes, videotapes, transcripts, and memory, there is a substantial body of data that documents the process of inscribing Ted Rios's Native American life story.

So let's retrace the process of collaboration and inscription that produced the first paragraph of Ted's narrative. This too is a story, albeit episodic and limited to a specific relationship and goal and supported by only meager documentation and memory blurred by intervening years. It begins with Ted, struck by a car in South Tucson, injured badly enough to be hospitalized for many weeks in Sells, the headquarters of the Tohono O'odham tribe, isolated from family and friends and generally bored.[7]

Meanwhile, seventy miles away in Tucson, a student has completed reading several lengthy interviews with Papago individuals, one of whom is Theodore Rios.[8] She's taken with his narrative for—in hindsight—all the wrong reasons. To her, a doctoral student in literature embarking on ethnographic training, Rios represents a "typical" male Papago severely affected by the "breakdown" in traditional Papago culture, a man "caught between two worlds." The "she" is obviously me, but it's hard to face up to and admit publicly how stereotyped my responses were and how ignorant I was. It is so much easier to keep at least some rhetorical distance. At least she was also taken with the voice of the narrator, a rhythm and phrasing that was distinctive and vivid, and she admired his capacity to relate a lively anecdote.

Reading Papago life histories had been undertaken as part of an independent study under the guidance of Dr. Bernard Fontana of the University of Arizona Department of Anthropology. He had directed me to the Doris Duke collection of Native American life histories archived in the Arizona State Museum on the university campus. When we met to talk about my reading, I probably expressed my enthusiasm for Ted's narrative style—memory is fuzzy here about just what might have been said. He suggested that I meet Ted. As it turned out, Fontana and Rios were acquainted, and Fontana knew Ted was laid up with multiple fractures and time on his hands.[9] Fontana thought it would be a fine project to do another series of interviews with Rios that, with my training in literature, I could turn into a edited and polished Native American autobiography, maybe a dissertation.[10] He even offered to take me out to Sells to meet Rios. Who could resist? Certainly not that graduate student with romantic notions of what anthropologists did—and absolutely no training or experience in fieldwork and limited reading background in Papago culture and language.[11]

So to Sells we went, me with little more than curiosity and interest as tools for beginning fieldwork, and Fontana with a great deal more confidence in me than I deserved. I remember the trip and the first encounter vividly but very inaccurately. In my memory, I have no recollection of Fontana in the car. Surely we must have talked about something in the hour and more it took to get to the tribal hospital. I imagine that I drove; actually he did. I remember the desert, the isolation on the highway with only a rare oncoming car, the spring-blooming yellow of mesquite trees and the lavender blossoms on ironwood trees, and, most of all, the cattle guard at the entrance to the hospital and the fear that vibrated through me as the car crossed over it. I have very little recollection of the rest of that day, but fortunately I have a record. Whether my notes are any more reliable than the images that stick in my memory is, of course, debatable. But at least they contain more detail.

When I go back to read my fieldnotes, made the evening after returning from my introduction to and first conversation with Ted, I'm amazed by what they include and by what they omit. Here they are:

April 29, 1974
We drove out at mid-morning from Tucson, through the spring desert to the central Papago reservation community of Sells, Arizona. I was grateful for Dr. Fontana's company on this first visit to Theodore Rios. It was through him that I had been introduced to the biography project, and his support and enthusiasm offset my apprehension about meeting Rios, a man I know intimately from the Dunnigan-taped interviews but had never met personally. How he responded to my request to pursue the interviewing with the publication of his autobiography as the purpose hinged on his response to me personally as well as professionally, and I was nervous. I needn't have been. The halls of the Sells hospital smelled like the halls of every medical institution. We were told Ted was sitting outside in the sunshine, but instead found him in room 69 of the one-story building, sitting quietly in a wheelchair beside his bed. The image I had formed from reading the transcripts of the Dunnigan tapes was of a more robust man than I met. My first impression was of his dark, lined face, reposed and unsurprised by our visit, and of the thick iron-gray hair swept directly back from his face. Despite the casts on both legs he did not look

pained or uncomfortable, his slender arms resting lightly on the blue and white hospital robe that covered his lap. [See photo 2.]

Dr. Fontana introduced me to Ted and explained my interest in working with him to produce interviews that would be the basis for a book about him. Ted made no comment. Instead, he and Dr. Fontana spoke briefly about mutual friends, and then I explained to him that I would like to begin interviews soon. When he asked where we should start, he answered the question by suggesting that we begin at the beginning, anticipating my own wish. Though he showed no overt enthusiasm, he seemed pleased with my interest in him and that I had read the interviews he had done with Dunnigan, and assured me that he would be glad to begin, his only reservation being uncertainty about the length of his treatment and hospitalization.

He went on to tell us that Sunday had been an unpleasant day for him because he had been confined to his bed and was anticipating a visit from his son Michael, who had been unable to come. Though the room was pleasant and the window looked out on a fruitless mulberry tree, his morning sitting outside had obviously pleased him and relieved some of his boredom.

Ted shared the room with an old acquaintance, also from San Xavier, Marcellino Barcelo, an elderly man lying motionless and apparently unconscious on the bed next to his. Though he [Ted] did not say so directly, the man seemed near death. Rios's comment on the man brought him to another friend whose death related to his own accident and confinement to the wheelchair. Just one week before Rios himself was struck by a car in South Tucson, his friend, Jose Ignacio was hit at the same place. Ignacio never regained consciousness and died five days later. Rios told us his death was on his mind when he himself was hit, leaving him in a coma for a time and breaking five ribs, both his legs, and causing liver damage. The relationship of the two events was strongly implied though not directly articulated. Maybe coming

7

so close to dying made him interested in making his life into an autobiography.

He expressed impatience with his confinement and a desire to be home again so he could plant squash and pumpkins, "because people were asking him to."

We left after about an hour of conversation. I felt encouraged by the ease of his stories and the subtle humor he revealed in our conversations. We left him sitting as we had found him, the stark white of his hospital gown accenting the dark wiry form of his body, at ease despite the casts and discomforts of surgery and injury.

Why this initial encounter was not tape recorded, I don't recall. It should have been, but perhaps we all thought of it as a preliminary meeting, not part of a field project. Had I been more experienced at the time—or had the benefit of current ethnographic theory—surely I would have recognized that this initial dialogue as being every bit as important as any of the interviews that would follow. Not only did I not tape this meeting, I have no evidence that I took any notes during the encounter, so the above field record is likely tainted by faulty and/or selective memory.

Without what anthropologists currently refer to as "headnotes"— recollections documented in either "scratch notes," fragmented jottings made on site, or formal fieldnotes (Sanjek 1990: 92–100) typed up from the previous two after the encounter—I now have no recollection of the topics discussed that day in Ted's hospital room. The above fieldnote entry is all I have to go on. I wish I could go back and ask Ted what he remembered and what his impressions were, but I never did that. Maybe not discussing our personal reactions to one another is not surprising since, at the time Ted and I did our work together, interpretation of field experience was a one-way process, with no consideration for the input of the Native American individual. And even now, I'm not at all sure Ted would have thought it appropriate to express his views on the experience.

Left with the fieldnotes cited above, I can only speculate that he probably thought that being interviewed by me would be a reprise of the methods he had engaged in during his interviews with anthropologist Timothy Dunnigan in 1969. I would ask questions and he would supply answers, but this time the interviews would somehow be transformed into a book.

What the notes do reveal is that Ted was not reluctant to talk about his experiences or his current circumstances and through them make connections between himself and other members of his community. They also suggest that he was at ease with the interview process and accepted Dr. Fontana's presence as tacit assurance that I was capable of conducting interviews and making them into a life story. In time, though he never voiced this to me, he must have been disappointed that I did not produce the book he expected.

The most distressing omission from the above fieldnotes is the lack of any specific discussion of how the project was presented to Ted, or even who presented it. From the notes, it's obvious that Dr. Fontana introduced me in terms of the project I hoped to pursue with Ted, perhaps as a reprise of a telephone conversation they may have had about my interest in working with Ted, though I don't recall whether such an event actually took place and maybe never knew in the first place. What's absent are any mention of details of how the project was to be accomplished. In retrospect, what's glaringly present is the term "biography." It suggests that even on first meeting my notion of an autobiography project was faulty, and I was unconsciously moving toward redesignating the inscription that would result from the interviews. Also, Ted's lack of verbal response is puzzling and opaque. Did he perhaps nod his understanding of what was wanted? Did he indicate agreement by a facial expression? I have no recollection. The statement in the notes that I explained I would like to begin the interviews soon suggests his assent to the project, but there is a gap in the notes exactly where they should contain the most detail. Given that gaining Ted's agreement to be interviewed for a book was the purpose of the trip, the absence of a description of that negotiation is strange and, in retrospect, unfortunate. The omission suggests that both Ted and I already had assumptions about what the encounter would produce. We each had conceptions of our own and of the other's roles in a collaborative endeavor. So while our general life experiences were cultures, generations, and genders apart, his experience with a previous interviewer and my study of standard ethnographic and literary procedures created a meeting point and a tone of reserved cooperation from which the project could be undertaken. In retrospect, I think Ted really did know what he was agreeing to and how he intended to narrate and that he acted consistently on that idea throughout the project. Equally clear is that I had very little idea of what I was getting into or how the project goal would be accomplished. I had models for interviewing in the Duke Collection transcripts but no models for transforming interviews into a life-story text. And I really had no idea how the commitment to Ted to produce a book from his narration would gnaw at me over the years.

Haphazard as the encounter was, agreement clearly was made to undertake the interviews because we began them seventeen days later. Somewhere during that period I drew up a letter of intent for both of us to sign at our first taping session. What follows is a written contract Ted and I signed before the interview began:

May 16, 1974
In the event of publication of the autobiography of Theodore Rios as told to Kathleen M. Sands, the above parties will share equally in publication credits and royalties from the book.[12]

Mr. Rios will have the right to advise changes or deletions in the completed manuscript of the taped interviews upon which the completed autobiography will be based. The original tapes and typescript will be turned over to the Arizona State Museum for use by scholars with a valid interest in the information they contain.[13]

Mrs. Sands reserves the right to edit the information gained during the interviews into publishable form and to preface the material with an original introduction.[14]

It is also agreed that the completed autobiography may be submitted to the Department of English at the University of Arizona to meet requirements of Mrs. Sands's doctoral degree, either prior to or after publication in book form.

Since some use of the taped interviews conducted by Timothy Dunnigan in 1969 will be made in preparation of the final manuscript, his collaboration will be acknowledged in a preface, and any monetary compensation he receives upon publication of the book will be taken from subsequent royalty payments, drawn equally from the shares Mr. Rios and Mrs. Sands receive, the exact percentage to be negotiated with Mr. Dunnigan prior to publication.

I recall clearly that we began our first session together discussing this letter document and signing it. Precisely what we said is a blur, though I'm reasonably sure Ted raised no objections to any part of it. With our signatures affixed to this document, the first series of negotiations, badly documented and remembered as they are, were complete, and the interviews progressed over the next three weeks.

The above documents describing the beginning of our project expose the improvisational nature of our field collaboration. Anthropologist Hein Streefkerk says that all fieldwork is "necessarily improvised," particularly when it is "carried out under circumstances which are characterized by fundamental contradictions between dominant and subordinate groups" (1993: 2), which this fieldwork was. Our meeting was in many ways accidental, as was the methodology by which we worked. Ted already had a framework in his mind for narrating his life experiences based on the interviews he'd done five years previously. I had a framework in my head gleaned from reading many published Native American autobiographies and from reading his previous interviews, but I had absolutely no field training. I was escorted into the field to either sink or swim; mostly I sank.[15] As the following transcript of the first part of our first session—the part that appears in edited form at the beginning of this chapter—demonstrates, I was not a skilled interviewer:

TAPE ONE[16]
Subject: Theodore Rios
Interviewer: Kay Sands
Place: Sells Arizona Hospital
Date: May 16, 1974
Time: 9:45 A.M.

SIDE ONE

KS: Okay, the first thing that I want to know is when your were born.

TR: October first, 1915.

KS: Okay, some of the other things that I need to know are things about your family—your grandfather's name—your father's father.

TR: Jose Rios.

KS: Okay. And where was he from?

TR: I think he was from San Xavier.

KS: He was from San Xavier?

TR: Mm hmm. He stayed there.

KS: Do you know when he was born? Any idea?

TR: No. No idea. 'Course I was just a little tot when he died.

KS: Oh, you were? Do you remember what year that was?

TR: No, I never did.

KS: About how old were you? Six, seven? You were a full-timer? You were just a child?

TR: Mm hmm. Well, yeah. As far as I can remember, little.

KS: I see. What did he do for a living?

TR: Oh, he done farming, and then he was—represents San Xavier. He went to Washington.

KS: Was he tribal chairman, then?

TR: He was. 'Course, at that time they don't have that many officers. Just maybe one or two or—you know.

KS: For the whole reservation?

TR: The whole reservation, San Xavier.[17] So he's got to go to Washington. You know, he went once. You know, they settle disputes for the lands and all that.

KS: But did he represent the tribe for the—with the government?

TR: Mm hmm.

KS: Had he had schooling? Was he an educated man?

TR: I don't think so.

KS: Did he speak English?

TR: Maybe he understands it, but he speaks Spanish.

KS: Oh, I see. Do you speak Spanish too?

TR: Yeah.

KS: Most of the time he spent farming, though, and that was at San Xavier?

TR: Mm hmm.

KS: Did he hold any other jobs? Did he ever work in Tucson?

TR: That I don't know because it was hardly settled at the time, you know.

KS: Yeah. What about your grandmother? Do you remember her?

TR: On my father's side?

KS: Yes.

TR: Not too much. She—well, she was older, so I—I seen her then.

KS: What was her name?

TR: Agnes.

KS: And was she from San Xavier, too? [See photo 3.]

TR: Mm hmm.

KS: Okay. Can you tell me anything about her at all. What she looked like? Do you remember?

TR: Mm—just like an ordinary old lady.

KS: Okay. What about on your mother's side? Your grandfather's name?

TR: They call him Arnito Williams.

KS: And was he from San Xavier also?

TR: Oh, probably he's from Santa Rosa, but he was—-he moved from there, but he was—he spent his time most any place.[18] He was settled down at San Xavier.

KS: Oh, he moved around a lot?

TR: Moved around a lot.

KS: Okay. Was he still alive when you were born?

TR: Mm hmm.

KS: Do you remember very much about him?

TR: Well, he—he's in cattle business. A rancher.

KS: Now, did he live near you, or did you live with him, or—

TR: Sometimes. Close by—he's close.

KS: Did he have a lot of cattle?

TR: Mm hmm.

KS: That was a pretty new industry then, wasn't it?

TR: Mm hmm.

KS: Was he educated?

TR: No.

KS: He never went to school. Do your remember when he died?

TR: I know when, but then I don't know the year when it was.

KS: Do you remember about how old you were?

TR: Yeah, I was pretty old—about eight or something. You know, that—them people, they don't know what their age is, or you know.

KS: Yeah. What about your maternal grandmother, his wife?

TR: Born about the same place, around . . .

KS: Around Santa Rosa?

TR: Mm hmm.

KS: What was her name?

TR: Martina.

KS: Martina—that's pretty. Well, do you remember about how old you were when she died?

TR: Just about that—well, she's pretty old. Of course, she died not too long ago. I don't know when, but she claims she's real close to—about ninety or something.

14

KS: And did she live at San Xavier when she died?

TR: Mm hmm. Yeah.

KS: So you saw her . . .

TR: Yeah, I seen her all the time because I was around there most of the time.

KS: Yeah. Okay, what about—what was your father's name?

TR: It was Frank Rios.

KS: You have any idea when he was born?

TR: I know it, but I never—about the year, but he was pretty old, about seventy-two, I think, when he died.

KS: And he was from San Xavier, right?

TR: Mm hmm.

KS: What was his occupation?

TR: He's a farmer—rancher.

KS: Both?

TR: Both.

KS: Okay. Had he been to school?

TR: Mm hmm.

KS: At San Xavier?

TR: At Santa Fe.

KS. Oh, at Santa Fe. Was he active in tribal government?

TR: Oh, he's been to Washington too. He represented most of the tribe—at the time, you know.

KS: Just from San Xavier or the whole reservation?

TR: The whole reservation and San Xavier.

KS: And your mother's name?

TR: Anselma.

KS: Okay, and was she from San Xavier also?

TR: Mm hmm. Yeah. (1–5)

This poor excuse for an interview[19] goes on for another twenty-four pages of leading questions and monosyllable answers. There is no real narration, just sentences strung together at most. It's not that Ted was not capable of giving the history of his family in narrative form. In later

15

interviews he spoke more discursively about his parents and grandparents. But in this session, I gave him no chance to affect the direction of the "interview" or to speak anything but the barest data. And even then many of my questions were, in fact, statements to which he pretty much muttered agreement or dissent. As I read back through the transcript, I'm embarrassed that I didn't have the sense to ask open-ended questions. That technique would have encouraged spontaneity, which would have exposed what Ted himself thought was important—or at least what he thought important to tell me. Equally importantly it would have allowed me to learn how he conceptualized and thought about his own life (Langness and Frank 1981: 48). But at the time I did not understand that "the interview is probably the most crucial single act anthropologists in the field engage in, and much of their success depends upon how skillful and perceptive they are in the interview situation" (Langness and Frank 1981: 43). I was neither perceptive nor skillful. I'm ashamed of how I ruthlessly attempted to gather data at the loss of story. Even so, what results is actually a minimum of data, and it's data that fit my idea of setting up a genealogy, a standard procedure for autobiography, but certainly not Ted's idea of his family origins. It's a wonder he was willing to continue work after such a rude— and I mean that as a descriptor of the approach I took—first session.

Obviously I was nervous. Too eager to fill the slightest pause, too concerned with information. I wasn't listening, and I certainly wasn't giving Ted a chance to speak. As I look back on this transcript and review the tape, it seems he was remarkably tolerant and patient but also resistant.[20] He hesitated each time before he spoke, and he made me work for each bit of data and gave nothing more than exactly what had been asked. His way of being polite but not cooperative. The questions I did not ask, and the ones I did, if they had been properly phrased, might have elicited a narrative, or several narrative anecdotes.

The initial interview also reveals how devoted I was to creating an autobiography in the Euro-American mode—beginning with the birth of the subject, providing the family context and history. But I didn't even do that adequately. And in retrospect, generic autobiography was as uninspired and probably, from Ted's cultural point of view, as inappropriate a mode of development as could be found.

Had we talked discursively about how a book about Ted's life would come about, perhaps the interviewing would have been more fruitfully directed and his responses to questions more detailed and fluent. Perhaps we might have started not only where but how he wanted to start. But I was shy and shaky on my own, feeling inadequate to the task but armed with a passel of prepared questions to cover my nervousness. And Ted was looking to me to lead. And did I ever lead, even supplying answers to my questions which Ted merely confirmed by repeating my phrasing or with assenting vocables. Had I known Ted better at the time, or even been a more sensitive reader of the interviews he did with Dunnigan, I'd have known that leading was not Ted's way. He was willing to answer questions but presumed that I was in charge, that I knew what I was doing. In fairly short order, I think, he recognized that my lead was inept and began to narrate to suit his own purposes, but I didn't catch on to his subtle tactics until I started reviewing the transcripts and attempting to organize the narrative years later. Far too late to accommodate a more effective recording methodology.

From the onset of our fieldwork together, I think we both had set notions in our heads that inhibited explicit negotiation. We were strangers. I knew his life story from what I think of as the Rios-Dunnigan tapes, but I had barely met him in person, and I was a total blank for him. We began the project in what Hein Streefkerk calls "an instrumental relationship" (1993: 11), from which we both hoped to produce a book but by a means—interviews—that put us in tension with one another. Ours was "a historically contingent, unruly encounter involving both conflict and collaboration." Recognizing in hindsight the "political, ethical, and personal cross-purposes that undermine any transmission of intercultural knowledge" (Clifford 1983b: 154), I see how naive I was to believe that I could ameliorate all the contingencies that were present in our project. So much for the naive notion of fieldwork as "an innocent attainment of rapport analogous to friendship" (Clifford 1983b: 140).[21] The project demanded mutual cooperation, but at this stage it was very tentative. Barbara Tedlock's observation that two individuals attempting to work cross-culturally work across a gulf that makes them "vulnerable experiencing subjects, working to coproduce knowledge" applies (1991: 80).[22] The gulf we were attempting to work across was great. As strangers we were both too vulnerable to confront and attempt to ease the tensions that we felt. As time progressed and we worked together day after day, the relationship between us eased as we engaged in small talk before and after interviews and became more familiar with each other's personal sensibilities, but as the initiator of the project, I missed a crucial opportunity for creating a dialogue that, while given the disparate nature of our experience and the contingent nature of cross-cultural representation could not erase conflict from our relationship, could have improved our interview sessions. I didn't have the experience or a sound instinct to do it, and at the time Ted was too reserved with a female, Anglo interviewer to set me straight. He would do that later, but the pattern set in the above sample was hard to break; I never consciously tried any other technique, my education in alternatives having been acquired only in the last few years. Coupled with Ted's vagueness—note his poor recollection of dates above—the tense, nondiscursive pattern set in the first interview seriously undermined the potential for a well–fleshed-out life story. What resulted from this interview was, in the end, not much more than a skeleton.

There are several observations that might be made regarding the material from the presentations of samples of Ted's narrative, both in "raw" and edited form. First, the transcript is a standard but minimal facsimile of a dialogue, a poorly conducted exchange, but nonetheless an oral interaction with intonation, emphasis, silences, hesitations, etc. Ted's voice is especially hard to catch because there is no extended verbalization in the transcript segment. Ironically, his voice is much more accessible in the edited version that introduces this chapter. Perhaps because I know his voice and have recently reviewed the tapes, I can catch the rhythm and particular idiom of English that identifies Ted's voice in the edited excerpt. I know that preserving his voice was one of my intentions in editing the material into a sustained albeit rather predictable and data-focused narrative, and by the time I did any editing on the transcripts I had had substantial experience as editor of a written autobiography by another Native American man.[23] Which of the two forms of representation — raw or edited — comes closest to Ted? Neither, or either, depending on the intended reader.

Without specialized interest in Native American autobiography or in certain aspects of Tohono O'odham culture, the tape transcripts are tedious, especially in the beginning. And they are every bit as unreliable as any edited version might be, both dependent on Ted's often faulty memories and significantly interfered with by the collector-editor. The edited version is still very spare; follow-up questions during the next session could have elicited the details that would have made Ted's family members vivid and animated instead of merely reported upon. But I didn't ask them. The edited version reads much more smoothly than the transcript, but then it's supposed to. The "as told to" appellation of the period presumed a fairly heavy hand in turning field collection, often fragmented and haphazard, into narrative. Several considerations go into that convention of editing. I would hope that the foremost one would be to present the subject effectively as an able narrator. Part of the motive for that is respect for the narrator, but part also is concern not to be embarrassed by revelation of shoddy field methodology. The edited version is spare, but it does hide the painfully abrupt and terse exchanges on the tape transcript. However, it loses much of the sense of oral performance — no vocables, hesitations, repetitions, emphases, etc. The trade-off is disturbing.

One more document, this one representing the first round of editing I did on the transcript printed above, gives some further insight into how the edited excerpt at the beginning of the chapter came to be.

What follows is editing done in 1984 during a sabbatical leave, when I worked on making the interviews into part of a book-length study focusing on Ted's life and his relationship to Papago culture.[24] In the edited transcript, insertions are shown in square brackets, and deletions are shown with strikeout. Changes in capitalization have been marked with either double-underline, to indicate that a lowercase letter should be capitalized, or double-strikeout, to indicate that an initial cap should be made lowercase. The material in parentheses has either been moved from one of my questions or statements that have been deleted or combined from separate responses given by Ted. Italicized material in brackets is from fieldnotes I made during the interview.

TAPE 1, SIDE 1

~~KS: Okay, the first thing that I want to know is when your were born.~~

~~TR:~~ (I was born) October first, 1915.

~~KS: Okay, some of the other things that I need to know are things about your family—your grandfather's name—your father's father.~~

~~TR:~~ Jose Rios (was my grandfather).

~~KS: Okay. And where was he from?~~

TR: I think he was from San Xavier.

~~KS: He was from San Xavier?~~

~~TR: Mm hmm. He stayed there.~~

~~KS: Do you know where he was born? Any idea?~~

~~TR: No.~~ No idea (where he was born) [*shakes head*]. 'Course, I was just a little tot when he died.

~~KS: Oh, you were? Do you remember what year that was?~~

~~TR: No, I never did.~~

~~KS: About how old were you? Six, seven? You were a full-timer? You were just a child?~~

~~TR: Mm hmm.~~ As far I can remember, little.

~~KS: I see. What did he do for a living?~~

~~TR:~~ Oh, he ~~done farming~~ (farms), and then he ~~was~~—represents San Xavier. He went to Washington [*nods*].

~~KS: Was he a tribal chairman, then?~~

TR: He was (tribal chairman). 'Course, at that time, they don't have that many officers, only maybe one or two ~~or—you know.~~

~~KS: For the whole reservation?~~

TR: (for) ~~T~~he whole reservation. So he's got to go to Washington. You know he went once. You know, they settle disputes for the lands and all that.

~~KS: But did he represent the tribe for the—with the government?~~

~~TR: Mm hmm.~~

~~KS: Yeah. Had he had schooling? Was he an educated man?~~

~~TR:~~ I don't think (he was educated).

~~KS: Did he speak English?~~

~~TR:~~ Maybe he understands [English] ~~it~~, but he speaks Spanish.

~~KS: Oh, I see. Do you speak Spanish too?~~

~~TR: Yeah.~~

~~KS: I do a little. Most of the time he spent farming, though, and that was at San Xavier?~~

~~TR: Mm hmm.~~

~~KS: Did he hold any other jobs? Did he ever work in Tucson?~~

~~TR: That I don't know, because it~~ (Tucson) was hardly settled at the time[,] ~~Y~~ou know.

~~KS: Yeah. What about your grandmother? Do you remember her?~~

~~TR: On my father's side?~~

~~KS: Yes.~~

~~TR: Not too much. She—well,~~ ̲she was [younger] ~~older~~, so I—I [saw her more]~~seen her then.~~

~~KS: What was her name?~~

~~TR:~~ [Her name was] Agnes.

~~KS: And was she from San Xavier, too?~~

~~TR: Mm hmm.~~

~~KS: Okay. Can you tell me anything about her at all? What she looked like? Do you remember?~~

~~TR: Mm—~~ [She looked] just like an ordinary old lady.

KS: ~~Okay. What about on your mother's side? Your grandfather's name?~~

TR: They call [my mother's father] ~~him~~ Arnito Williams.

KS: ~~And was he from San Xavier also?~~

TR: ~~Oh, probably~~ <u>h</u>e's from Santa Rosa, but ~~he was—~~ he moved from there~~, but he was—he spent his time most any place—~~ [and] he was settled down at San Xavier.

KS: ~~Oh, he moved around a lot.~~

TR: Moved around a lot [before that].

KS: ~~Okay. Was he still alive when you were born?~~

TR: ~~Mm hmm.~~

KS: ~~Do you remember very much about him~~?

TR: ~~Well, he—~~ <u>h</u>e was in cattle business[,] [a] rancher [*nods*].

KS: ~~Now, did he live near you, or did you live with him, or—~~

TR: [I lived with him] ~~S~~ometimes. Close by[,] ~~—he's~~ close.

KS: ~~Did he have a lot of cattle?~~

TR: ~~Mm hmm.~~

KS: ~~That was a pretty new industry then, wasn't it?~~

TR: ~~Mm hmm.~~

KS: ~~Was he educated?~~

TR: ~~No.~~

KS: ~~He never went to school. Do you remember when he died?~~

TR: ~~I know when, but then I don't know the year when it was.~~

KS: ~~Do you remember how old you were?~~

TR: ~~Yeah,~~ I was pretty old—about eight or something (when he died). You know, ~~that—~~them old people, they don't know what their age is[.] ~~or, you know—~~

KS: ~~Yeah. What about your maternal grandmother, his wife?~~

TR: ~~Born about the same place, around . . .~~

KS: ~~Around Santa Rosa?~~

TR: ~~Mm hmm.~~

KS: ~~What was her name?~~

TR: [My grandmother was called] Martina. [She was from Santa Rosa too.]

KS: ~~Martina—that's pretty. Well, do you remember about how old you were when she died?~~

TR: ~~Just about that—well, she's pretty old. Of course,~~ she died not too long ago—I don't know when, but she claims she's real close to—~~about~~ 90[.] ~~or something, or maybe around there.~~

KS: ~~And did she live at San Xavier when she died?~~

TR: ~~Mm hmm. Yeah.~~

KS: ~~So you saw her . . .~~

TR: ~~Yeah,~~ (She lived at San Xavier) so I [saw] ~~seen~~ her all the time, because I was around there most of the time [*nods*].

KS: ~~Yeah. Okay, what about—what was your father's name?~~

TR: ~~It~~ [My father] was Frank Rios.

KS: ~~You have any idea when he was born?~~

TR: ~~I know it, but I never care about the year, but~~ he was pretty old, about 72 when he died.

KS: ~~And he was from San Xavier, right?~~

TR: ~~Mm hmm.~~

KS: ~~What was his occupation?~~

TR: ~~He's~~ a farmer. Rancher.

KS: ~~Both?~~

TR: Both [*nods*].

KS: ~~Okay. Had he been to school?~~

TR: ~~Mm hmm.~~

KS: ~~At San Xavier?~~

TR: ~~At~~ [He went to school at] Santa Fe.

KS: ~~Oh, at Santa Fe. Was he active in tribal government?~~

TR: [He went] ~~Oh, he's been~~ to Washington too. He represented most of the tribe[,] ~~the time when, you know.~~

KS: ~~Just from San Xavier, or the whole reservation?~~

TR: ~~T~~he whole reservation and San Xavier.

KS: ~~And your mother's name?~~

TR: [My mother's name was] Anselma.

KS: ~~Okay, and was she from San Xavier?~~

TR: ~~Mm hmm. Yeah.~~ (1–5)

The pattern continues, condensing the data into a continuous narrative by eliminating the questions while borrowing clarifying phrases from them to flesh out Ted's brief replies, changing words to make his comments more grammatical, and deleting the vocables and speaker initials. Such a brief excerpt — a lengthier one here would just be tedious since the same pattern of editing is used throughout — does not, however, address how the interviews, which bend back on themselves in variants of the same stories and after this section are never chronological, could be shaped, as I intended, into a continuous linear narrative of Ted's life.[25] I can't demonstrate that for you because I could not figure out how to do that fifteen years ago — or even now, for that matter. The editing was easy, just supply the language where Ted didn't. But, but even in 1984, that felt too intrusive; it turned collaboration into manipulation pure and simple. Moving words around was bad enough, but whole sections — a comprehensive cut and paste job — was beyond me. I did do the cutting and even sorted the anecdotes into periods and categories in 1984 but quit when I realized either system did major harm to Ted's narrative intentions and style. The project as it existed suggested no organic shape of its own, and I had none to provide. So after this initial stage of editing and the further round of line editing, a sample of which opens this chapter, I reassessed what I had and decided that what I needed to produce was not a conventional personal narrative but a heavily contextualized autobiography — what I would now call a collaborative ethnographic biography of Ted Rios since there is no attention to literary or performance aspects of the narrative in the plan. I outlined the volume I envisioned in some detail, as follows:

AUTOBIOGRAPHY OF THEODORE RIOS
Preface and Acknowledgments
Ch. 1 The Autobiography as Document and Literature
Discussion of ethnographic and literary autobiographies of Indians, particularly Indian men and Papago narratives. Methodology of as-told-to form, its history, problematic nature, and uses.

Ch. 2 The Rios Autobiography: Methodology and Style

Discussion of choice of subject, linguistic proficiency and narrative patterns, subject's audience awareness, control of elements of narrative, creation of dramatic persona, etc.

Ch. 3 Cultural Backgrounds and Biographical Sketch

Discussion of the land and culture of the Papagos and a brief biography of the subject, including a genealogy

Ch. 4 The Autobiography

Edited text of Rios's narrative divided into five parts

1. Family background, birth, early childhood (farm and ranch)

2. School (mission, Phoenix Indian School, Tucson High School)

3. Marriage and work (especially mines)

4. Travel (World War II period, including Hanford and aircraft jobs)

5. Later Years (jobs, events, reflections)

Ch. 5 Interpretations

Omissions, amplifications, clarifications, and analysis of the subject's narrative

1. Family background, birth, early childhood

2. School

3. Marriage and work

4. Travel

5. Later Years

6. Evaluation of subject as representative and individual

Ch. 6 The Editing Process

Discussion of the editing and structuring process and rationale for decisions. Should include substantial samples of raw text, edited text, final text for comparison and discussion.

The plan set out here seemed workable, had precedent in many ethnographic texts using individual lives as case studies, and incorporated theory current in the 1980s and some discussion of the editing process and sampling of raw text that was rarely offered in published works. But it wasn't what Ted and I had agreed to, nor did it solve the problem of structuring the edited transcripts into a chronological narrative. It presents Ted as little more than a representative Papago male in a period of cultural transition, ignoring his oral style, his sense of audience, and how his narrative relates to other Native American collaborative life-story works. This plan addresses Ted as an ethnographic subject but not as a performer of narrative and certainly not as having told "a good one," a phrase with which he often ended the telling of an anecdote he especially liked. The plan looks tidy, looks like the kind of book an academic press would publish, but I didn't like it very much then and still don't. It's flat and too documentary. Even the proposed title is boring, and inaccurate too, since the plan is clearly dominated by biography rather than auto-narrative. More importantly, even as I first penciled the outline, I knew it violated Ted's sense of himself as a narrator, as a roving, talking man who had articulated a self into being with the assistance—and sometimes interference—of a well-intentioned but often inept collector-editor.

The 1984 sabbatical ended; I filed the tapes, transcripts, edited texts and outline, and I pretty much abandoned the project, turning it into psychological and literal baggage as I pursued an academic career. I carted it around on several yearlong teaching exchanges in the United States and Europe, thinking I'd get back to it when I had few distractions. But, of course, I never did. There are always distractions, always other responsibilities and projects less vexing and more inviting, and even if there aren't, they can be invented.

Now as I look at the outline, I realize that many of its components are essential to making a story out of Ted's narration, but in a more vulnerable and insightful way, which is why I changed my mind about beginning this volume with discussion of theory and have begun with a narrative about the narrative that is the reason for the book.

What I've presented in sample form here is what existed until right now. You have the original contexts for the project. Placing Ted's narrative in the context of the new ethnography and theory of autobiography is the next step in sorting out how Ted's narrative can be presented as a story—"a good one."

ꝯ 1

THEORIES OF INSCRIBING

COLLABORATIVE PERSONAL

NARRATIVE

The cross-cultural encounter between a Tohono O'odham man and an Anglo woman for the purpose of producing a publishable life story exposes a complex set of circumstances and expectations.[1] It begs for a paradigm or methodology for presentation that elucidates fully the narrator's and the collector's roles in the collaborative process. As in all cross-cultural field encounters, it is "always difficult, if not impossible to know what happened." Readers are left to rely on "ex post facto narrations," accounts which mask the encounter by providing only "limited and foreshortened evidence" (Clifford 1983a: 123). Because the authority of the text-maker has been the criteria that has determined the value of most representations of the Other, challenging the institutional criteria that support the idea of writing—not oral narration—as the determiner of value is difficult. Escaping the limitations of ascribing authority to the collector-editor-contextualizer may be impossible. However, recognizing the ethnocentricity of this criteria and the falsity of collector authority, without authority first and ultimately residing in the oral narrator, provides a de-centering strategy that at least in some measure exposes the vulnerability of the inscriber and the fragility of the cross-cultural enterprise.

Ultimately, I think that neither the field interviews Ted and I did in the 1970s, nor my attempted editing of them in the mid-1980s, nor this volume as it attempts to probe and expose all aspects of the process can successfully evoke Ted Rios's life or the narrating of it. Specifically, I doubt that it can escape the inhibiting conventions of life-story collaboration as an ethnographic or literary work that mitigates against full disclosure of life experiences. Had the project been initiated and completed in the past few years under the benefit of new theories of representation and inscription of Native American lives, perhaps past practices would be less influential, but I do not believe they would disappear. They would just be more fully exposed and more experimentally expressed. I think, in fact, that all such attempts to turn the oral narrativity of Native American life stories into written texts are at best only partially successful and never fully successful in terms of Native American criteria for narrative expression and aesthetics. But inscribing individual Native American lives is a firmly entrenched form of cross-cultural collaboration that, despite its problematic nature, deserves scrutiny and comprehension and a greater appreciation of the Native American collaborator's role in the production of text. These lives express meaning and value that to date are best understood in terms of the ethnographic and literary tools we can bring to bear on them.

The methodology of the encounter with the Other is rooted in ethnographic practice, while the intention of the collaborative personal narrative, if not primarily literary in many cases, dictates attention to readability and style. Those two elements of the life-story project have not changed appreciably in the last quarter century. Thus, it is useful to look at the institutional influences that have shaped and still shape Native American personal narrative in order to understand why this process and form of personal/cultural expression is so hard to access and so troubling. And specifically why the Rios-Sands project is so difficult to inscribe accurately and effectively even with the best of scholarly tools at hand.

Because the encounter between Ted and me and the work that developed out of it is historically situated in relation to both ethnographic-methodology and literary-genre conventions and the theoretical frameworks dominant in each in the 1970s, examining both the

28

fieldwork and editing expectations and actualities in terms of those concepts is a way of opening up the process in terms of its period. But because the actual making of a book attempting to challenge conventional forms of cross-cultural inscriptions is also significantly affected by 1990s theoretical models, it is useful to discuss the Rios-Sands project in relation to the current emphasis on self-reflexivity in ethnographic inscription and the focus on subjectivity in personal narrative theory.

The Rios-Sands project fits most immediately into an ethnographic paradigm, so viewing it in terms of fieldwork and inscription serves to open up the narrative process to scrutiny. It is also a point of departure in the search for theories and models for presenting Ted's life story in publishable form.

The project that Ted Rios and I undertook in 1974 began in a conventional way, with a member of Western society seeking collaboration with a member of an indigenous group. When Ted and I met in that tribal hospital room in 1974, he was not a self-selecting subject for a personal narrative.[2] He did not initiate the encounter, nor did he define the methodology of the enterprise. As was typical for the time period, the project came about because an ethnographer — in this case a pseudo- or would-be ethnographer — sought agreement from a particular individual she saw as suitable for a life-story project intended to make a book out of his narrated experiences. However, the choice of Ted Rios as narrator was not entirely mine. He could have refused. Instead, he assented to once again become a Papago narrator. (See photo 4.) Our mutual agreement demonstrates that "the selection process, when it comes to an intensive life history, involves two parties, and both come with their own desires and needs, some of which are unconscious" (Langness and Frank 1981: 44–45).

Ted was already familiar with the role of "informant," and he had his own reasons for agreeing to the project though he never articulated them to me.[3] Perhaps he was simply bored, or needed attention, or he recollected working with Timothy Dunnigan as pleasurable, or he harbored a desire for understanding from his family and/or for some status in his community. Maybe his cooperation was motivated by hope for payment, though that was not discussed in the initial meetings.[4] Whatever his reasons, he already had experienced a fieldworker-narrator relationship and an intensive interview process, and I had considerable familiarity with examples of personal narratives collected, edited, and published by anthropologists. The framework of established anthropological methodology as we individually understood it promoted a good many assumptions that directly affected our work together.[5] Most obvious is that at least at an easily observable level, Ted gave over control of the project to me. As the letter contract I drew up indicates, he allowed me to define the project and, in general, its methodology, though, as further examples of our dialogues will reveal, he resisted that methodology. In our initial encounters he never told me how he thought we should proceed. Of course, I never explicitly asked him questions that might have generated such a response either. I simply took for granted that the fieldwork that would occur between me — Self — and Ted — Other — would, as nearly as I understood it, repeat countless such encounters in the history of ethnographic research among colonized peoples.[6]

In the discipline of anthropology, what was then called personality-in-culture study had a long history of legitimacy by the 1970s,[7] making what I saw Ted and I undertaking an "authorized" form of inscripting his life story as an example of the effect of cultural transition on the individual Papago male. I proceeded on the assumption that his life story was valuable because it would contribute to the dominant society's knowledge of a Native American culture by providing a record of individual experience within broad categories of Papago culture. I don't think it ever occurred to me — or to Ted either, though I don't know that for sure — that we were engaged in this one-to-one colonial encounter for the purpose of producing a strictly literary inscription that would be valued primarily for its aesthetic quality. In a period when Native American "as-told-to" autobiographies were still being shelved in the anthropology sections of libraries and listed under the sole name of the collector-editor, literary value was clearly a secondary issue. That I hoped to edit Ted's spoken words into a literary autobiography proved an overly ambitious and unrealistic aspiration, given the conventions of the time.

In retrospect, Ted and I were actually playing out given roles in a first world–third world relationship. He would supply a lengthy personal narrative that I would edit and contextualize to give it authority and value as a representative male life from a transitional period in Papago cultural history. As Roger Sanjek points out, "Authority is neither bad nor good in itself, but it is always tactical" (1990: 58). How authority is established and maintained, and for what purpose, is hard to evaluate in the messy moments of field engagement, but it becomes clarified in retrospect. One tactic I employed for achieving authority in the collaborative partnership is especially troubling as viewed from the present moment.

Concrete proof of how deeply our relationship and definition of the project was shaped by institutional attitudes and practices exists in the fact that, with the help of Dr. Fontana, I obtained a one thousand dollar grant from the Doris Duke Foundation. It supported ethnographic research, not literary scholarship, for fieldwork with Ted. The issue of money changing hands between field collector and Native "informant" has generated a long history of ethical debate. It is a debate I was quite unaware of at the time Ted and I engaged in fieldwork. The grant came after we had made our agreement to work together toward a book. I was totally inexperienced in grant application procedures and would not even have thought of seeking grant money on my own, and I did not know that the Doris Duke Foundation offered grants. I appreciated Dr. Fontana's support and was thrilled to receive the grant money, all of which went to Ted during our work together, but not until quite late in the taping—1975—well after our formal interviews were over. My attitude toward the monetary relationship this grant established between Ted and me falls into a typical pattern of abdication of financial influence. As Langness and Frank note, "Most ethnographers who have done successful ethnographies or life histories [meaning here, I think, published] deny that their informants were motivated by financial considerations but, of course, there almost always are indirect rewards of one kind or another" (1981: 37). I, too, want to think that money was not a major motivator in Ted's cooperation.

Even now, I think Ted would have narrated his life without monetary compensation; I want to bring evidence to bear that such a vulgar motive could not have dominated our relationship. So I note that payment to him was actually made after we had completed very nearly all of the interviews. By then I was just verifying information and collecting variants of some stories. In spite of the fact that I know how influential payment to an "informant" can be, I want to convince readers that Ted originally agreed to our project simply to break the boredom of his enforced immobilization, because that's what suits my sense of propriety and ethics. But in reality that may just be the influence of ethnographic convention and my guilt at work. Certainly Ted was not adverse to or embarrassed by the payments he received. I think he welcomed them since his injuries dictated unemployment for many months. He asked that the money be paid to him in cash, and we agreed on several substantial payments. However none of this, I have to admit now, argues convincingly that payment was not a significant factor in my authority to direct the project.

I realize all this talk of payment is discomforting. It's very uncomfortable to discuss because the ethics of such a practice are questionable. But at the time, I don't think either of us saw the arrangement as anything but positive. I saw myself simply as an agent of the Doris Duke Foundation, for which he had done previous work. I think Ted saw the payments as fortuitous. Perhaps they affected his commitment to follow through on the interviews after he was discharged from the hospital and returned to his home at San Xavier; he knew I had applied for the money for him well before it was granted. Probably I used the promise of payment as a tacit inducement, not for initiation of the project, but for completing fieldwork when Ted was no longer held captive by injuries and casts. Surely the payments encouraged Ted to meet with me in follow-up sessions for verifying facts and collecting variants of stories told earlier.

As Langness and Frank observe, other forms of compensation also occur. Throughout our relationship and, in fact, well beyond the interviews, I almost always came to see him with fruit or other snacks, with magazines—he particularly liked *National Geographic*. I bought mesquite wood from him, and on two occasions I bailed him out of jail when he was arrested for disorderly conduct, but that aspect of Ted's story is best told by himself in several anecdotes that will be presented later.

At the time, it never consciously occurred to me that these monetary and material compensations placed me in a position of power. I don't think graduate students feel that they have much access to power. The acts described above seemed, at the time, more courtesy that coercion. How Ted felt about them, I don't know.

Almost nobody talks about money in published ethnographies or, for that matter, in collaborative autobiographies.[8] What little evidence there is of compensating "informants" is the stuff of field diaries, grant reports, and perhaps ledgers, but these are usually hidden records kept apart from reports and publications because public admission of paying "informants" evokes a sense of impropriety. Admission of payment seems just a little too close to bribery; it suggests the possibility of tainted data. Yet discussion of the impact of payment is important in assessing the material collected and inscripted. In my relationship with Ted, it obligated him to meet with me for interviews, and it defined our collaboration, not as an equal partnership but as one in which he repaid material and monetary compensations with narrative. Ours is a classic example of the colonial relationship.

On the other hand, I think it needs to be acknowledged that payment, in a world that assigns value on the basis of material worth, affirmed the value of Ted's contribution to the project.[9] His time and words were worth not only the serious attention of a presumed professional; they were worth money. Both factors gave Ted status and bragging rights among his cronies. I observed this on several occasions. Also, Ted never talked about me paying him. I presented payments as coming from the foundation, not me personally, and he always, in my earshot, spoke of them in those terms too.

Does that let me off the hook as some sinister colonialist? I hope my actions and attitudes were not sinister, but were they colonial? Yes. I think all relationships that have produced Native American personal-narrative volumes have been essentially colonial, not only because of commodification of the Native American part and partner in the collaboration but because rarely have Native American narrators had equal control in the actual presentation of their stories.[10] This volume is, then, an example of the dominance of the collector-editor in the publication process of a collaborative project. Unlike many contemporary collector-editors, I did not consult — as promised in our contract — with Ted on the edited versions of his narrative except at the very earliest stages of editing, when I showed him sections like the one in the previous chapter so he could see how I crossed out the questions and rearranged wording. He read the transcript of the first interview but was not very interested in the process of editing at that point and made neither positive or negative comments nor offered suggestions. The attempt was premature. Had there been something to hand to him that actually looked like a narrative on the page, he may well have been more interested. But by the time I got to an editing stage where there was a substantial piece of continuous text for his appraisal or revision, we had lost contact — my fault since I was the one who was healthy and had mobility — and I had pretty much given up hope of completing the project. At any rate, his disinterest relieved me of the responsibility of collaborating on the editing part of the project — or so I thought at the time. If he didn't care, I was free to do as I pleased as long as it respected him. As fate would have it, his death makes edi-

34

torial collaboration impossible now, but it does not give me a sense of freedom to manipulate his narration to fit my genre expectations of a life story. In fact, it obligates me to be far more respectful, not only of him but of his narrative style, than I was in the earlier stages of the project. But even now, a quarter century after our collaboration ceased, the colonizing continues even as I attempt to make his narrative into a coherent expression of process.

The colonizing aspect of my relationship to Ted and his narrative is a significant part of the process and result of our collaboration. However, colonial theory is limited in its usefulness in addressing collaborative life story because it focuses exclusively on the power balance between the two parties and deflects attention away from the actual performance of narrative except where incidents or omissions support the colonial thesis.[11] Moreover, it presumes that the collaborative power balance is consistently unidirectional and tends to define narrators as victims rather than essential and usually willing partners in a dialogic enterprise. Analyzing the colonizing aspects of a collaboration is most useful when it is addressed within the broader process of inscription, where it can be legitimately and usefully discussed as an initiating and shaping factor in a project, but only one factor among several. Because colonial theory is a way of analyzing encounter and resultant text that generally discounts the subversive, resistant, and/or cooperative power that the narrator can and, certainly in the case of Ted, does manifest in the oral mode of narrating life experiences, it tends to be dismissive of the Native elements of control in the life-story collaboration. Colonial theory may, in fact, be not only limited but misleading as an interpretative strategy for Native American life story.

Examining a broader range of contemporary ethnographic and literary theories offers several approaches to comprehending the inscripting of the Other that are potentially more useful than colonial theory in analyzing the Rios text and its collaborative contexts. One is dialogic ethnography. Dennis Tedlock calls his concept of dialogic anthropology a mode, not a methodology. His definition of dialogic as "a

35

talking across, or alternately" offers a way to assess how Ted and I did and did not collaborate in our attempt to communicate his culturally situated experiences. As Tedlock explains, "the anthropological dialogue creates a world, or an understanding of the *differences between* two worlds, that exists between persons who were indeterminately far apart, in all sorts of different ways, when they started out their conversation" (1983: 323). "This *betweenness* of the world of the dialogue," he continues, replaces what earlier ethnographers called *rapport,* a state of benign good will or even intimacy they claimed existed between the fieldworker and the "informant." I make no claim to *rapport,* nor do I believe Ted would; even well into our interviews a level of formality and difference dominated our exchanges. Perhaps we both instinctively knew that "too thorough an investigation of the presenting selves might prove destructive because it might reveal the mismatch of our intentions" (Crick 1992: 177) that would contradict our contractual goal.

Tedlock claims that what distinguishes the dialogic mode is the negotiation of comprehension out of difference, not the closeness and understanding that *rapport* would suggest. Take, for example, the following interview excerpt. While this falls within Tedlock's definition of dialogue in that we are speaking alternately, also note how often distance is revealed, how often we talk past one another or clarification is required. Mutual understanding eludes us. Ted struggles to bridge the cultural gap, but I often cut him off before he can give a full answer, or I change the topic when follow-up questions would provide more fully developed and perhaps more specific and descriptive responses. I'm so anxious for information that I don't recognize "just how perplexing the question can be" (Cohen 1992: 221). Difference is certainly exposed in this dialogue, but the dialogue alone does not elucidate the nature of difference or the circumstances of the exchange. As in all the taped interviews, Ted and I speak to one another from a liminal space. The exchange is divorced from ordinary life, suspended in time and occurring in a place foreign to but comprehensively influenced by both our ordinary lives. We function strictly according to a conventional ethnographic model which constricts our exchange to data collection and suppresses Ted's cultural conceptualization of his own experience and especially his narrative style. This dialogue defeats Tedlock's goal of mutual comprehension. We never achieve a balanced dialogue because our intentions are at odds.

TAPE ONE

May 16, 1974

KS: The inside of the house—how big was it? Can you give me any indication?

TR: They had different sizes.

KS: Was it all one room?

TR: Sometimes two. It's just like an ordinary house. It's not all the same.

KS: The house you that you grew up in—your family had?

TR: Oh, they got different sizes.

KS: You had more than one house, then?

TR: Sometimes. Sometimes, you know, they got—sometimes they got a bigger house, more rooms, lot of space.

KS: So you lived in more than one house as a child?

TR: Sometimes.

KS: But you kept the other houses when you moved into a different one?

TR: Oh, yeah. There's a lot of things that's in there too [*nods*].

KS: And you just left everything in that house?

TR: Yeah.

KS: Why?

TR: Storage. Storage—we don't—well, we store in there and then just like they got food or surplus food someplace, and there's other in the other one and whatever—bedding and all that.

KS: How was the food stored?

TR: Oh, they pack it in that—'course now they got boxes. Just like any other place.

37

KS: Did you use pottery to store? . . .

TR: No. We never—they only use it for grains, syrup, or something like that—something that wouldn't spoil, make the rats want to go in. That's the only place for pottery. They don't use it for any other thing. It's just for food.

KS: What kind of floor did the house have?

TR: Oh, dirt floor. Dirt floor but it's packed.

KS: How did they do that?

TR: Oh, they just—just like any floor. Sometimes they got to mix in something like certain kind of soil, where it's hard. Of course, you know, it's just like—bring the water in there and smooth it off and then it's just—it's pretty hard.

KS: When your mother did the wash, how—what did she have to do?

TR: Oh, in a tub.

KS: Where did you get the water?

TR: Right in the well. We got wells. Most any—everybody had wells who lived around. [See photo 5.]

KS: Each house had . . .

TR: Each house, or maybe if that water is hard to get, well, then all the community and that's for everybody. Just like if you're on a farm like that if you want to dig a well, you dig a well—that's you're business. Or the place where someone lives. Of course, someplace like—like it was, it's got a lot of water. Now it's—you can dig so much at that time, you know, to get to the water. But now they're pumping so much, well, it went down so much. They pump and there's no pond around—it's got a lot of water. Even sometimes that—in a shallow river, you know, bed, there's still running water there. Sometimes people living all across from a river bed, you know, down—especially that Santa Cruz—the water's running most of the time, day and night.[12] They just get their wells, and that—what they just grab on their roof, you know, they make a— like a washtub but it's there, on the roof, and they kept it there and go right in there and get that water off the—off that river. Use the river—sometimes they'll just put it right by that river and start

38

scrubbing and then—that river, you know, just rub it there—it runs off. That's the way they do it most of the time. You know, if they're close by there.

KS: What kind of cooking utensils did your mother use?

TR: Oh, we had *ollas*—you know *ollas?*

KS: Yes.

TR: 'Course, they had that—we had all this—just whatever we have now, because it's got—it's not too long ago. 'Course, when they go to Mexico, they might stop at . . .

KS: Pottery?

TR: Pottery and all that—that dishes, cups and all that. Of course, people like Tucson, maybe somebody'd come around peddling all that—saucers and dishes, spoons and whatever, you know, most any different time in the old time. Because they go to every town and pick for everyone, like a frying pan or coffee pot or whatever.

KS: When you had meals, did you all eat at once—gather around the table to eat?

TR: Yeah, sometimes too, but, you know, sometimes they got a lot of kids or whatever. 'Course, they'll be cooking the same time and working, or they're doing it while they're eating, and then they say, "Why don't you do everything—clean up." Just like—just like now.

KS: Did you have to help do the dishes?

TR: No, they got ladies, and they got sisters maybe there—they do the whole—of course, they're not the whole crowd. It's just like, you know, maybe one family, do it only one. Just like now. It's no different from that time until now as it is. (18–20)

This sample of dialogue makes the case that "interactants must have something in common in order to be able to enter into and sustain a dialogue" (Graumann 1995: 1). Here, there is a desire on my part for Ted to narratively express his Otherness, but Ted attempts to place his childhood memories in a framework of universal experiences. Our intentions are not common, and asymmetry is the dominant feature of the exchange; there is little reciprocity and nearly no mutuality.[13]

Hence, there is no flow, and no opportunity for what Dell Hymes would call break-through into performance (1981: 79–86, 131–41).[14] Though there are topics for narrative, there is no story of Ted's childhood in this interview segment because Ted has no confidence in my capacity to comprehend his experiences and may even be leery of revealing his culture as inferior or "primitive" in the eyes of a middle-class Anglo woman.

The appeal of the exchange is immediacy and exposure of speech interaction. The interview has a perpetual present, but even that is false. As Johannes Fabian notes, language is "an eminently *temporal* phenomenon" (1983: 163). No interview goes instantly from speech act to published text. The moment the words are spoken the experience of verbal exchange is past. While dialogic anthropology avoids the pseudo present tense of conventional ethnography studies, it presents an equally contrived sense of the present. It works best, regarding this project, to demonstrate the improvisational and largely unsuccessful nature of the process for Ted and me. For Ted's life story to be accessible and comprehensible, the dialogue that gives a sense of being present during the interview needs interpretation — discussion in the past tense — from the privileged viewpoint of the collector's acquisition of knowledge from the compilation of subsequent interviews and from other sources. As it stands alone, the dialogue reflects the required commitment to cooperate, but the cooperation is severely limited; discrepancies between the requested and supplied information are notable, and hence there is little construction of shared understanding. But knowing that, in order to achieve genuine dialogue, "the dialogical partners are not merely 'subjects' speaking to each other but *participants* in the dialogue" (Bernstein 1996: 37) provides a way of understanding what is otherwise an instinctive negative reaction to the tensions of the above excerpt. Ted and I are not dialogical partners; we are participants in only a very limited sense. We are discovering "that we don't quite understand what is being said. We are both interrogating the other's range of knowledge and capacity for understanding or articulation [me overtly, Ted covertly]. We discover that our prejudgments don't quite fit the meaning of what is being said" (Bernstein 1996: 37). We don't know how to understand one another's intentions or culturally formed expectations; we do not share "frames of meaning" (Webster 1982: 94). Rebecca West sums up the limitations of verbal exchange across this chasm of mutual ignorance: "Only stupidity fails to recognize that each of the parties in such a relationship has command of a store of information almost wholly forbidden to the other: so that each, in the other's sphere, is helpless and astray unless his host is generous" (1994: 934). Ted was generous — with his time and tolerance — but it would take time for his generosity to elicit the kind of generosity in my verbal technique that would allow him to give of himself in language.

Dialogic anthropology, if the circumstances are good — where conversation is clear, specific, and mutually directed — is a very desirable mode of collection and a useful published representation of fieldwork. When the awareness of difference does not produce on-the-spot informative and insightful verbal exchange, however, dialogue is not a very practical or even comprehensible form of representing culture, speaker, or interviewer. The transcripts of the Rios-Sands interviews do not incorporate enough self-consciousness or sensitivity to serve as inscriptions that adequately evoke Ted as a narrator. They do not create what Tedlock calls *betweenness*. Also, the interviews Ted and I did are incomplete and only minimally communicative to readers. Without the discussions that have preceded this excerpt, this dialogue would be nearly incomprehensible, as would all but a few from the twelve formal interviews we taped. So while this theoretical approach makes preservation and subsequent analysis of field dialogue more accessible for examination, it does not provide the contextualizing elements that are carried in memory and field records, and it does not overtly present either participant in the exchange as self-reflexive. Such dialogues have the same limitations that fieldnotes have. They can't — were never intended to — tell a comprehensive story of a cross-cultural encounter.

41

Taken together with fieldnotes and metanarrative volunteered or solicited from the Native Other, reflexive commentary by the collector, and stylistic analysis of performance, presentation of dialogue in unedited form can expose the process of encounter. Dialogic theory has, then, limited application in presenting Ted's life story.

Though I will return at several points in this volume to analyze the dialogic strategies of the taped interviews Ted and I made, the contemporary ethnographic theory that I find most useful for analysis of the Rios-Sands project and the one that dominates this volume is narrative ethnography.[15] This theory builds on dialogism by developing a strategy for presenting and interpreting cross-cultural talk that incorporates methodological as well as modal strategies. Barbara Tedlock, in her discussion of the recent emergence of narrative ethnography, notes that the dialogue between the collector and the narrator aims "to create a world of shared intersubjectivity and to reach an understanding of the differences between two worlds." She further states that, in "phenomenological terminology, this communicative interaction, or 'we talk,' belongs neither to the realm of objectivity nor to that of subjectivity, but rather to 'human intersubjectivity'" (1991: 70–71). As words bridge "the gulf between Self and Other," they reveal "both parties as vulnerable experiencing subjects working to coproduce knowledge" (1991: 80). She argues the case for representation not only of collected data but field experience "re-presented by a situated narrator, who is also present as a character in the story," that focuses "not on the ethnographer herself, but rather on the character and process of ethnographic dialogue or encounter" (1991: 77–78).[16] Accomplishing that is exactly the intention of this volume. Barbara Tedlock further recommends that this be accomplished not by simple reflectiveness, where "one is conscious of oneself as an Other" — that is evident in the dialogic sample given above — but in reflexivity, where "one is conscious of *being self-conscious* of oneself" (1991: 85). Somewhat similarly, Shaobo Xie, recognizing that in a "world burdened by a few centuries of coloniality, it is impossible to construct identities and forms of knowledge uncontaminated by universalist or Eurocentric concepts and images," argues that it is necessary to "take up a third space of revision," which she calls "the Third Space of enunciation, the hybrid, ambivalent, in-between space of signification." This she calls "an interstitial locus of meaning, between the indigenous and the European" (1997: 17).

Scrutinizing one's own terms and procedures follows directly from recognizing a space of cultural revisionism and a system of doubled self-consciousness (Babcock 1980: 1). Such reflexivity places the collector-editor in a simultaneously powerful and vulnerable state. It eliminates the distance between inscripted text and Self. It exposes the fallibility of the collaborator, who in conventional representations of the Other is protected by the didactic deadpan of academic rhetoric. It makes both participants in the encounter Others and examines how they work to co-produce knowledge out of consciousness of difference. It exposes multiple connections between the collector and the narrator — many of which are not recorded in dialogue — despite the cultural and personal differences that separate them. These are connections and negotiations the reader needs to become privy to, in order to comprehend the multiple influences on the subjectivity of the persona developed in the narration of collaborative life story. By foregrounding the "interpretation of the details of reality that eludes the ability of dominant paradigms to describe" (Marcus and Fischer 1986: 12), ethnographic narrativity reconnects the speech-act of dialogue to event so that writing may become "the full manifestation of discourse" (Ricoeur 1976: 25–26). It reanimates the shared time and space of encounter. As Johannes Fabian explains, "reflexivity asks that we 'look back' and thereby let our experiences 'come back' to us. Reflexivity is based on memory, i.e., on the fact that the location of experience in our past is not irreversible. We have the ability to present (make present) our past experiences to ourselves. More than that, this reflexive ability enables us to be in the presence of others precisely inasmuch as the Other has become the content of our experience" (1983:

90–91). Narrative ethnography makes the Self, or the character created to represent the Self in the interpretation of the encounter with the Other, responsible for both process and text and the success or failure of both.[17] And it shifts the critical focus and criteria away from the finished text to the process of entextualization.

Being self-reflexive, writing vulnerably about the encounter with the Other, according to Ruth Behar, "challenges autobiographical isolation" by placing exploration of the Self—which most theorists now agree is the actual result of inscribing Otherness—in the role of mediation of the subjectivity of the Other (1996: 132).

Mediation has always been and still is the collector-editor's role and responsibility in the production of a Native American personal narrative.[18] For Ted, I was first a mediator who, through questioning and listening, elicited the spoken words. Through our engagement in dialogue, he separated his private and public selves, turning the internalized self of his sixty years of experiences into the narrated subject of a life story retrieved from his memory. Now I am mediator between Ted's narration and a reading audience. In that capacity I function as "mediator between distinct sets of categories and cultural conceptions that interact in different ways at different points of the ethnographic process" (Marcus and Fischer 1986: 31). I am an intrusive mediator rather than the suppressed collector-editor of conventional collaborative Native American personal narratives. However, in spite of a considerable amount of scholarship on narrative ethnography, I am quite without models for making this new, self-reflexive mediating role work. I know that whatever turn this volume takes, it will never accomplish the original goal of the Rios-Sands project—a polished personal narrative by a Native American man. It will not meet the expectations of a reading audience, even one made up of scholars who ascribe to new theories of cultural inscription. What began with a failed application of conventional methodology cannot be saved by a better-late-than-never attempt to inscribe fieldwork in an experimental form. So while I credit advances in ethnographic and literary theory for providing an opportunity to attempt this experiment, I have no illusions that they will carry it to success or closure for either Ted's or my purposes. I am also aware that I am sacrificing Ted's narrative to the examination of process, an act every bit as ethically dubious as making a conventional narrative from his part of the interview dialogues.[19] To publish or not, and in what form, is a dilemma every collector-editor of a Native American personal narrative has had to face. The emergence of new theories of inscription make me more self-conscious of being self-conscious — more reflexive — but they have not solved the problem of inscribing cross-cultural life story. My solution — if indeed it can be called that — is to abdicate the editorial role of shaping a continuous and comprehensive narrative from the interviews. Instead, I choose to expose the fallibility of the original collection process, but that does not, in the long run, produce a successful personal narrative for a reading audience. It probes the problem without offering any method for solution. So what is the point of this self-examination and speculation about Ted's motives? I think it is to show readers the complexity of the dialogic and narrative-ethnography methods of inscription and the difficulty of ever representing the Other without exposing the fallibility of the Self.

As I look back at the first interview Ted and I did, I wonder what might have happened had I begun by saying to him, "Tell me about your life." Where and how he would have started, and what form the narration might have taken, no one will ever know. He might have been incapable of directing his own narration, especially given his previous interview experience. But capable or not, he never received the opportunity or the challenge. On page eight of the transcript of tape one, after bullying genealogical data from him, I preempt Ted's potential control of the narrative when I tell him, "I'd like to start pretty much with the beginning of your life and the memories that you have there and work forward. Do you remember your family telling you anything about your birth? Did they tell you stories about when you were born?" This is clear directive that a chronological narrative is required. When I say "I'd like," I speak from genre expectations; hence, what I am really saying is "the projected readers would like." And the request to "work forward" demands in polite terms a linear plot told in chronological order. None of this takes into any consideration what Ted's idea of a life story might have been or his sense of what constituted structuring a personal narration. It totally discounts cultural and expressive style. Life history is not a universal form, nor is interview. Ted resists the conventions of both. He makes it quite clear that it's one thing to ask for a narration based on Western conventions and quite another to get one. Ted did not resist my request openly. He answered the questions I asked about his birth, baptism, childhood, schooling, work, etc. pretty much in chronological order, but close attention to his responses to my directive questioning shows that his surface cooperation masks resistance and an assertion of his own cultural style. The following sample, again from the first interview, demonstrates his resistance.

TAPE ONE

May 16, 1974

KS: What time did you get up when you lived at the ranch?

TR: About as soon as they get up. We get up pretty early. They got up. They got to water the cattle and all that, and then they would start in milking the cows — pretty soon not only the cows but the horses come in and drink there, get their water.

KS: Did you have to bring them in or did they just? . . .

TR: No, they just come. You know, because they're — well, because they need it.

KS: Did you have more milk than you could use? Did you sell the milk?

TR: No, there's no need of selling any. It's too much 'way out. Use it all in the cheese.

KS: How'd — can you describe how you made the cheese?

TR: Well, you got to cook it, cook the milk, then they got to start on that — start in and they got to break that cream in there [*stirring*

46

motion] or that—they call it, stomach from a cow, and then from that something and they start doing that, and by the time it gets solid and they make a kind of cheese, you know. They got little rings [*makes about a ten inch circle of his fingers*] that are made of wood—it's round [*repeats circle*]—set it in there and press it, put a big fat rock on top—keeps it, you know, let it stay for awhile until it gets all whatever's in there, all that juice, water or whatever, it's out, and then it's time. Just like any cheese.

KS: That's interesting.

TR: Sets in and then—and then day by day they keep it and of course it takes a long time in there. By the time [*inaudible*], haul it to town, you know, down to the village, something—down to the Yaqui village, too. They like it. Mexicans and everybody. They'll go and pretty soon it's all gone [*skids palms together*].

KS: Did you do this continuously all year 'round? . . .

TR: No, just at certain time when—like the summer, the summertime when there's grass and newborn calves come in. You can only get it when the milk—from the mother—not any other.

KS: Did your grandfather have a lot of cattle? Can you estimate at all?

TR: I can't. Well, he's got enough to go by with. You know, of course, the range, food . . .

KS: It was open range? . . .

TR: Open range. Of course there's some other ranches besides this one there, all around there, see, 'n' the whole cattle stretch all over.

KS: How could you tell them apart?

TR: Well, they're branded.

KS: Did they round them up once a year, or? . . .

TR: Year. Mm hmm.

KS: And you sold them off?

TR: Well, if you're going to sell anyway—just like any other place. Sell 'em or—like to these dealers.

KS: When they were sold, were they driven down to San Xavier then?

TR: They were driven, slaughtered or whatever—whoever buys them.

47

Of course, at the time, they don't use any trucks as it is now. Hardly any. (11–12)

In this transcript excerpt, Ted often cuts off the questioning to supply an impatient answer. Only when he thinks my ignorance is justified, in the section on making cheese, does he amplify his answers. The rest are abrupt, curt, and devoid of detail. Even the cheese-making section is relatively general. Though I know from later tapings that the time he spent at his maternal grandparents' ranch generated some of his fondest memories and that he could narrate with specific images and particularized anecdotes about these summer stays, here he is disinterested in amplifying. He has picked up on my tone and pace from the beginning of the interview and turned the tables on me, cutting off questions, letting me know my ignorance is not worth his patience. Rather that educating me to his cultural and personal experiences, he makes them generalized and impersonal. There are no characters in his narrative, nor any specific images or scenes. He does not identify who milks, who makes cheese, who the stock dealers are and where they come from. He doesn't refuse to answer, but he refuses content. Later narration makes it clear that he is capable of, in fact quite talented at, narrating richly detailed stories and anecdotes. But at this point, he is holding back, being minimally cooperative, assessing me and my ignorance of his culture, and considering how he, not I, will control the project. His resistance comes early and stays late in our project, as further transcripts will illustrate.

The above discussions and analyses of my relationship with Ted Rios in the project to publish a book-length narrative of his life verifies that cross-cultural inscription, whatever form it takes, while it is based in experiential reality and purports to constitute fact, actually produces a fiction, one largely shaped by the collaborative partner from the dominant society. The story Ted tells is neither narrated spontaneously nor structured according to his idea of how and in what order a narrative should be told. In the words of James Clifford, who is perhaps the most influential spokesperson for the "new ethnography," representation of the Other is "something made or fashioned" (1986a: 6). The transcripts of the interviews Ted and I made show clearly that the making is directed by the questions. The data and style of answering are Ted's, but his responses are directed, limited, and controlled by the circumstances of the interviews and the intentions of the questioner, who is attempting to make a particular kind of cultural and personal representation. Clifford argues that the maker cannot "avoid expressive tropes, figures, and allegories that select and impose meaning" (1986a: 6–7). It is clear from the directive approach I took to eliciting Ted's narration that, as maker—as opposed to narrator, and the relationship is clearly oppositional at this stage of the work we did together—I impose Western tropes upon Ted's life story from the outset of the collaboration by means of the terms I use in the questions I ask and the comments I make. I restrain and orchestrate Ted's narration by giving to my voice "a pervasive authorial function" and to his the role of source "to be quoted and paraphrased" (Clifford 1986a: 15). I overtly control the discourse; his control comes from covertly resisting. His responses work to defeat the imposition of my authorship onto his life. He resists sufficiently to thwart the production of a conventional personal narrative from our dialogue. In doing so, I think he demanded—though I did not recognize that demand at the time—that I find an unconventional form for the expression of his life. The form that this book pursues is no less a fiction—in the sense of a made or shaped thing—than the one we originally agreed upon, but as a self-reflexive inscription of our project it might more accurately be termed a metafiction.[20] I do not wish to claim that by remaking the dialogue Ted and I tape recorded, by reinscribing it in a radically different form than that originally planned, I am reversing the hierarchy of cross-cultural inscription. My deconstruction of the 1970s and 1980s phases of the project maintains, perhaps even empowers my authority, but I anticipate that the authority I have established thus far will be undermined if not negated by presentation and analysis of the texts of Ted's narration later in this volume.

Examining the dialogue Ted and I engaged in demonstrates that although they are not "really 'verifiable'" even when presented in "raw" form, "the fictions of ethnography are 'appraisable'" (Webster 1982: 102). I think they are best appraised by means of narrative-ethnography methodology, in which the reader is made privy to the collector's self-conscious participation and doubly self-conscious hindsight.

Discussing the work Ted and I did together in relation to traditional and contemporary ethnographic theories and practices provides a way not simply to salvage a narrative I misconceived and misdirected but places that narrative in the framework of process rather than product. It establishes that textuality is always "in progress and unfinished — thus undecidable" (Davis and Schleifer 1994: 302). It makes the field interviews "not really 'verifiable'" but at least "'appraisable'" as texts in process. It does not, however, address Ted's narrative and my role in mediating either Ted's life story or his use of language in expressing his story in terms of the conventions of literary narrative. For a project originally conceived as both ethnographic and literary, attention to Ted's narrative as autobiographical expression is as important as ethnographic appraisal of the process of collection. If ethnographic inscription is now recognized as producing unstable, ambiguous, partial, and untrustworthy texts, the same insight can be attributed to contemporary literary theory applied to the inscription of subjectivity.

ℰ 2

COLLABORATIVE LIFE STORY AS

LITERARY EXPRESSION

Telling a Good One, even though it was originally conceived as an "as-told-to" autobiography, transgresses most conventions of autobiography as a literary genre. By every standard, the project was ethnographic in its methodology and results. Does that make the edited text of our interviews a literary failure? As genre-defined autobiography, yes, I think it does. As cross-cultural experience-based discourse, emphatically no.[1] In fact, the resistance of Ted's life story to Euro-American conceptions of autobiography makes his narrative genuinely cross-cultural and points out the inadequacy of Western criteria and genre terminology as it is applied to orally narrated Native American life story. That is not to say that the process of inscription and the text made from the interviews Ted gave are not heavily influenced by conventions and theories of Western autobiography or that those conventions are not useful in examining the process of collecting and editing Ted's narrative and assessing his mode of personal expression.

In 1974, producing a conventional autobiography of Theodore Rios, based on the narrated experiences of his life as he recollected them, was, though uninformed by any substantive study of autobiographical theory, my intention.[2] I came to the project with no theoretical base in literary scholarship on autobiography, and I seriously doubt that Ted had more than a superficial familiarity with the concept of autobiography as a genre; his reading during the time I knew him was limited to periodicals and newspapers. We never discussed the project in terms of literature, only in terms of interviews that I would somehow make into a book. Neither of us had a clear notion of the "how." But I had a firm intent to make the events he narrated into a conventional story of his life in a linear trajectory from his ancestry and birth to his recovery from his hit-and-run injuries.[3] As time passed, that proved unworkable. The ethnographic methodology of our interviews did not produce a chronology of his life or even a clearly topical narrative. There was plenty of data with revelations of moments in Ted's life embedded in the discourse but no continuous life story and only occasional detailed narrative episodes, because my questions did not focus sufficiently on Ted's personal experience. I thought they did at the time of the interviews, but when I reviewed the tapes after each interview, they clearly did not adequately elicit Ted's responses to and interpretation of his experiences. Even knowing that, I seemed unable to correct the methodology to fit the intention.[4] Having collected Ted's narrative both superficially and unsystematically, the edited texts of the interviews are neither chronological nor comprehensive, a clear violation of basic characteristics of Western autobiography. When I finally came to edit the transcripts in the 1980s, I could not get the events Ted had narrated into linear order, nor could I choose which narrations — there were many repetitions in the interviews — to use or figure out what to do about substantial gaps in the narrative.[5] Even when I tried to file his narrations by topical category, a strategy that even then I felt violated his narrative style, I found the material did not lend itself to a comprehensible story; it remained choppy and discontinuous. I left the cuttings in a folder, stymied by the complexity of the task. By the 1990s I consciously resisted tampering further with the order or content of his narration, having become convinced that my inept interview technique had severely contaminated the project as an autobiography but also that the value of making Ted's narrative into a meaningful inscription would be in exposing the process and letting the narrative appear in its various stages, none of which was structured as a conventional retrospective chronology.[6] The transcript of the second taped interview and the edited version that follows it demonstrate how the question-answer format produced a narrative that thwarted my attempts to shape Ted's narration into a conventional chronology.[7] Given my form of spontaneous questioning and his style of narration, production of a conventional autobiography was a naive and, in retrospect, ill-conceived goal since it totally disregarded Ted's conceptualization and style of expressing his life experiences.

What follows is actually the second half of the first interview on May 16, 1974:

TAPE TWO, SIDE ONE

KS: I asked you as the other tape ended how you learned to do the chores.

TR: Like I said, they taught us to watch what they're doing, so—and the way we learn—or sometime they just have us—"You take it over. We'll see how you do it." And then just keep on, keep on— maybe the—you do it a lot of times, then you know how it's done. Or else maybe you've got to stay on. Of course, like we do most of the farming work, agriculture, certain way—you've got to cover the—little chilies growing up or squash or whatever it is, and they'll show us how to do it at the beginning, you know, and then when they get older, spreading out, then you do it different, and then on and on and then finally when it gets so and so you—all you do is watch the weeds and all that. But there's certain—well, everything like that, at the beginning there's a certain point and you've got be told this and this and that.

KS: Did you do all the farming by hand when you were a kid?

TR: Well, some. There's certain plants you got to do it by hand. Some you got to go by the planter, just like corn and all that. But out here on the ranch, where my grandfather lives, you got to do it by hand.

KS: Just with a plow?

TR: Just with a plow and you got to put 'em in by hand and then kind of squish 'em—how far apart and all that [*presses down with both hands*].

KS: Did you do work with the—did the women show you any work?

TR: Oh, yeah. They know how to do it. When he's around—he's not
around, well, she's the boss [*lifts chin and shrugs*].

KS: Still works that way doesn't it? What about learning to use some of
the equipment you had on the farm?

TR: Well, it's the same thing. We're told before we get—like hoes and—
'course, the hoe is nothing, you know, any different. Every tool
we've got they've got to use it just like they do, at the beginning.

KS: What kind of tools did you have?

TR: Oh, like pick, hoes, or shovels—all that.

KS: Did you have any equipment that was self-run?

TR: Mm hmm. Cultivators, plow—mostly horse pulled, you know.

KS: Did you have to harness the horses and do things like that?

TR: Mm hmm. Yes.

KS: How was the work divided in the family? During certain seasons
did your mother help in the fields, or? . . .

TR: If she had time. We always—we done all the work, all the time.
What we're doing we didn't stop till we finished. And then the next
different, you know . . .

KS: You planted several crops during the year?

TR: Several crops.

KS: What order did they come in?

TR: Oh, they come all together. When you get around to the certain—
you know you're through. Then you do the same, just like you got
to do for a little while, then start in to plant in there, when it starts
growing you go from there this way or this way. Or . . .

KS: Did the whole family—did relatives help too?

TR: No.

KS: Just each family?

TR: Each family. Oh, once in a while when they'd—when somebody's
got a whole lot and can't do it, well, they got to hire somebody to
tell somebody, and a lot of people, well, they got—you know, out
in the country they haven't got much—a hand, you know, to do, or
planting a lot. They go over there and do it—a certain, you know,
certain route. And in the meantime they might be planting

something on it—like for money or staple food or whatever when it gets ripe or—you know, harvest.

KS: At harvest time, did you hire people?

TR: Mm hmm. Yeah. People always get rid of it before it spoils.

KS: How did you market what you had? How did you sell it?

TR: Oh, people come and—people come around and they'll ask me— you got to know who—it's just like ordinary, usually—it's got so much for this if you're big enough or you know for so much.

KS: Is that the whole crop then?

TR: No, they just—here and there, just like . . .

KS: Did you like to? . . .

TR: Sometime come somebody, some big dealer comes around—they look at it and they know what they want and then they say, so much of that and so much that [*nods twice*]—well you haul it down there and they know what it's worth and they always—it's already settled, on the farm, and you know. Or else go up there and tell 'em for so much and this—well, if you comply with, well, they sell it.

KS: Did you ever go with your dad?

TR: Once in awhile.

KS: Did you like to?

TR: Well, you know, it's—I guess so much about this and that. I'd stay home and do this or go with him. 'Course, it's a long waste of time.

KS: How did you know whose land belonged to who? Was it fenced?

TR: Well, it's fenced—fenced and the people living on it, and they know—they got their stuff and their horses. It's already lined up— boundaries.

KS: What kind of fencing did you put up?

TR: Oh, the same thing. It's wire fence. Posts.

KS: What time of year did you like best when you were a kid?

TR: Summer.

KS: How—I know the land is different now, the environment is—how did the seasons change or whatever? Is it different?

TR: Mm, same. One season from another. Get cold.

KS: Ever snow?

TR: Once in awhile, like now, every so often. But it rained a lot and now it doesn't. See a lot of rain when I was a kid. See the storm coming, and we know it's going to rain.

KS: When you know there was a storm coming, did you make any preparations for it?

TR: Oh, yeah, yeah. We take in a lot of stuff that's going to get wet, spoil. Like anything. 'Course, we had more rains than any other time I know of—hard rains, like all this hail and all that. Now we don't have it.

KS: Did it ever flood out there?

TR: 'Course, it goes only one way.

KS: Did it damage the village?

TR: No, it's well taken care of. Just go in the ditches along the— wherever the irrigation water goes, it goes right there, and down on the arroyos. Lot of times.

KS: When you were up on the ranch, when it rained did you ever drive the cattle in, or did you just leave them?

TR: No. No, they can stand the rain. They're out there for good. They got the arroyos there. They like the rain.

KS: Did you like it?

TR: The waters come along in that big—them big arroyos [*stretches out arms*] we had right close by the house. We dam it down there where—we had a little ditch to the *charco*[8] where they water in there. If it doesn't go by the other creeks, you know, it goes right into there, where they hold the water for the cattle. A big one, like a lake. And then—or else that comes out all by itself—runs along. That is, if you got a hard rain. And then that big water comes down there [*sweeping motion*]—we'll have to do a little dam in there, you know, where it come into it as a little, goes in the same thing. Used to. Now, never [*nods*].

KS: Were you ever afraid of the storms when you were a child?

TR: Mm.—I mean, I was used to it.

KS: Were there any special places that you like to go when you were a child? I mean just around where you lived.

TR: Well, around there. 'Course, we haven't seen that other place where it's another place, where it took 'em down or someplace, you know. I don't—I won't go around myself—well, they've got to take me around and take me back. Hardly anybody like to take me—a child or—you know, every once in a while.

KS: When you did, say, go into Tucson or go out to Santa Rosa, what kind of preparation did you have to make? Was it a big project?

TR: Hmm—it's all up to the family, how long they going to stay and, you know, how far it is, the trip—you know, food to come by with.

KS: Did you ever sleep out while you were traveling? [See photo 6.]

TR: Oh, they—they don't want to get there, they—they got roads, you know, with the short cut. And they figure so much, how long of a distance to get there, you know, they take that direction.

KS: I see.

TR: Of course, they would be shooting anything, like rabbits, maybe deer, on the way.

KS: Were there special hunting expeditions every? . . .

TR: Well, not all of that—it's just up to the household. Just like up at the ranch, just—these old people, well—old man there and they'll arrange it together and then they make—they get their ammunition, some certain food, go alone, horseback. They might camp over there, you know, maybe two days, three days.

KS: They ever take you with them?

TR: No. They don't—we're not allowed [*shakes head*], 'cause it's too far. And they got to watch what they're doing out there, you know. And then when they're lucky they get that—they kill a deer and then they got to bring it back.

KS: What else did—what other kinds of game did you get, besides deer?

TR: Oh, mostly any—like antelope, if there's any around. Whatever comes along. Same thing as they do now. Mostly deer.

KS: Did you ever hunt birds, or did your family—

TR: No.

KS: Did you have any special kinds of celebrations during the year?

TR: Oh, over there at San Xavier where the church is, when everybody gets together they got some certain days for saints. That's the only time.

KS: What happened then?

TR: Oh, you know, they got—you get to go to church, the priests and all that. People around town, Mexicans and all, they know what's going on—they come there. Fireworks, dancing [*circles arms and sways*], praying.

KS: Were the kids included in the celebration?

TR: Not exactly. Just grownups. 'Course, kids, they don't know what they're going to do, what it's for. Play around. It's just for the grownups. They butcher a cow or whatever. They got a certain committee on it, and they do the whole thing. Butchering and cooking and all that, greeting the people.

KS: What did the children do? Nothing special for them—no races or—

TR: No, no. Just only at Christmas. Christmas time when they get their candy. Oh, there's certain things. They have races—most of the time it's dance, for the old . . .

KS: What was Christmas like, then?

TR: Same—same as it is now.

KS: Did you celebrate it in your family as well as your church?

TR: No, uh-uh. Just the whole thing. Of course, they give presents— they give so this and that and that from each, you know, any family. There's no special—it's for the whole crowd, I'd say.

KS: Did you celebrate the Fourth of July?

TR: Once in a while.

KS: When someone died in the family, were there special rituals that you remember when you were a child—when your grandparents died—

TR: No. It's just like—as it is now. 'Course, I don't know—back—how they did it—they buried 'em—like in the graves where there's made out of rocks, you know, piled up, and that—I don't know so much about that. I just heard about it. But I don't know, on the contrary,

58

you have seen graveyards 'way up in the mountains — it's that old one — how they tear 'em out of there and how they do it — still there.

KS: So when somebody died in your family it was mostly a religious service, then?

TR: Mm hmm.

KS: Did all the relatives come home then?

TR: They're there. Not any far out. Just right in there. Whoever's there is there. 'Course, there's not much you can do. Only praying the rosary — call the priest in there and everything — take 'em to church and then you take it to the cemetery.

KS: Did — do you remember when you were a child — did the first time someone died in the family really affect you?

TR: I never paid attention. Of course, we're not allowed, you know. They'd tell us, "Get away out of there" [*shooing motion*]. They — you know, we be doing this and they'll just send us — "Go play — go play someplace. Just don't hang around. You're bothering — ." You know, they're doing this and this and that.

KS: Preparing the body, and —

TR: Yeah, preparing the body and they're praying and then mostly the children, they'll be — somebody will tell 'em, "Well, go and play over there," you know, just like they do. Just like in that — certain bodies that — taking care of it. If they don't like you hollering or chasing around, they tell you to get over there. Just to get you out of the way.

KS: We talked about illnesses a little bit and about medicine. Were there government doctors that worked around the reservation at all when you were a child?

TR: Mm hmm. Yeah. Oh, there used to be stationed on right in — you know where it is. Sometimes he'll go house-to-house or else you go to him, or that man, he's now there all the time — they got to make a run around. And then sometimes when you're too sick he'll come around, give you medicine and see — pills or whatever they got.

KS: Do you recall when your family ever called in a medicine man?

TR: Yeah. Lot of time I seen 'em. Well, you get too sick and then tell 'em what's wrong with you, you know, whatever it is. They'll probably send you some cures in the night—they sing this and that, certain songs to heal 'em up. Different kind—I don't know the songs. Supposed to be one for certain—certain kind of whatever it is. Like if something—well I don't know—most anything to heal you. Well, they got whatever this medicine man says that's what ailing him; then they—whatever it is. Wind, or whatever it is.[9] So they got to know certain songs about that, or they go with these home singers—they know that; they know to sing that song. Well, they come around at night and then start.

KS: Does that last all night?

TR: Sometimes and sometimes not. A certain part.

KS: Did you stay in your house when they were there?

TR: I never paid attention. It's up to them to cure them. I never—there no special—never anything special for the whole—just if you're sick, that's all.

KS: Did they ever call a medicine man for you?

TR: I don't think so [*cocks head to left*]. Maybe so, but then—

KS: You were too small to remember?

TR: Mm hmm.

KS: Were your parents Catholic?

TR: Yes.

KS: Did you attend church regularly?

TR: Yeah, they used to, when they—when you know, the olden people, you know, they really when I saw them, well, they're in for religion. But now everybody's just stay away from it.

KS: Mm hmm. Did you go to church with them?

TR: We go to church, yeah.

KS: Did the priests ever come to visit you at home?

TR: Mm hmm, yeah. Priest—always priest.

KS: What happened when he came? Did you just—was it a social visit or—

TR: No. It's the mass. 'Course, the priest is right — always there, and they live right by the church.

KS: Mm hmm. Did he ever come to your home to visit?

TR: Once in a while. He never goes around unless he has to. He stays by himself. He doesn't go visiting with the — unless he's got some message or something.

KS: Does the mission look different now than it did when you were a child?

TR: Oh, not too much. Of course, they just work it all — whatever it's — like painting or — keep it up. Never did — only the painting. Of course, they tore some buildings — the school buildings as we call it — and they build another one on the side. They don't use it any more. But it's there to store everything in. Almost the same as it was.

KS: Did you play over around there a lot?

TR: Yeah. Around the church we're not allow to bother the — you know, the priest, when they're having their time in there. They don't need bothering.

KS: You went to school at San Xavier, didn't you, at the church there?

TR: Mm hmm, day school.

KS: The sister teaching there then?

TR: Mm hmm. Yes.

KS: Did you speak English before you went to school?

TR: No. Too young to speak English.

KS: Spoke Spanish and Papago?

TR: You've got to pick it up. English is the main language there. They don't speak that Spanish — you got to pick it up while you're traveling.

KS: I see. But they taught in English at the school, didn't they?

TR: Yes.

KS: Did they ever teach in Papago?

TR: No.

KS: Was it difficult when you first went?

TR: I guess it was [*shrugs*].

KS: Were there things that you liked there or—

TR: Not at all.

KS: No? Did you like the sisters?

TR: Not too much [*shakes head*]. [See photo 7.]

KS: How long did you go to school there? Do you know?

TR: I don't know. I don't know—till I—well, nobody knows. Sometimes when you're of age they just take you out and then they send you some other place. The government, you know.

KS: I'm interested in that. How do they decide where they're going to send a child to school?

TR: Oh, well, they got—they got an arrangement with—well, they got certain places where them send 'em a lot, like in Phoenix and in California, or maybe the priest is—they got schools in California too. And they—they might ask our parents or the parent wants them to go to the Catholic school, you know, down there. They got a lot. I know they sent a lot of them—then they sent 'em over. Or else their parents want 'em just to go to the government school in, you know, Phoenix, or they might want 'em to go to Saint John's where that Catholic school is, priest, you know. It's up to the parents [*nods*]—wherever you want. And then they send 'em there.

KS: Your—you had older brothers, right? Did they go to school at San Xavier before you?

TR: Oh, yeah. Everybody did.

KS: Then did they go on? . . .

TR: Then after then they sent 'em—when they're old enough to take care of—you know, themselves.

KS: Mm hmm. Did they go to school somewhere else, then, after that?

TR: Mm hmm. A lot of them. When they're of age, like ten or something—when they're able to get around. Put their clothes, wash—you know, their—do the same when they get over there. Boarding school.

KS: You were about ten or so when you went?

TR: Mm hmm. Yeah [*nods*].

KS: Were you glad to go?

TR: I don't know. I never was thinking about it or what I wanted. I just didn't think about nothing. What is happening is what's happening. Most of the time, eh — they don't care where they go.

KS: Was it hard for you to leave home?

TR: No.

KS: Did you go? . . .

TR: Got to — it's not hard because there's a lot of children there when they send me.

KS: You knew them?

TR: And then I know some of them. Then after then I get to know most.

KS: How did you go up there? Did your parents take you to Phoenix?

TR: No, they got certain — they got special — well, somebody's got to do something and that they got this — all of this figured out and then they send you either by bus or the train.

KS: A whole bunch together or by yourself?

TR: Together.

KS: Did somebody go with you — a grownup?

TR: No. They're already notified down there and there's a guy about there — with a bus there. When you get off they pick you up and they take you. They just mostly — they do it mostly — place — anyplace among the Indians. At that time when they're — had that big boarding school in —

SIDE TWO

KS: Okay, we were talking about the school — that they sent you all together at one time. What kind of boarding situation did you have up there?

TR: Just like boarding school. Of course, there a lot of children — girls and all. And then they're — we're given assignments where you — numbers for lockers, numbers for clothing, and all that. Well, they go by numbers, and all the — you know, when you look at clothes in the laundry they got numbers, and you know who it belongs to.

KS: Did — who was in charge, then — did you have? . . .

63

TR: They got employees there, just like working there—they got to do certain somebody's got to watch this. Somebody's got to look after the boys, and some lady got to—matron, they call it—girls.

KS: Did you all go to school together or were you separated?

TR: Separated.

KS: The boys weren't together and . . .

TR: No, we go together. 'Course they got certain groups—we're in groups, you know. Whatever they can hold. They go over there and—mornings. In the afternoon they do different kind of trades and then the rest go to school, you know.

KS: Oh, I see. So they alternate.

TR: Alternate, well—same time, but that same time they got to know how many they go so they won't make it so crowded.

KS: How old were the children when they began to teach them trades?

TR: Well, as soon as they're there, you know, and—ten or maybe younger.

KS: What kind of? . . .

TR: All depends how young they are—how their parents sent 'em early, well, they're there early. Or they're there old, well—

KS: What kinds of trades did they teach?

TR: Cattle, farming, dairying, carpentering—most anything. Engineering.

KS: Did you then work part of the time?

TR: You work right on it and that's when you learn. If you're poultry—working with poultry now, like—you got to work with the chickens. And there's always a boss looking after you. Taking care. And they tell you all this and this and that. And you got to gather the eggs—'course, they use the eggs—you got to gather 'em and they take 'em to—where they cook 'em. And then if you're a farmer you got to go out on the farm. There's always somebody to tell you how to do it and—like that. And then if you're a dairyman, there's always somebody there. They tell you how to run the machines or milk. Of course, they haven't got much machines, just very few, but you've got to know. Of course, the cows, you know, they—they know better than you [*nods*]. They know their numbers. They just know where there's—where to lie and whether they can stand and they got numbers on them. There's no certain place were they're supposed to be. When you drive 'em in they just go like that and just go in come certain—one goes 'way up there and walk right up there and go and just start eating that grain or whatever, oats or whatever. 'Course, you got to put 'em in there before you—before you take 'em in. And then they'll teach you—of course, at certain time they'll get you in a class with 'em there and teach you—tell you all that—places, you know, dairying and tell you all about the cow and all that. 'Course, every once in a while they get together and get in a big class, tell you all about the vocation and—whatever it is.

KS: So you—did you have a choice of what you did?

TR: Well, you're—they—if you want a choice you can have a choice but if they see if you're doing the—what you're supposed to do, well, they keep you up, or else if you're not doing—if you're not smart enough, they might change you, you know—they might tell you— ask you—you can do better on this, all right, put you there.

KS: What kind of trades did you do while you were up there?

TR: Oh, well, I—well, you just got to be all over, from the starting point as landscaping you do all the rounds, like parks and all that, around the buildings, cleaning up, cutting those weeds and fence, whatever it's—to be done. And then when you get it you go from place to place and then when you get higher, you know, you get older I mean, and then that when they—pick your choice, whatever you want—carpenter, mechanic, or—then they send you and that's where you belong. And then that's when they start teaching you this—what you do. Instead of that it's—the bosses tell me after that I was doing all right in each and every. I had good grades, you know; they got to test you. I know I had 90s and 98s there. But— and in engineering—I don't know why, I just didn't—didn't like it I guess [*shrugs*]. And I turn around and went to mechanics. Then I stay with mechanics. And then after that engineer, that main

65

engineer told me, "I though you were going to be an engineer. You had good grades there, and then you changed."

KS: Did you like mechanics better?

TR: Oh, about the same. 'Course, I got good grades too but—I should have stayed there, learned more about that, on account of they got so many mechanics right along. Everybody liked it. Lot of them liked it. But I guess maybe engineering is better for me at the time, or right now.

KS: So you also had to go to regular classes.

TR: Mm hmm.

KS: What kind of things did they teach?

TR: Oh, regular, just like an ordinary school.

KS: Did you like that?

TR: Not too much.

KS: Were you a good student?

TR: Well, of course, I've got a lot of big boy, girls and all. Take test in that and that. I don't know—you know how it is—it's—good grades or bad grades—most everybody.

KS: Did you have activities? Did you play sports?

TR: Sports, everything. Most everybody did.

KS: Did you—you didn't have school on weekends. What kind of things did you do?

TR: Oh, you—put you to work, painting around, or whatever you work—you know, like I said before. If you work on the poultry farm, well, you go over there at that—when you're supposed to be there, Saturdays. And you got to do a lot of cleaning—rake and clean out and water the chickens and yard work all over, gather the eggs, feed the chickens, you know, or on the same time they bring in that sacks of mash and you've got to unload it, stack 'em where it's supposed to be. Then you're done.

KS: Did you go to work on Sundays, too?

TR: No. No, we had free days. We go different—you know, certain— not mission like Catholic, Presbyterian, they go—'course, the priest

gets over there and the sisters and all, and they teach us this
catechism and all that.
[*Taping concluded when Ted was served his lunch.*]
(2: 1–16)

In Euro-American autobiography, dramatic presentation and reflection interweave to create a composite of the interior and exterior life
of the subject (Shapiro 1968: 439). Phillipe LeJeune defines autobiography as "the retrospective prose narrative that someone writes concerning his own existence, where the focus is his individual life, in particular the story of his personality" (1971: 14). In the "autobiographical
pact," the autobiographer "explicitly commits himself or herself not to
some impossible historical exactitude but rather to the sincere effort to
come to terms with and to understand his or her own life" (Eakin 1989:
ix). Jeff Todd Titon applies a similar criteria to the broader concept of
oral life stories as narratives that "expose the inner life, tell us about
motives" and affirm the identity of the teller (1980: 290). Ted's narration fits LeJeune's definition in being retrospective, but the method
of addressing the past from the present of his hospital room is directed by my questioning, not his sense of retrospective. Ted provides
a chronicle of some events — directed by my choice of questions —
but the material does not develop a progressive, individual development nor fit the paradigm of autobiographical revelation of personal
identity.[10]

Ted's responses to my interrogation consistently lack interpretation.[11] Though, like all autobiographers, he reconstitutes his past in
language from the present perspective, he does not overtly evaluate
his circumstances or experiences or claim any personal volition for the
incidents of his youth. In this sense he fits Paul Smith's definition of the
term "subject" as one who is "the object of determinant forces" (1988:
xxxiv). He follows the direction of others — elders, teachers, bosses,
even when the choices are not much to his liking — a pattern that persists throughout his narrative and one that reveals both his cultural

perspective on the concept of human agency and his personal relationship to circumstances and authority.[12] Unlike Smith's concept of the "individual" as one "who determines the character or constitution of his/her own subjectivity" (1988: xxxiv), Ted accepts whatever tasks and roles circumstances thrust upon him without apparent resistance or resentment. Moreover, his narrative rarely acknowledges emotional or even analytical responses to events. Though Ted sometimes exhibited emotion about an event through tone of voice, facial expression of humor or puzzlement or irritation, or even on rare occasions by tearing up, the actual words of his narrative betray little passion, regret, guilt, or joy, or inclination to examine his intentions, motives, or desires. Even when he does articulate reaction to his experiences, as in his regret at switching from engineering to mechanics as an area of specialization at the Phoenix Indian School, he expresses his emotion only indirectly, as a missed opportunity. Or as in his statement that he did not like the nuns at the mission school "too much," he does not offer any explanation why. Or in the instance where I asked him to remark on the effect of a family death, he dismisses the query altogether when he says, "I never paid any attention." Most telling is his claim, "I just didn't think about anything." Obviously the claim is an impossibility, but it firmly limits the dialogue between Ted and me to behavior, not emotional or interpretive responses.[13] Though, as the transcript reveals, I did fairly consistently ask him to comment on his feelings about particular events or conditions, I did not probe his emotions aggressively.[14] But even if I had, I doubt he would have been forthcoming. Whether his reticence was cultural, influenced by generational and gender differences between us, deliberate resistance, or simply part of his personal habit of mind—or all four—is irrecoverable. But what is interesting about the lack of interpretation and emotional expression is that he resists the autobiographical convention of self-disclosure.

Unlike the literary autobiographer, Ted does not project meaning into the past. In fact, I believe he consciously delegated discovery of meaning in his life story to me as part of my responsibility in the collaboration.[15] Ted's narrative is not one of self-discovery through language. He refuses to bear witness to the meaning of his life by withholding expression of interior states of mind, a stance not uncommon in Native American collaborative narratives, but nonetheless a thwarting of reader expectation. Autobiography readers familiar with Euro-American models take up a personal narrative with a culturally specific system of signification firmly in place; they anticipate revelation of not only socially directed actions but of agency, and they seek insight into the intimate thoughts and feelings of the subject and a pattern of cause and effect that reveals motivation. Readers want to participate, to feel an intimate relationship with the narrator accessed through the narrator's memory and self-awareness as revealed through a personal style of expressing "emotional color and context," which provide the reader with an integrated recreation of a knowable world and individual (Shapiro 1968: 433). Never mind that the persona developed by the narrator is a fiction based on personal intention and the highly selective and frail properties of memory. Readers expect a verifiable, authentic person to be depicted in the narrative and want to know the interior life of a narrator who claims authorship with his or her signature.

However, even in that basic element of authorizing, Ted's narrative violates convention: his life inscription is a collaboration that carries two signatures.[16] As LeJeune points out, it is not collaboration that is disturbing to readers: it is the dual signature, which "reveals the secrets of fabrication" (1989: 186), that distresses them. Publicly acknowledged dual authorship "necessarily subverts the concepts of the unified author and person" (Eakin 1989: xvii) and undermines the intimacy of autobiography's presumably confessional quality and revelation of interior life. As LeJeune colloquially argues, two signatures "let the cat out of the bag" and violate the rules of the game (1989: 186, 190). The "true self" is demonstrably an artifact in publicly acknowledged collaborative "auto"biography. The *"division of labor* between two people (at least) reveals the multiplicity of authorities implied in the work" and elaborates on the authority of the "I" who seems to write but is more source than author and who may be induced "to narrative and descriptive methods that might be quite different from his own" (LeJeune 1989: 188–89). Given the reader's desire for a transparent relationship with the narrator, the acknowledged mediation of the collector-editor inhibits the sense of intimacy assigned to the genre.

In the case of Ted's narration, exposed collaboration is not the major determiner of a reserved presentation of the subject. Rather it is Ted's own style of narration, which he maintains in spite of prodding toward greater self-disclosure, that frustrates the readerly expectation shaped by genre familiarity. Deliberate exposure of dual authorship creates a situation, and a text, that challenges genre expectation. Because the narrative is cross-cultural, monoculturally imposed expectations are thwarted. But more important to his narration's resistance to genre convention and reader accessibility is that Ted maintains his culturally determined methods of self-presentation. In doing so, he minimizes his authorship by diffusing his personal presence in the text as well as by resisting elicitation of interpretation of his experiences.

The following edited form of the second interview more nearly fits reader expectation of an autobiographical narrative because it appears to be continuous and progressive, though when analyzed it is clearly sporadic and disjunctive. It also more clearly reveals how tentatively Ted authorizes his own past, how much more comfortable he is in describing others or generalizing than he is in telling his own life. Grammatically, he, as authorizing narrator, is barely present in his own life. Frequently he depersonalizes the experiences he narrates by avoiding the personal pronoun "I." He consistently generalizes by diffusing the experiences to "we" and even detaches himself from his own past by talking in third person about what was actually happening to himself.[17] As Elizabeth Bruss points out, "Language is itself positional, a vivid reflector and also a shaper of pragmatic situations." Her observation applies specifically to Ted's choice of pronouns when she notes that linguistic features include "whole ranges of cultural distinctions regarding interests and capacities, appropriate social relationships, and possible relationships to the world" (1976: 19). While establishing "distance with regard to himself in order to reconstitute himself" in language is a recognized characteristic of the autobiographer's strategy for creating "unity and identity across time" (Gusdorf 1980: 35), Ted's rare use of "I" is more closely associated with non-Western modes of life story in which the narrator does not define himself as unique but explores a "sense of shared identity" expressed in "fluid ego boundaries" (Friedman 1988: 44). Ted's use of multiple pronouns reflects multiple subject positions that he engages in relationship to his community and as narrator in a cross-cultural project. Experience, shared within his culture and shareable with a non-Native readership—rather than the uniquely individuated self of conventional autobiography—is the rhetorical strategy in Ted's narrative. He sees himself and his experiences as ordinary, again a stance contrary to the exalted individual, the successful achiever and self-appointed model of Euro-American autobiography. He does not posit himself as culturally central; by defining his identity in terms of "we," he emphasizes his experiences and himself as typical, which brings his narrative closer to ethnographic life story than literary autobiography.[18]

The edited text of the above transcript follows. Without the apparatus of question and answer, several other rhetorical strategies Ted employs for resisting conventional autobiography are more accessible.

They taught us to watch what they're doing, or sometimes they just say to us, "You take it over. We'll see how you do it." And then we just keep on, keep on, do it a lot of time; then we know how it's done. Of course, we do most of the farming work—cover the little chilies growing up or squash or whatever.

They show us how to do it at the beginning, then when the plants get older, spreading out, then you do it different, and then on and on and then finally when they get so big, all you do is watch

71

the weeds. At the beginning you've got to be told this and this and that. There are certain plants you have to do by hand. Some we put in with the planter, like corn. But out there on the ranch, where my grandfather lived, he'd do it by hand, with a plow, and we'd put 'em in by hand and then kind of squish 'em in so far apart [*presses down with both hands*]. My grandmother know how to do it too. When he wasn't around, well, she's the boss [*lifts chin and shrugs*].

We have picks, hoes, or shovels—all that. There's cultivators, but we mostly used horse and plow. We done all the work, all the time. We plant several crops during the year. Once in a while when somebody has a whole lot and can't do it, they have to hire somebody or tell somebody and a lot of people do the planting. They go over there and do it. Harvesting too. People always get rid of it before it spoils. People come around and they ask about the crop, some big dealer comes around; they look at the crop. They know what they want and then they say, so much of that and so much of that [*nods twice*]. We haul it to Tucson, and they'd know what it was worth because it's already settled on the farm. The land's fenced and people living on it, and they got their stuff and their horses. It's already lined up with boundaries. There's wire fence and posts.

It rained a lot then and now it doesn't. I saw a lot of rain when I was a kid. We'd see the storm coming and we'd know it was going to rain. We'd take in a lot of stuff that's going to get wet, spoil. The rain goes in the ditches along where the irrigation water goes, or down the arroyos. Cattle can stand the rain. They're out there for good. They got the arroyos there and they like the rain. The waters come along in them big arroyos [*stretches out arms*] we had right close by the house. We dam it down there where we had a little ditch to the *charco* where the cattle water. If it didn't go into the other creeks, it goes right into there, where they hold the water for the cattle, like a lake. That is, if you got a hard rain. And when that big water comes down there [*sweeping motion*], we'd have to make a little dam in there. Used to. Now, never [*shakes head*]. I was used to the storms, not afraid.

When we traveled, they would be shooting anything, like rabbits, maybe deer, on the way. Up at the ranch, to go hunting, these old people arrange it together, and then they get their ammunition, some certain food, go alone, on horseback. They might camp over there, you know, maybe two days, three days. We're not allowed [*shakes head*] 'cause it's too far. And they got to watch what they're doing out there, you know. And then when they're lucky, they kill a deer, and they got to bring it back, or antelope, if there's any around. Whatever comes along. Same as they do now. Mostly deer.

Over there at San Xavier where the church is, when everybody gets together, they got some certain days for saints. Then you've got to go to church, the priests and all that. People around town, Mexicans and all, they know what's going on and they come there for fireworks, dancing [*circles arms and sways*], praying. Kids don't know what they're going to do, what it's for, so they play around. It's just for grownups. They butcher a cow or whatever. They have a committee on it, and they do the whole thing, butchering and cooking and all that, greeting the people. At Christmas there was something for children. Christmastime they get their candy. They have races, but most of the time it's dancing for the old people.

When someone died it was as it is now. 'Course, I don't know way back then how they did it; they buried 'em in the graves made out of rocks piled up. I don't know so much about that. I just heard about it. When someone died, there's not much you can do, only praying the rosary, call the priest in there and everything, take 'em to church. I never paid any attention. Of course, we're not allowed around. They'd tell us, "Get away out of there [*shooing motion*]. Go play, go play someplace. Just don't hang around. You're bothering." They're preparing the body and praying, and they they'd tell the children, "Well, go over and play over there."

If they don't like us hollering or chasing around, they tell us to get over there, just to get us out of the way.

There used to be a government doctor stationed right here. Sometimes he'll go house-to-house or else you go to him. And then sometimes when you're too sick, he'll come around, give us medicine, pills or whatever. Or they call a medicine man. Lot of time I seen 'em. If you get too sick, tell 'em what's wrong with you. They'll probably send you some cures. At night they sing certain songs to heal, different kinds. I don't know the songs. There's one for each sickness. Whatever the medicine man says that's what ailing the person, wind or whatever it is, they got to know certain songs about that. Well, they come around at night and then start.

And priest, always the priest. The priest is always there, and they live right by the church. Once in a while, he come to our house, but he never goes around unless he has to. He stays by himself. He doesn't go visiting unless he's got a message or something.

School was difficult when I first went, I guess [*shrugs*]. I was too young to speak English. You got to pick it up. English is the main language there. They don't speak Spanish. I didn't like the sisters too much [*shakes head*]. After mission school, they got an arrangement with—well, they got certain places where they send 'em a lot, like Phoenix and in California. Priests got schools there in California too. They got a lot. They might ask our parents whether they want us to go to Catholic school. I know they sent a lot of them over. Or else the parents want 'em to just go to the government school in Phoenix, or they might send 'em to go to Saint John's where that Catholic school is. It's up to the parents [*nods*]. They send 'em to boarding school when they're old enough to take care of themselves, like ten or something, when they're able to get around. I was ten [*nods*].

I never was thinking about it or what I wanted. I just didn't think about anything. But it's not hard because there's a lot of children there where they send me. I know some of them. They send us together either on the bus or the train. They're already notified in Phoenix and there's a guy with a bus there. When we get off, they pick us up and take us. There's lots of children — girls and all. And they're giving assignments: numbers for lockers, numbers for clothing, and all that. They go by numbers; when you look at clothes in the laundry, they got numbers, and you know who they belong to. [See photo 8.]

They got employees there; somebody's got to look after the boys, and some matrons for girls. We're in groups. In the afternoon we do different kinds of trades, and the other half go to school. Alternate so they won't make it so crowded. They taught us cattle, farming, dairying, carpentering, engineering. You work and that's when you learn. If you're in poultry, you got to work with chickens. And there's always a boss looking after you, taking care. And you got to gather the eggs. They use the eggs. You got to gather 'em, and they take 'em to where they cook 'em.

And then if you're a farmer, you got to go out on the farm. There's always somebody to tell you how to do it. And then if you're a dairyman, there's always somebody there. They tell you how to run the machines and how to milk. Of course, they haven't many machines, just very few, but you've got to know. Of course, the cows, they know better than you [*nods*]. They just know where to lie and whether they can stand, and they got numbers on them. There's no certain place where they're supposed to be. When we drive 'em in they just go up there and walk right up there and start eating that grain or oats or whatever. You got to put the feed in there before you take 'em in. And they'd teach you, tell you all that.

If you want a choice you have a choice, but if you're doing what you're supposed to do, well, they keep you at it, or else if you're not smart enough, they might change you. They might ask you if you can do better on something else and put you there. You got to be all over, from the starting point at landscaping, you do all the rounds, like parks and all that, around the buildings, cleaning up, cutting those weeds. And then when you get it, you go from place to place, and then when you get older, that's when you pick your choice, whatever you want—carpenter, mechanic. Then they send you where you belong. That's when they start teaching you what to do.

I had good grades, you know; I know I had 90s and 98s there except in engineering. I don't know why; I just didn't like it, I guess [*shrugs*]. And I turned around and went to mechanics. Then I stayed with mechanics. And then later that engineer, that main engineer told me, "I thought you were going to be an engineer. You had good grades there, and then you change." Course, I got good grades in mechanics right along. Everybody liked it. Lot of them liked it. So I guess maybe engineering was better for me.

On weekends, they put us to work, painting around, or whatever. If you work on the poultry farm, well, you go over there Saturdays. And you got to do a lot of cleaning, feed the chickens, raking and cleaning out and watering the chickens and yard work, gathering the eggs. They bring in sacks of mash and you've got to unload it, stack 'em. Then you're done. We had free day Sundays. (edited tape 2: 1–6)

In this edited and condensed version of the second taped interview, the retrospective quality of the narrative is obvious, but it exhibits no attempt by Ted to "come to terms with and understand" himself as a historically situated individual (Eakin 1989: ix). Though there is some sense of time period—most of what is discussed has to do with Ted's childhood—no dates are used, and his age is not clear except in terms of San Xavier experiences and the Phoenix Indian School period. Comparative terms appear—older, later—but no specific time markers. Spatial markers are equally vague—farm, ranch, river, school. Without a particularized articulation of time and place, the events are abstracted and lack connection or coherence. The narrative, even in edited form, achieves no continuity of discourse because the dialogue of the interview was sporadic and disjunctive, held together only by regional location and a broad concept of Ted's youth. Further, the questions allow Ted to generalize about rather than personally claim his experiences. The tape and edited narrative are therefore somewhat useful as a source of ethnographic data but disappointing as a narrative of emerging subjectivity.

A progressive time-line, a continuous and comprehensive story, singular authorship, and narrative interpretation are the central characteristics of Western autobiography that Ted's oral telling and edited text refuse to inscribe. Ted's resistance to Euro-American criteria for autobiography as defined by literary critics makes his narrative a failure by generic standards. But I don't think it's a failure. It's simply something other than autobiography. But if his narrative isn't autobiography, what on earth is it? Since ethnography defines personal narrative much more broadly, Ted's oral, collaborative narrative is at least in some measure successful as ethnography since it communicates cultural data and personal behavior. But even as traditional ethnography narrative, Ted's story seems valuable primarily for positing generalizations about the role of Papago males in a period of transition, which reduces his narrative to case history and entirely ignores his style of expressing himself. Even as performative storytelling, Ted's narrative is only marginally significant since it incorporates a limited number of anecdotes and stories that meet folklore criteria for authentic performance. Yet, I don't think Ted's narration can be dismissed because it does not fit Western notions of specific genres. Ted's narrative is not sui generis. Except for the fact that I have not edited it into chronological order and deleted questions and repetitions, it is very similar to hundreds of texts generally grouped under the term Native American autobiography, a term I find both inaccurate and misleading, one which continually forces producers and critics of these texts to attempt to justify them within the constricting limits of a Western literary genre.

From my present perspective, I view our project as collaborative biography. While Ted's narrative violates in some measure every criteria of autobiography, his life story meets most biography expectations, especially in that it recognizes collaboration as a legitimate methodology.[19] Though the term biography is also a Western literary designation, it is much more accommodating to the methodology as it actually exists in the collection and editing of Native American personal narrative.[20] I hope that the ensuing discussion of what is most commonly called Native American autobiography, and Ted's narrative in relationship to that designation, will make a case for incorporating Native American collaborative biography as a category and term into future studies of similar works.

ℰ 3

NATIVE AMERICAN

COLLABORATIVE PERSONAL

NARRATIVE

There are no models for *Telling a Good One*. Even among the over six hundred published texts usually termed Native American autobiographies (Brumble 1988: 10), there are, to my knowledge, no presentations of Native American life story that concentrate on addressing personal narrative as a process rather than a product of briefly acknowledged and then firmly suppressed methodology. I don't mean to imply that I think that this attempt to reveal the process of the collaboration Ted and I engaged in is therefore somehow superior to previous publications of Native American personal narratives. I know that this presentation of interviews and inscribed text is far less "literary" and thus less readable than most of the works that have preceded it, and far less successful as a coherent narrative. In many ways it sacrifices Ted's intention in agreeing to be interviewed to a text that uses rather than forefronts his narrations. It's disjunctive to juxtapose narrative and analysis, to expose methodology. I believe, however, that there is a gap that this volume can fill, that the work that Ted and I did together as it appears here might provide some insight into the *how* of Native American personal narrative that has been glossed over in most previous presentations.[1]

Revelation of the process of collecting, editing, and structuring collaborative Native American personal narratives is consistently relegated to methodological introductions, if it appears at all. Presentation of interviews and material in the order it is narrated, in the rare cases when they are incorporated into a volume, appear in appendixes. Almost never are both participants in the collaborative process overtly present in the text, and when they are, the format is not dialogic.[2] Rarely have those who control the presentation of Native narrations — collector-editors — ventured outside the conventions discussed in the two previous chapters.[3] And with good reason. Text, not process, has traditionally been the central concern of collaborators and their audiences, and of publishers.[4] Understandably so, given the Euro-American generic conventions that influence the production and presentation of Native American "autobiography" and the expectations of largely non-Native American audience for them. Until recently, even scholars, especially literary critics — and I count myself among them — have done little more than lament the lack of methodological material in published texts.[5] In fact, until fairly recently, scholars have not intensively probed published texts for evidence of methodology embedded in the narratives.[6] Furthermore, because many of the scholars whose work centers on analysis of Native American "autobiography" have no experience of actually collecting and editing personal narrative, examinations of published texts tend not to incorporate very well-informed speculation on the actual composition of the narratives under study. Literary critics, especially, I think, have an idea that what goes on in the collaborative process is much more deliberate, organized, and fruitful than is generally the case. Recent introductions and critical essays by ethnographers who collect personal narrative are beginning to crack open naive notions of collaborative intimacy, common intention, and narrative tidiness.[7] But even most of those, in order to keep the narrative dominant, do not integrate discussion of process directly into the text.

I'd feel a lot less anxiety and a lot more competency about composing this volume if there were an established tradition of reflexive Native American collaborative narratives on which to rely for models. It would be much more comfortable to fit this study into an established scholarly context than to write against the grain.[8] When I described what I intended to do in this volume to a friend and colleague, his comment, none too gently proffered, went something like this: "So now that you've read up on theory, you think you're ready to make something out of the stuff you haven't been able to use." I bristled, made a case for my project as working against most existing theory, and fumed some more. But when I thought about what he said honestly, I had to admit his observation is fair and a well-considered warning that theory and disciplinary history could easily become the shaping elements of this volume, and deflect the project away from the fact that this book is in some sense an extended admission of incompetence and a long apology to a narrator who expected better of me. My colleague's caution that scholarly discourse could easily deflect this study away from analysis of the Rios-Sands project to justification of it in theoretical terms, while discomforting—or maybe precisely because it is discomforting since it demands I discard a strictly academic form of discourse for a riskier one—has merit.[9]

Ted often used the phrase "braved himself up" in his narratives. I guess that's what I've been doing for two decades by reading ethnographic and literary theory and the history of each. "Brave" is overstating the case, but despite the fact that I define this project as resistance to conventional inscription of Native American collaborative personal narrative, yes, I do value the scholarship that has developed since the mid-1970s, partly because it legitimizes Native American personal narrative as a valid form of expression but, more selfishly, because in the last decade it has increasingly authorized writing about the dialogic process and inscription of narrative. It grants license to self-reflexivity and permission to try new forms of presentation.

Though I have no intention here to reprise the history of Native American "autobiography"—that would be redundant since comprehensive critical studies of the "genre" are already in print[10]—there are several published narratives that I think have bearing on the Rios-Sands project and facilitate discussion of methodology of inscription, each for a different reason. My unconventional approach to presenting Ted's narrative, *Telling a Good One,* becomes more comprehensible when placed in the context of other of works that also resist or expand upon the conventions of Native American "autobiography."

The one that most closely parallels the Rios narrative is a recent publication, *Corbett Mack: The Life of a Northern Paiute as Told by Michael Hittman* (Mack 1996). From 1965–1972 Hittman interviewed Mack over fifty times (1996: 6), beginning work with him as a graduate student in search of data on aspects of traditional culture, especially food lore, among the Yerington Paiute tribe of Nevada (1996: 2–3). In 1968, the project evolved into a more concentrated study of the use of opiates among this Native American group and then proceeded as a collection of Mack's life experiences, incorporating revelations of his addiction to narcotics. While Hittman's overall structure is conventional — introduction, narrative text, epilogue — his level of self-disclosure and discussion of methodology are unusually forthcoming.[11] Hittman's introduction to Mack's life story, besides giving a brief history of opiate use and a summary of Mack's life, is a methodologically revealing discussion of his relationship with Mack, making it an exceptionally self-reflexive analysis of his work with the subject of the "autobiography" whom he characterizes as an experienced informant (1996: 3). In the introduction, Hittman discusses the circumstances of their first meeting, payment of commodities during their work together, his own admission of using dope as a catalyst for Mack's candor about his use of drugs, his timetable and a sample of what transpired during their first four encounters, a rationale for his organization of the narrative in the ensuing 241 pages of Mack's text, and a transcript of his final interview with Mack in an epilogue.

While there are not a great many similarities in Mack's and Rios's lives, there a few: both were rather ordinary tribal males, both worked in ranching and agriculture, both suffered from substance addiction, and both lived during a post-traditional period. What is more interesting and useful for my purposes is that Mack's narrative, although it has been put in chronological order by Hittman, is presented in brief episodes, many personal in focus but many others on cultural topics. This structuring of the narrative does not attempt to suppress the disjunctive process of the interviews; in fact, it calls attention to the sporadic and dialogic process that produced the content of the narrative. What in my case was an abortive attempt at organizing Ted's narrative topically/chronologically, Hittman brought to a coherent conclusion, weaving in Mack's narratives of traditional lore into the personal narrative where the material connected topically. Hittman employs a standard chronological strategy to organize the narrative material into eight chapters by time periods and broad predictable topics such as "Birth and Family (1892)," "Boyhood (1892–1905)," "Boarding School (1905–10)," and so on through chapter eight, "Retirement Years (1954–74)." Within each chapter, there are numbered entries in a fairly continuous narrative, 159 in all. However, though the chapters break the narrative into chronological segments, the continuously numbered entries reveal the episodic source of the narrative from interviews. The resulting narrative is somewhat choppy but preserves a sense of narrative expressed orally, jumping rather than segueing from place to place and topic to topic. While Hittman does not specifically discuss or demonstrate his editing of individual entries in the narrative, the text retains clues to Hittman's techniques for preserving Mack's oral style. For instance, in the following passage that covers material somewhat similar to that addressed by Ted in his recollection of learning to do ranch work, Mack's voice, speech rhythm, and grammar are evident as are Hittman's insertion of explanatory words and identifiers. Hittman's transcription and editing technique appears to be very similar to that which I have used in transforming Ted's tape-recorded oral language to inscribed narrative. There is no attempt to make Mack's narrative literary; conversely, Hittman seems to make every effort to resist editing for smoothness or even total clarity: Paiute words are not translated, false starts are retained, and elided sounds are indicated:

Big Mack, he learn me everythin': you know, how to irrigate, stack hay. . . . Then after I get older, why, I can do it myself. And call that *tuuvaroi'ee*, that irrigatin' work. . . .

'Cause the Old Man, he take care the beddin', and [also] cook on them cattle drive we go on for Frank Simpson. Cook as good as any woman, too, by God! Yes, sir! Same way, too, after Old Man [Dan] Simpson's boy [Frank] cut up that ranch, he can feed cattle in winter. 'Cause that's the only kind of job there is in Smith Valley wintertime . . . before the *Aytayay* come. Yes, sir! Feed cattle for Al Trielof. . . . 'Cause them rancher, you know they're always askin' for him [Big Mack] to work. . . .

And so that's what I [also] do: help Frank Simpson on that cattle drive to Leavitt Meadow every summer. Then feed 'em all winter. Then no more cattle, when Simpson sell out, I can irrigate and stack hay. (1996: 83)

Besides compiling a continuous narrative, Hittman includes alternate versions of certain incidents, again calling attention to the interviews, and in the final chapter includes seven traditional tales.

Ted's life story might have come out very much like Mack's had I followed through with the cut-and-paste strategy I started but gave up on in the 1980s. The advantage of Hittman's organizational strategy is that Mack is the dominant figure in the volume; Hittman is a facilitating figure. The disadvantage is that the methodology, as usual, is constrained by placement in a brief introduction, and there is only a three-page sample of interview transcript. While Hittman is more candid about his role in the production of the volume than most collector-editors, much is still left to speculation on limited evidence.

A much earlier volume, *The Fifth World of Forster Bennett: Portrait of a Navaho* (1972), by Vincent Crapanzano, probably better known for his ground-breaking ethnopsychiatric studies of Moroccan men and essays on ethnographic theory, provides an example of life-story inscription that incorporates the collector-editor into the narrative text and concentrates on the field relationship between the subject and the ethnographer. Like Corbett Mack's and Ted Rios's narratives, it is a life story collected while the editor was still in graduate school,[12] and Forster Bennett, the title figure in the volume, is another "ordinary" Native American man of the same generation as Mack and Rios. The volume begins with a disclaimer that introduces Crapanzano's self-reflexive bent two decades before such a concept was recognized as legitimate in ethnography. In the book's foreword, he specifically informs readers that the narrative is not the conventional Indian auto-biography audiences for this "genre" might expect. He says, "*The Fifth World* is, rather, a personal account of the reaction — sometimes naive, often arrogant — of an 'Anglo,' an East-Coaster who had been oriented more toward Europe than toward his own country, during one short summer on the Navaho reservation" (1972: v). He also warns that the book "touches upon material dear to the anthropologist, but it is not, at least in any technical sense, a work of anthropology and was never meant to be one, despite the fact that readers who insist on classifying a work not in its own terms but by whatever particular label society attaches to its author will inevitably judge it as such" (1972: v). The fact that he emphasizes his disciplinary identification as the determiner of classification of the ensuing work is indicative of how firmly Native American personal narrative is connected to ethnography even as it oddly bears assignment to a literary genre. The subtitle of the book, *Portrait of a Navaho,* suggests ethno-biography, but the text is actually a field diary.

Interestingly, Crapanzano cites Irving Goffman's metaphor of back and front stages of action to define his intention and role in the book. He says it is the graduate student "I" of the narrative who has prevented him, the retrospective analyzer of his own field journal, "from dressing up the manuscript in the years that have gone by since the book was written" (vi).[13] He resists convention to reveal process. He notes that foregrounding and interpreting the "backstage," the author's role in the production of the volume, is his intention. He then admits that "*The Fifth World* has had a long and difficult history" (1972: vi), entailing unconventional choices for representing his inter-action with Forster Bennett, some of which he discusses in the intro-duction. About his choice of a journal format, he says, "I found that a journal provided a temporal framework through which changes in my informant's behavior and in my own perceptions could be re-corded. . . . To have written an account of Forster's life, for example, in the standard life-history form would have been like putting together a jigsaw puzzle in which none of the parts exactly fit" (1972: 16). The puzzle metaphor aptly describes my sentiments about Ted's narrative when I tried to fit it into a conventional life story.

What Crapanzano does, instead of forcing the data he collected in the field into a continuous narrative, is portray Bennett by means of on-site interpretation of the verbal and observational interactions he has with him. He begins his narrative ethnography with himself and the disorienting experience of his arrival, exposing the same anxiety I recall when I drove out to Sells to begin my work with Ted.[14] He writes, "I was naturally apprehensive when we drove out to the Navaho reser-vation. I had never been on a reservation before." He admits that as an adult he had "never spoken to an Indian" (1972: 25).[15] He goes on to detail his sense of alienation as he comes to the community where he will do his work in the company of an acquaintance who lives on the reservation:

> The desert, opening suddenly below us as the car climbed up and over a ridge, managed to obliterate every certainty of scale and space. It could have been a moonscape. It was the color of weath-ered rust, but it was splotched with green here and there until the reservation itself began. Then there was no more green—noth-ing to fix on, nothing to orient the eye. We were halfway through Little Bluff before I realized that we were there. I caught a fleet-ing glimpse of Forster Bennett's camp and the hogan in which I would be living for the next seven weeks. (1972: 25–26)

86

The day-by-day entries in the field journal detail the family activities at Bennett's camp and at a ceremony, conversations with family members, some direct questioning of Bennett to which Bennett responds with no lengthy narrations, information about Bennett gleaned from other sources in the community, incidents of conflict between himself and Bennett, and a good deal of introspective interpretation of the experiences of his seven-week stay at Little Bluff by Crapanzano.[16] The entries each begin with the month and day, but no indication of the year is given anywhere in the book. So while the interactions are clearly situated in a specific landscape, they are not embedded in a time-line. And aside from the brief introduction, there is no further retrospective commentary by the author.

Precisely because *The Fifth World* is very different from most Native American personal narrative volumes in that it does not actually present a comprehensive life story as the title suggests, it offers some precedent for *Telling a Good One* in that the field collector selects an unconventional way of presenting data about the title character. It also interprets the process of collection and personal reactions to the field experience and integrates them into the narrative. As a psychoanalytic ethnographer, Crapanzano's intention is to probe the mind-set and expression of Bennett's personality,[17] while my interest in Ted's narrative focuses more on his style as a narrator, but *The Fifth World* provides a rare example of a volume that deliberately exposes the field side of life-story process.

Two more recent works, Margaret Blackman's *During My Time: Florence Edenshaw Davidson, A Haida Woman* (1992b)[18] and Julie Cruikshank's *Life Lived Like a Story: Life Stories of Three Yukon Native Elders* (1990),[19] written in collaboration with Angela Sidney, Kitty Smith, and Annie Ned, have also challenged traditional conventions of Native American personal narrative and influenced how I have addressed and interpret Ted's narrative.[20]

In the preface to the revised edition of *During My Time,* Blackman makes an observation that is pertinent to both my attitude about life stories and about how Ted's personal narrative has eluded resolution:

> Squeezed between hardcover is the text of a life, its beginning, its turning points, its closure at the time of the telling. It represents in some ways a final statement, an authoritative text on the life lived and recalled, but in reality a life story is never finished. . . . Story and the text are further subject to alterations over time as the narrator ages, rethinks, revises and retells, and as the editor reconsiders the representation of life-history material. (1992b: xi)

The afterlife of the project, then, allows the collaborators to reinterpret the original encounter and the inscription that grows out of it. In the best of cases—unfortunately not with the Rios narrative—both parties in the collaboration contribute to an open-ended reassessment of the original narration, as they do in the republication of *During My Time*. This destabilizes the authority of the written text and points to the impossibility of fixity and closure even for published inscriptions. Blackman explains the effect of on-going reassessment further, saying, "Every life history interviewee obviously edits the telling of his or her story, and consequently every life story is a partial story." She also points to the asymmetries in collaboration that "give the advantage to the editor" (1992b: xiv). That advantage is irrefutable—*Telling a Good One* demonstrates Blackman's observation aggressively—but the partiality of the story is a shared element of collaboration, not just the editor's responsibility. Editors do not conventionally use everything they collect. To do so would probably produce an overly long, unwieldy, and unreadable book. But neither do narrators tell everything about their lives. Memory fails, sometimes words fail, and often events and recollections do not suit the narrator's sense of an appropriate public story. In these separate but related processes of redaction, two editors work, sometimes at odds with one another. The collector-editor always wants more; the narrator-editor resists full disclosure by omission or perhaps by ameliorating memories.[21]

While the organization of *During My Time* is conventionally ethno-graphic — with chapters on Haida women and a biographical sketch of Davidson introducing the actual narrative that runs seventy-six pages and is framed by a discussion and an appendix that gives a four-page interview transcript sample — the addition in 1992 of a new preface and an epilogue add considerably to the interpretive elements of the volume.[22] For instance, Blackman incorporates some personal history of her own, the birth of a child, and admits after the publication of the 1982 edition that she "thought often of the questions I might have asked, but had not" (1992b: 180). Her statement indirectly confirms what is obvious to me about my relationship to my interviews with Ted. Aging and experience make a huge difference in how we read what we have collected and how we become aware of and regret what we did not have the insight to explore. But she also points out that second chances do not guarantee more or better material when she describes an interview in 1989: "The tape rolled on, but nothing else came" (1992b: 179). The reservoir of memory is not limitless, not a bottomless well, as I discovered in interviewing Ted.[23] His responses, while often circling back to add some detail to a previously covered topic, became very repetitive as our interviews extended into 1975. A life holds only so much experience, so many memories, or at least memories a nar-rator deems worth telling.[24] After hours and hours of interviews, the story runs out. Memory is indeed fragile. In some measure, that makes the role of the interviewer perhaps slightly less negative. Though in-vasion of the narrator's past is intrusive, and sometimes even painful, it is the interaction with the collaborator that activates memories and produces the language of narrative. So while the interview process pro-duces only partial and unreliable and usually discontinuous narrative, it does produce what might otherwise be entirely lost.

Life Lived Like a Story interestingly preserves the narrators' memo-ries, not only of their personal experiences but of cultural history and oral tradition that shape them. Julie Cruikshank's ten-year collaboration with three Yukon women, Angela Sidney, Kitty Smith, and Annie Ned, is my idea of an exceptionally fine example of inscription of Native American lives. I admire *Life Lived Like a Story* primarily because I think it comes closer to evoking oral narrative in a manner that both exposes better than anything currently in print the process of inscripting and inscribes narratives that create a dialogic relationship between the individual lives of the narrators and the traditional storytelling of their cultures.[25]

In keeping with most contemporary ethnographic collections of personal narratives, Cruikshank frames the Native women's life stories with an introduction discussing her methodology and a concluding analytical chapter. She also supplies an introduction to each of the three personal narratives that addresses methodology. That format, along with the juxtapositioning of traditional and personal narratives in the individual life stories, provides for considerably more methodological information than is usually available and effectively details the collaborative process of producing the personal narratives as an emerging one largely controlled by the Yukon women. Cruikshank explains that, over time, her understanding of *our* [emphasis mine] objectives shifted significantly. She writes that initially she

> expected that by recording life histories we would be documenting oral history, compiling accounts that would be stored, like archival documents, for later analysis. I was interested in hearing women talk about events chronicled in written documents and records and tried to steer our conversations in that direction. Although the older women responded patiently to my line of inquiry for awhile, they quite firmly shifted the emphasis to "more important" accounts they wanted me to record — particularly events central to traditional narrative. Gradually, I came to see oral tradition not as "evidence" about the past but as a window on ways the past is culturally constituted and discussed. (1990:14)

She goes on to explain that she came prepared with questions to each interview session but soon "began to take increasing direction from the narrators" and as a result "the kinds of questions changed" (1990: 14).

Looking back at my experience with Ted in light of the success of *Life Lived Like a Story* in evoking personal narratives that are clearly tribally composed, I'm compelled to speculate on a number of "what ifs." Had the initial twelve interviews we did together been spread out over months instead of three weeks—May 16–June 6, 1974—and the questioning in each been much more thoroughly thought out ahead of time—there were the earlier Dunnigan interviews to refer to—might I have elicited more narrative rather than mostly data? Had I persisted in interviewing Ted over a period of years, might I have learned the right questions to ask? The transcripts of our interviews certainly demonstrate that I was asking too many questions and not ones that elicited narrative fullness. Thus Ted's narratives only rarely evoke experience rich in sensate detail and emotional content. Might Ted have tutored me as Sidney, Smith, and Ned did Cruikshank, or—and I suspect this is the reality—might we have worked together *ad infinitum* without ever really achieving a collaborative process that would allow us to do more than accumulate multiple accounts to be boxed in an archive for some later use? I believe the latter. Ted and I did continue follow-up interviews over the span of about a year without any appreciable change in the style or content of the interviews; the interview sessions amounted to collecting variants and verifying information with very little additional material forthcoming. We probably could have gone on in that vein for years with no appreciable change in our relationship or methodology. Ted did not think of me as his student except in the sense of being interested in Papago culture and his life story. He did not see me as coming to him for instruction on traditional Papago culture except where it impinged directly on his experiences—we had agreed on a specific personal narrative intention—and certainly not for instruction on how to inscribe his personal narrative in a culturally appropriate way. I do not think Ted conceived of himself as anything other than an "informant" expected to contribute data to the project. Nor do I think that he was familiar enough with Papago oral tradition to deliberately formulate his own life within traditional mythic or legendary conventions.[26] Of course, my speculations about his inadequacy as a tutor might just be a self-defensive rationale to lighten my burden of inadequacy as a student of Papago culture and oral narrative style. But I'm not trying to place blame here. I think Ted gave generously and fully what he knew to give and that I bear the responsibility of over-controlling the process and not recognizing at the time that he was narrating in a culturally authorizing style. But examining his strengths and limitations as a Papago narrator is helpful in assessing the inscribed text of our collaboration. Realistically, the documentary character of our collaboration may also be in some measure accounted for by his limited knowledge of Papago literary models. He did not live a very traditional life, not even residing within his own community much of the time, and by his own admission regretted that he had not listened more carefully and learned traditional stories when he was a youngster. Also, the model closest to him in time was the format of the Dunnigan interviews.

While I sometimes wish the collaboration between Ted and me had been as complete and productive as that described and narrated in *Life Lived Like a Story,* given the times and the circumstances, there wasn't a prayer that we would break out of the documentary mode into conventional Euro-American literary expression, or that I would recognize Ted's nontraditional but distinctly Papago way of narrating during our interviews. Viewed within the framework of *Life Lived Like a Story,* Ted and I were not so much mismatched as collaborators as we were individually lacking in the skills and cultural resources that might have allowed us to develop a more evocative inscription of his life story. His narrative style does not even meet criteria for what is usually termed and increasingly criticized as ethnographic realism, let alone achieve evocation.[27] No matter what form I might present Ted's narrative in, it would not change his usually unadorned reportage into highly evocative literature because the process of eliciting narration was not literary. And at the time we worked together, he was either unconscious of or chose not to educate me to the influences of Papago expressive style on his narrative.

Which bring me full circle back to Corbett Mack's narrative, with which I think *Telling a Good One* shares the most similarity. Both are documentary, and both, in comparison to many Native American personal narratives, are rather ordinary, even dull in that they recollect day-to-day lives centered on, for the most part, pretty unglamorous work and social interactions. Neither of these men narrates the persecution and heroic resistance of a warrior hero like Geronimo, nor the religious vision and responsibility of a leader like Black Elk, nor the achievements of a figure like Charles Eastman or William Apess. Both are born too late for traditional, heroic lives, and neither is an extraordinary storyteller.

Does that reduce the Mack and Rios narratives to purely documentary value? I don't think so. It simply means that the results of the collaboration require much more interpretation than many other narratives in order to be appreciated as cultural expressions of a nontraditional but distinctly cultural sort.

The edited version of the third tape in the series of interviews with Ted is useful for demonstrating how episodic narrative alternating with collector-editor interpretation offers a form of life story that is a possible alternative to the usual continuous narrative, one which can open up otherwise opaque elements of the narrative to the reader better than unmediated episodes.[28]

TAPE THREE
May 17, 1974
To get Saguaros we go right up by the side of the Tucson mountains. 'Course, everybody went there and helped the people there. We used to stay, I'd say about two or three weeks. It all depended

on how much they gathered of how much syrup they get for jam. They use a long stick. You know the ribs of that saguaro? Put 'em together and put a little cross-piece [*crosses index fingers*] on the side where it's swept down [*downward motion with right arm*]. We're pulling ripe ones, not the green ones, red ones. They fall on the ground, or they'd fall right at the bottom, at the foot of the saguaro. There's a whole load of it. We just thresh them. Then they'd just peel 'em off and get something like beets, and they just dump 'em in one old big round basket, till it would get full, you know. And then they pour water on it and let it soak and kind of stir it, and the juice that comes out of it is just like strawberry soda, and you can drink it if you want to. They just tell us [*nods*], "Go ahead and drink it." Almost tastes just like the sweetness of soda. And then, after, that is started cooking, just like you cook anything else. They build a fire, and they dump the whole bucket in there and start to cook it. The ladies stirred and stirred and boiled it. When it started to get soft, the meat porous, that's where the syrup comes in. They keep on stirring but don't burn it. If you burn it once, it sticks. They boil it and boil it and when it's ready, take it off. Then they put it in ollas and then they get some kind of cloth and wrap over it, tie it good, cover it with something like wet mud.

It's around June, when they get ripe. June when it's hot, you know. We just make a ramada beside the tents, and besides them the wagon with coverings, like in the olden days. If it rained, you get in there. I helped around with the wood but I was too small to handle that long stick. Women alone did that. The old ones stayed home. Just the ones that are able to gather or cook went. All that little dry fruit that's already fallen, they gather that too. They separate it and put it in another sack to take it home. And that's good stuff too because it's still got the same flavor. They take it home and then grind it. It comes out like mash. And they make it for their soup, especially when they're sick. It's good stuff, cream [*nods*]. They bring it home. You know, they just do it, just to have something. But they could do it at home.

There is a special ceremony that goes with that too [*nods*], for rain, for the rain — that is, if the people wanted their way; it's up to them [*shrugs*]. It's not always a schedule that comes, a system. When they want they talk it over. Only when they want it to rain will they do this. There was lots of singing, lot of drinking [*brings right thumb toward mouth*]. They sing the rain songs. In the olden times they say when they get this settled the rain comes [*slight shrug, palms up*].

My grandfather never comes down here. He's too old. He was an old man. He seen everything before everything happened like not these days. He's fought the Apaches, when they come to the village, you know. He told stories about things he really saw. I was too young to listen to them. I just remember parts, you know. He'd be saying that the Apache chased them or whatever, and the people got killed and all that. And I wish that I could have written down so many of them [*nods*]. (edited tape 3: 1–2)

In this segment of the third interview, Ted is very general in his recollections of the annual saguaro fruit harvest, mentioning himself as part of the experience only once — gathering wood for the fire. He is equally general about the wine ceremony performed to pull down the clouds and bring the rains in late summer. Even memories of his grandfather's stories about wars with the Apaches, which must have been exciting sagas for a youngster to hear, are only vague. Was Ted simply not paying attention to the events and stories that filled his childhood? I don't think that's a likely explanation for his lack of specificity. I know that as the taping progressed, his memory was stimulated, and later versions of many events and experiences became more fully rendered. As the interviews continued, Ted circled back to certain events mentioned in earlier sessions to embellish his narrative with more detail. I think in this taping session, as in the two preceding ones, my questions often caught him unprepared, threw him into topics and times he had not thought about in years. Between tapings, I think he plumbed his memory, and as the interviews progressed, he became more and more a narrator of substantive episodes and even stories.

As the edited version of tape three continues, it is apparent that a drastic shift in topic takes place, prompted by my question, "Do you remember very much about the government influence when you were a child?"

> When the government took over, they put in a lot of projects, like putting in dams, ditches where the water flows in by itself. 'Course, at the time the water comes from way out there where they build a dirt dam and then it's stored and it comes through the ditch. I played a lot in that water, stream, when I was young because it runs by our house. But of course, the rain water, the dirty old muddy water, comes through there and makes puddles there, you know, and it goes fast. Then after it's all gone, we start cleaning up again. The agent lives right there, and he's the one that's taking care of things. Some people work for him, even the policemen. He's put in by the people. It was for the tribe. Whoever they want to put in there, why, they make a choice. (edited tape 3: 2–3)

Because I wasn't listening carefully enough to anticipate how vague this section would appear when I would actually use it, I did not ask the follow-up questions that would place this recollection in a specific time period or identify exactly the role of the "agent" and whether this person was a government employee or a tribal official. Again, a topical shift is evident as Ted's responses to the deleted questions continue:

> They only go to Tucson when they run out of certain things, because they raise the other things. But certain things they don't have, like sugar, flour [*counts on fingers of right hand*]. But they make their own flour too, out of wheat [*nods*]. They grind it on a stone—a metate, they call it. And everybody's got one 'cause

they've got a lot of use for the wheat flour. They thresh wheat with horses. They circle them around a post there, and they get so many horses and tie 'em like that in a row. Then the horses pranced around, around, and around. They have a solid ground. They put water in there and make it solid as cement. They dry and stomp it, and in a while, it was hard enough. They don't want to make any cracks. So the wheat is just like on the cement. It's dried so all the wheat just fell out. And then they get it and make piles in the wind, like bumps. The chaff flies off, and the wheat settle right in there [*nods*]. And they sacked it up. The women help. They make brushes out of certain bushes, and they just brush chaff, clean the wheat. Each family got to do their own. If there's not enough they might hire somebody along. Everything goes like that—corn, you know, it's harvested then, watermelon—June, July, or August. We pull corn off the stalks, pile 'em up, take 'em home. It's dry already. When the corn is ripe, it's already dry when it's in the stalk. All you got to do is pull 'em off and pile 'em up and they'll be dry enough. In my days, they owned one of those grinders. Run 'em through by hand. And there's green corn. They make tamales out of it. And you can cook it. They know how to cook it well, like the Mexicans. Make tamales out of it or cook it just like you need it. Everybody does [*nods*].

The Yaquis keep to themselves, but they danced for fiestas. They do the same for their own belief and rites, you know. They do it now. It's like now they do it to lead the procession. They take out the saint. They're the leaders.

We had a Yaqui wood cutter. He kept down there where we owned that wood, the land with the trees on it. He'd camp up there, and then he got the wood out of there and cut it. 'Course it's cut by the cord. And then when he got so much, he'd bring it down by a wagon, sell it. The land was way up there. It's got a lot of wood all around, all over. The timber, the wood, is owned by individuals. If you know where it is, you fence the land where it's supposed to be. Except, you know, most of them, they don't know where it is, and they don't bother. It's too bushy.

See, the rain come and then it irrigates the crops. 'Course, out there they do better than out on the farm because the land out there has more fertilizer, and it's got more of everything. There's always fertilizer in there once you put something inside. Just like in a desert, see, it spread out just like that. We get better crops at the ranch, only they're smaller but they're sweeter—like watermelon, so big [*measuring with his hands about twelve inches apart*], or maybe a little bigger, but they're the sweetest of any, you know. And then when there's a fiesta going on, there's a certain place way down there where they do it every year, on a ranch. My grandfather used to go down there all the time. It's in the mountains. My grandfather would take his harvest down there and sell. By that time, it gets ripe and everything. It comes late, September or October. People come from ranches. You see, there's no boundaries there, no fences. And we lived right in the closest part of the mountains. And then all the Mexican ranchers around there, they come over. The ranch was near the Papago line, the Papago border, the Papago boundary. (edited tape 3: 3–5)

The preceding section is Ted's first extended narration. The section on threshing and corn harvesting and the part about his grandfather and melons are narrated with almost no questions or prompts. It is also the first evidence of Ted's capacity to narrate in some detail, though at this point it is still quite sparse, and Ted is still reporting rather than making himself a participant in the events he describes. He continues in response to my reference to a previous interview: "I also remember from the other tape that you were talking about the river, that you learned to swim. Was it in the Santa Cruz?"

I learned to swim in the Santa Cruz at the Midvale dam. That's where everybody went even the outsiders when they'd come, like whites, Mexicans, everybody [*nods*]. 'Course it was right close to the road. You could see where it was, you know, picnic going on and everything. They'd get a big picnic, and they'd go there. 'Course it not too deep, but just enough to wade around in. 'Course this other dam that belongs to the tribe is bigger and it's deeper. We go there once in a while and swim all day. Everybody, all the kids, whoever want to go would get together, just like any ordinary kids. We'd be playing around and then we'll set a date and say a certain day we'd all go there and have a swim, go just like a bunch. There was not as much danger as there is now. It was just a free country. Nobody bothered us. Not many people come around. But there was the machinery, pumps going there. We're not allowed near there because some of the machinery would be running water through, and there were electric lines that come in.

We know how far we can go from home. We just know where we're going. When you grow up in the wild like that you always can see where you're going. It's not like now; the people, you know, they don't know where they're going. That why they fall off a cliff or get bitten by a rattlesnake. It's just they don't know where it is. We could see a rattlesnake coming; we know how to take care. We got used to it. There always was a storm coming; then we'd be gone. Or else we knew where to get under, where to keep dry. All the dust, splatters, big drop. It splashed, oh, just like somebody playing with water [*downward motion with open-fingered right hand*]. And it started. It's very, very strong. Now I never see this kind of rain. All of a sudden the water is just like somebody splashing around like that. I'm used to it. I just stay in the house and watch it. And then, pretty soon, the water'll start running. That's how it used to be. Now I don't see it like that. (edited tape 3: 5–6)

This section emphasizes a pattern that dominates much of his narrative, the comparison of the present to the past. Looking back on his life, the landscape, and the social practices of his youth, he imbues them with a superiority to his experience of the present. This is not an uncommon pattern in many Native American personal narratives, but in more fully edited texts that are structured chronologically this comparison is not as overt or dominant as it is here. Unlike some of the early Native American narratives in which the reservation experience is contrasted negatively to the earlier period of little contact with Anglos, Ted narrates a world in close proximity and close contact with members of other Indian tribes, Mexicans, and white people. Still, the world of his youth is depicted as more manageable and fulfilling, and safer. Nearing sixty and in poor health, his present state may have affected his perception and narration, as might a nostalgia for the "good old days" and ways of Papago life. I don't think it's accidental that he warms up to the memories of his youth more and more as the narrative continues and provides, while not highly specific detail, more sensual language, especially in describing the storms and running water. Both the contrasting pattern and the detailed description of storms continue:

We lighted the houses by kerosene and we slept outside in summer. Everybody did, out under the trees, of course, peach trees, pomegranates, carnovales — hard nuts.

Used to keep livestock out on the range. The people that owned the stock — not everybody owned any except nowadays when they issue out stock, hardly anybody, just very few — mind their own stock, well, corrals, and of course, it's open range. All they did is see that they're watered. They give 'em water.

Sometimes the hail ruined the crops. The hail does it, not the rain. The hail, when it comes, will knock everything over, but it doesn't knock off the whole thing, just the leaves. The roots were still in there [*spreads hands downward*]. And then it starts in again [*nods*]. There weren't many times when the crops were bad because at that time, it would rain all the time. Now we don't have it. That's the trouble with the whole country now, everybody, everyplace. At that time everything is beautiful [*sweep of right hand*]. The wind started blowing all the dust; then you knew it was coming. Mostly from the southeast. Then it would be coming, and you know it was coming.

Before the summer, before the start of summer, there was roundup. When I was old enough, I watched close and careful. All the ranchers from around there, they'd get together, with their horses and all, Mexican and all. They'd build a camp — a big camp, and they might butcher a cow or so for everybody. There's always a lot of buyers because they know the schedule when they're supposed to be there. And then they started buying them. They had the trucks. They had the trucks when I was around. But it used to be when the roundup started, if the ranchers want to sell some, they just tell the buyers down there they're selling some stock and they'd drive 'em home. 'Course, it wasn't far. All the buyers around, they'd all come, even the Mexican buyers — slaughterers. 'Course, they're mostly Mexicans then. They know the people.

At Santa Rosa, they did rain farming. They do mostly, all over. It's just like all over the country. They didn't have irrigation; they got wells. Every ranch had a well.

I was still a boy, oh, in '26 or '27 when my father got a truck. (edited tape 3: 6–7)

The material in this section repeats and expands upon the very brief mention of roundups and selling stock during the first day of interviews. Ted is still an observer, but in this telling, he places himself as a careful watcher of the roundups. This absorption of ranch activities and the skills required to perform them is influential in his own adult participation in roundups, rodeo competitions, and even working as a rider in western films shot in Arizona. The points of amplification grow as the interviews proceed and begin to reveal a pattern of what is of importance to Ted within and outside his own culture and landscape. When he runs with a topic, it is one that interests him. One line answers, as at the end of this section, show his disinterest. Better follow-up questions, rather than shifts to related topics, might have garnered more, and more detailed, responses.

Ted shifts topics again in response to my lead when I say, "We talked yesterday about Christmas, just a little bit, and you said that there were races for the children. Can you describe some of them?"

> We don't want to run. We were standing there and somebody would say, "Hey, go in there and get a race; get on in line." Then we would go hide some place around there, around the village. Once in a while we'd get caught and then I would have to do it [*nods*]. They'd put oranges, apples, whatever, a bag of candy, lined up way out there where the race finishes, and then you'd get whatever you could. They'd draw a line there, and once you hit the line, then you go right over and pick out what you wanted.
>
> Most of the time, there's no recreation at all. There's just work. Of course, somebody might come around, and they'd gossip, gossip. On Sundays, though, they'd go visiting among themselves, maybe two families. (edited tape 3: 7)

Ted's comments on avoiding participation in the holiday games reveal a sensibility that dominates throughout his recollections of his life. He consistently depicts himself as a reluctant participant. "I don't want to, but I got to," is a phrase he uses again and again to indicate that forces beyond his control — social pressures, directions from teachers, orders from employers, and even global events like World War II — compel him to act or take on responsibilities he would prefer to avoid. He does not examine compelling causes, nor does he offer them as excuses for mediocre or poor performances of actions or duties — most of which he is very competent at — but the cumulative effect is that he is more acted upon than actor.[29] The next section responds to my follow-up questions about his school experiences:

At the mission school we had showers and everything [*nods*]. We had to go to the shower in the morning, the whole group. We would eat together. 'Course some older girls, they'd help the cook. Sometimes they need help, putting in the dishes, whatever. And the older boys, too, they'd chop wood. They had to work together on it, chop wood. Well, the sisters too, of course, they used to work. We worked only when we were out of class, like before class or after class—the evening. Just certain ones did, older ones who know how to chop.

They taught something like they teach now, like reading, arithmetic, all that, and religion, catechism [*sweep of right hand*]. 'Course we were right at the Church. As soon as we were able to understand it, like eight, different ages, we made our first communion in a group. Whenever you're ready, understand it. We were confirmed too. We had sponsors. Often times it was somebody close to you, our godfather or godmother, something like that. They gave us gifts, but because I was too young, I didn't care much about it. You know, no one did. They were kids. Whatever they tell us to do, we did [*nods*].

It's my parents business to decide the school after the Mission. They know where. If you want to go to Catholic school, you go. If you want to go to government school, then it's up to them. My brother went to Phoenix before me. He was still in Phoenix when I went. He stayed over there. We went by train. All the parents that had kids, take 'em to Tucson. Then from there we're on the train. In Phoenix we have to get off. See, the conductor there told us, and when we get there, we get off, and there is somebody there to pick us up. And then we got on the bus.

The school was a lot like home—it's just like home. We know everybody there. It's set up according to how old or how big you are. We register right then and then we're given numbers. Then we stand by that number. The lockers got numbers, the bedding got numbers and we go over there and find out where it is. Once you got there, you're just in the whole family. Everybody knows you, and they miss you, and it's just like coming home. I must have been in fourth grade when I got there, about ten years old. There were kids from other places, different tribes. We had to speak English to understand each other. They go by the standards, regulations, whatever the government wants — that's that [*nods*]. And at certain times they might put on dancing, Indian dancing, or whatever they want, just for an official.

You had a chance and if you get a job; then on Saturday morning you go out to that place, and then you'd work — yard work or whatever, and get paid.[30] When I got old enough to get around, I'd go out every Saturday to a certain place to clean their yard, cut their grass, whatever they wished to be done, for so many hours, and I'd get paid for it and could keep it. They had movies every Saturday night for the whole school. Sundays we had all the time after church. We'd go hiking, all of us boys, not the girls, but the boys, go hiking, up to the mountains, wherever they want to go. Came back when supper comes. If we miss it — out of luck. The streetcar comes there from Phoenix. We'd go look around, maybe buy some clothes, shirt, pants, whatever. They got their own orchestra. They got everything, everything. They bake their own bread, cook their own everything. (edited tape 3: 7–9)

Ted's descriptions of his school experience amplify only slightly what he narrated on the first tape. They are interesting in that they depict both the mission and the boarding school experiences as demanding a good deal of physical labor but not as punishing. Ted seems to thrive on group experience, to view himself as an undistinguished part of a greater whole which gives him a sense of communal rather than individual identity.[31] Ted's concept of selfhood is connected to specific experiences — shared experiences — not to a developing sense of individuality. As he begins to narrate more about his adulthood, his personal actions begin to dominate, but clearly, until he leaves the predominantly Indian communities of his childhood and early teens, he does not speak about himself in individuated terms. As he continues, the emphasis shifts to his personal desires, motives, and actions:

During the summer, come home to the farm because I wasn't old enough to do anything else. I think about seventeen, eighteen, I left. I had to come home, and then I didn't go back, but I was supposed to go back again. I went to Tucson High School because it's closer there. In the first place, I really wanted to go to Kansas, where the big college is, Haskell Institute. But I really want to go in the first place before I went to Phoenix. But they wouldn't take me because they weren't taking any more western states — crowded, I guess [*shrugs*]. So I came back to help with the work on the farm.

I like Tucson High, but it was too crowded because it was the only high school at that time. I stayed two years, sophomore and junior. I dropped out in 1933 [*cocks head*] or '34 because of a lot of bad things happening, and I had to be at home, farming, ranching, all that. My brothers are all dead. Died at home. Disease. I was the only one.

I married two year later, around 1936. Ramona. Well, she stayed in town. It's like a village, next to town. She's Papago and partly Creek — from Oklahoma. We moved 'way down there on the Pima reservation; they had a big job going on, big project. 'Course everybody was staying all over [*sweeps right hand*]. Around '36, I think. It's got a big camp there. 'Course, she got some relatives living there, working. We stayed there. They're all living in a big camp, but living there alone, got a house. We stay with them. Oh well, it's a big project where the water runs underground — big pipes.

I was in Ajo when Junior [his first son] was born. We rented a house. You could rent from Mexicans mostly. In '37 Junior was born at Sells hospital. It's better to be in the Indian territory, in the first place, so you'll know where it's born. All that red tape, you know. I didn't come. She came. (edited tape 3: 10–11)

Boarding school begins Ted's pattern of extended stays away from the San Xavier reservation that continues throughout most of his young adulthood. The pace of his narration accelerates as he describes the shift from childhood to maturity, but that is actually due to my questions, which push him forward in time. The topics covered on this tape are revisited for amplification in subsequent narrative, though he resists certain topics—the deaths of his family members and his relationship with his wife Ramona Tiger—and I did not push him, though later attempts to bring him back to fuller narration on these topics made it clear that they were ones about which he would not be forthcoming. The final section of this edited interview centers on his work at the Phelps Dodge Copper mine in southwest Arizona, the site of Ted's most continuous employment during his life:

Ajo's like any ordinary town. There were houses there, and there were shacks there, and there were certain little spots—a store there, a bank there, churches here—just like a real small town [*nods*]. And then they start putting in the company houses, but we didn't live in a company house. 'Course it's a small town. Everybody knows each other, Mexicans or whites, or anybody. You know your way around. They got a lot of different stores. Trade with you. [See photo 9.]

Nobody's just living in Ajo for nothing, for just a home. Some work in the mill; some work in the mine. All depends on how much work we're going to do. Maybe four, maybe five on a crew. See, down there, every time the train's to go in that hole—the pit, every time they blast, bang, the gauge got to be moved. I mean the rail, the track. Track got to be moved. They blast. Then the bulldozers come and grade it. And then it's going to be put back again. Where the train will come in they got big shovels, like pick shovels. They got a track, and you got to move it back and forth. Lot of trains, diesels, hauling the waste, and this waste, they dump it out of there. If it's good ore, they haul it to the mill. Back and forth.

They got their seniorities. Not like competing, but then you just do whatever's supposed to be done. If you're good at anything, they know you could do it for a certain length of time. Then you go back to where you belong again. And then a lot of time I got to interpret at the meetings right in there. We got meetings, too — first aid meeting, most of them. They had their own meetings, and while I'm there, they put me in there to interpret for whatever they're talking about. Safety meetings for work. They got to be safe, or else they can get hurt or get killed. It's dangerous. If you know English, they know you understand them. So much of them hardly speak English, you know. Course, they come from Mexico. You represented your crew. They have that, I guess, every month. The big bosses come and the superintendent comes to the main meeting building — everybody, all the big shots. They ask how the work's going, if it's safe enough. I reported back, when they were talking.

It's a big pit, you know, big. And then there everything gets hot when it gets hot in summer. The rocks get hot, tracks get hot. Have to stand the heat. If you can stand the heat, you work. Make you sick, but never did that to me. Other people got sick. Get 'em out of there. They examine you before they accept you, before you were hired. Then you're on [*nods*].

Thirty-nine is when Michael was born. We were there twelve or fifteen years. I moved up on a different mine, but same company, different places. When you're working underground, it's all right, but — it's hotter. You got to strip clear to waist. And then you sweat. And everywhere you struck, water falls out of the rocks. Used to go in there and drink the water [*cups hand*]. It's sweet, sweeter than what you get in the city. 'Course it's fresh water. And then you can't see your finger if you go like this [*placing his hand an inch from his face*]. Don't see nothing — dark. You got to have a light all the time. I helped set up the machinery, or else empty the chutes. See, they got some chutes in there, empty to another hole, and then goes down to the loading chute. Tiger Mine — it's the one where the San Manuel mill gets their ore—that's a big mine where their ore comes from. It was an independent company. Then, at one time I went back over to Ajo. I don't know when it was. I went back over there again, for a few times. I don't know how long. For a few months, I guess. At the time the war broke out. We worked six days a week at the time when the copper was in production. And then everybody left. Then I left, and I went different places. (edited tape 3: 11–13)

As this extended piece of narration demonstrates, Ted liked to talk about work, about his capacity to perform hard labor well, and about his endurance. In subsequent interviews, I returned to the topic of his mining experience because—along with his work in the movies—it was the topic he was most willing to talk about with little prompting. I thought at the time of the interviews, and believe even more firmly now, that Ted's subjectivity was most clearly defined by work. Questions about his adult family relationships were neatly deflected as unfit topics for discussion. Social experiences were secondary to his sense of himself, perhaps largely because they were fleeting or areas of conflict or failure, but work was public and a topic in which he could narrate his competence and even bravery.

Alternating narrative and interpretive analysis, while it clarifies some elements in Ted's narrative that would otherwise be confusing and also connects episodes to the larger patterns of his life experience, creates a form of presentation that is nearly as discontinuous and disruptive as the question/answer format of the interview. That may explain why this is not a commonly used form of life-story presentation. Usually such interpretive and informational commentary is relegated to footnotes or an epilogue in order to spare the reader the interruptions in the text. The above alternating format is one that I considered and discarded as unwieldy and overly intrusive when I was attempting to figure out a way to organize the edited tapes into a publishable text in the 1980s. As a model for inscribing a Native American life story, I think it is a poor choice, because it makes the actual narrative simply material for analysis, and not very substantive or extensive analysis at that. It reduces a life story into a case study, that outworn ethnographic model where "informant" quotations are used to support generalizing observations. Foregrounding my comments on each segment of the taped narrative has only one useful aspect; it recovers elements of the process of the interview—verification and clarification of previously collected material, attempts to develop thematic elements, concern for eliciting a narrative that depicted a developing persona, movement forward in the interview to previously unnarrated experiences, and more and fuller continuous narrative responses by Ted. But all but the last in that list of process-exposing factors focuses, not on Ted and his narration, but on my role in the collaboration.

Most published Native American personal narratives underplay the collaborative process. Collector-editors generally edit the narratives they collect so that they can stand on their own. That is, in fact, the dominant model for Native American life-story presentation. Numerous variations exist—framing with methodological introduction and interpretive epilogue; use of footnotes; brief introductions to life-story sections; contextualizing with cultural data—each dictated by the publishing intention of the collector-editor and perhaps narrator, or by the content and narrative style of the Native American person. Finally, I think it is the latter, the narrative itself, not academic or publishing theories or restrictions, that should be the determining factor in the mode of presentation. Easy for me to say, of course, since I'm experimenting on material that resists choosing a more conventional form. But I think by now it's evident that Ted's narrative could be presented in a traditionally chronological format. With extensive editing, it could be set up almost exactly like Corbett Mack's narrative. Or it could be inscribed in a way similar to *During My Time*, with cultural and personal essays framing the text and a sample of the interview transcript. It could even be presented somewhat similarly to Crapanzano's inscription of his relationship with Forster Bennett, though that would throw the focus almost exclusively onto me, not Ted, since it does not accommodate extensive interview material. It could not, however, be set up like *Life Lived Like a Story* without the collaboration between Ted and I having gone on over a much longer time and his having had determination and knowledge to narrate his life in relation to traditional Papago literature.

My search for models has led me to examine numerous engaging and provocative forms of Native American life story. *Telling a Good One*'s analysis of methodology and presentation of Ted's narration share some commonalties with nearly all of them, but in the end examining other examples of Native American personal narrative provides only a context for analyzing the Rios-Sands project, not a model for its inscription. For the most part, collaborative Native American personal narrative falls somewhere between "ethnological life history" and "self-expressive autobiography" (Bloodworth 1978: 67). It is consistently about—and presumably by—the Native American person who tells his or her life story, not about the relationship or the work that transpires between that person and the non-Native who inscribes the narrative. This volume, then, is not Native American "autobiography." It is a volume about a particular Native American narrator in relationship to a particular collector-editor at a particular time in both our lives.

Telling a Good One is about how difficult it actually is to tell "a good one," an experiment in the dialogue between collector and editor, between editor and transcribed narrative, between editor and life-story conventions, and between narrator and editor and audience. It's also a dialogue between then and now, between presumptions about personal narrative inscriptions and the realities of the process.[32] And it is an attempt to see how Ted's narrative fits into past and current ethnographic and literary theories and into a small but distinctive number of oral and written Tohono O'odham personal narratives.

ℰ 4

PAPAGO PERSONAL NARRATIVES

Ted Rios is not unique as a Papago narrator of life story. Three Papago personal narratives already exist in published form, one written and the other two orally narrated by members of the Tohono O'odham tribe. The best known of these is *Papago Woman,* narrated by Maria Chona and collected and edited by anthropologist Ruth M. Underhill in the 1930s. It focuses on Chona's youth and adulthood in traditional Papago society.[1] The other two, *Papago Traveler,* written by James McCarthy, and *Papagos and Politics,* told by Peter Blaine Sr. to Michael S. Adams, narrate the stories of Papago males living and working in the bicultural world of the early to mid-twentieth century.

Besides these three published works, there is a bilingual autobiographical text by Juan Dolores, who worked with anthropologist Alfred Kroeber to document Papago language and culture.[2] This unpublished fifty-six-page, handwritten text traces his village and boarding school experiences.[3] Further, eight sets of taped life-story interviews are archived in the Doris Duke Collection at the University of Arizona, including the Rios interviews collected by Timothy Dunnigan. Finally, a brief, episodic narrative of the life of Ella Lopez Antone, a cousin of Ted Rios's residing at Santa Rosa village and whom I interviewed in 1982, also exists in unedited and unpublished form. Taken together, they constitute an unusually substantial body of personal-narrative texts from a single North American tribal culture. This makes them useful to the investigation of the specifically cultural themes and tropes that permeate Native American life stories narrated from a particular culture. Most pertinently to this study, numerous Papago life-story texts are valuable for comprehending both the content and style of the Rios narrative as a bicultural work that demonstrates not only accommodation to the expectations of a non-Native readership but expression of a distinctly Papago sensibility manifest in culturally specific thematic, linguistic, and stylistic elements.[4]

All of these life stories overlap — some only slightly but several almost wholly — with the time period Ted covers in his narrative. In all of these narratives, the protagonists' identification with a particular landscape and articulation of common themes indicate a shared cultural perspective. The temporal and thematic relationships among the narratives confirm that Ted's narrative exhibits patterns of life-story telling that are arguably cultural in origin.[5]

Life history is neither a natural or universal form (Langness and Frank 1981: 87–116); it always carries the marks of the culture from which it originates, and in cross-cultural narratives such as all those listed above, it also carries evidence of influence by factors from a soliciting culture outside the Native one. Cross-cultural textual interaction, then, is characteristic of Native American personal narrative.[6] Examining a body of Papago life-story narration and how Ted's narrative fits into that group of texts sets up the possibility of uncovering how Papago culture shapes even a narrative collected and edited by an outsider. Placing Ted's narrative in the context of other Papago narratives facilitates examining his life story as both Papago expression and the telling of a distinctly individual life. It reveals the process of his narration, not only from the collector-editor's experience of the Rios-Sands project, but also reveals Ted's concept of how a Papago life is made out of memory and language.

Of the thirteen personal narratives of Papago men and women, the bilingual text by Juan Dolores is by far the shortest and most limited in time frame and topics.[7] It contains brief descriptions of his family's trip north from Mexico to the Arizona reservation where they decide to remain, the building of a *charco* for watering horses[8] and a house for themselves at Rock Bend Village, the recollection of a trip north to visit the River People (Pimas), Dolores's memory of going on a mountain-

lion hunt with an uncle, remembrance of a snow storm and an earthquake that took place in the same year, and a fairly detailed narrative
about his very difficult stay at the Indian Presbyterian Mission School
adjacent to the San Xavier reservation. Though his parents bring him
to the school and stay nearby for a lengthy period of time to assure
themselves—his mother is particularly reluctant to leave him in the
hands of whites—that he is being well treated, his fortunes change
drastically when they leave. The text ends as he runs away from the
school, heading back to his family. All of this predates Ted's birth, but
Dolores's full lifetime overlaps Ted's by over twenty-five years.

Though this bilingual autobiography fragment—in Papago with
an interlinear literal English translation by the author—is undated
and contains no internal dates, other documents indicate that Juan
Dolores, originally known as Juan Lolorias, was born in Mexico on
June 24, 1880.[9] He attended the Indian Presbyterian Mission School
sometime in the 1890s and found the experience brutal.[10] He writes
repeatedly about loud, angry scoldings and of severe physical punishment for very minor infractions. Describing one staff member, he
writes, "He would be talking and will be seemingly angry while talking. I was afraid of him. When one something not will understand,
he right away there will take him by the ear and back and forth, back
and forth will be yanking him along" (19).[11] Even more fearsome was
another who used a whip. Dolores describes it as "loaded with buck-
shot, when it is thrown hard it pops like a gun and makes holes in mule
hides. When this thing popped near my ears I ran faster than a deer"
(34). Even worse, he writes, is his recollection of being locked in a dark
room and given no food (27–28). Dolores's boarding-school experience is a far cry from Ted's, but there is a similarity in the initiation
of his education and the fact that Dolores's schooling leads the Lolorias family to farm at San Xavier, where Ted's family resided. Dolores
describes how the decision to send him to school is made his by the
parents, as in Ted's narrative:

In the time that we finished our reservoir and there from not long after, thus said father of mine that it was time he will take me there Black Bottom[12] toward, I would go to school. My mother yet disagreed. . . . If you very much desire that will go to school the child, we there will go and there will be living. . . . My father made good for himself that he will pay (rent) each year the farm and there will be living. There he planted two years. (9–10)

Dolores's father had been a cattle rancher in Mexico and becomes a farmer at San Xavier, similar to Ted's father and grandfather.

Ted and Dolores also share perilous births; Ted was premature and Dolores was born in the midst of a smallpox epidemic. He writes: "It was killing all the children, my mother prayed, and made a vow to donate a certain amount of money to the church at Matalena [*sic*] in Sonora. I remember we went to that church every year" (14). Ted, too, recalls trips to Magdalena for the feast of St. Francis.

Brief narratives about the 1888 earthquake are also common to both Dolores and Ted. Ted's is a family anecdote. At the time it happened, his father was an infant in a crib hanging from the beams of a ramada. "The roof started leaking—like leaves," he says. When it started shaking, someone yelled, "Earthquake, earthquake, everybody get out," and they saw "all those rocks start rolling, rolling, rolling." His grandfather was out collecting the horses, and the relatives were worried that the rocks might have crushed him, "so worried about him." But when he returned unharmed he told them he'd hardly noticed the quake. "He braved himself up," Ted said (untranscribed tape, April 3, 1975). Dolores narrates a similar story (7–9). He writes: "Thus said the father of mine that there he went and there he saw, that there was marked, that there ran down great rock, that there was smoking, and that there was humming, in that time that the earth shook" (9). Dolores actually remembers this event; Ted's is a version of a family story that predates his birth by twenty-seven years.

Admittedly it requires a stretch to relate the events of Ted's and

Juan Dolores's narratives, but there are stylistic similarities between the texts that I think point to the influence of the Papago language on Ted's narrative style. Ted and Dolores share Papago language as their first language and the cultural perception and way of expressing experience that goes with it. The relationship of English to Papago in the direct translation by Dolores is obvious in the syntax, but attention to the rhythm and grammatical construction of his phrasing, and a similarity with Ted's rhythm and phrasing, suggest that Ted's narrative style is also strongly influenced by Papago. For instance, Dolores quotes his father talking about the San Xavier farm going bad: " 'My partner is lazy, just sleeps in the nights that we irrigate, for that reason spoils the ditches' " (16). Ted's oral narrative displays similar enjambment and phrase layering. In the transcript of tape four, Ted answers my query about going to the mountains in the summertime saying, "They go and gather whatever they can get over there, like cactus fruit when they're ripe enough to — you know — to harvest. And besides, the old men, you know, they go out hunting, hunting for deer or whatever they can get — rabbits" (edited tape 4: 4). Take out Ted's trademark "you know" and the meter and phrase layering is very similar to the direct translation from Papago Dolores makes. So while there is little direct correlation between the events and experiences in the Dolores and Rios narratives, there are elements of the Dolores text that illuminate the Papago nature of Ted's way of telling. It is also a stretch, but again an informative one, to compare Ted's life story to the published narrative by another Papago born in the nineteenth century, *Papago Woman* (1979), the life story of Maria Chona, collected and edited by Ruth M. Underhill.

Primarily because Ted's narrative is two generations removed from Maria Chona's, which begins with her childhood in the 1840s, there is little beyond landscape and identification of the narrators as Papago to link these two life stories together. Gender difference also makes the perspectives and experiences articulated in the narratives markedly different.[13] Chona's narrative, despite the fact that she lived until the mid-1930s, documents almost exclusively her life in traditional Papago culture. Unlike Ted, who narrates a world of multicultural influences, she makes few allusions to the impact of Anglo society on tribal life and only undetailed references to trips to and work in Tucson. Helen Carr argues that this monocultural focus is a result of Underhill's desire to evoke sympathy and admiration for Chona with a white readership.[14] She points out that Underhill "stresses the Papago's sensitivity to natural rhythms, and the calm peaceful tempo of their lives." She continues:

> Underhill has chosen to emphasize the ritual and harmonies of Chona's life. Relations with government officials, references to the support the Papago gave to the U.S. against the Apache, the eventual establishment of the reservation—all of which must have been part of Chona's experience—never appear. The dual allegiance of the Papago to Catholic and native religious rituals is touched on only evasively. Shortages, most bereavements, illnesses (apart from their shamanic cures) are passed over. The only distresses that the narrative encompasses are romantic ones— Chona's mourning for her first husband, not abated until her second husband severely lectures his rival's bones; the muted sadness as she herself faces death. (1996: 245–46)

Carr's argument is persuasive. Underhill's selections of narrative episodes from her interviews with Chona seem deliberately to omit Chona's experience of white culture, but because Underhill does not discuss the process of inscribing Chona's life in detail in either the original 1936 or the 1979 introductions to Chona's narrative, it is impossible to tell whether the omission is entirely Underhill's decision. Carr's conclusion is, however, supported by Underhill's admission during an interview shortly before her death (Sands, November 3, 1981) that she deliberately translated Chona's words from Papago into a style of English modeled on the King James version of the Bible in order to give the narrative a rich and dignified style befitting the dignity of traditional Papago culture.

While contrast to Chona's narrative is easily illustrated, some similarities do exist between Chona's and Ted's topical choices. As with the similarities in Dolores's and Ted's narrations about horses and a story about his grandfather's experience of the 1888 earthquake, Chona and Ted share some narrative topics. For instance, both describe the saguaro fruit harvest, which has changed little in the time between Chona's telling and Ted's. During the seventh interview, recorded on May 23, 1974, Ted recalls:

My grandparents take me to harvest saguaro fruit. We'd travel by about half a day, or maybe not quite one day. It's right in the Tucson mountains. Mules or horses pulled a wagon. I was too small to help. I couldn't even harness a mule or anything. I had to go. Nobody's going to look after us when we're left there. They got to take me.

The pole comes like that [*indicating a downward dragging motion*], or if you want you can push it off like this [*upward movement*]. But it's too heavy for us, you know, because we're small. We can't balance it. The men are the ones that's doing it—not the ladies. The ladies, they're doing only the cooking. The men do all the—ripping them off. Mostly men. There's only one family that's in one group, in one place. Other family'll be over there, and the other family maybe 'way down there. They're not always in a group because they carry their own food, water. They do their own work, maybe a week or two weeks. Just as long as they want to stay. They want to keep on doing it, they do it. Over there is nothing but desert. Just a few families, certain families. They want that syrup and all that—jam, you know. All the ladies say well, they want to go and make some of the jam, you know, or syrup. While the other—"No, we don't want to go." Then the others got a lot of things, like farming, they've got to be doing. They don't want to go. My father never went because he's too busy with it. And my grandfather, because he's out at the ranch. Well, they got to water the cattle. So I went with my mother's parents. From the ranch. (edited tape 9: 9–10)

Ted goes on, giving a brief description of the rain ceremony that followed the harvest, but this section contrasts with the harvest in that he describes it as no longer practiced or understood as it was in Chona's time. He continues:

And then they wait for that rain. Just like any big occasion. They do that Indian dance. They've got certain custom. They've got to go by that dancing the way they're supposed to, not just like any dance. It's the old ways. I don't know much about it. They make their wine. Like beer. They know how to make it. Gets you drunk, too [*closed fist, thumb toward mouth*]. Whoever comes they give you so much. They go slow. Everybody gets at least a drink [*drinking gesture again*]. Some will get drunk. You're supposed to be praying for the rain. That's why these old-timers they make special speeches. But now, they don't keep track of how it's supposed to be run. They don't have enough speeches. They don't have the guys that know how to say it in there the way they want to do it, praying in Indian, you know. It's all gone. And like I said, now we've got everything just mixed up. (edited tape 7: 9–10)

Chona's description of cactus camp is similar, though expressed more personally and lyrically. Whether that lyricism is Chona's or Underhill's, of course, is debatable. Nonetheless, the text reads:

At last the giant cactus grew ripe on all the hills. It made us laugh to see the fruit on top of all the stalks, so many, and the men would point and say, "See the liquor growing." We went to pick it, to the same place where we always camped, and every day my mother and all the women went out with baskets. They knocked the fruit down with cactus poles. It fell on the ground and all the red pulp came out. . . .

It was good in Cactus Camp. When my father lay down to sleep at night he would sing song about the cactus liquor. And we could hear songs in my uncle's camp across the hill. Everybody sang. . . . Then the little rains began to come. . . . Much, much liquor we made, and we drank it to pull down the clouds. . . . We heard them singing all day all over the village. (1979: 40)

Both Chona and Ted, though forty years apart in their oral narrations, also tell stories about going to the Pimas to gamble—Chona on horseback with her first husband (64-66) and Ted by auto with his father and stepmother (edited tape 6: 15-16)—and both discuss incidents of witchery connected with races and gambling. But there is little substantive overlap in the topics they address because Chona looks primarily to a traditional past for her story, while Ted's memory generates stories of change and experience beyond tribal culture.

Another aspect of the Chona narrative that is very different from Ted's is the level of detail in descriptions of both events and the landscape of the Papagueria. Chona's are rich in detail, as the following childhood memory shows:

The girls used to crawl laughing out of the houses, with their long black hair hanging to their waists, and they would pick up their carrying nets. Fine nets we used to have in those days, all dyed with red and blue. Shaped like a cone they were, with tall red sticks to keep them in shape. When the net was on a girl's back those red sticks would stand up on either side of her face. (1979: 36)

Chona's memory of the home place she lived at when she married for the second time is equally specific:

Standing Rock was a nice place under the hill slope, with a big rock standing out like an eagle's beak just above us. There was a pond there for my husband's horses to bring: the yucca that we use for our baskets grew up on the hill; there was good clay for pots. (1979: 79)

Compared to these descriptions, Ted's narration is spare indeed. For instance, the edited fourth tape from May 21, 1974, begins:

Right around there they mostly used wood for heating and cook-ing, most of the families around there. And they need it, must be close to all year 'round. Green or dry, especially dry. Just plain wood. Sell it by the cord, hauled it out in a wagon, but now they haul it out by the trucks. You deliver some wood to somebody's place and the neighbor'll be right there. And then everybody starts come 'round and they want to know about price of the wood and they want it. Then you got buyers there [*nods*]. The last time I know, it was eight dollars a cord. It depends on how much you have. Your good wood, well, it's good. And besides, they got wood yards along there where you can sell it right in there, right in town. And then you can just haul it right in there and then whoever runs the wood yard, he'll buy right off. And he's the one that sells it out. For heating and cooking and I don't know what else they might—Oh, yeah, for fencing too. Somebody might need posts, you know, for their corrals and all that. (edited tape 4: 1)

The contrast in narrative style and language is striking. Chona's lan-guage is specific in terms of both action and place; the effect is visual. Ted's language is generalized and the effect is abstract. How is it that two Papago narrative can be so different? I think the answer is in the language used for each narration. Chona narrated in Papago with Underhill using a translator most of the time but also having some facility in Papago. According to Ella Antone, who translated for part of the interviews, Underhill pressed very hard for details and clear understanding of Papago words (interview, November 20, 1981). Her persistence seems to have paid off. By contrast, Ted narrates in English. Though I consistently asked for detail, I got little. For example, the transcript of the fourth tape shows that after Ted said, "And besides, they got wood yards along there where you can sell it right there," I asked, "On the road to Tucson?" but he responded with "Right in town" (edited tape 4: 2). The whereabouts of the wood yards is undefined, as are all other locations in the above discussion of wood selling.

A major difference between Ted's and Chona's narratives is in locatives. Chona locates action precisely; Ted, only generally. From my knowledge of Papago language, I think that this difference is directly related to the precision of locatives in Papago—for instance a single word can indicate where a man is positioned in relationship to a mountain and a cactus and in what direction he is moving—compared to English, where location given in a single word is reduced to "here" or "there."[15] That does not, however, entirely account for the generality of Ted's narration. Ted, throughout the interviews, resists precision. Whether that is because his memories are often vague, or he merges separate memories into typical events, or he deliberately typicalizes to avoid revealing data that he thinks might be too personal about himself or others, or he assumes more knowledge on the part of the audience than it has, or generalizing is simply his style, or several of the above in any given narrative segment is impossible to trace. But linguistic and cultural factors do play a role, for instance, in his extremely rare use of personal names. Since culturally Papagos do not usually call one another by name but rather by kinship terms, Ted's use of names only when I make specific queries about individuals and name them myself is not so much a disregard for specificity but a cultural sensibility that translates across cultures poorly.[16]

Had the process of the Chona life story been fully discussed in any venue by Underhill, this narrative of a Papago life might be more useful in comparison to Ted's narration. Without such information, I can only speculate here on why Chona's narrative is so much more vivid than Ted's. But Underhill does not give a revealing account of her methodology, and because the relationship of these two lives as they are inscribed is so tenuous, and because much has already been written about the Chona-Underhill collaboration, it is more pertinent to the discussion of collaborative process and Papago narrative themes to look at tellings and inscriptions more similar to Ted's.[17] Let's move on to the narratives of the two Papago men whose lives most parallel Ted's in time and, in some measure, in experience. Of particular interest is the Peter Blaine Sr. text, *Papagos and Politics* (1981) because it is inscribed from oral narration collected and edited by a non-Native American, Michael S. Adams. The process of this volume, unlike the Chona narrative, is traceable because the tapes and manuscript are accessible for study.[18]

Though there is no indication in the archival records that Adams had training in anthropology, the introduction to the published text is typical of the ethnographic convention of only a brief description of methodology. Adams begins by explaining that he met Peter Blaine Sr. through his son, Peter Blaine Jr., a school guidance aide, while Adams was revising a workbook on Papago history for his eighth grade class at Indian Oasis Junior High School in Sells, Arizona. It was Adams who solicited Blaine after he found out Blaine Sr. had been the second chairman of the Papago Tribal Council. At their first meeting, Adams became aware that Blaine was not only a willing narrator but also a knowledgeable observer of both important Papago events and Papago-Anglo politics — his skill in English and tribal employment led to many stints as an interpreter for outsiders and Papago officials — and he could recall participation in a wide range of events over a period of more than sixty years. The interviews took place from May 1978– July 1979. Adam's purpose was to document political and economic changes on the Papago reservation; Blaine's purpose is not stated, but given that the balance of the text is on his activities in Papago government, his purpose seems congruent with Adams's. The similarities between the Blaine-Adams and Rios-Sands projects are immediately evident. In neither project is the intention of the narrator explicitly articulated; each is solicited by an outsider on the basis of information about the subject gained from another source; each is recognized by the collector as a source of information on a range of topics over a significant time span; and each is interviewed on tape. A major difference is equally obvious. Blaine is a public figure in Papago society and in relation with Anglo society; Rios's life is marked by avoidance of public life. In one instance Ted says he could have been on the council at San Xavier, as his father and grandfather had been, but he chose not to; he never discussed any other potential entry into public life or desire for public recognition. Blaine, as Adams describes him in the introduction, "inherited from his father and grandfather and uncles an ability and willingness to 'mingle,' as he puts it" (1981: 2). Rios does not follow in his paternal ancestors' roles. He says that, if you hold tribal office,

> You always gotta argue this and they gotta argue you and you gotta argue with the common people and pretty soon they say you're not good. You know, I'd rather just be on my own side. . . . I can do my own thinking, my own way, my own, you know, on my own instead of somebody telling me do this and tell this and tell them and all that. They tell me, "You're no good." Something goes wrong. It goes against you. That's why I don't like it too much. (Dunnigan 215)

Ted never tests his ability to function as a leader because he has no willingness to take on responsibilities or potential criticisms from the community; he's sociable but not willing to volunteer or lead. The fact that at one point he explains that he has never been a godparent (unusual among Papagos), though he's been asked to be one several times, illustrates his reluctance to participate in even common social relationships that require performance of public duties. Asked why he never accepted the honor, he claimed, "I don't want to have to do it. I might have to pay for the funeral if the person dies, or raise the child if its parents die—too much work" (audio tape, March 14, 1975).[19] Not that Ted was afraid of work, but wage labor and ceremonial or social duty were not equitable to him. For Ted, labor occurred in manageably short time periods and was directed, while ceremonial or social duties were ongoing and required voluntary assumption of responsibility and self-direction, and perhaps equally importantly were judged by the community at large, not by non–Native American employers. Also, the rewards were less tangible than those he earned for wage work.

Blaine and Rios are, then, quite different in terms of their attitudes about public service and social responsibility and also in their public standing in both the Papago and white worlds, but their narratives share some striking similarities.

Though Blaine was not born at San Xavier as Ted was, on tape he begins his narrative with his move to the reservation when he was seven.[20] He says, "I came to San Xavier in 1909, after my aunt died in Tucson. I had another aunt at San Xavier living at the time. After my mother died, my aunt that died in Tucson kept me. When my Tucson aunt died, my aunt at San Xavier took me in" (transcript: 1).[21] Adams then directs him back to his birth and lineage, to which he responds, "I was born in Tucson. All of my parents were born in Hermosillo.[22] My Grandparents. My mother and those aunts of mine that I had were here before. But the rest of my grandfolks, whatever's left they were still down there" (MS: 1). In response to further questioning about his family and birth, he relates, "My mother was full Papago. My father was a mixture. But both my parents had the last name of Garcia" (MS: 1). These three sentences open the published text of Blaine's narrative (10), having been rearranged from the taped interview. Blaine is not sure whether his father is part Yaqui Indian or part Mexican but comments that he grew up speaking both those languages as well as Papago because they were spoken by all his relatives. He goes on to explain that his father was Jose Jesus Garcia and that he lived on the Sells reservation, but that Blaine met him only a few times during his childhood. He explains, "I didn't have any use for him. I talked with him, but not like a father-son thing. He had seven children; they were my half-brothers and sisters" (1981: 11). He goes by the surname Blaine because it is the last name of his older brother Lorenzo and his stepfather Jim Blaine. His narrative continues with memories of his mother tending house in Tucson and of his aunt Josefa, with whom he also lived in Tucson after his mother's death until, upon her death, he was delivered to the aunt at San Xavier where his brother was already living (1981: 12–14). Included in this section is recollection of his aunt Josefa's activities as a medicine woman and midwife, which, while more specific than Ted's responses to my queries about traditional medicine practices during his childhood, recalls similar experience.

As Blaine's interview responses continue, the parallels between his and Ted's childhoods become more striking. They both attend boarding school, and both leave school before graduating because they are needed to work the family farm. Blaine explains that when he was about nine years old, his brother brought him to "the Indian boarding school out on Ajo Road. I could walk from my aunt's place. 'Escuela,' we called it. It was a Presbyterian school about a mile from the Santa Cruz River" (MS: 3). When the priests at the mission discover he is attending the Protestant school, they determine to rescue him. Blaine continues:

Father Bonaventure took me to this mission school, after he got me out of Escuela. Bonaventure then took me up to St. Johns.[23] I was there for one month. He brought up my half brother and took me back to San Xavier. I finished the school year at the mission school. The following year he took me back to St. Johns. That was the time my aunt who had me was sick, about 1913. After . . . after I came back from St. Johns I went to Phoenix Indian School, north of Phoenix. That was 1915. Three years. I had to leave school. They wanted me to help out. My brother, this Lorenzo Blaine, he was with them at the time, and he was kind of sickly, too. My uncle was too old to do work, farming. So they wanted me back to help out on the farm. Mostly it's winter crops: barley and wheat. Then in the fall, well, it's beans and melons, you know. We had irrigation. We used to dam this water up. (MS: 3–3a)

He then goes on to discuss the effect of white farming south of the reservation on the water supply and on the Santa Cruz River, much in the same tone that Ted laments the abatement of water during his youth. Blaine continues, saying he got married in 1919 and lived in the adobe house that was his uncle's, and that he farmed and did government irrigation work; this material appears in the second chapter of the book (MS: 7–12).

The first chapter is clearly a compilation of material from several interviews that cover a range of topics, topics Ted also addresses in the course of my interviews with him: the origin of many families at San Xavier from Santa Rosa village and its environs; trips to Magdalena in Sonora, Mexico, to celebrate the feast of St. Francis; baptism and godparents; serving as an altar boy at San Xavier Mission;[24] Phoenix Indian School education, outings, and sports; harvesting crops; and elegiac laments for the quality of community and environmental life on the reservation in the first quarter of the century.

Blaine is somewhat more explicit than Ted in his recollections, and he does identify most of the people he talks about by name. In particular anecdotes he is sometimes quite specific, especially about locations. For instance, he says, "The edge of Phoenix was about three miles south from the school" (1981: 25). Later he says, "In between was nothing but orchards of oranges and lemons, and two dairies" (183). Ted never gives any location for the school. Blaine also gives more detail on the day-to-day routine and the layout of the school:

There were not only boys at the school but girls too. They had their own dormitory. It was in the middle of campus. There was a park surrounding the girl's dormitory. I took shop in the Industrial building. This is where I learned the printing business. . . . I wore a uniform: a regular one and a dress one. Both had stripes down the front and on the sides of the pant legs. We had to get up at 5:30 in the morning. We had to be in bed by 9:00. The night-watch man [*sic*] came around and checked. I used to laugh at some of these Indian boys that would sneak out at night from the dormitory. They'd make a dumby [*sic*] in their beds, with pillows and sheets. Then they slipped out and went to town. They weren't mean. They did it just for the fun of it. (183–84)

Despite Blaine's description of resistance to the school regimentation, like Ted he offers mostly positive reactions to experiences at the Phoenix Indian School. Blaine says, "The food was good, everything was good" (1981: 25), though he admits that he had to obey orders or get ten days of bread and water as punishment (185).[25] It was still a military-style school when he attended; it was not when Ted was there more than a decade later. According to a summary statement in parentheses in the middle of Blaine's description of the school, Blaine goes on a "diatribe—the Papago kids today get up anytime of the day and don't want to go to school. We had to go to school. We had to go or we had to work hard in the fields" (184). What's characterized—presumably by Adams—as a "diatribe" is a pattern of contrasting then and now, in the same way that Ted contrasts the present unfavorably with the past throughout his narrative.

Like Ted, Blaine also discusses the running of cattle on the reservation, indicating that his uncle was both a farmer and rancher, much as Ted's father was. And he recalls working eighteen years for a Tucson construction company, performing jobs similar to those Ted describes when he returned to San Xavier after World War II. So while the time frame is quite different, there are several parallels in the narrative. Where they diverge significantly is that in the thirties Ted was in Ajo working in the open-pit copper mine, and Blaine had moved to Sells and taken a position as a tribal policeman, though both describe serving as interpreters for meetings. The move to Sells begins Blaine's involvement in political work; at this point Ted's and Blaine's narratives diverge completely, though Blaine and Ted, experiencing essentially the same historical milieu, refer to the same or similar events at many points in their narrations.

Adams sets the edited Blaine narrative up much as Michael Hitt-man organizes Corbett Mack's narrative, using date spans—1902–1918, 1919–1931, etc.—to give the narrative a chronological tether, but the table of contents for the archive lists 192 separate topical entries:

Traditional ones
calendar sticks
the San Juan's Day rooster pull
the wine-drinking fiesta
Tribal government issues
chiefs' meetings at San Xavier
the Papago constitution
land allotment
political structure
Tribal relations with the region and nation
draft registration
the bombing range on the reservation during World War II
employment of Papagos at the Ajo mine
water disputes with Tucson
union wages
The impact of particular anthropologists on the reservation
Portraits of a wide range of individuals
Father Bonaventure
various Papago leaders, including tribal chairman Thomas
    Segundo, whose tragic airplane crash death Ted also recalls
John Collier, a director of the BIA who had significant impact on
    the Papagos.

Unlike Ted who, though he spends a good deal of his childhood and adult life away from San Xavier, always returns to his home place, Blaine does not. When Blaine retires from public life, he moves to an apartment in Tucson, where Adams interviews him. If location and life work mean anything, Blaine seems to identify much more strongly with the white world than Ted does. The bicultural facility both Ted and Blaine exhibit seems stronger, or maybe more deliberate in Blaine's case; he works with government officials, travels to Washington DC to testify before government commissions, interacts with the white world primarily in official capacities, and retires to live among whites. Ted, on the other hand, travels more broadly, but his interactions with the non-Papago world are directed primarily at gaining and maintaining employment and are often discussed in terms of his reluctance to be away from San Xavier for extended periods. Unlike Blaine, Ted's identity is permanently connected to the immediate landscape of his childhood. Perhaps the difference is that Ted was born at San Xavier, but Blaine was born in Tucson, so his retirement there is analogous to Ted's return to San Xavier.

Travel and eventual return to the Papagueria is the central trope in James McCarthy's written autobiography, *A Papago Traveler* (1985), edited by John G. Westover. The pattern of his life, and even of much of his traveling, parallels Ted's pattern of work away from San Xavier but intermittent return and eventual residence there.

In his forward to *A Papago Traveler*, Larry Evers writes: "For those who think that an Indian can only be truly at home when he is living in a tribal community attuned to the natural world around him, here is an Indian who seems to be comfortable and "at home" with himself whether he is in England or China or a trailer park in California. . . . For those who would have their Indians disinterested in contemporary American culture, here is an Indian who yearned to see "the country" because there was always something new and interesting to learn" (1985: ix–x). The same might be said of Ted, for whom seeing the country held a magnetic pull. Though born twenty years apart—in 1895 and 1915—and though part of McCarthy's travel was initiated by his service in the U.S. military during World War I and took him to several foreign lands, Ted and McCarthy share both similar work experiences and a map of wanderings in the United States.

McCarthy's memoir, published in 1985, was begun in the 1960s after his retirement from a job at a Tucson hotel. It was during interviews with military historian John G. Westover that McCarthy confided he had hand-written a book-length narrative about his life (1985: xxi). They proceeded to work together to put it into publishable form. How they did that beyond condensing some stories and expanding others (1985: xxiii) is not revealed in Westover's introduction to the narrative text. Nor does he say whether he incorporated any of the material collected over five months of interviews with McCarthy into the written narrative. No discussion of who structured the book into chapters is given, though it was probably Westover. Like the Blaine narrative, it is divided by dated chapters — "The Early Years, 1895–1906," "Indian School Days, 1906–1917," etc. As usual, the volume is short on analysis of process, but it's long on episodes that parallel and even overlap the events Ted narrates.

McCarthy begins his story with his birth near Santa Rosa on the main Papago Reservation. He was brought as an infant to San Xavier, where his grandparents farmed. He was baptized Macario Antone at the Mission, but explains that his name was misunderstood and changed to James McCarthy when he was in the army.[26] McCarthy's early memories are inscribed in much the same way as Ted's. He writes:

> I first remember when I was about three years old. I remember that my grandparents grew many things in their fields — like beans, peas, corn, wheat, canes. The first thing which I learned to like was watermelon and other melons. At that time there was plenty of water to irrigate their plants. They had their own dam on the Santa Cruz River. In those days we had plenty of rain; sometimes it rained for several days. . . .
>
> When I was five years old, I used to walk along the river with my older brother and uncle. On each side of the river it was all swamp, and water drained into the river from both sides. The mesquite trees were thick and large. By 1968 we could only see big stumps standing among the new trees. For many years the trees had been chopped down by our people and sold to the people in Tucson. (1985: 2)

McCarthy summarizes in a couple of paragraphs much of what Ted observes in the first four interviews we did and intermittently thereafter, and he uses a then/now pattern of judging the present in terms of a more verdant past in the same way Ted does. However, he does not place blame as Ted does when Ted says, "It's not like it was then. When the white man came they spoil everything. They got no rain; they couldn't make rain. The people used to say they could make their own rain. They drink that wine off the cactus. And then they sing and dance for the gods, and pretty soon—clouds" (edited tape 6: 13). But McCarthy does go on to describe swimming in the river, flooded fields during the rainy season, and how green everything looked in the spring (1985: 2–4).

Like Ted, he recalls starting school at the San Xavier Mission, though his parents didn't send him voluntarily; the tribal truant officer forced them to send him, and he was scared. Like Ted, he didn't much like the mission school and says, "It was hard for me to learn," and claims he didn't learn much in the year he attended (1985: 5). Unlike Ted, there is a hiatus in his education when the family moves to the outskirts of Tucson and both parents take up wage work and set him the task of minding younger siblings. He escapes the classroom until he is eleven, when the same truant officer forces his parents to send him to Phoenix (1985: 6–27). McCarthy's experience is not as pleasant as Ted's. It is still a military school when he arrives, and he's ashamed when his hair is clipped and he is given his first pair of shoes. Again, he says he didn't learn much because he didn't know English (28–29). Like Ted, McCarthy's wandering begins with school and blends fairly seamlessly into a work pattern. By the early 1920s, he is working in Ajo at the mine. He writes only briefly of the experience:

Most of the men in the pit mine were Papagos. Everything was done by hand. They drilled, shoveled, and moved track. It was hard work at first but John [one of his brothers] and I got used to it. A few months later I was hurt while carrying a big water

131

pump with three other boys. One stumbled on a rock and fell. The weight shifted and pulled my shoulder muscle, so I was taken to the hospital for treatment. I stayed for awhile, but my younger brother continued working. (1985: 115)

Jobs that McCarthy doesn't like get little narrative attention. Ted, on the other hand, returns during nearly every interview to his experience in the mines.[27] Of course, Ted spends years, not months of his life, in the Ajo pit, so the danger and frantic activities there play a larger role in his memory. It is also a period of stability in his life and one in which he earned respect for his work skills, so it has a more positive value to Ted than McCarthy's accident-ridden stint does for him.

During our fourth interview (May 21, 1974), Ted talks again at some length and considerable animation about his mining experience. This tape contains some of the most extensive narrations by Ted, suggesting three things: topics he likes make it easier to narrate — mining and his work in the movies dominate this interview; he was becoming more at ease with narrating; and I was finally learning to shut up and let him talk. The following edited section was interrupted by me only for brief clarifying questions, which do not break the flow of his narration:

I was on the track crew. That's the one they start you on, the first one. Putting rails, rails for the train, you know, railroad. And then the track keeps moving all the time, 'specially down there. The main line is the line that comes in from any place like the smelter or shops. Then it goes on every level. You go around in a circle all the way around the edge [*circling motion with right hand*]. That is, if it'll come in a circle. Sometimes it ends and has to come back [*indicates switch-backs*], you know, because it's too steep. They got to make it some way. They can make it come in a circle but not — quite always. It always has to come in. So the trains back down, so they could go forward going up, because they're loaded. They're moving the tracks, just like I said. See, they're drilling, big churn drills, holes about this big [*circles his arms*], so deep, here and there along the bank. And then they drill, drill all along the bank, and they shoot the whole thing, and all of that collapses right in there. And then you've got to put the track over in there, wherever it's clear, see, so in that way they load it. The shovels get in there and then they load the train right off. And when it gets so far, you've got to move the track some more in there closer, where they can load it. And at the same time another bank comes down, and you got to move the tracks. And then, after it's all set down like that, well, they've got to carry it over and then you've got to lay that track where they started hauling it out just like that, all the way. Continual. It's got to be done [*nods*]. There's so many gangs on that track. Then you've got to be one of them.

And then you go to maintenance. There's some crew that maintains the track all the time where the main line comes in. It doesn't move. Then you've got to take care of it where it won't sag, because they're heavy. It's heavy when it's loaded, all that. And you've got to block it to keep it from sinking. Just the sections. You have to disconnect 'em where it's connected. And the hoist just pick 'em up or load 'em, take 'em someplace else and pile 'em. And when it's cleared the same hoist comes in there and picks 'em up one by one, put 'em in just like that, and you're there with the hammer, to put the joints on, plates on, and all that. And at the same time someone'll be jacking it up. It's got to be level and they got to block it some. Like that all the way. Up to wherever they started working. Trains start coming, and there's another one. You've got to go all over. Going deep. And then sometimes it gets so bad that maybe the train jumps off the track, cuts the ties off [*skidding motion with hands*]. Then that's got to be fixed. Then sometimes it happens right on the main line, and then they have to block off the trains coming in, and then there's no stoppage in the work and the whole bunch, whoever they can get, get together and fix it, you know — spiking by hand. Just got to do it fast. And then you've got to know how to spike. If you know how to spike, you're on it. If you can't spike, you can't. Then you swing the ax, like when you're chopping wood [*demonstrates a chopping motion with his right hand*]. Another guy standing and you're partners, and the other one's on big rod. It's got — like a hoof, where he can dig it in and just lift the spike off if you want to. They've got to have one like that, and he's your partner. Then he's got to hold the tie up under, you know, when you're spiking on the rail. And then you got to have the spikes. Sometimes if you're a spiker, you have 'em in your pocket — heavy. But you can always thrown 'em and pick 'em up, and most of 'em there have 'em spread out. The fewer times you hit the better. You don't have to keep on tapping. We call them woodpeckers. If you're good enough, maybe you hit it two or three times, just as well as your partner, and you're good. You got to have a good partner. When we work together, we're just doing teamwork. You always get the same man. Just like three of us, we're in a bunch, and we know what we're doing. The other guy knows what he's doing. If you've got to do it fast, you do it fast. If you've got a lot of time, you just take your time. Once you're in a big gang like that, you know he knows what he's doing and he knows — everybody knows. Just say, "Just take it easy. We'll go slow." "Okay" [*nods*]. But sometimes, they got to do it in certain time; well, you got to do it fast, too. And then you move. See, that's how we get in there. That's how I got in, because I could spike either way, left and right. When you get on and you get used to it, then you know if a spike is way on the other side of the rail. You never hit the rail. If you miss the spike, then the thing will fly like a nail, and it's dangerous. And if you hit the rail, sometimes an old rail, a chip might fly to you. I know somebody that got hit in their eye. It's dangerous. That's why they had a lot of these safety precautions. That's why they had meetings then. Tell 'em what's bad for them and what's better.

For hauling ties, rails, they got all the machinery. They got all the little cars that got trailers on 'em. They load it on 'em and haul it down like that. Unloading the train takes a lot of men. Grab, throw on more [*grabbing and throwing motion*] and then get all the stuff ready and then start in building.

I used jack hammers, drilling them big boulders. They've got to be drilled in there and then they've got to be dynamited. They drill it in there so far and then put the sticks of dynamite, load 'em in there, and then they block it in there, and then when it's time to shoot 'em off, there's a certain time. They're together, and they know how many. They've got to count, count how many, how many you've got to shoot. And then they start a big whistle that warns everybody to get away from there—shooting going on. Stop the trains for so long, a certain length of time. Then it's up to them. And they start it, blowing 'em all up, and they scatter like nothing. They blast bounders because the shovel won't carry them, see, and then everything scatters and then the shovel can pick it up. Jackhammer's too heavy and they make too much noise. Oh, once in a while, if you have to. I don't like it. It's too heavy, heavy and makes too much noise like all that. 'Course, nobody liked it.

Oh, I done a lot of hauling—hauling the materials that come in. You've got to stack the ties, or the rails. That's the worst ones. The hoist got to be there. They got to tie so many on there, one end and the other end. Then you've got to signal the operator when you're ready and then you go. Then you got to watch 'em which way it swings—out of everybody's way—and drops on the train. They unload it and stack 'em. If it gets on your foot because it slips when it's laid down, I don't like it. Oh, it's dangerous. Every place is dangerous in a mine [*nods twice*]. And then you have to have gloves. You've got a foreman. 'Course, the gangs don't work together. Some will be here and this other one way down or some will be away up there. One gang is in a certain place; another gang is doing the same thing, but they're maybe on the next level, or so on. Just like that.

Hot! Hot! 'Specially if you're handling them rocks. You know, down there mostly it's that ore and all that, and no wind, no nothing. And then the sun, you know, not enough air in the hole. But it's worse, worse underground, worse than on the pit. I've been both. Underground's the worst one. Not much air. And then you sweat—just running. 'Course, you got a lot of water there. Then you can't see nothing. You have a light. And you can go like this [*hand about an inch in front of face with fingers splayed*] with your fingers—you can't see that far.

They got a lot of bosses. And I don't want to be, either. When they all get together, that's when the gossip starts. They're kidding everybody around. When they get to know you, they know who's the big talker. And then when there's news about something around Ajo any place, they already knew it too. Because somebody's liable to tell it in there, and somebody don't know—well, they found out right there. You can always find out working there what's going on. All that rumors come around. Everybody knows. Lot of fun. And there's a lot of people from different places, you know, like across the line—Mexicans and all that—and down this way—Pima. They tell you what's going on. Everybody knows each other. And then when payday comes, well, certain times when the payday comes, well, they get their checks. And then the gossip starts. They say that they're going to the store and get stuff, and then somebody—"What about some beer" or some wine or whatever. "Let's get one, you know, drink before we go" [*lifts right fist with thumb toward mouth*]. And the night, it goes like that [*repeats thumb motion*]. Oh, it's a lot of fun when you know everybody in town, even the Mexicans. Small town and everybody's walking down the street anyway. You know where you live—just one family. (edited tape 4: 5–11)

Ted continues his description of his experiences at the Ajo mine on tape five (May 22, 1974), starting with a reprise of his description of blasting, again emphasizing the danger of the job and by extension his skill and bravery, a marked contrast with McCarthy's terse report-

136

age and dismissal of his experience in a single paragraph. The edited narrative reads:

> Rocks are dynamited. They're drilled and then they put in all the explosives, and they bust 'em up in order to put 'em on the train where they won't be so big, because when they dump it in the chute where the mill is, they got to smash it. And they got to be so big, so they just slide in there. And then the machines—they got to smash it into powder anyway.
>
> At night I worked with the hoist where they carry loads that come in—unload it, unload it, just all that. Oh, they got lights; they got lights in there. It's just like a town in the mountains. It's lighted, 'specially where somebody's working. Like bulldozers, see, they got to make a clearing in there. They work at night. Everybody works at night. We couldn't see no spikes or anything to lay track at night. We do it in day. Mostly machines, they just go, and shovels and trains. If a train jump the track at night, the hoist got to be there and lift the cars up and then set 'em on the track and then move out. But a crew will have to be there in the morning to fix the wreckage.
>
> They mostly do it at night, you know. It's dangerous. Dynamite explodes, you know, kills somebody. I don't handle dynamite. It's dangerous [*nods*]. Sometimes one would be in there, you know, just like I said, if they don't count. The dynamiters, they've got to count how many—how much got to be blasted or whatever. They got to know so they're sure after everything's over so if maybe one doesn't explode, there's dynamite in there, and if you're not careful—they got to drill it again. They have to drill twice, and it gets so hot and explodes—kill all the drillers. Dangerous [*nods*]. You can't just go ahead and do whatever you want to. You got to watch the other fellow, yourself. Especially them power lines—carry so much voltage for the shovels. Like a hose, rubber, but you've got to handle it. When you move it, you've got to handle it by tongs, or they shut the power off at certain

places, and you've got to move the cable in when you shovel there. Be careful. That's why they had to have them meetings all the time. They've got a big office. All the big shots and all — everybody that's responsible. Certain representatives, you know, like me, I'm representing a crew.

If a man's hurt, well, there always fifty men right around there, and they got telephones all along there, and they can call 'em right in, call up the ambulance or something. See, the ambulance, they just go right in there and pick him up, take him to the hospital. They got a big hospital. Got a big hospital 'way up there because there's always somebody — doctors and all.

Lot of changes now. Oh, yeah. Used to have an old train, made a lot of smoke, and now they've got this one. It's just like you see on the main railroad. I didn't stay there after I'm divorced [1941]. I was out. Because it was wartime, I had to go down to that plane factory and all that. I was traveling. Everybody left when the war came. See, a lot of them, even a lot of my friends, because they're tired about the mine. 'Course they got good jobs there, but when you're there for a time, well, you feel like just going away somewhere. That's what happened. And then they opened a lot of jobs, like defense workers. Everybody start moving out. The big bosses want to keep me. And I told 'em, "No, I'm going. I'm tired of them rocks." And they couldn't hold you back if you say you're going. Well, they asked me if I wanted to come back, but I never did. (edited tape 5: 2–4)

For Ted, mining is a success story. For McCarthy, it is not, though he returns to work at Ajo in 1936 to hold a less perilous job as a shop helper:

No more pit for me. I liked that work, and they put me at different jobs helping on the engines and trains. My regular job came to be taking care of locomotives that ran on the company line from

138

Ajo to Gila Bend. I cleaned and oiled the engine each day when
it returned to Ajo. (1985: 153)

He continues to work there until 1944, and it is very likely he knew Ted,
though there is no specific evidence of that in either narrative. Mining
work, of whatever variety, does not inspire more than brief reportage
from McCarthy. He treats a stint with a motion picture company in
the late 1920s with the same brevity:

> Sometimes a man came asking Indian boys to take parts in
> movies, playing the part of Indians. I took a part one time in win-
> ter. We had almost no clothes on, and they wouldn't let us start
> a fire. I almost froze. I only hired for the movies one time—no
> more. They paid us four dollars a day, but I wanted a different
> kind of job. (1985: 121)

Ted treats his experience in the movies with the same enthusiasm he
treats his mining work. During the fourth interview he speaks at length
of his motion-picture career.[28] The following edited section sums it up:

> I've been in about sixteen or seventeen different movies. I know
> the people. Mostly it's westerns. Oh, they come over there. See,
> they come around and hire people. When a movie comes, then
> they've got to come around and then they see me over here, and
> then I got to go around and pick whoever can ride horses, ride
> or race. Not the real old one, somebody that's active, that can
> ride. 'Course, you've got to fall, and then you got to get knocked
> over, and all that. Then you meet a lot of people there, some from
> Hollywood. Yes, it's a lot of fun if you don't get hurt [*nods*]. Once
> my horse bucked me off—landed me in the hospital. Eighteen
> days in Tucson General Hospital. Broken ribs [*grabs right rib area
> with left hand*]. (edited tape 4: 5)

He then goes on for seven more pages of recollections about working on films with Audie Murphy, a cavalry-Indian film in Yuma, a segment of the TV series *High Chaparral,* and *Dirty Dingus McGee* with Frank Sinatra, all these film experiences extending over two decades.

The mining and movie treatments by each of these narrators speak to the individuality of sensibilities and experiences even within narratives that are very similar in many respects, especially in the travel themes. In fact both narrators cover much of the same territory. While McCarthy goes as far north as Alaska—a destination Ted considers but rejects—and Ted gets only as far as Seattle, the primary motive for leaving Arizona is similar—restlessness. Ted says, "I was tired of that Ajo. Can't stay one place too long. Besides, maybe I could get a better job outside" (edited tape 12: 6). Each voluntarily left "familiar ground in search of difference" (Clifford 1997: 90). McCarthy says, "I was young and could not stay long in one place" (1985: 139). He heads north in the 1920s, before he is married. He spends time in Portland and at The Dalles on the Columbia River to fish for salmon for three months. Then he moves on to Toppenish on the Yakima Reservation, where he stays until the weather turns cold, then decides to make his way down the coast to Los Angeles. He travels by way of Seattle, Portland, and Klamath Falls, where he works two months on a tunnel, then on to Escondido doing gravel and cement work until it turns cold there (1985: 130–39). Delete Klamath Falls and Escondido and add Ted's job at the Hanford nuclear energy plant near Pasco, Washington, and the itinerary is nearly identical. While at Hanford, Ted goes to the Yakima reservation, and when he leaves the nuclear energy plant he works briefly for Boeing in Seattle, then visits a friend from the Hanford job in Portland for awhile before stopping to see San Francisco and moving on to Los Angeles, where he picks up odd jobs cleaning bars, helping to load and clean ships (edited tape 5: 7–13). Even their responses to the social situation in Los Angles, where a great many Indians from all across the country live, is similar. Both dislike the fact that acquaintances are constantly cadging money and determine to leave, McCarthy north again, stealing rides on trains. "I was getting to be a regular hobo," he says (1985: 139). Ted, always lonesome for home when he's away,[29] heads from Los Angles to San Xavier in December of 1944 (edited tape 5: 14).

The time frames are different; Ted's travels are twenty years after McCarthy's and are in some measure motivated by a desire to avoid the World War II draft by working in defense industries, while McCarthy has already served in World War I and in Panama and China before leaving the service and embarking on his civilian travels.[30] But the desire to see new country and find new experiences is similar, as is the capacity to make one's way in new places.[31] As James Clifford points out, leaving home and returning allows the traveler to enact "differently centered worlds, interconnected cosmopolitanisms" (1997: 27–28). Both of these Papago travelers cross geographical and cultural borders with considerable ease,[32] which may account for their ability to cross narrative borders to tell their life stories. McCarthy does not take up residence at San Xavier again until 1950, but when he comes home, he stays (1985: 186). Ted comes back to San Xavier to live in the mid-1940s and resides there, farming a little and taking jobs in landscaping and agricultural work with an occasional stint on an Anglo ranch until his health begins to fail in the mid-1970s.[33]

Reading Ted's narrative in the context of the Papago life stories discussed thus far convinces me that there is a Papago way of expressing life experience. Topics and themes resonate from one narrative to the other; stylistics, where they are not obliterated by non-Native editing, show the influence of the Papago language; and a consistent framing of experiences in terms of Papago relationship to land and particular cultural values provides evidence that Ted's narrative is part of a nontraditional, culturally adaptive form of Papago expression. As Edward Said notes, emergent movements—in this case a modest but definable narrative movement—develop in spite of Western cultural hegemony; "there is always something beyond the reach of dominating systems, no matter how deeply they saturate a society" (1983:

246–47). Granted, these Papago narratives are solicited and, except for the Dolores narrative, edited to conform to the expectations of a non-Papago readership. But in spite of the influence, even interference of Euro-American cultural and disciplinary norms and the individual biases of non-Papago collector-editors, each is marked by uniquely Papago experiences and by a culturally shaped way of articulating those experiences. Yet each is individual, marking not only the dynamics of culture change over a period from the mid-1800s to the 1980s on the Papagueria, in Arizona, and throughout the nation but also tracing a range of subjectivity created out of language. *Telling a Good One* is unique as the narrative of an individual, but it is tightly connected to a way of telling one's life that is shared with other Papago narrators.

There are two other texts by Papago narrators that are of particular interest in relationship to the Rios-Sands project in that the methodology — taped interviews — is nearly identical. In one case, in fact, the subject is Ted, and in the other, a female cousin of his of the same generation is interviewed by me. Because Ted's interviews with Timothy Dunnigan are lengthy — 349 pages of transcripts based on twenty-two interviews [34] — and offer so many parallels with the ones Ted and I did together as well as some striking differences, I intend to address them separately as variants of the same life story. My dialogues with Ella Lopez Antone, though never edited into a narrative that could be called a coherent life story, do contain a partial record of her life that intersects with Ted's and other Papago narratives in themes, specific topics, and oral style and provides a contrast to all but Chona's in terms of the female perspective of the narrator. [35]

The interviews with Ella Antone, in November of 1981 and January of 1982, include a few comments on Ted, but most of the narrative is actually about Ella. I had not sought her out to verify data from Ted's narrative. Rather, I was introduced to her by a colleague who thought she might know something about the Chona-Underhill project, which

I was researching and writing about at the time.[36] She did. We talked informally for an hour or so, and I arranged to return to tape her on that topic. On November 20, we began talking about her recollections of translating for Chona and Underhill when she was fourteen and home for the summer from the Phoenix Indian School.[37] As she recalled her travels and talks with Chona and Underhill, she began to think of other memories and said she would like to record some for her children. At the end of the session, we made arrangements to meet again in January. The second tape is primarily about her recollections, and at one point specifically about Ted, whom she recalls playing with when she spent time in the summers at his maternal grandparents' ranch and with whom she attended classes at the Phoenix Indian school. Born a year after Ted into the same maternally related extended family, her life shares many common experiences with his. Both were raised in farming villages; both began their educations in the local school; both went to boarding school; and both lived a good part of their adult lives away from the reservation. For each of them, as for other Papago narrators, parents sent them beyond the boundaries of the reservation to become educated. Ted describes his father, the force behind going away to school, as "not for the olden time people. He's going the other way. You've got to have a good education, all that," and quotes his father saying, " 'What's coming on? White man's way. You got to tackle it' " (edited tape 12: 7). Ella explains a different but no less compelling reason to leave her family home in Santa Rosa:

> Dad was sick with diabetes. And he knows he's going. At that time there was no medicine and we just know that Dad's going to die. . . . Mom never went to school a day in her life but she was very, very smart woman. She knew that we [eight children] would have to look after ourselves because we wouldn't have a father, and so she figured if she sent us away to get educated that we would get jobs to support ourselves. That was her idea and that was the reason she sent all of us away to school. (tape 2: 7)

Her first boarding-school experience, at St. John's School near Phoenix, was as difficult as it was for other Papago narrators. She was the same age as Ted when she was put on a bus. About going, she says, "I was all excited, but that night I changed my mind. I got up there in that strange dorm, with a whole bunch of all kinds of tribes and everything, and I laid down and, boy, the tears came out" (tape 2: 7). During seventh and eighth grade she went to the Phoenix Indian School. Here her recollections about courses contrast with Ted's memories of dairy farming, mechanics, and engineering. Ella describes training in domestic work, "sewing, sewing clothes, or how to bake" and housekeeping skills (tape 2: 10), and unlike Ted recalls enjoying academic classes except for math. Like Ted, she leaves school because she is needed at home. When her father dies, she reluctantly stays in Santa Rosa to be with her mother, saying, "She was heart broken, you know" (tape 2: 11). She marries a local man, and in 1948, when he has a job offer in Marana, a town about thirty miles north of Tucson, they take their children and apparently make the adjustment to a bicultural life easily. Ella recalls being active in clubs and holding jobs at the local school and a daycare center. Again, unlike Ted, Ella does not give up her house on the reservation, where they finally return in 1971 (tape 2: 3–4).[38] Unlike Ted who seems to slip back into village life easily, Ella found readjusting hard, life in the village boring after so many years away. "I had to learn people all over again . . . and I gradually began to take an interest back into my culture," she says (tape 2: 5).

Much of the tape is taken up with reminiscences of her childhood, like a pilgrimage to Magdalena, Mexico, in a wagon train and being hidden when bandits posing as soldiers took everyone's money. She says, "I was scared to death. My Grandma was crying and she pulled us in the covered wagon and covered us up with a shawl, or whatever, a blanket" (tape 2: 1). She also had many memories of cooking and cheese-making and roasting coffee beans brought back from Mexico (tape 2: 2–5). Ella and Ted, unlike the other Papago narrators, pay a great deal of attention to traditional foods and food preparation;

neither had to be interrogated to get them talking about food. For instance, during the sixth interview (May 23, 1974), Ted brings up the topic of cheese-making at the ranch. He says, "All the ladies got to make it. It's not a man's business" (transcript 6: 16), but then goes on for seven pages to detail exactly how his grandmother made cheese (transcript 6: 17–24). Ted never claims to prepare food, but he raises both animals and farms vegetables and takes a keen interest in traditional ways of cooking and incorporates his lament for the passage of time and the changes in culture into his narratives on food.[39]

It may well be that family ties and some shared childhood experiences account for the topics they narrate, but more likely Ella's narrative, though brief, simply fits into the patterns of Papago narrative outlined above. Though the style of her narrative shows the effect of a quarter century living in a world dominated by English-language communication—she exhibits almost no traces of Papago in her oral style—the topics and themes of her life story center on Papago experiences.

From generation to generation and across genders, Papago life stories document a distinct tribal culture in a specifically cultural way. Whether written or told, each narrative aims at communicating life lived Papago to a non-Papago audience. How individually each life is lived, recollected, and narrated speaks to the range of experiences, attitudes, and expressive modes available within traditional and bicultural ways of being Papago. How a dialogic process of narrating a Papago life affects the topics, style, and themes of one life—Ted Rios's—becomes apparent when two sets of interviews by two different collectors are examined as variants of one life story.

5

MORE THAN ONE WAY TO TELL

"A GOOD ONE"

When Ted and I met in that hospital room in Sells in 1974, I knew more about his life from the interviews he had done with anthropologist Timothy Dunnigan than I would learn directly from him in our interviews. The transcripts of the Rios-Dunnigan tapes (1969) contain narration of many facts, events, and experiences in his life that Ted did not tell me, or at least would not talk about when the tape recorder was running. Part of the difference in the narrations is clearly due to different interview techniques. Dunnigan was more skilled at eliciting narration than I was and more insistent and precise in verifying information. I also think that Ted's memory may have been clearer during his work with Dunnigan than when we worked together; the earlier interviews give more evidence of dates and more complete and specific data.

I am also convinced that the difference in gender in the interviewers produced differences in how our taping sessions worked and in the narration they produced. Ted had a strong sense of propriety and a differential attitude toward "ladies," the term he always used for women. I think that attitude affected what he thought was appropriate behavior and what he thought was appropriate to discuss with a woman, especially a white woman twenty-five years younger than he. The informality and male camaraderie established between Dunnigan and Ted is quite different from the almost genteel relationship Ted and I shared. Even the taping circumstances were different. While Ted and I met at the Sells hospital and later sat outside — never inside — his home about a hundred yards southwest of the San Xavier Mission, Dunnigan and

Ted taped both outside Ted's residence and inside Ted's room and discussed topics he never acknowledged or treated much more circumspectly with me.[1] About two-thirds of the way through their taping, when Ted obviously felt at ease with Dunnigan, he freely began to discuss his drinking.[2] He relates one incident that reveals the seriousness of his alcohol problem, saying,

> I was drunk then, when I got off at the bus stop, I had a bottle. . . .
> I thought, "I'm on the wrong path, I better go back." So I sit for
> awhile, sat there with them rocks and pretty soon when I sit for
> awhile, I heard something coming, some clicking on the rocks,
> hitting something. . . . Something was shining ahead. That's the
> devil! So, right then I realized, "I'm in trouble. I better get out of
> here!" So I scrambled up. . . . I took the trail out and I got here.
> See, what happens when you get so nasty about this . . . "D.T.s."
> (1969: 279–80)

He never related that story to me, and he never drank in front of me, though a couple of times during the sessions at his home his buddies came by and offered him a beer.[3]

Nor did he ever admit to me any promiscuity or harsh treatment of women. But he tells Dunnigan about women he meets at the fiesta in Magdalena, Mexico (1969: 78–85), and he also tells him an involved and long story about a spur-of-the-moment trip to Nogales to visit a whorehouse where he is recognized by the woman he engages and admits, "I didn't know what to say, just stunned, you know" (1969: 329–35). He wasn't about to tell that incident directly to me even off the tape, and I never dared try to get him to relate it—my sense of propriety enters in here too, I guess. Even if I had led him toward it, I'm certain he would have avoided telling me, despite the fact that he knew I had read the transcripts of the interviews with Dunnigan. Even in the description to me of his trip to Magdalena for the feast of St. Francis, a narration very similar in content to his narration of the event

148

to Dunnigan, he mentions women only obliquely, saying simply that he danced.

Drinking was also a topic he rarely broached with me. The few times I tried to get him to talk about his drinking, he usually deflected the questions. The only times he discussed alcohol on tape were incidental and in the context of broader topics. Throughout the interviews there are several brief references to alcohol in relation to ceremonial wine-drinking, complaints about friends cadging him for drinks in Los Angeles, a description of one of his weekend trips from Hanford to the town of Toppenish on the Yakima Indian reservation, and another brief but pointed description of drinking in a fairly lengthy narration on the activities during the St. Francis fiesta in Magdalena.

During our fifth interview (May 22, 1974), Ted relates in some detail a visit to a friend's place in Toppenish:

TR: Where we been to a friend's place—he makes his own brew. That's when I first tasted—made from plums.

KS: Oh, wine.

TR: Wine, right. Put in the refrigerator, pull it out, drink it [*fist with thumb extended toward mouth*]. Boy, it gets you drunk [*nods*]. No kidding. He told us before he did it, you see, he warned us—oh, Jonathan, he told us, "If you want to drink this stuff I'll let you have it, but you know, you get drunk." Well, we're drinking like— any punch, right? My friend, he says, "Ah, I don't think it gets you drunk. Take another." He was drunk already [*nods*]. Pretty soon I got drunk. You know, it tastes good when you drink it. Everybody's drunk. (5: 18–19)

The context of this brief anecdote is a narration of exuberant release from the garbage detail at Hanford and the barracks living conditions that went with it, as well as Ted's amusement at thwarting the prohibition against alcohol sale and consumption on the reservation. He narrates the occasion as an innocent indulgence.

His drinking at the fiesta in Magdalena, Mexico, is also amelio-
rated by the context of celebration and its relatively brief part in the
larger description of the festivities. In the seventh interview (May 23,
1974), he talks at length about going to Nogales by wagon and then on
to Magdalena by train, then as an adult driving there in his own car.
The transcript reads as follows:

TR: Musicians, drinking, all that, all that dancing there, the Church is
full of people—you're crowded. You never get to see that—what
you want to see in there, like the statue of Christ 'way down in
there. Keep pushing, pushing, pushing the crowd and when you get
there, sick and all, ladies and all, and . . .

KS: Where did you stay when you went down there? It must have been
crowded.

TR: Oh, there's a lot of people that live down there, well they have a
certain farm that—lots, where they had the storage for—you got a
car, car or wagons or whatever. Well, they let you in there and then
you get your own blankets or what. Hotel's so full. You can sleep
any place—you get your choice. But it's dangerous there—you're
supposed to watch, you know. Lot of bad people coming there. Too
many people. Hand pickers, pocket pickers. Lot of people [*nods*].

KS: You said they sold herbs down there during the festival.

TR: Lot of things—saddles, serapes—whatever they make down there.
It still is—just like if you go down the parkway there, you know the
big parkway that—just like that. Serapes there and there and all
you got to see along down there in the parks—tents where they
cook and sell food. If you want to eat any place, well you can—
right along there. They cook it and then they sell it, just like in a
restaurant, just set up. And different people—they make those, you
know, spurs, silver spurs, bridles, saddles, bits—everything, right
on the table. Pick it yourself.

KS: You bargain for it?

TR: If you want to. You've got to be good—they're good, too. It's good
stuff, but they're cheaper than here. And they sit and make 'em,

just like I said, right in there. If you know what you're getting, you get it. But I don't know.

KS: Did you ever buy anything down there?

TR: Oh, I bought a [*shrugs*] — long time ago — you know, jackets, ladies' jackets, for my wife, you know. Oh, they got the — they're made in Mexico. . . .

KS: Leather?

TR: No, they not — they're made from — I don't know. It's got Mexico on the — you know.

KS: Oh.

TR: Lot of different kinds — anything you're — they want to sell, they got it. They bring their wares from wherever they make 'em. Lot of things. But its cheaper than here. Lot of guys — lot of people, they buy stuff there.

KS: They set up everything in the square there? It's not very big.

TR: Mm hmm.

KS: It must have been. . . .

TR: Big one. As big as here [*nods*]. Church there, and then they sell the beer right along in places like that. And they get musicians, I don't know how many — mariachis. Some will be standing over here where they're drinking that beer. They'll come over and say, "Hey, you want to hear some music?" "Okay" [*nods*]. Then you drop in that — whatever you got, Mexican money, Mexican — maybe a dollar or fifty cents or whatever, and they start right in there. And they'll be standing over here someplace — some people's crowd — they'll be doing the same thing. Usually they just — they have a player here and there.

KS: Pretty noisy, huh?

TR: Noisy. And, you know, it's got a crowd, too. And the kids and ice cream and everything — see 'em around. And then the evenings they got special — you stand there, where the orchestra sits up there and — stand, dance floor right around, and you dance there. And there's another place, another place — music going on, whatever — and drinking going on. Somebody be selling soda pop, beer, and all. Just like that. Lot of people. Big carnival. I don't know, I haven't been there for a long time. I go there once in a while when I'm home. I don't know how long since I've been there. But it's too crowded. Of course, the buses go now, and they've got a good highway through there. It's easier now than it was. Won't cost you so much, because — Greyhound. It's Greyhound there, too.

KS: Mm hmm. Yeah, they have a good bus service in Mexico. Were there — did you ever see Indian dancers down there, in the square?

TR: Oh, yeah. Yaquis. They were better than anyplace I ever saw them. You know, they come from the Rio Mayo.[4] They can to this stuff you never see, even in the Yaqui fiesta. Probably so, but then they came from where — originated. They got musicians, just dance with their own.

KS: What kind of costumes do they have?

TR: Be nearly bare.

KS: Oh, really.

TR: You know, that's what they're supposed to be like. They don't do it so much here. Just a little thing here, there — maybe got an antelope head right up here [*pats the side of his head*], or they used to be.

KS: Oh, the deer dance.

TR: It's got all that — yeah [*shaking his left hand up and down imitating a rattle*]. It's got all that thing. . . .

KS: Gourds?

TR: Mm hmm.

KS: Like rattles?

TR: Got all these — lot of things. Musicians. They do it all day, all night. Old men too, grownups — they do a lot of that dancing. And then pretty soon — well, they do it for money. After awhile somebody will get a — throw a piece of coin, somebody else — they won't ask you, but you just — their own, it's their own idea. Pitch in.

KS: Did Papagos ever dance there?

TR: Well, they dance where they have that dancing places.

KS: But not Indian dances?

TR: No.

152

KS: Did they have religious processions outside the church?

TR: They used to. They used to do it — good ones, too, but I don't think they do it any more on account of it takes too much time, and they're too crowded. And the people in the church, just like I said, just packed in there. They go and then they come out and then another one will go just like ants going into the hole. Some get there first, come out, well, the others'll go in. That's why you never get there when you get in the church. You've got to wait — moving, moving, moving — somebody will be going on their knees, like that, and all them sick ladies by that — by that opening, you know, they got square, be sitting against the walls, blind, maybe deaf, sickness — oh, it's awful. Never see that — there wasn't — you never see any here. They're coming to be cured by the church or by the God or whatever. It's why they're there. Lot of old people, ladies. And then you see a lot of these stands like tacos, whatever, you know — eating. If you want — if you want money, you just set up a little business like that, you know, here and there — tacos, tacos and all that — probably drinks, too, soda pop, whatever — just to make money. That's why they're there.

KS: Lot of people from here go down?

TR: Lot of people [*nods*]. If you're such a religious person, you go from here to there, and you make sacrifices. You just walk from here up to there.

KS: Oh!

TR: They do it — used to do it.

KS: Do you meet a lot of people down there?

TR: Lot of people. That's why I don't want to be there — because I know a lot of people down this way, Sonora, that I work with. Sometime there'll be some, and when I'm there, I meet 'em, out in the crowd — "Oh, you" — "All right, how are you — let's have a shot." So we buy it. "Here, drink yourself." I drink the bottle. "You want a beer?" I won't refuse it. I got to take it. Maybe see my friend, I say, "Okay, you want a shot, I'll give you a shot." And soon you know you're drunk. I don't care so much about crowds. No, because if I

go like that I'll meet a lot of my friends there; everybody knows me
from someplace. Sure, sure, they say the same thing. It's all they do.

KS: Were these people you knew in Ajo and the mines, or—

TR: Oh, yeah. Anyplace—maybe here. It's all they do—that's why a lot
of them just go over there, just drink. And you won't have much
good time if you're not drunk, which I did a lot of times. But if you
go, come right back, you're all right. The only time I want to go is
when they—when there's no crowd. (13–18)

In this segment of Ted's narrative, drinking takes up only a small part
of a larger description of the fiesta, but its inclusion is important to
understanding how this topic works in his narration. Ted builds toward
it slowly and characterizes his drinking as reluctant. "I got to do it" is
a phrase Ted uses when he talks about anything he is compelled to do.
With drinking, this is his stance. He can't refuse. Friendship, even ele-
mentary politeness, demands participation and reciprocity.[5] Once in
the situation, he must go along. I don't think this is a pose on his part,
since this attitude of reluctant capitulation and a sense of guilt that ac-
companies drinking is also consistently voiced in his interviews with
Dunnigan. Once he is in the midst of the fiesta, he seems, or at least
represents himself as, compelled to drink. Once into the fiesta topic
narratively, he's compelled to talk about drinking. Context seems to
dictate at least brief admissions of alcohol consumption. This is born
out on the 1975 videotape *Papago Storyteller,* when he tells a funny
story about drinking wine made from saguaro fruit at a ceremony he
attended in the late 1930s. Talking about the ceremony seems to neces-
sitate talk about drinking. With amusement consistent with the tone
in the Toppenish anecdote, he tells of one of his friends, not realizing the strength of the wine, passing out: "There he go, there he go.
He fell over. He pass out."[6] Ted, by association, is of course drinking
too, though one infers he is more temperate. The tone of his narrations about these incidents speak to Ted's ambivalence about alcohol.
His narrations indicate that pleasure is connected to alcohol, but also

resistance, his rather painful acquiescence, and retrospective ruing of his behavior. I think the relatively rare mention of alcohol consumption during our interviews speaks clearly to a desire to downplay an element of his life about which he carried considerable guilt, and with reason, since it certainly affected his family relationships, his health, and his standing in his community.[7] What Ted accomplished during his lifetime, despite this debilitating problem, was what he wanted to narrate. I facilitated Ted's understating of the role of alcohol in his life by never broaching the topic directly and by not asking specific questions that might have prolonged his rare anecdotes about drinking.

None of Ted's attitudes about talking about particular topics was ever overtly discussed between us. He simply controlled what he would or would not narrate by resisting or ignoring my efforts to get him to talk about certain topics. He was never rude, just firm. I cooperated by not asking the specific questions that might have enlarged his references to drinking and also by never asking direct questions about intimate relationships or about any topic on which I thought he might feel I was judging him. He spoke with me because he wanted to, and I was certainly not there to push him into discomforting revelations or into representing himself in a way that violated his sense of himself. I felt that cross-cultural narration, delicate and difficult business on even the blandest of topics, demanded that I accommodate Ted. Looking back, I think my willingness to follow his lead on topics and ways of narrating was appropriate, even necessary, to our continuing work on the project. He had a lot at stake—inscription of a life story that would exist, and does exist, long after his death—so he used his narrative power to select and shape topics to his purposes.[8]

At the time of our interviews—though I was not unaware I was being manipulated away from certain topics—I might have realized more fully just how effective Ted was in determining the content of his narrative. I might also have been more aware that he had subtly but deliberately changed his strategy for narrating from the Dunnigan interviews to our work together to suit his desire to present a more positive image of himself to potential readers. Looking at the transcripts from both projects, what I believe is most influential in the difference between the two series of interviews is the fact that when Ted and I worked together, he clearly knew he was narrating "for the record." He expected what he told to be published. Dunnigan had been collecting ethnography for an archive, but our work together was to produce a life story. With the intention of a published life story on his mind, I think Ted emphasized certain aspects of his experience and character and made deliberate omissions in our dialogue by either not volunteering information or by deflecting some of my questions, because he had a strong sense that he was narrating a public version of his life. He had an idea of himself he wanted to communicate, so he actively edited his narration in order to inscribe a particular Theodore Rios.[9] He wanted to tell "a good one." Not only in the sense of an interesting story, but a story he could live with personally. I think he had a right to determine what "a good one" was and that I have the responsibility to see that Ted's subjectivity as he verbalized it to me is fairly represented in this volume.

In a sense this volume, in a rather unorthodox way, presents an authorized biography of Ted Rios. To include detailed information he did not narrate for the record would be to write his unauthorized biography, which would completely undercut the premise of collaborative biography that I think describes the intention of our project together — overtly stated by me and tacitly controlled by Ted's narrative strategies. So while Ted's full life-story inscription — which really begins with the interviews with Dunnigan and ends with several untaped conversations we had after the formal interviews were completed — would be more complete and detailed if I included a chapter incorporating incidents he did not narrate to me or did not allow me to tape, the life story published in this volume is largely the one he told to me for publication. I've added only a minimum of factual data gleaned from the earlier tapes that clarify what he narrated to me and some verifying genealogical data from mission records. This volume does not include any detailed accounts of experiences he withheld from me, nor details of material he explicitly asked me not to tape. I don't think Ted was prudish, nor do I think he was unwilling to admit he had a problem with alcohol, but certain topics did not suit his purposes.

In the case of things he told me "off the record," he explicitly made it clear that he wanted to protect certain individuals. He also let me know that his marriage to and divorce from Ramona Tiger were private. Though he had no objection to acknowledging it and gave me a bare outline of dates, places he and his first wife had lived, and some discussion of their sons, his courtship and married life were sparsely discussed. He never gave me any rationale for his avoidance of this part of his life, but whenever I probed, Ted responded tersely and redirected the conversation, perhaps because his wife was still living at the time of the interviews and he wanted to protect her privacy as well as his. I was actually more persistent about his marriage and divorce than with other "touchy" topics, because omission of information about his marriage, and especially his divorce, leaves the motives for his extensive travels shortly after the divorce only partially defined. When I suggested that I might interview his former wife, he objected strongly, so I did not. In fact, he did not want me to interview anyone but him, another mechanism of control he asserted over the project. He also wanted the identity of his second wife and his two daughters by that 1947 marriage left out of the book. That was an explicit request. When I reminded him that I had read what he had told Dunnigan about them, he stood by the request, even though later he had me give him a lift to the home of one of his daughters in Tucson. Life lived and life narrated were not at all the same thing to Ted. What may seem contradictory in the process we engaged in had a very clear logic for Ted.

I think he saw our relationship as cordially formal. I was certainly not his confidante or close friend. We were acquaintances with a broadly defined mutual goal, a book about him, which he saw as best serving his specific intentions in characterizing himself as a work-ing, traveling man deeply connected to the landscape and history of his home community. I don't think this goal was the dominant factor in his interviews for the Doris Duke American Indian Oral History Project.

When Timothy Dunnigan began his work with Ted in 1969, he was a doctoral student at the University of Arizona hired to conduct inter-views for the American Indian Oral History Project, which had in-vested a total of a quarter of a million dollars in several universities to gather life stories of Native Americans from many tribes.[10] Duke, apparently operating on the popularly held theory of the vanishing Indian, was concerned that older Native Americans be interviewed to preserve a record for the future. The materials were archived at the various participating institutions as a resource — of what or for what is unclear. Preservation, not publication, was the purpose of the project.

The Duke project appears to be the first and only intensive and ex-tensive collection of Native American life stories on the Papago reser-vation.[11] The institutional history of the project has become obscured over time, so there is no record of why certain individuals were selected as subjects for the interviews.

Ted's telling of his life story to Dunnigan, like all the other oral personal narratives discussed in this volume, was narrated in a non-chronological order, though Dunnigan, in standard fashion, begins his questions with Ted's birth and genealogy. It is interesting to ob-serve not only the difference in the topics Ted narrated as discussed above but the differences at a micro level in the transcripts. The data is similar but somewhat more detailed than what I collected in my first interview with Ted. The transcript reads:

June 27, 1969.
TAPE NUMBER 10 [This is, however, the first tape with Ted].
TIMOTHY DUNNIGAN INTERVIEWING THEODORE RIOS, SAN XAVIER

TD: First of all, your name is?

TR: Theodore, Theodore Rios.

TD: Theodore Rios. And how old are you?

TR: About 53.

TD: Let's see, that means you were born . . .

TR: 1915.

TD: Where were you born?

TR: Right up here about 12 miles from here, right in the Sirritas [*sic*]. It's in the reservation, but they call it San Xavier altogether, the whole reservation combining there yet. At that time they have ranches out there so that means all the same as here. So I guess it doesn't make any difference anyway.

TD: Was there a little village out there where you . . .

TR: Well there's just the ranching, ranching place, you know. The other side of the little mountain and the other side too around this side, about, oh, I'd say about six families on their side and about three on this side.

TD: I see.

TR: Two mostly. And what they do over there they raise cattle, first cattle raisers on the reservation.

TD: Did your father raise cattle?

TR: Of course we've got another place about another six miles back beyond where's another two more ranches besides them Mexican ranches. It's . . . it's right close to the reservation line on the south side.

TD: Did you grow up then on the ranch?

TR: Uh huh.

TD: Was this ranch your father's?

TR: My father's and my grandfather's. They got separate. One of them my grandfather on my mother's side, and the other one my father.

TD: What was your father's name.

TR: Frank Rios.

TD: And your grandfather's name?

TR: Arnito Williams.

159

TD: Let's see, was that your mother's father or your father's father?

TR: My mother's father.

TD: I see. Did your father have any brothers or sisters?

TR: Ya.

TD: Remember any of them?

TR: Ya.

TD: How many brothers did he have?

TR: Just one.

TD: What was his name?

TR: Juan Rios?

TD: Did he have a ranch?

TR: No. Just together. Of course he's the youngest, youngest of the bunch.

TD: And did your father have any sisters?

TR: Just one.

TD: What was her name?

TR: Sally.

TD: I see. Did Juan Rios marry?

TR: Uh huh, ya.

TD: What was his wife's name?

TR: Justina.

TD: Justina, ah, do you remember her maiden name?

TR: Justina Lopez.

TD: Did they have children?

TR: Ya.

TD: Are they living now?

TR: No. They're all dead.

TD: How many children did they have?

TR: About three and they all died.

TD: I see. Did they get married before they died?

TR: Ya, they got married before, ya. No, you mean the kids?

TD: Uh huh.

TR: No, none of them. They died young.

TD: How about your father's sister, did she marry?

TR: Ya. She married. He's got a son but he died too. Just one.

TD: How many brothers and sisters did you have?

TR: As far as I can remember I had, I don't know how many, but the living ones when we were young, I had two brothers besides me, and two sisters.

TD: Two brothers and two sisters?

TR: Uh huh, living at that time.

TD: I see. What were their names? What were your brothers' names?

TR: Juan Rios and George.

TD: Were they older or younger than you?

TR: One is older and one is younger, and I'm between.

TD: How about your sisters?

TR: The oldest is Marciana.

TD: And the younger?

TR: The younger sister is Lena.

TD: Were they older or younger than you?

TR: The younger is the youngest.

TD: I see. Did they have children?

TR: The youngest one.

TD: Uh huh.

TR: And the next oldest one had only one. They all died except the youngest.

TD: I see. Is she still living?

TR: Uh huh.

TD: Does she live at San Xavier?

TR: Uh huh.

TD: What's her name?

TR: Lena.

TD: What's her last name?

TR: Ramon.

TD: I see. You have cousins, lots of relatives that live here at San Xavier?

TR: Uh huh, ya, I got most of them, but I still got some down in San Pedro and Santa Rosa Village, scattered all over yet. The younger

161

children I don't know them because I've never seen them too well, but the older, their mothers and their grandfathers, well I know them when they come here and then they died too. And then a few of them I know step by step but most of them they're so scattered all down the cotton fields that it's hard to tell unless they come to me and if they know me who I am, say, well, "Is that you?" "Ya." Okay. It's me. And they'll tell me about it. Yet I won't recognize them if I just seen 'em off, you know, some of them, most of them, because they don't grow up here. They grow down some place else.

TD: Santa Rosa.

TR: Santa Rosa, San Pedro. All of them scattered in there, I don't know. I won't say just how many but some are dead, but most of the older they died off. That I know them too well.

TD: What was your mother's name?

TR: Anselma.

TD: Anselma?

TR: Ya.

TD: And her maiden name was?

TR: Williams, no, Arnita.

TR: Arnita.

TD: Where was your father from? Was he from San Xavier?

TR: San Xavier.

TD: Or was he out from the other part of the reservation?

TR: Well, he's from someplace where they call Gu Achi. But that was long way before I guess. And the people all moved down here at the time when he was young. And of course most of them these San Xavier people they're from, they came from here, you know, at that time. And then that's why they have relatives back there because they left quite a few down there and all them migrated down here at the same time and then they start living here then they grow up here then they called they're born here. I don't know. I couldn't say it.

TD: How about your mother. Where was she from?

TR: She's from Santa Rosa. Well my grandfather from Santa Rosa, and from some other little village on that side, this side of Santa Rosa. That's my grandmother. See and then they just, they call the place their home alright but from place to place them little villages. Well they don't know it off so much as you know because they're not so well known at this time you know.

TD: I see. Was that your mother's mother you were talking about?

TR: Uh huh.

TD: How about your father's parents?

TR: I don't know too well about them because they were older than them. I don't see them. I was too young when they died. See, but I know they're from some place around there but I didn't get to talk too much with them because I was too young when they died then when I was still, oh, about six, seven, or something like that.

TD: Are your brothers and sisters still living or? . . .

TR: Just one.

TD: Just the youngest girl?

TR: Ya.

TD: Where? Does she live here at San Xavier?

TR: Uh huh, ya.

TD: When you lived with your father, did he ranch all of his life? Was he mostly a rancher?

TR: Rancher and farmer.

TD: He had lands out there?

TR: He had land down there. We got land, about sixty acres.

TD: Is that near the Santa Cruz River?

TR: Ya, right near Santa Cruz.

TD: How old were your brothers when they died? Did they grow up and marry?

TR: One of them, just one, the oldest, but he didn't live too long. I'd say about in his twenties, I guess.

TD: When you lived out on this place, could you tell me some of the things you did? I mean how you were a youngster. I imagine you worked with your father, did things to help him out.

TR: On the farm?

TD: Ya.

TR: Well, as far as I can remember I had to do a lot of that farm work. Of course raising of wheat and barley, chili and watermelons, all that stuff. We harvested it.

TD: How old were you when you began doing this kind of work?

TR: As soon as I got to be able to do anything. So irrigating and you know all that stuff. Driving a team. And of course they didn't have tractors at the time, just horse-drawn, you know, plow, and they were threshing with the horses, you know, like that because they just sit on the horse and go around and you know. And then most of the time we'll hoe watermelon and the chili and the cantaloupes and all that stuff. Of course at that time, you know, it's very different from now, what they do now. At that time they get altogether. One place own so much land and other so much and when they ask for help, you know, get so many on the, your neighbors, well they all come and do the work for him. Next, same thing. And of course, when we raise corn like that we sell 'em through here, you know, to the people that don't have anything like that. Well they sell 'em through here or they buy 'em so much. Then we sell 'em down through the Yaqui, used to be a Yaqui village right close. Sell them Mexican people right down here, through this Midvale Farms along the river, they had houses along the river. Used to sell 'em all along there clear up to wherever, you know, how far it'll last. Just like that. (1–8)

Using the first interview with Dunnigan and my first interview, it is possible to put together most of Ted's lineage.[12] Throughout both sets of interviews, incidental factual information about Ted's family comes out, and a fairly complete family tree can be established. Even so there are gaps that only research in the records at the San Xavier Mission archive could fill in. I don't think Ted deliberately omitted information. My questions just didn't elicit it all, even though I had the Dunnigan-Rios interviews as a starting point. Dunnigan gets more, but he has to work very hard for it; Ted is equally terse on both initial tapes, partly

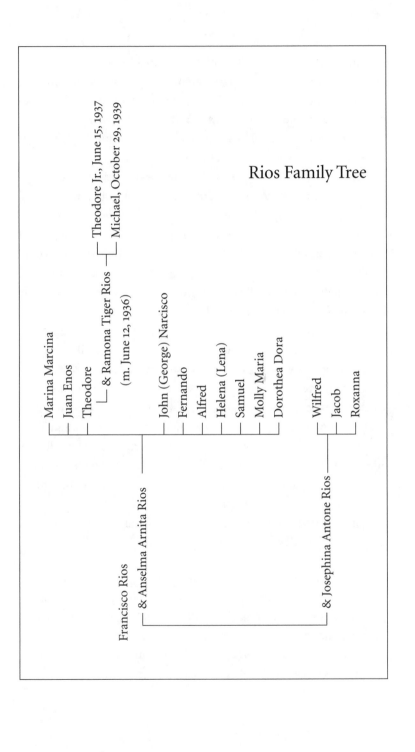

Rios Family Tree

Francisco Rios
& Anselma Arnita Rios

Marina Marcina
Juan Enos
Theodore
& Ramona Tiger Rios
(m. June 12, 1936)

Theodore Jr, June 15, 1937
Michael, October 29, 1939

John (George) Narcisco
Fernando
Alfred
Helena (Lena)
Samuel
Molly Maria
Dorothea Dora

& Josephina Antone Rios

Wilfred
Jacob
Roxanna

because he doesn't know either of us but also, I think, because—aside from his relationships with grandparents and parents, all of whom are deceased at the times of the tapings—he is not close to any of his relatives, so they are not central to his identity. Also, he is consistently a bit fuzzy on exact data. To clarify Ted's family relationships, I've brought data from all the source material into the following summary.

Access to Ted's family tree is useful in viewing his narration as life history, a term that connotes verifiability of data. It is, however, of only limited value in addressing his narration as life story, in which the congruency between fact and the incidents as told is less important than the creation of subjectivity. As a narrator of life story, Ted could be selective, telling a version of himself that suited his sense of how he wanted to be known publicly. Ted chooses not to narrate extensively about his family relationships or to place himself as a central figure in the welfare of his kin group. Instead, he narrates his life in terms of incidents and experiences that characterize him as an individual who shapes his identity through acquisition and practice of skills that make him a competent, independent person able to adapt to a multitude of circumstances in a wide range of locations. His skill as a horseman and the recognition it gains him at roundups, rodeos, races, and in the movies is a theme that is prominent in Ted's narrative strategy. Riding horses takes up almost as much of both the interviews with Dunnigan and with me as does his work as a miner, and he narrates the stories on this theme with much relish.

His experience with horses begins on his grandfather's ranch. On the ninth tape (May 29, 1974) he explains,

> Pretty soon, you know, you're riding horses. Pretty soon, you know, you're branding cattle. And pretty soon, you know, you want to get on the bronco—then you're on it. Everybody got to ride, once you're on the ranch. Just like the Mexicans—they're good riders [*nods*]. Good horses [*nods*]. You've got to be like them. 'Course, we break a lot of horses—my uncles, my god-

father—we break a lot of horses when we're kids. We'd see 'em, saddle 'em, lead 'em around and then pretty soon they'll be kind of tame. . . . [See photo 10.]

I rode a lot of time—tame horses, riding if I can get on there. Lots of times I get knocked off, too. I remember one knocked me off when I was just a baby. When you're a kid, once you get bounced off of anything you just bounce like a ball [*slaps heels of hands together*]. But when you're grown, there's always something broken. That's what I done. I got bounced off a lot of times but I never break any bones. At the movies we rode bareback. Slide off. Besides, you know, it's slick, the skin on the horse. . . .

I learned to rope at the ranch. Got to see how they do it, and they tell you to rope—seen some good ropers. Anyone that's been on a ranch, you've seen it. You've got to be everything before you be a rancher. You've got to learn how to tie knots—when you're tying a calf's legs, you've got to do certain things. There's a lot of different skills. But I was taught. (edited tape 9: 5–6)

By the time he's about seventeen, Ted takes the ranching skills he mastered as a child to the rodeo arena. During our seventh interview (May 23, 1974) he says,

There's a rodeo that's going on annually. See, when it first started, it's more colorful than what they have now. They put it on — 'way on the north side of town [Tucson]. They didn't have the rodeo ground that they are now, but it was an airport right where the rodeo grounds is. It's an airport, and they have to go 'way out there. I was out there once, someplace 'way back up there, where they had that rodeo. They used to have Indian Day there. Now they don't have it. Everybody from here—lots of competition. I was in it, mostly racing—horse racing, calf roping. I was still in high school. I don't get enough practice. Lot of competition because there so many—like Apaches. They were pretty good. They're always in business for cattle. They get the money. Indians come from all over the state and across California. Big rodeo [*nods*], you know, just like I said. . . .

If you enter a rodeo someplace you've got to haul your horse over. We got rodeos here. Got a rodeo grounds [Sells]. Every year they got one on Pima, Sacaton. Fourth of July is where they celebrate it. There's a rodeo there, up in Salt River. I got thrown down in Yakima one time, just for the fun of it, in that rodeo. They got a rodeo there, too. They coaxed me about it, these people I was with. You know how broncs are. They know how to buck. . . .

Of course, in racing, I always place there, maybe second. Then I get some money. It's all I need. Used to celebrate the Fourth of July here at Sells — rodeo, barbecue, everything, all Indians. But it's hot on the Fourth. I brought over my horse once. We had to haul a lot of watermelons — truck and a trailer and the horse. And I came down, with all them watermelons, and I won the race with a sorrel. (edited tape 7: 3–4)

He enjoys the recognition he gains during the five years he rodeos regularly. He tells Dunnigan essentially the same information that he relates to me with a similar sense of pride:

I've been there. I grow on a ranch. I know what it's all about. I got horses. Then we got a best horse, racing, farm, the best. I guess all over the Papago land. There's not another rider for the half mile horse race. . . . Once I got it. Everybody's hollering, "Theodore, Theodore. Come on. Come on." Give me the time. It's alright. . . . That's how good I was in my youth. I know what I can do. I went up there to Washington, same thing happened. (1969: 144–146)

He also tells the horse-race story to Dunnigan, but with even more verve. This is the day that he reaches the pinnacle of his fame as a Papago rider, and he relishes the telling of it and includes more details than is often the case in his anecdotes. Ted says,

168

We had a good horse, all the time, of course we're ranchers. See? When he came out he can beat anybody, anybody. So I took him to Sells, Fourth of July, I took him to Sells. One day I took him when we hauled watermelon with the truck and took this horse over there. I won first place in the mile. This was when they used to have no stadium, they have a *charco* where they used to held, hold that rodeos. On a hot day like this. Put a competition, all them ranches. I came out very good in it, one mile race, I won the one mile race. Besides, we sell all that watermelon. See? My girl was there. I wasn't married yet but I had my girl with me in the truck. See? So it is. How good a rancher I was when it was. We had the best horse. I race him over there with the competition, from all over, Maricopa, Pimas, right in the rodeo grounds. See? I rode it, bareback. That's the limit. (1969: 147)

If Ted ever sees himself as a hero, or perhaps more realistically, as achieving a full measure of success within his culture, it is most intensely articulated in stories about his equestrian skills. In a culture where men are ranchers, Ted acquits himself very well. His success is marked by his possession of a highly desirable Papago attribute — outstanding horsemanship. He is the son of one of the most successful ranchers in the history of the tribe (Fontana 1960: 151), and he publicly displays skills that come directly from a family enterprise respected not only by other Papagos but by Mexicans and Anglos as well.[13] Never is he more centered in terms of post-traditional cultural roles than in this period of his life. On that Fourth of July the world is his. He's admired by his fellow Papagos and by the woman he will marry. In both versions he tells of the event, he's a winner — youthful, with good prospects, and performing well in a tribally endorsed role. He's gone to "the limit." In neither set of interviews does he ever describe himself and an experience in such exuberant terms, not even when he talks about his work in the mines — where competency and endurance dominate the narrative — or in the movies — where prestige in relation

169

to the glamour of Hollywood sets the tone—does he narrate such a culturally positive subjectivity.

Horsemanship, of course, is what gets Ted into the movies. He's not the first in the family to be connected to motion pictures. His father was actively involved in the filming of *Arizona* in the 1930s (edited tape 4: 5). Ted does not get into the film business until the 1940s. Intermittently throughout the two decades after his return to the reservation, Ted signs on as a rider for Columbia Pictures. Ted initially told me about his work in the movies after we had finished taping on the first day of our interviews at Sells. I had so thoroughly controlled our first taped session that I'd not given him a chance to bring up a topic he wanted to talk about, but when I turned the recorder off and relaxed a bit, he told me he'd been in a lot of movies and began a story about playing an Apache attacking a fort in a movie filmed in the desert near Yuma. I think that at that time Ted knew I had read a version of the story in the Dunnigan transcripts (1969: 114–122), but perhaps he forgot since he told it to me spontaneously. At the end of the story I, of course, asked the name of the film, and he responded, just as he had to Dunnigan's identical query, *The Last of the Mohicans*—straight-faced, no hesitancy or hint of a put-on. I laughed and called him on his spoof. Then he laughed too and replied, "A good one." It was the first time he had even smiled in my presence. I still think of it as the break-through moment in our work together. His intent had clearly been to entertain me with a story on a topic he thought a white woman might find a bit glamorous—our interview had been pretty plodding and serious—but also to test me. He had no desire to talk to a total fool. I got the joke, and he was pleased. I think that moment sealed his commitment to the project.

I regretted the tape recorder wasn't on for the story, but I came back to it during our fourth interview, and he narrated it and other recollections about his movie riding in an extended narration. The portion of this recorded segment about the Yuma film, *The Last of the Mohicans*—he couldn't remember the real name of the movie—is not nearly as coherent or detailed as the version he told on that first day of our work together.[14] Once the story had been told to me, the edge was off. The original effect had been achieved on a fresh audience. This time it gets woven into other movie experiences, and while pleasurable to recall, humorous, and lively in the telling, it is not the dramatic or detailed rendering it was the first time I heard it.

May 21, 1974

I've been in about sixteen or seventeen different movies. I know the people. Mostly it's westerns. Oh, they come over there. See, they come around and hire people [*sweeping motion*]. When a movie comes, then they've got to come around and then they see me over here [*points to himself*], and then I got to go around and pick whoever can ride horses, ride or race. Not the real old ones, somebody that's active, that can ride. 'Course you got to fall, and then you got to get knocked over, and all that [*nods*]. Then you meet a lot of people there, some from Hollywood. Yes, it's a lot of fun if you don't get hurt. Once my horse bucked me off—landed me in the hospital. Eighteen days in Tucson General Hospital. Broken ribs.

Once I went all the way to Yuma. Paid all the way. Whole bunch. All the buses, they got buses coming. It's a lot of fun there. That is, if you know how. If you're once in it, you know what it's all about. Then you don't have to worry. Everybody, all them people, mostly around San Xavier, they were hired. And everybody goes. Sometimes women, children.

You get bucked off the horse, of course. In Yuma, that's where a lot of bucking took place, because out in Yuma, see, the movie company just landed in there, and we landed from here. We don't know anybody or we don't know the town. And they start hiring and it's in December—rain, kind of like winter—cold. They've got to strip you off, to the waist, put a costume on, and you're a fighter, an Indian. And there's the cavalry—that's the whites. They got horses; they're dressed in cavalry uniforms with rifles and everything. You got rifles too, and spears. An' then, you know, the horses have just been picked on the farms, on the ranches right around there. When we got there, we saw them. They were hauling in horses through the town. And then we know—we already know what's going to happen because we already been in the movies before. So we're already saying, "Hey, we're going to get bucked off." That was Sunday, I think. One day, the day we got over there, we got paid from here, and then next day we're supposed to be in the cast. We didn't get enough men then, so they just leave it until the next day and pick some more. And here we're gone on a drunk [*rubs palms against one another in a skidding motion*]. But we got paid then.

And then, next day early in the morning we were in a campground. We got to travel about twenty miles inside of California where they had it set up. Buses. The horses were there and everything's ready there—tents, costumes, everything was already there. Whatever they put in there—the buildings, church—then it's way out in the desert, kind of rocky, rough, open. Where they're going to shoot. And then, that's when it was starting to be cold. But the clouds bother too much because they need the sun before they shoot. Sometimes we don't work till the sun comes out. And the horses get cold. Sometimes you get a horse that'll throw you, buck you off. They're not used to it. The cast got their own horses. After they get used to it for maybe a day or two, well, then, you're all right. You can do anything you want to—shoot. Guns. Guns, but then they got caps in 'em. Sound like a gun but nothing is fired. You know how horses are. They'll do anything— throw you off [*throws up his hands*]. And you're just there, no saddle [*throws up hands again*], no nothing. A lot of fun. And that's a real movie too. It's when you see it with your own eyes you know what happened. Once in a while I see myself in the movies.

The first movie I was in was the same way, the same way. They come in and they want actors and all that. They need some Indians—chiefs, you know—and they call you up and you pick up

172

whoever wants to go out. They got to know if you can ride the horses 'cause if you got a big belly or something, you can't.

They mostly come either to Tucson or some other place. The directors, they've been there before, and they can pick the good riders because they know; they've already been there. The Yumas, they don't know. I think me and one of my friends were the first ones to sign. And I told him, "Well, we'll be the first ones to sign on and get our things all set up so we can get the horses first, before anybody." So when they saw us strip, it was cold—all this bunch, they'd never been into the movies and all.[15] And they look at us all stripped in this cold—windy like this, kind of cloudy, drizzling, you know. And then they backed up, said, "We can't work like that." But my friend said, "Sure you've got to work. I can do it. I can." We really did it. And they saw us half-naked. It's cold—sure it's cold. What else can you do? We've been there before trying to get that money. "No, I can't do it," when their turn comes. They beg off, a lot of them. They didn't have enough. They had to take 'em when they said they want to go back to town, but they said, "We can't take you there now. Why didn't you say so in the first place, right there. We won't have to take you this far too." So, you know, they waited. "We've got to set them up first and then when we got time we'll take you back" See?

And then the horses. Started getting our weapons and everything. And then the wranglers—there were wranglers drawing out the horses, you know, bunches. And then they told us, "Take your choice. Pick your choice" [*making pointing, stabbing motions with index finger*]. And you never know the horses—which horse is which [*shrugging*]. Then you got to make your choice. Take a gamble [*hands palms up*]. I ride a good horse. Some of them are thrown off. So as soon as the horses are like that, then they put 'em out, keep the ones that aren't bad. And then that's—when you know you're—in there [*nods*].

I make movies in Bear Canyon too.[16] The last one we made, it was I think, a year ago, way down near Benson, in the mountains, way down there.[17] The sets are still there, where they put 'em up. Well, you could see some of the higher ones, still there. Good buildings, like a town, small town, but it's just fake. Lot of shooting there. Good horses. They haul 'em in. I know the fellow that takes care of the horses. He's got good horses [*nods*]. Separate the bad one from the good ones. And then we hear Frank Sinatra was there. 'Course you got to gallop. It's a lot of fun. I know the lady, she's a rider and driver of the buggy. She can really ride. The other day I was working for Cactus Nursery at the time—over at her house. And this other fellow was with me. He was with me at the movies at the same time, when we saw her. I can kind of remember her face and he did too and so he said, "Looks like that was her, wasn't it?" And I said, "I think so." She's got a good house in Tubac.[18] And then we were there and I guess the boss said something about me, about the movies, right then, or she said something about the movies, either one of 'em. And then he brought me out. Then pretty soon, she came over. He came over and met her and said, "You know this fellow?" Okay [*nods*]—then she told me. She's been there and I noticed it. She's hired to stand in, stand in for the main actress. She can ride.

Up at Bear Canyon, up in the Catalinas, that's where I got hurt. I picked the wrong horse that time [*shrugs*]. This one is *The Last of the Comanches* or *The Last Outpost*. So many different names. I played a bad Indian, where we kill somebody, you know, like the old time [*grins*]. They got the same kind of long hair, you know, the wigs they put on there—bands, maybe a feather, paint.

Only once I went to the television filming, *High Chaparral.* I been there I think one day or two days. At *High Chaparral* they don't keep you long. It's just a few days, then you're off.

'Course, we did some right in there, behind the Catalinas. Lot of shooting. Wouldn't think I carried so many rifles, pistols, a rifle here and yet I wasn't using all that. The pistol, I was using that, fighting the bad banditos, the bandits. They you play dead [*flat, palm-down stroke toward ground*]. They spill all the red paint. I've been dead a lot of times. Blood all over like in Yuma. Cold lying down in the sand. Play dead and you can fall off from the horse just when you're shot [*nods*].

That's why they want somebody who that knows horses. You do just what they want you to do, but a lot of times you've got to do it over and over. They got to lead you all the way. The camera's up in the hills, and they're going to lead you there and lead you around the church where you're going to circle and shoot them around the church, 'cause you've got to start from way off. And that's when you start galloping. Of course, then the main actors from Hollywood, they've got their own horses, and they can gallop right ahead of us. We're following, and they start shooting first. And when the horses hear all this — you know horses — they do anything. Rest of the time you eat, drink coffee, eat doughnuts, wait around, and they're shooting for so sudden, and call you "Riders!" And you get your horses. Lot of time you do a lot of riding, but sometimes you don't [*shrugs*].

Old Tucson's got no room.[19] It's too up and down. Too many gullies and then you can't ride around there. But in other places they got a wide range, and it's not much like Old Tucson. It's better riding than Old Tucson. There might be a lot of brush or anything, but you can really go. Old Tucson's too close. In Benson, people were set up way around out in a big canyon. All the Indian tents, and the ladies start cooking on the ground, you know, out in the open. And here the enemy came. We had to rush through it or else run over somebody or run over the olla or whatever they got there — fire. Maneuvering very close in there [*tight reining gestures*]. They've got to start running or else some of them ladies just stay — set there on the ground — and you've got to watch 'em too. Then you've got to go right through, meet the enemy. Then we start shooting. It's a good place because the mountains are, you know, behind it. And then if something goes wrong back here, on their side, not on our side, then they got to rerun it. And that's a lot of fun, too, you know. You know you're doing it right, but

somebody down there in the main cast, they're doing something wrong at the same time. And you rerun maybe five or three different times before you get it. And you like it because you've got a lot of time to talk, talk, and talk, and when they're ready, then —
"Action!" Start the same thing.

Audie Murphy. He's nice, Audie. We had some kids, boys in the movies. Always when we had time, well, he'll set 'em up and put 'em in a race, old Audie. Just line 'em up way up there, you know a race. Then he'll call 'em. "The winner gets this dollar" — and there's a dollar in his hand. "Hurray!" [*holds out his hand*]. And they start coming for that dollar. Oh, that Audie's a lot of fun. I like Audie [*nods*]. Since the first time that I met him there. He was a good fellow. He's really friendly, too. He likes Indians pretty well, especially them boys. Likes to play with them. Races. And he'd have the dollar right in his hand and say, "Here you come boys. Come and get it." The winner gets all.

The children — they're earning — they're getting paid so much. They show you, and they're holding a baby or it's hitting the ground or maybe playing around while the acting's going on right in front of it. It's just background they use 'em for. Ladies, they'll be doing this or making food or carrying ollas or just backdrop. The main ones, they're shooting. (edited tape 4: 4–11)

The following day, May 22, 1974, we began tape five with his continuation of his work in the film *Dirty Dingus McGee:*

In that movie is Frank Sinatra. He's the main one. I don't know the rest. We moved into the Holiday Inn at Santa Rita. Stayed down there at night. They took us over there in the bus morning and night. But we have to be out before sunrise in the mornings. Then we go and about sunrise we're already on the place. Oh, the set's something like a settlers' town — church, store, and everything. Barber shop, street, one street, lot of background. Of course, it's level ground — kind of sloping toward the south. You could see everything. You could see the village from the highway [*sweeping right-hand gesture*].

They hired a lot of Indians, maybe a hundred, but they couldn't get 'em. I guess they got about eighty or so. There was mostly men until the last two days. We worked, I think, three weeks [*holds up three fingers*].

Well, the action, I think it was in the frontier, where somebody's trying to get all the land. And the cavalry—they got about maybe ninety, eighty men on the cavalry. Horses and all, rifles, everything. And all we got to do is try to stop them some way or another—fight and shoot 'em, chase 'em, or they chase us—either way. And at the same time we chase the buggy. And there's that big building—I don't know what it was—quite a ways from there. We usually chase the buggy right up to it.

Same movie, at the finish and last, they had to move to a canyon, a narrow canyon where you couldn't see anything. They set up the tipis here and there along the bushes, and that's when the women came. And then they had 'em doing that hot cooking or whatever they done. And then the fire—and then the cavalry were right behind. And then that's when we start fighting right there. (edited tape 5: 1–2)

Timothy Dunnigan recalls that "Ted seemed happiest when recounting how he died in spectacular fashion as a paid movie Apache shot from horseback" (personal communication, 1998). Certainly he enjoyed talking about his work in films, I think for the same reasons he enjoyed talking about his rodeo and racing days. He was getting recognition for his horsemanship, just as he had in his youth. I think talking about being a movie rider connected him to those earlier equestrian achievements and restored a sense of virility and activity, which he especially longed for sitting on the hospital patio in his cast and wheelchair. He gives no indication, either in his narrations to me or to Dunnigan, that he saw any irony in reenacting the cultural conflicts that had destroyed many Indian lives, nor does he comment on being dressed up as an Apache warrior, the traditional enemies of the Papa-gos. As Ted tells it, play-acting was play for him, and he was getting paid and paid well for doing it, just as he had been paid when he ex-celled at the sport of rodeo. As in his earlier riding anecdotes, in his narration about the movies, he knows his role and can fulfill it ably. Thus, these stories of his sporadic film career support the image of himself as a competent, tough, even courageous, man, the image that he wants to inscribe for his potential readers.

I think it is significant that the narration of his movie experiences to Dunnigan, while they are considerably more detailed and longer, place much less emphasis on horses and the perils of riding unfamil-iar mounts in noisy, fighting scenes than does his narration with me. In his narration to Dunnigan, Ted gives a lot more attention to other aspects of his film experiences. He talks in detail about costuming, especially wearing fake braids and being painted with "war paint," and he even explains that if riders were not dark skinned enough, they would be sprayed with a brown dye (1969: 117–120). He also gives a lot of attention to film company logistics, food, time waiting for film takes, weather, guns, movie plots, his treatment in the hospital after he breaks his ribs, and the skill of the stagecoach-driving stunt woman he mentions in his narration to me (1969: 114–29). Looking at the two versions of Ted's narration of his movie career is instructive. It dem-onstrates the value of variants in interpreting narrative intention. In his discussion with Dunnigan, Ted is much more comprehensive about movie making and less focused on his own role as a horseman than he is in the interview with me. Again, I think this can be traced to his per-ception of how the interview material will be used. With Dunnigan, Ted seems to aim at thoroughness. Dunnigan asks very few question; Ted volunteers detail after detail. This points to a sense of narrating life *history.* He is equally fluent in his conversation with me, but the emphasis is on skill, danger, and activity, pointing to his sense of nar-rating life *story.* Stressing his horsemanship in the narration with me is consistent with his goal of depicting himself as a member of a select group of Papago riders who epitomize a high value in tribal terms. This section of the interview, then, is congruent with his rodeo narrations, another high-point life story that is told with the same vitality and pleasure as the racing incident.

Ted's narratives about his movie work come very close to breaking into storytelling performances. When we recorded them, he was animated, gesticulating more than when he talked about more mundane jobs. Similarly, in talking about his movie work with Dunnigan, he is enthusiastic and detailed in describing incidents. But never in his narrating incidents from his life does he actually structure an event or series of events into a dramatic, unified story. The interview form prevents that much of the time, demanding digressions, clarification, connections to other events, but, more importantly, I don't think Ted thought of the taping session with either Dunnigan or me as a storytelling event. Despite the difference in intention in the two interview series, he recognized his role in both as essentially documentary. Telling traditional stories or making up experiences for the sake of entertainment or specifically defined cultural instruction were not goals of either project, so he treated the events he narrated as essentially factual reportage, though there are a few examples of anecdotes that meet the criteria of story. It was only near the end of our formal taping together, when he repeated to me stories told to him by or about others, that he crafted his narrations into authoritative storytelling performance.[20] How he achieves the breakthrough into performance is an element of his total narrative style that broadens the image Ted presents of himself in the narration of his own experiences. It's in performing particular parts of his life narrative, and especially stories that are not part of his own experience, that Ted exhibits another aspect of his subjectivity and yet another way to tell "a good one."

$\tilde{\mathcal{C}}$ 6

PERSONAL-NARRATIVE

PERFORMANCE, STORYTELLING,

AND AUDIENCE

Telling "a good one" sums up two of the most important qualities of Ted's narration of his life story—his sense of what constitutes a good story, and his sense of how his narrative reflects on him as its teller. The former has to do with Ted's concern with plotting and embellishing episodes and stories to create attention and interest in the hearer/reader. The latter has to do with Ted's narrative development of subjectivity. Not only does he want to tell "a good one," he wants, by means of his narration, to be understood as "a good one"—a respectable Papago man in the eyes of the eventual readers of the book, in the eyes of his community who might perceive him differently than he narrates himself, in the eyes of his family where his behavior and neglect have left some hard feelings, and, most of all, in his own eyes or, more accurately, ears. He wants to tell a story he can live with, and he brings a great variety of editing and performance skills to bear on creating, from the experiences of his life, a story to leave for future generations. In his narrative, Ted emphasizes his role as a versatile and hardy, even brave, worker. Understandably, he downplays his failures and weaknesses. He tells a very human and complex story that incorporates several categories of oral discourse, from experiential and eyewitness reportage to aesthetically shaped storytelling.

Though collaborative Native American personal narrative is a form of oral performance, it is rarely addressed as performative discourse. As a form of dialogue with the Other and with one's own communities, it engages the narrator in a series of oral episodes that add up to a life story told to a particular individual, the collector-editor. How the identity, personality, and even gender of the collector affect Ted's life-story narrative performance is demonstrated in the previous chapter. How his performance — or more accurately, range of oral performances — is affected by a larger and more complex sense of audience is equally significant in understanding the process of oral life-story narration. Telling his life to me was Ted's effort to establish a permanent, accessible — or so he anticipated when we were working together — record of his life as he wished it to be known. As I look back at our work together and review the transcripts of our interviews, I'm pretty well convinced that Ted saw collaborating on a book as an opportunity to tell his life as he wanted it told. Not so much to set the record straight, but to create a record of his life as he wished it plotted and thematically developed.[1] That probably wasn't how he thought of the project at the beginning, but as it progressed, he came to control the telling of his life more and more in a number of ways. He omitted or gave only cursory narrative attention to episodes and people in his life that were not congruent with the subjectivity he was shaping. He selected experiences to narrate that supported his desire to present himself with characteristics that would gain him respect from the multiple audiences he recognized. And he emplotted and connected the episodes and stories that he told in order to maintain audience attention and develop a consistent subjectivity by means of a variety of experiences and acquired knowledge. Ted's recognition of and performance toward multiple audiences can be traced by looking at a particular story made up of two connected episodes in his life — a prophecy and fulfillment of the prediction in potentially fatal mining accidents. They provide a focused and unified episode in Ted's narrative that lends itself to analysis as story performance better than many of his other, more digressive narrative experiences. This section of our eleventh interview (June 5, 1974), begins with a discussion about defense work and his decision to leave mining for work at Consolidated Aircraft in Tucson, and then

182

1. Above: Papago adobe house at San Xavier. AHS 41,982, courtesy of the Arizona Historical Society, Tucson.

2. Left: Ted Rios during an interview. Courtesy of the author.

3. Left: San Xavier Mission with women processing corn in foreground. AHS 91,793, courtesy of the Arizona Historical Society, Tucson.

4. Above: Ted Rios. Still taken from *Papago Storyteller* (1975), courtesy of the University of Arizona, Tucson.

5. Above: Papago women at a well. AHS 57,566, courtesy of the Arizona Historical Society, Tucson.

6. Top right: Papagos traveling by wagon. AHS 55,355, courtesy of the Arizona Historical Society, Tucson.

7. Bottom right: Nun scolding Papago boy. AHS 9,969, courtesy of the Arizona Historical Society, Tucson.

8. Above: Phoenix Indian School. Photo Sato-6 N-1778, courtesy of the Arizona Historical Foundation, University Libraries, Arizona State University, Tempe.

9. Below: Pit mining at Ajo. Photo # RW-245, courtesy of the Arizona Historical Foundation, University Libraries, Arizona State University, Tempe.

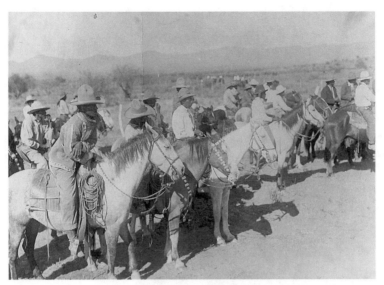

10. Above: Papago
cowboys. AHS 21,395,
courtesy of the
Arizona Historical
Society, Tucson.

11. Below: Ted Rios.
Still taken from
Papago Storyteller
(1975), courtesy of
the University of
Arizona, Tucson.

12. Above: Papago Children's Shrine. AHS 48,843B, courtesy of the Arizona Historical Society, Tucson.

13. Below: San Xavier village. Photo WCB-39, courtesy of the Arizona Historical Foundation, University Libraries, Arizona State University, Tempe.

14. Right: Mine tailings. Photo MCC-8, courtesy of the Arizona Historical Foundation, University Libraries, Arizona State University, Tempe.

15. Papago women with pottery.
AHS 24,808, courtesy of the Arizona
Historical Society, Tucson.

the series of jobs that take him to the West Coast. Thus he connects these episodes to the larger theme of his adaptability to changing work situations within the framework of the World War II period of his life. He begins this three-part narration:

TR: It's wartime. I was working at the mine. That's when she told me that—"you're earning a lot of money here, but that money doesn't do you any too good. And besides, the place is not good for you, the way—as it is, so I think you better just leave."

KS: Was this a Papago woman who told you this?

TR: No, no. She just said she was part Indian. She's with the carnival. Old Lady.

KS: Oh. Is this in Ajo?

TR: Big carnival came. That's when—I heard so much about this, but I never did believe it, or even go in. I just look at them and I say, "You pretend." My friends told me so much about it [*nods*]. We're together in there and they're—when they were announcing it. That's when it started off. So I had to go in there. Instead of coming out for just them three questions, it sounded so interesting to me, I thought, "Maybe I'll ask a little—some more." So the money started—I had the cash—there it is, maybe a dollar—okay. Then it started so interesting—well, another dollar. There it went [*lifts right hand, palm open*]. See, that's when it came up and raised that point about my past. She told me about my past.

KS: She knew?

TR: Mm hmm. Of course she told me but she didn't say exactly, but she said it, what happened and all that. I don't belong there, you know, something like that. And this and this and just like they say. Because she knew I didn't believe in it. And then she said, "You don't believe in what I'm trying to tell you. All right, I'll tell you." Right off my left hand [*turns palm up*].

KS: She read your hand?

TR: Uh huh. Started from there and just went like this. She knew I was a Catholic—she knew the church, because she even mentioned that—she said, "That big house, that's where you belong, not here." Then I knew she meant the church. You know, them religious people, and the reservation, where I owned the land, money, and everything. "You don't have to be here. It's no good for you here." Yeah. And then I went to the mine, and then—again—that's when I almost got killed there and then I got out.

KS: You didn't tell me about that.

TR: Up in Tiger mine where that rock almost hit me, fell on me— boulder.

KS: Oh, no, you didn't tell me about that.

TR: I thought I did.

KS: No.

TR: Somebody I told. Where that boulder came off from the ceiling— missed me about as much as from there to that bench [*gestures to a space of about a foot*]. Or could have been right here on this table, if I was still standing where I was, but I moved up—kind of thinking about it. Then I moved out into the other tunnel—POW! [*slaps palm down on armrest*]—took the whole ceiling, the cross joints, all that.

KS: Right through it?

TR: Uh huh. Right through it, and landed on the ground. Before I was standing right there where it was. Or if it'd come this way, if it wanted to come right in there on top of me, but it wouldn't. It was from there and yet I wasn't there then—walked off. I knew that it was gonna happen—a kind of feeling. If it had wanted to kill me, it could have killed me right there, but it didn't. Then I thought about that, what she told me—"That business is no good for you." Then I know it [*nods*].

KS: Did you leave the mine then?

TR: After a while I left. Then everybody got scared when I told 'em about it, what happened. It was too dark—you can't see nothing, except that little light in there where I was working. You can't see what's going on 'way up there. Well, it was raining—water's leaking in there and it got wet in there. That's what they told me—the boss told me afterwards. "I better watch it. I better quit this job and go out down there. It might come some more again." And I went.

KS: You just kept on working after that happened?

TR: Well, I didn't work there. I worked down another level, 'way down below, not at the same place—'way down there with them other guys. I was working along there where it happened. Nobody would have seen—known what happened, but they'd find me.

KS: Did it close off the tunnel? Was it that big?

TR: No. No, there's a big wide tunnel about that big as from here to there [*gestures from his wheelchair to the wall, a space of about eight feet*].

KS: Oh.

TR: Tracks go in and it's another tunnel. It's got a lot of tunnels going each way. But there's another hole—there's another tunnel down there, and another one down there, and that little train comes—hauls it up. Sometimes we'll be working together, maybe two or three, doing this, maybe one another place. It all depends on where they put you. Sometimes I have to stay 'way down the bottom.

KS: Must be hot.

TR: Hot. Where they—water just going like this—then it trickled right around—

[Side Two]

KS: Okay, you were talking about being a thousand feet down at the bottom and the water.

TR: There's a big pump there. All that water gushes in like—when you're standing on a big arroyo or something, sliding down that—little rocks start rolling, make a little crack. It's going like this and goes in around that pump—big pump—twenty-inch pipe—that runs all the time, draws that water out, keep it from coming up. Just blue and clean as it is. And all around there where that water comes, it's just gushing from the rocks.

KS: Seeping through, huh?

TR: Seeping through. And it's hot. Any time, you don't have to wear a shirt—just go—fresh water, splash yourself over. You're sweating—

185

no air. And then the water goes in there just seeping all along. Keeps going all the time and the pump's running all the time. And when it rains down in Coolidge, there, around there someplace, where the power comes, it'll kind of knock the power off. It'll stop the pump, and the water starts coming up like that. "Oh, yeah, we have to go." And that elevator start—they'll signal the elevator, and all the water will be on the floor—carrying the whole ore. And us will be there—the water will keep coming, coming like that [*gestures to indicate about eighteen inches above the floor*].

KS: Oh, my gosh. Up your legs?

TR: Fast. Coming fast. Pretty soon it'll be in my boots—they we'll say, "Well, I think we have to go." 'Course they got another pump there, but it's run by—either battery or gas. It doesn't draw well. So—"I guess we'll go." There's a ladder there, another ladder. We'll be coming away up here. We'll get out. Up we go to the next level.

KS: Sounds pretty scary.

TR: Lot of water, lot of water just coming in like this, you know. Of course, when you leak water, that's where it starts running like that. It won't go any place—it'll be going down. But once it goes down to the nearest—that's where it's starting. It'll draw up. Lot of water. And they take that—pump that out, and they wash that ore with that water, clean it up, and then whatever's left goes down that arroyo.

KS: They use it for the leaching process?

TR: Yeah, and they just—I don't know whatever they do with it. There's no mining there now—well, there's mining at San Manuel. It's moved up.

KS: That night that you almost got killed, what kind of work were you doing there in the tunnels?

TR: Oh, I was emptying the chutes. See, they got little chutes just like that, in there where the ore comes from another level. See, they got so many levels, like this tunnel's maybe about half a mile, quarter mile, down. And then when they bring that ore on top, they dump it in that hole and it goes to another tunnel where they have them

186

chutes, and they keep on filling them chutes till they're full, and then I have to empty them and dump it into another hole and it goes to another chute. Then finally it goes on where it meets the train, that little train. And then it goes on that and goes up.

KS: So there was a train on every level?

TR: No. It goes down on the lowest level. Everything was going down, you know, down. If they don't find any good ore, well, they go down some more—just keep on like that. Lot of work but not enough men, that's why.

KS: Because it was wartime?

TR: Wartime. And besides, who wants to work underground? It's too dangerous [*nods*]. (11: 20–25)

Ted's narration of this episode is one of a handful of moments in our interviews that meets the criteria for a story as outlined by John A. Robinson, who says, "As there is no story without a plot, we may readily accept the claim that complication and resolution are obligatory features of narratives" (1981: 74). The plot of Ted's story is quite clear: he is warned away from mining work, but he doesn't heed the prediction of peril. Only when his life is twice put at risk does he follow the advice of the fortune-teller and take up other work, which eventually—outside the parameters of this set of episodes—brings him back to the church at least symbolically—since his home is very near the San Xavier mission church. Robinson also notes Teun van Dijk's more specific criteria, saying that to succeed as personal narrative, an incident must be "remarkable" and "must meet one or more of the following criteria to be tellable as a story: (1) the actions performed must be difficult; (2) initially the situation must pose a predicament, that is, there should not be an obvious or predictable course of action which the narrator could have followed to resolve the situation; (3) in an otherwise normal sequence of events unexpected events occur; (4) some aspect for the situation—the participants, objects, or processes—must be unusual or strange in the narrator's experience" (1989: 59).

As a distinct part of Ted's personal narrative, this three-part narration—prophecy, boulder, flood—meets not only one but all of the criteria that van Dijk sets out for a story. The actions he performs in the mines are difficult and dangerous. At the beginning of the set of incidents, Ted is posed with a predicament—whether to continue working in the mines despite the fortune-teller's warning. His course of action is initially unpredictable. Suspense is established. Then, "development of the reported event proceeds from that starting point," and he replays his experience in dramatic form (Goffman 1974: 504). When Ted does return to the mine, unexpected events occur, the first of which, the boulder dropping, is not only unanticipated but mysterious. These incidents are told with considerable animation and detail. Further, they connect to Ted's other episodes of his narration about work, risk, and survival. However, they are also strange and unusual in his experience, as is the palm reading by the fortune-teller, which is a singular instance of prophecy in his life story.

Robinson comments further on stories orally performed in the context of a personal narration, saying: "As van Dijk notes, all of these qualities or criteria must be defined by reference to the norms of experience in the narrator's speech community. Put differently, when the narrator and the listener(s) share the same model of reality, then the 'remarkableness' of events is consensually defined. In those circumstance the narrator may safely assume that what seems interesting or remarkable from his point of view will be interesting or remarkable from the listener's point of view as well" (1981: 59).

Ted may not consciously calculate the effect of each episode he narrates on the multiple potential audiences for his life story, but as the one above indicates, episodes generated from his life experiences are chosen and presented to engage listeners by means of suspense, mystery, and selected narrative detail, and they are intended to communicate his subjectivity to more than one audience.[2] His narrative episodes attest that he is "remarkable," not just the representative type of oral history but an individual whose unique experiences, expressed in a distinctive style, communicate his sense of himself as a man able to negotiate the perils of life in both his tribal community and the world at large. He narrates to make a story of his life—his story. He narrates for his own community, which is familiar with the history of Papagos working in mining, and for his own family, to preserve for them the details and perils of his work history.[3] He also narrates cross-culturally to an audience to whom fortune telling and the hazards of mine labor are not alien topics. The central elements of the narrative are accessible and supportive of his goals in presenting himself within and beyond his own community. As his most immediate audience, my listening vocables and clarifying questions demonstrate comprehension of the remarkableness of his story, but also my confusion about the exact location and sequence of action in some instances. I am a surrogate for his wider cross-cultural audience, and he accommodates my—and their—need for clarity and specificity by confirming or correcting my understanding of his verbalizations. I am also his most immediate per-formance audience, privy to the kinetic aspects of his narration as no other audience will be; I actually hear his voice volume, pitch, tone, and also see his facial expressions, gestures, and emotional registers. I get a sense of his performance that the reader of the inscribed text gets only a hint of, though it's probable that Papagos would be able to visualize typically Papago body language as well as much of the content of his narration.[4] Were he telling this only to a Papago audi-ence, especially one made up of his peers who share mining experi-ence, his minimal use of nouns and the abundance of pronouns with-out clear referents would not be problematical, since Papago speech frequently omits specific identifiers when it is understood that par-ticipants in the dialogue know the references. Ted's characteristic use of pronouns without establishing their referents, then, is not idiosyn-cratic but cultural. Papagos often have conversations on commonly held knowledge, beliefs, or attitudes in which nouns are omitted be-cause the topic is mutually understood. My interventions, then, are a

189

means of reminding him he is also speaking to strangers, who require more information to follow his narration.[5]

The fortune teller/mine incident, despite the fact that it is a report of just one of many experiences in Ted's life, is an oral performance. He has an audience, my physical, interacting presence that influences what and how he tells the incidents of his life. But a larger audience is present in his mind, and he performs his narrative for that diverse audience by controlling how and what he tells of his life episodes. Parts of his life he tells multiple times—horse stories, movie work, mining experiences, work for various landscaping and farming outfits around Tucson, school incidents—suggesting that for him they are key episodes in his life narration, experiences that develop his idea of himself in a particularly telling way. These repetitions, when analyzed in the larger context of his narrations, function as stories, each meeting the criteria van Dijk sets out, indicating that Ted has consciousness of what topics and modes of presentation engage his multiple audiences. The fact that I did not recognize his storytelling strategies at the time of the interviews is largely a matter of my concentration on collecting a comprehensive life story and my lack of training in folkloristic approaches to narrative. During the fieldwork, I did not recognize that Ted was an active performer of selected episodes of his personal narrative, a collage of interconnected, often repeated narrative incidents that accumulate into a coherently presented and performed life story. None of these central incidents Ted tells should be considered recitation pieces, but they are oral performances to which he brings a particular style of telling. Ted is not a raconteur. The telling is not an end in itself, nor is it primarily for entertainment or instruction. Ted narrates his life for a very specific purpose—to create a permanent, inscribed version of his subjectivity. In his dialogues with me, it is the drama and variety of his life that he focuses on, creating a particular kind of performance that, in its accumulation of incidents and observations, makes a story.

To call Theodore Rios a Papago storyteller is a stretch. As the narrator of his life experiences, Ted does not create a unified, dramatic narrative. Many anecdotes he tells about himself achieve or come close to genuine story, but he does not claim to know traditional Papago stories or to be recognized by his community as a raconteur. Nonetheless, he does have a repertoire of stories that he tells in a more dramatic way than he narrates his own life. These are not traditional narratives but stories told to him by others, usually about identifiable Papago people, though he has a few episodic pieces that might fit into the categories of myths and tales. Both are informal and conversational in style, not polished recitations; they do, however, evidence characteristics that set them off from his experiential narrative.

Not until Ted and I had been taping for some time did our conversation about his life generate narratives that are so clearly different in content and style from his personal narration that they could be identified as examples of deliberate storytelling. During the eleventh interview session (June 5, 1974), he told one story, then another one about the same protagonist came in quick succession. The context for these stories is a conversation about the progress of Ted's recovery from the injuries of his accident. He was chaffing, quite literally with the body cast, but also with inactivity, and he was eager to get back home to San Xavier. Doctors had told him it would be another month before the cast would come off. He was clearly disappointed but resigned; having had previous fractures, he knew the doctors were right about the slow process of mending broken bones. Talking about his own healing probably put him in mind of a medicine man with close ties to his family. But I also cued him to the first story, not realizing his health preoccupation and my query about an egg tied together. In a brief conversation I had had with Dr. Fontana a short time before this taping session, he had suggested that I ask Ted about the egg. Dr. Fontana wouldn't give me a clue as to what significance the egg had; he just laughed and said I should ask Ted about the medicine man who got arrested with an egg. And so I did. As we began taping on June 5, 1974, I said to Ted, "Tell me about the egg." The initial anecdote establishes the medicine man's power and sets up the comic story about a mysterious trick he plays on the Phoenix police, and then Ted tells a story about how the man gained his healing powers. The lead-in to these stories begins:

TR: Egg.
KS: Uh huh.
TR: What was that egg?
KS: Well, the medicine man is arrested — the magic egg?
TR: My uncle's — my uncle and my — my mother's side. They grow up together, and they're like this [*holds up two fingers together*] all the time. Some relation — I don't know what kind of relation, but it's a close relation, so, you know, he comes. When he got — when he got in a wreck, my uncle, that night, and got killed there, he knew it already. He knew it already, what happened.
KS: The medicine man did?
TR: Mm hmm.
KS: He . . .
TR: I think some way he said. Yeah, I know that someone came over there — he came over there [to San Xavier].
KS: And he knew?
TR: That's all I know. I don't know how, but — just like I say, they know everything. I don't know. I know when it happened, then, see, I know he came.
KS: What was your uncle's name?
TR: William. William — Bill.
KS: When did this happen? How long ago?
TR: Oh, it's — in the '30s sometime. It's quite a long time ago.
KS: What was the — do you remember the medicine man's name?
TR: Roy. I know it's Roy. He lives down there in — by Santa Rosa in this other village. It think they call it Ak Chin — there's another village beyond, before you get to Santa Rosa. There's another village where he lived, I think.
KS: He's still living, the medicine man?
TR: No.

KS: No.

TR: I don't know what happened, but then all of a sudden somebody told me he's gone already. Yeah. He could be living as an old man now, but—you know that—he's the one that—he's the one that's been curing everybody around here. He's a good one, and then he knows everything, and about that—I guess it's before he ever came to be a big—known all over, but like anybody else, he fools around like all these guys. And it's when he was in Phoenix. That's when they try to arrest—policeman tried to arrest him, for drunk or something. But he—but I guess he knows himself. But he told him that he wasn't drunk or something, but they want to put him in jail, I guess. They were right in the office. Everybody came in there and came in, you know, like they—"What happened?" "Oh—oh, yeah," he said—somebody. It's one of them policemen. He was asking the time—anyway, something like that, and this policeman pulled out his watch, a good watch [*nods*], a gold watch, and he said, "It's the right time here." And he said, "Well, let me see that," and it's a good timepiece—a good watch, too [*nods*]. He said, "No, I don't think so," and he knocked it down on the desk there [*hits his hand on the wheel chair arm*], bang it [*hits the arm again, harder*], whatever—whoosh—everything fall apart [*gestures with hands about a foot apart; looks down*]—"Ah, you spoiled my watch! You shouldn't do that!"—you know, he got mad. "Oh, it's still going" [*holds his fist up to right ear as if listening*]. You know, the hands—I guess the hand go 'round. "See, it's going now. It stopped but it's going" [*hand to ear again*]. No, it isn't." And you know, the policeman still has that watch. Put it right back [*hand toward pocket*]. He was afraid he might do it again. And then everybody started coming in, you know. And he was trying—they were amused by him, you know. They really want to find out something—before they lock him up. Then finally, think he took that egg out, and he said, "Well, I'll show you something, too." Set that egg down like that [*slaps at the wheelchair arm*], but it didn't break. They said, "What's that?" "It's an egg. Look at it." Started moving you know [*walking motion with fingers*], running just like it's kind of steep, you know. "Oh, that egg's gonna fall!" "Yeah, it's gonna bust!" "Better watch it!" Well, everybody was watching while it's dancing around on the table or whatever counter, when it's going to go off to the ground, grab it, you know. While they're doing it, he walked out the door [*slaps left fingers to right palm in sliding gesture*]. They were trying—I don't know what happened after that. Walked down the street—got away.

KS: Oh, that's great!

TR: Then after whenever happened, he's gone.

KS: That's a good trick.

TR: So he got out of it.

KS: And he was a friend of yours, too?

TR: Uh huh. I know him.

KS: He told you about this, huh?

TR: No, my—somebody told me about it, you know, around. I heard it so many time, you know. But he's the one that cured my dad up while he was there curing somebody. That's the first—when he got witched down in Pima country. He came and—I know he was there some place. He told me about something was going around— "Well, I'll get you a medicine man if I can." Then I found out he was curing somebody down in the village, right over there—he was there and I told him about it. So we went over—came over there, and he's the one that got that thing out, that thorns or whatever, got it out. Good man—he's very honest [*nods*]. He don't go like the rest. That's why most of these no-good medicine men, they witch him too, because they don't like him. But he'll get himself up. And the way I heard this story came—I don't know when—before—but it happens like that. When something starts like that, you've got to—so—at the time—he tried to—he saddled a horse. It's a tame horse but kind of wild horse. The corral—I don't know what happened there, when he got on—that horse bucked him off. Laying there unconscious. He don't know nothing, but it's the time when those fellows came out, when he was unconscious. He knew

194

that some guys came around, took him up, told him, "Go with us. We'll take you." Set him on another horse. Off they went, gallop, right straight on [*points*]. Two of them I guess — one on each side. They just went — some hill down there, some black, dark hill, and they were going straight in toward it. Before — just about the time they're reaching it, it opened [*spreads hands*]. They just went right in there and then — in that hill, or down the dungeon or some place, "Here we are." "Yeah." "Look around and see what you like." He looks around. Everything was spurs, bridles — silver — saddles, whatever. And there were horses, good horses [*nods*]. And they try to ask him if he can ride one. "No, I can't." And it happened like that. And all because it's down here, he won't do it. But he won't. Well, they show him around, all the way — I don't know how long, but finally they said, "Well, I think if you want to go, we'll take you." "Okay, I want to go." "But we'll give you some medicine first, a drink of something, before you go. By this we're going to give you, you're going to be just like a good one." I don't know what they meant by good one, but he says, "All right." So they dish [*pantomimes holding a cup and scooping up liquid*] him out a glass or whatever it was, a bowl or whatever. And he drinks whatever it was [*raises hand in drinking motion*]. "Take it, take it whole — take all of it, if you can — take all of it. Drink it all at once." Took it, and he tasted it some way [*lifts right hand toward his mouth in a drinking gesture*], I don't know how, but he was drinking, drinking [*makes drinking gesture again*] — before he got it all, he felt it was BLOOD [*voice drops dramatically and draws out "bloooood"*]. Turned around — some left, still some left. It was BLOOD [*deep-voiced drawn-out "blooood"*]. "You didn't drink it." "Oh, no, that's all I want to drink." He knew it was blood. "Why don't you drink it all?" "No, I can't." He wouldn't drink it. "Okay." And then while he was leaving, while he was leaving they told him, "Since you didn't drink all that, when anybody's so sick like that, you won't be able to cure him, whether he's dead, half-dead, for the reason you didn't drink it all. If you had drunk it all up, well, you'd heal better than anyone." He points. "So if you want to go, go ahead." He picked out a gold piece, brick, gold. "Take it home." He went. Then when he was coming to—I don't know what—"Why am I carrying this? I'm not supposed to be carrying it." Threw it away [*backward tossing motion*]. And then, finally, when he came to, he was right in that corral, in that coral where he was bucked off. He was still there, out in the sun. And he came to—nobody around [*looks around as if in a daze*].

KS: Nobody there, huh?

TR: Nobody around. He got up, thought about the horse. Horse was over eating grass, saddle on, everything when he got up. So, there it is [*nods*]. From then on, he started over as a medicine man. He knew it then, that he was a medicine man. But it happened like that. (11: 1–7)

At this point Ted explains how he heard the stories: "I think my uncle told my grandfather. That's the way it goes" (11: 7). Then the interview goes back to Ted's personal narrative and his experience with another medicine man who set bones. The two stories above are related to but separate from Ted's own narrative.[6] Significantly, he identifies them as stories repeatedly told within his family. About the egg story he says, "I heard it so many times." The fact that Fontana knew the story also suggests that Ted had told it many times, and the nearly word-for-word similarity of later retellings of this story to me indicate it is something of a set piece for Ted. The same can also be said for the cave story. These two stories, then, demonstrate Ted's participation in an oral tradition, and his telling of them fits into what Dell Hymes identifies as performance. Hymes explains the criteria for this designation, saying that "performance is situated in a context, the performance is emergent, as unfolding or arising within that context. The concern is with performance . . . as creative, realized, achieved, even transcendent of the ordinary course of events" (1981: 81).

In the interview format, the stories are somewhat hesitant, but each centers on a single episode that incorporates suspense. Thematically, they are like mirror images—same protagonist, but the theme is reversed. In the first, the medicine man is a trickster; he creates confusion and escapes. In the second, the medicine man is tricked into drinking blood, and by not finishing it all forfeits some measure of healing power, though his reputation seems to indicate his powers are indeed strong. Both plots dramatize mysterious events that are never fully explained: how is the watch restored? why doesn't the egg fall and splatter? are the riders and the cave full of precious things hallucinations or real? No attempt is made to answer these questions. In fact, the effect of the stories hinges on the mysteries being unexplained. The theme of power—its acquisition in one and application in the other—is heightened by the mystery of each.

Like all of Ted's narration, these stories show evidence of biculturalism, but in very different ways. In the egg story, the medicine man is not portrayed in a traditional setting or doing traditional things. He's in an urban police booking office, and his interactions are with policemen who are disrespectful to him. In the second story, while it is presumably set somewhere in the Papagueria and involves a culturally specific experience, there are echoes of European fairy tale motifs in Ted calling the cave first a castle, then a dungeon, and in the fact that the mountain admits the riders in an "open sesame" way. And the cavern is filled with treasure, albeit of a sort that would be meaningful to modern day Papagos, or maybe the saddles, spurs, and horses are Ted's own fantasy, given their importance in his personal narration. At any rate, though caves do figure in several Papago mythic narratives, these are not motifs from traditional Papago stories.[7] Ted's stories, then, like his personal experiences and narrations of them, are permeated with cross-cultural references.

I find it interesting that Ted tells these two stories together. While I cued him to the egg story, the cave story follows with no prompting from me; I didn't know it was in his repertoire. Taken together, they form a progression from comedy to serious depiction of the source of healing power. As Ted progresses from the egg story to the cave story, the telling becomes more dramatic and detailed and artful. The story is framed by the scene in the corral, then by journeys to and from the cave, with the cave and the drinking of the contents of the bowl as the central focus of the action. This is a much more complex structure than the egg incident, though presumably both originate with the same teller, the medicine man who experiences them. For Ted, I think the structure of each is received; it comes from hearing the stories repeated within his family. He puts a bit of his own spin on them in the cadence, hesitations, and phrasing that are recognizably his, but essentially he is telling them as "authentically" as he can; he knows "a good one" when he hears it and passes it on.

Presented as part of Ted's prose, it is hard to see precisely how clearly these stories stand out as different from his personal narration. But by taking the egg story out of the context of the continuous prose narrative of the interview and formatting it into lines that reflect his pauses and emphases, it becomes much easier to see that it is both understood and told by Ted as a type of discourse different from his personal narration. In 1980, I was asked by Larry Evers, editor of the Suntracks series of books on Native American literatures published by the University of Arizona Press, to edit a version of Ted's egg story so that it could stand alone for publication in *The South Corner of Time*.[8] I chose to line it out rather than leave it in paragraph form in order to call attention to Ted's narrative techniques.[9] The story as it was published follows:

> Egg.
> What was that egg?
> Oh, yeah, yeah, yeah, that one.
> It's a good one.
> He's gone,
> all of a sudden disappeared.

My uncle — my uncle on my mother's side —
and this man,
they grow up together, and they're like this all the time.
Some relation —
I don't know what kind of relation,
but it's close relation.
So, you know,
he comes.
When he got —
when my uncle got in a wreck that night
and got killed there,
he knew it already.
Nobody,
nobody said anything or nothing.
He just —
I don't know how, but —
just like I say, he knew.
I know when it happened, then, see,
I know he came.

Oh, it's in the '30s sometime.
It's quite a long time ago.
He lived down there in —
by Santa Rosa, in this other village.
I think they call it Ak Chin.
There's another village beyond,
before you get to Santa Rosa.
There's another village where he lived.
I don't know what happened,
then all of a sudden somebody told me he's gone already.
Yeah,
he died.
He's the one that —
he was the one that's been curing everybody around here.

He's a good one,
and then he know everything.
And about that egg—
I guess it's before he ever came to be big—
known all over—
but was like anybody else.

He fools around like all these guys.
And it's when he was in Phoenix.
That's when they try to arrest him—
Policeman tried to arrest him for being drunk or something.
They didn't know he was a smart man.
They were yelling at him and saying,
"What are you, a drunk, chief?" and all that.
But he told the policeman that he wasn't drunk,
but they want to put him in jail, I guess.
They were right in the office.
Everybody came in there and came in,
you know,
like they wanted to know what happened.
He was asking the time,
and this policeman pulled out his watch,
a good watch,
a gold watch,
and he said, "It's the time right here."
And the medicine man said, "Well, let me see that,"
and it's a good timepiece—
a good watch.

The medicine man said,
"No,
I don't think so," and knocked it down on the desk there,
bang it,
whatever.
Whoosh—

everything fall apart.
"Ah, you spoiled my watch!
You shouldn't do that!"
You know,
that policeman got mad.
"Oh, it's still going."
You know,
the hands — I guess the hands fell off.
"It'll be going," he told the policeman.
Like this,
took it back —
"See, it's going now.
It stopped, but it's going."
And you know,
the policeman still has that watch.
Put it right back.
He was afraid the medicine man might do it again.

And then everybody started coming in, you know.
They were amused by him, you know.
They really want to find out something before they take him and
   lock him up.
Then finally,
I think he took that egg out,
and he said, "Well, I'll show you something, too."
They said, "What's that?"
"It's an egg.
Look at it."
That egg started moving, you know,
walking around, running just like it's kind of steep, you know.
Just when it would come to the edge, where it would fall over,
it never did.
It just went right around.
And everybody was so excited about it.

"Oh, that egg's gonna fall!"
"Yeah, it's gonna bust!"
"Better watch it!"

Well,
everybody was watching while it's dancing around on the table or
    whatever,
counter—
when it's going to go off to the ground—
to grab it, you know.
While they're doing that,
he walked out the door.
walked down the street,
got away.
He's gone.
So he got out of it.
Somebody told me about it, you know.
Heard it so many times, you know.
He's the one that cured my dad when he got witched down in Pima
    country.
I found out he was curing somebody down in the village,
right over there.
He was there and I told him about it.
So we went over,
came over there,
and he's the one that got that thing out,
that thorn or whatever,
got it out.
Good man—he's very honest. (1981: 151–54)

A number of narrative techniques become apparent when the story
is lined out.[10] This formatting clarifies the dialogue and gives a better
sense of the exchange between the medicine man and the police officers. The movement toward the climax—"He's gone"—is more dra-

matic. The framing of the story is also more obvious;[11] the opening establishes the reliability of the story; it is about someone real with ties to Ted's family. The ending reaffirms the reality of the protagonist and his relationship to Ted himself. Both are credibility statements typical of what folklorists call "memorates," stories that circulate in the oral tradition about purportedly actual events. Lining the story out also exposes its incremental structure. First comes the watch trick, which establishes the protagonist's uncanny ability. I think it's no accident that he plays tricks with a timepiece, Anglo-American obsession with time being the butt of many Native American jokes. The egg, of course, is in itself a motif connected with mystery, the basis for riddles — which came first and all that — and the disappearing act plays into the notion of the elusiveness of Indians and their ability to fade into the scenery. Examining the story line by line, which is hard to do when it is in paragraph form, actually heightens the comedy and reveals why the story is funny. It also strengths the oral quality of the story, a characteristic of Ted's narration that is easy to forget when his articulation is edited into paragraphs.

The egg and cave stories are not the only ones that Ted tells. Though he laments that he did not listen to his grandparents closely when they told stories when he was a child, he does have a few stories about experiences from their generation and a small repertoire of traditional Papago stories.[12] None of these were told to me during the course of the taping on his life story. Only later, when I went to San Xavier to continue talking to him informally and to verify data on the first twelve tapes, did these story types emerge. When the producers of the *Words and Place* video series on Southwest Native American writers and storytellers asked if they could try on-site filming by making a videotape of Ted telling stories, my job was to cue him to tell, not personal experiences, but stories I knew he knew and told well from my experience of hearing them during the course of our dialogues together.[13] The point of the videotaping was to represent Ted as a storyteller, not a personal narrator.

Among the stories he told were versions of the egg and cave stories, though the latter is a bit disappointing since he kills the suspense and mystery of it by explaining at the beginning that the protagonist is unconscious when the cavern scene occurs and does not dramatize the "blood" element nearly as much as in the version above. But that is understandable, since he knows that I already know these stories. The rest of the videotaped stories are from our post-interview sessions that extended into 1975. I've selected one family story and two traditional stories that Ted told for the videotaping to demonstrate Ted's narrative range and his sense of himself as a storyteller. The first is a memorate from his grandfather. Ted says,

> The earliest time from here they tell me — when the railroad come across this line where it's still there now, all those people that are gone now, still lived. As boys, they'd go over to those railroad tracks, just for catch a ride on that train. You know how it is — the locomotive, it doesn't go as fast as it is now. That's why they're just like kids — you know.
>
> When they saw it coming, pulling slowly — well, they'd hop on — for a long way and then they'd jump off again. Wait for next one. Next one, they hop on, back again. Back and forth.
>
> At the same time when they're doing that, one day they could see all that dust — all that dust from there from up at the mountains, coming this way, you know. They know there are Apaches coming, so they know there's going to be a raid here [San Xavier] — and sure enough, they came here while they were out there. To be safe, they just stay there until everything settle and they come home. "The Apaches were here." And they said, "We know. We saw it — coming this way."

This is a story grounded in remembered history and connected to the present by location and the enduring presence of the rail line. It is an incident that Ted tells as amusing, despite the fact that the raid is a serious matter. He keeps the focus on the boys hopping the freights and using their absence from the village to spare themselves the danger of the raid. As Ted tells it, it is essentially comic. It bears some relationship to his telling of his grandfather's experience during the earthquake, where he treats that danger lightly, and also to another story his grandfather tells about hunting with four other men. In that story, when Ted's grandfather returns to their camp, there is a man in the shadows outside the fire and a deer carcass. Ted's grandfather greets the man, thinking him one of his companions, but the man starts and flees into the desert, and Ted's grandfather realizes he has come into an Apache hunter's camp. He flees too, and a potentially deadly confrontation is avoided. All of these family stories emphasize the unusual and stress ignoring or avoiding any inherent danger in the circumstances. These are not family hero tales—no really heroic action takes place—but rather survival tales with a comic spin that suggest recognition but also some disregard for the dangers of life. They fit into a dominant theme of Ted's personal narrative—recognizing danger and surviving it by acting judiciously.[14] Ted tells each of them with considerable pleasure, claiming them but also clarifying that these are stories handed down to him in the oral tradition of his family. He treats them quite differently from stories he tells from Papago oral tradition, for which he makes no personal claim to any talent for telling (see photo 11).

Ted introduces traditional Papago stories with signals that they have been passed down to him by no one in particular and are not part of his family tradition. He used phrases like "the story goes," "from time to time," and "from generation to generation" to mark his tellings of ancient myths or tales. Ted tells very few stories that could be described as mythic in the sense of set in the time before recorded history—a total of only five, and each one is actually less a telling than a summary. The one that follows is also from the videotape and is about I'Itoi, Elder Brother, who is a creator and protector of the Tohono O'odham. He begins,

People living down there on the coast[15]—and where the water, you know—and there—this is were this monster, whatever it is, it comes around there and grabs everybody, see, to feed on—even the humans. And the people couldn't get rid of it some way or the other. So, they had to come and talk to I'Itoi about it. And when he just said, "Okay, it'll be four—be four nights," or something like—you know, we call everything in a four. And so on that fourth day, he went over, up to the village and—I don't know where it is—and [they] said, "Right on the pond," swamp or wherever it is. "Okay, well, I'll go." He went. When he try to grab him, I guess he just kill him right off. And that's the end of that monster. And from that time, he's been all over, all over the place, all over the villages.

It's interesting to see how abbreviated this story is. Full versions of this myth are long and complex, with many episodes. Ted gives a bare-bones summary typical of his versions of ancient stories. They're good evidence that he wasn't exaggerating when he said he didn't listen when traditional stories were being told. His style is hesitant: he's not sure of locations or times, and at one point he actually uses the words "I guess." He does not claim mythic narrative or tell it with authority. He likes to tell monster stories—most of his traditional stories have some form of man-eater in them—and tells a much longer one about three men swimming in a pond and being chased by a monster; only two are ever seen again. In this story the monster is scaly and it's tail goes slap [*he makes horizontal clapping motions*] on the rocks above the hiding men. But typically his traditional stories gloss over detail; he reports rather than performs them.[16] Another example, this one a traditional story about the origin of the Children's Shrine—a holy site just off the highway between Casa Grande, a central Arizona agricultural town, and Santa Rosa village—is equally abbreviated (see photo 12).

Ted begins by alluding to the fact that there is story in Papago oral tradition about a flood that predates the one he is referring to, then begins the shrine story:

It's not really a flood, but the water sprang out of the ground and keep coming, you know, start running like that out of the ground. And the people got so that—they got scared about it, and they been talking about how to stop that water because they know—if they don't, it will rise and they're gonna have another flood. And so they said—the medicine men said, the only thing we can stop this water—get some of those children over. So they got four, two boys and two girls, and they just throw 'em right—throw 'em right there in that, in the water hole where the water's coming from—every one of them. Finally settle down and stop. And now days, it's a shrine—shrine now—then because after that you could hear them kids hollering at night where they were—where they are, and they made a shrine for that same reason. . . .

Why they have to stop that water when they need that water there . . . irrigation and all that? And why they have to kill those children? . . . People afraid of ghosts [they don't want to go there at night]. Medicine men go over there, and "They're just happy, that's all. Leave 'em alone. . . ." The story goes that way.

Ted's manner of telling this last story indicates a considerable personal investment in it. He gets quite emotional, blinking back tears, and his voice shows his distress. The issue of needed water is not part of the traditional story; instead, it links to Ted's consistent concern for the lack of water on the Papagueria.[17] And the sacrifice of children is disturbing to him. The fact that he is holding his grandson on his lap as he tells the story for the video camera also may be an upsetting factor.

As a teller of ancient stories, Ted is very cautious. He is consistently explicit about his limited knowledge and the reason for it. Having ignored them as a child, he is unable to access authoritative versions of them as an adult, a circumstance he laments. At one point in his personal narrative he says,

You hardly see any old people nowadays. That's why I'm lost. Sometimes I think about something that I didn't ask in the first place. I should have asked some of them smart people, old people, that used to tell me certain things. I should have listened, asked them, and now that I want to they're gone. Used to be a lot of them. Now — you don't see any old people — very few. And I don't know how come. But you can't ask them anything because they're too old to answer you either. They've forgotten. But at the time, I used to hear a lot of this talk. Now I don't. (edited tape 8: 8–9)

I don't think accommodating my questions about tribal oral tradition was the reason for his lament about not knowing the stories. I think he realized that such knowledge would give him a role and status in the community that he could never achieve as a narrator of his life story or even of family stories.[18] Ted would have liked to have an on-going audience for his verbal performances, and a repertoire of traditional stories would have provided him a way to interact with his peers and the younger generations of his community. Without a catalog of stories to tell, his life-story narration offers a way for him to command an audience — a physically present one for several months, but also an unseen enduring audience for his words as he expected them to be inscribed in his autobiography. To be an oral performer whose words are transcribed and edited into a narrative on the page is surely not as compelling to Ted, or as culturally endorsed, as being a traditional storyteller. But for him narrating his life is a means to impart his knowledge, attitudes, values, and experiences and demonstrate his capacity to engage and entertain an audience. No small achievement in a world where few are heard or leave a lasting record of a life for generations and an audience beyond the borders of family and community. Ted wasn't a traditional storyteller, but he was confident throughout our work, as the transcripts of our interviews together confirm, that he had a story to tell. Putting that story together into a continuous narrative was my responsibility in the process of inscribing Ted's life story.[19] How to do it has been the unresolved question of the post-interview period of this project. I guess it's time to tackle putting Ted's life story together.

7

LIFE-STORY STRUCTURE

AND CONTEXT

Ted Rios's life story, as it has been presented in this volume, is episodic, incomplete, and frequently repetitious. The topics and types of narratives presented thus far *attempt* to replicate the process of Ted's oral narration to me.[1] During our interviews Ted sometimes narrated related episodes, but as often as not—largely but not entirely due to my topic shifts in the interviews—he related episodes seemingly held together by nothing more than the fact that they were his observations and experiences and he was the teller. Listening to him address, and often later re-address, various topics from his life was dizzying. Just when I thought I could see a progression, a cause-and-effect relationship, a theme, or a chronology emerge, he made an association I couldn't follow or reprised a topic so generally that I was lost. Sometimes he repeated an episode with such subtle changes that I wasn't sure whether he'd forgotten the earlier telling of it or wanted to amplify or give it nuances omitted in the earlier version. Only through the accumulation of many hours of dialogue between us was I slowly able to begin to make some of the connections, which I think were so apparent and familiar to him that he felt no need spell them out.

Despite the fact that he often recognized my confusion—I quickly learned to verbalize it by asking questions, as the tape transcripts demonstrate—he did not talk about his life for my narrative comfort. He talked with me to present his life as he perceived it, organized and expressed in ways that suited his own narrative comfort, except when I directed him to clarify or connected ideas. And he did look to me for direction at the beginning, but as the interviews went on he relied on my lead less and less and determined his own method of narration, a method I've come to appreciate more and more as I work with the tapes of the interviews. Eventually I figured out that if I was patient, the story would become comprehensible. Sooner or later, but mostly later, Ted would connect episodes, get back to the point of the story, bridge the narrative to some present issue that was on his mind, suggest a motive for the action. I became familiar with his narrative style. I learned to wait. And I began to recognize his patterns. The fortune-teller/mine sequence illustrates his associative style; toward the end of that segment of his narrative he returns to the fortune-teller, who precipitates his telling of the mining incidents. In other words, the structure of this and many segments in Ted's narrative is circular in design; a topic or particular memory precipitates an extended narration that is associative but reconnected to the initiating topic or thought toward the end of the segment. All this, of course, attests to the fact that as an "act of memory and an act of creation, performance recalls and transforms the past in the form of the present" (Worthen 1998: 1101). Though his narrative purpose is not always clear, his retrospective view of his life has purpose in the present moment and circumstance. His narration is digressive and meandering, but followed carefully its emplotment becomes evident and the connection of incidents is comprehensible. On a larger scale, Ted also tells his story in an associative, digressive way. Starting at the beginning of his life was my idea, not his, and even when I tried to force him into a chronology, Ted resisted and told his life in terms of his own logic and cultural constructs. W. S. Penn likens Native American life-story narration to oral tradition, noting that such narratives are not "linear or temporally sequential" but freely digress dialogically in what he calls "supplementation" (1995: 108). This is a useful term to apply to Ted's narration, since he takes up topics, relating incidents that pertain to them associatively, and makes fairly dramatic shifts temporally. His narrative style, then, is "recursive rather than linear" (Harris 1990: 83). He supplements a single anecdote with related anecdotes that layer elements of a theme into a complex narrative. His discussion of his motion-picture experiences illustrates the nonlinear character of his narrative style. The particular films he discusses are identified geographically, not in terms of the sequence in which they occur in his life. Weather, location and terrain, costume, quality of horses, and type of action determine the order of telling and connect filming experiences together into a major element of his dominant theme—work. Despite my determination to structure Ted's narrative according to the conventions of a sequential narrative, Ted resisted and thereby controlled the style and shape as well as substance of his life story in its oral form.

Life stories—until they are edited to fit Euro-American norms of autobiography—also incorporate substantial amounts of repetition, another factor that resists linear plotting.[2] Ted's narrative is no exception. Partly because I asked him to talk about certain subjects more than once in order to clarify and verify data, he covers some episodes repeatedly. However in many instances, because a particular episode is pertinent to more than one theme in his interpretation of his life or to more than one topic he identifies as significant to his subjectivity, he also repeats himself voluntarily, sometimes for emphasis, sometimes for clarity, sometimes to cast an incident in a new light, and sometimes because he doesn't recall having told the event to me before.[3] His repetitions confirm that, as in oral tradition, there is no "wrong" or "right" version; variation in repeated tellings of episodes demonstrates the fabricated nature of narrative and make "the issue of authenticity ultimately unresolvable" (McCooey 1996: 106). Memory, intention, contextualizing narrative, audience awareness, cultural norms, a desire to revise subjectivity, and even physical well-being all have an effect on the details and emphases of Ted's multiple narratives.

Another element that resists Euro-American narrative conventions is his attitude about specificity and detail. The generalized level of his narration is not attributable simply to weakness of memory. As with most narrators he began to recall more, and in more detail, as our interviews and his interim thinking about them activated his memory.

He almost never told me he couldn't remember something, except for dates. His level of abstraction, then, as I see it, is another manifestation of his cultural sensibilities, his personal mind-set, and his narrative style. During our fifth interview, when I asked him to be more specific about an episode he was narrating, Ted said, "I don't keep track. I just know where I've been. I never did — I didn't ever care what year it was or when it was. I just kind of remember some things (edited tape 5: 28). W. S. Penn points out that a narrator "still tied to his or her oral roots knows how trivial too-particular details are. . . . Too many details burden the spirit . . . too many fixed and transfixing details kill the fluidity" (1995: 166–67). Details were not Ted's narrative priority. His aversion to pinpointing dates is especially problematical in establishing the sequence of the events of his life, but Ted clearly thought making the episodes of his life into a linear narrative was unimportant. Or he considered that chronology was my job, and he was therefore not very attentive to temporal or sequential specifics. Thematic association, the priority that emerges within episodes and in the overall Rios narrative, resists the chronological structure I anticipated, attempted to elicit, and would have found comfortable.[4] Narrating primarily for his own purposes, Ted's associative style of narration has both cultural and personal integrity and consistency that demands respect and provides more insight into his construction of personal identity and narrativity than a chronological narrative might. As I have worked with his narrative, I've come to appreciate more and more his skill at shaping his own life out of memory and language.

I am, therefore, loathe to obstruct Ted's narrative style by imposing chronological sequence upon it. His associative way of telling is a major part of his narrative subjectivity. Perhaps, as postmodern theorists would tell us, it *is* his subjectivity. Ted creates his life — emphasis on *his* — out of his thoughts as expressed in his words selected and ordered in terms of his own sense of himself and of the way life narrative shapes the self he wishes to impart.[5] The life story I have made in the course of presenting his narratives thus far, while no more chrono-logical than Ted's utterances, is quite different from what his oral nar-rative originally produced. It is a narrative that is analytical, inter-pretive, deconstructive. While it inscripts the episodic and associative nature of his way of telling his life, it suggests rather than actually rep-licates his narrative structuring and style. It connects Ted's narrative to his culture and its narrative traditions, but it does not reproduce the cultural contexts of his way of ordering the events of his life.

Firmly situated in his own culture, Ted narrated out of his cultural knowledge of places, people, and events that were obscure to me as his immediate listener. He knew how ignorant I was about Tohono O'odham history, culture, and landscape, and he accommodated my questions about all three—if and when I asked them—but usually not very precisely. Detailed descriptions of the land or other narrative scenes, I think, seemed unnecessary. "Just like anything else," he'd say, though I don't think he believed that about what he had seen and ex-perienced. He tended to be most specific about places away from the Papagueria because, I think, his home space was so deeply embedded in his sensibilities that it seemed beyond the need of extensive de-scription. Besides, we were right in the middle of it while he spoke—a gesture would do, pointing to the west with his chin when he spoke of I'Itoi, or nodding down the slope to the mission when we sat under the tree by his home, or toward Tucson, visible from our elevation.

The context of Ted's life was thoroughly available to him; it pro-vided the unarticulated motives for his actions, his perceptions, and his attitudes. Resituating him in the cultural and historical context from which he narrates makes his narrative much less vague and gen-eralized, his attitudes much less arbitrary, and his perceptions much better grounded in time and space. In other words, contextualizing, and providing a historical time-line and personal chronology based on research I did for this volume, offers his audiences the narrative com-fort Ted's narrative withholds. Placing Ted's narration of events into a broader cultural and temporal framework also provides insight into his life and, most importantly, reveals his narrative strategies. Therefore, I have worked through his narrations to both myself and Dunnigan in order to establish a biographical sequence. But in presenting a chronology of Ted's life, I make no pretense that it stands in any appreciable measure for his own idea of his life. It is simply an efficient way to enable me to relate Ted's experiences to the history of his community and the larger flow of history that impinges on his life.

The convention of including historical and cultural background chapters in most published Native American personal narratives has practical merit. As cross-cultural narration, the texts of Native American life stories incorporate events and circumstances beyond the experience of most readers, even those from other Native American tribes, and certainly those from generations removed from the lifetime of the subject. Background chapters usually precede the life-narrative text, reducing the sense of distance the reader feels from the subject. I've resisted the urge to position Ted's narrative antecedent to a discussion of the sequenced events of his life and their cultural contexts, because I've hoped that letting Ted's words carry cultural and historical experiences in this volume up to this point might destabilize the conventional reader-text relationship by forcing the reader to participate in the process of figuring out Ted's way of telling. I've also considered that accommodating to some degree Ted's associative narrative style might preserve a greater measure of the sense of strangeness that is usually mediated, if not entirely obscured, by the editorial process. I intervene now, not because I still think Ted's narrative needs or would even be well served by a linear emplotment, but because cultural and historical data that parallel and affect Ted's life and narrative is not readily connected to his life story without a clear time-line. The chronology, I hope, makes Ted's narrated episodes more comprehensible in relation to clearly defined increments in his life.

Rather that write a biography of Ted's life, which at this point would be redundant—not to mention dull, since it is his voice that makes his life story engaging and distinctly his own story—I've chosen to make a chronological listing of major events in his life *history*—as distinct from his life story—and to connect them to documented historical, cultural, and narrative contexts. The following data is compiled from interviews both Timothy Dunnigan and I conducted with Ted and from archival records at the San Xavier Mission:

1915
Theodore Rios is born at San Xavier del Bac Reservation (October 1). Baptized at San Xavier Mission (November 14).

1921
Enters San Xavier Mission School.

1924
Enters Phoenix Indian School. Returns to San Xavier part of each summer and sometimes for other holidays, especially at Christmas, often riding the rails with Depression victims when he is a teen. He works at the family farm and on his grandfather's ranch.

1925
Mother dies while he is in Phoenix. Given cattle to raise as his own. Flu epidemic at Phoenix Indian School. Ted and most of the students and staff ill. Epidemic forces cancellation of traditional Thanksgiving football game.

1932
Returns to San Xavier from Phoenix Indian School reluctantly, but needed at home because of family difficulties, especially his brothers' deaths. Helps out at grandfather's ranch and father's farm.

1932-33
Part time work with the CCC putting in fences, charcos, pumps, wells, and irrigation on San Xavier reservation.

1933–34

Attends Tucson High School, dropping out as a junior. Works part-time for El Paso Wholesale Grocers for two years, unloading freight cars and stacking goods until warehouse burns down. Begins three years of competing in rodeos and horse races.

1935

Sells off the cattle he was given as a child to buy his first car, a sporty blue Ford roadster with a rumble seat.

1936

Marries Ramona Tiger, a Papago-Creek originally from Oklahoma but living in Tucson when they meet at a rodeo. Works five months on the Pima Reservation south of Phoenix on an irrigation project. Works for Marana Cotton Growers Association building worker housing. Returns to San Xavier. Takes job at Phelps Dodge Ajo Mine. Steady work in the open pit mine, with one layoff when copper prices dropped in late 1930s and the mine is briefly shut down. Attends Rain Ceremony (Wiikita) at Santa Rosa village, where one of his friends passes out. Makes trip to Magdalena for feast of St. Francis celebration.

1937

Theodore Rios Junior born June 15 at Sells, Arizona, baptized August 15 at San Xavier Mission.

1938

Marriage to Ramona Tiger Rios in Catholic ceremony at San Xavier Mission, June 13. Michael Rios born July 5, 1939, at Sells, Arizona, baptized October 19 at San Xavier Mission.

1941

Divorces. Quits the Ajo mine.

1942

Moves to Morenci, Arizona, to work on copper ore concentrator tailings for about six months. Goes back to work at Ajo mine. Visits carnival fortune-teller. Works the San Xavier underground mine. Works the Tiger underground mine.

1943

Works for Consolidated Aircraft in Tucson, riveting ball-gun turrets for World War II bombers.

1944

Hanford Nuclear Energy Plant job hauling debris and garbage for six months. Weekend trips to the Yakima Indian Reservation. Boeing Aircraft riveting job in Seattle for two months. Visits former roommate from Hanford barracks in Portland. Stops briefly in San Francisco for sightseeing. Los Angeles Shipyards job cleaning ships and working as a longshoreman's helper for two months. Returns to San Xavier, where he takes temporary jobs cutting fence posts and chopping cotton, some farming.

1945

Does government agency work on reservation charcos, fencing, and dam building.

1946

Works three months for Tucson Transfer, hauling and stacking, and for a plumbing supply company.

1947

Father dies. Second marriage and residence in Tucson. Works for R. E. Miller Construction as mason's helper. Job is intermittent over a five-year period.

1950s–70s

Part-time work for Hernandez Landscaping and Southern Arizona Landscapers. Sporadic motion-picture and television work. Planting pecan orchards south of San Xavier Reservation. Intermittent work at local restaurants. Planting and harvesting at San Xavier.

1968

Second wife dies. Returns to live at San Xavier.

1960s–70s

Weeding and chopping cotton seasonally. Work on Arivaca, Arizona, ranch. Weeding and harvesting pecans. Harvesting fruit and corn in Wilcox, Arizona. Harvesting lemons in Yuma, Arizona, and produce in El Centro, California, cutting and selling mesquite firewood.

1969

Interview with Timothy Dunnigan for Doris Duke Indian Oral History Project.

1974

Victim of hit-and-run accident that results in fractures, surgery, and long convalescence. Interview with Kathleen Sands for life-story project.

1975

Continuing interviews and *Papago Storyteller* videotape

The sequence of major events in Ted Rios's life is reductive and deadening. Certainly, it does not make a story. Without Ted's narratives there is little to be made of this data and certainly no development of Ted as a protagonist in his own life. Some of the data contained in the chronology is verifiable from documentary records, but much of it is imprecise. The dates and the sequence he gave to Dunnigan are not always the same ones he told to me. I'm not very bothered by these time discrepancies.[6] Though life story purports to be verifiable, critics consistently point out that autonarration is more fabricated than factual. Consistent with the idea that narrative authority resides in the mode of telling, not in the data of the narrative, is Ted's method of relating his experiences. Precise factuality and even veracity are not issues for Ted. For him, the authenticity of his life and his narrative is a given. I have to admit that I am nearly as disinterested in the chronology of his life as Ted was. It's Ted's voice that makes his experience authentic, alive, and compelling; the chronology I supply is nothing more than a list that places him in time and space. To inject some energy into this bare-bones record of his life, I want to return to Ted's narrative and provide some cultural history that augments his chronology and his episodic style of narration in order to contextualize his narrative in the cultural events that impact on his life and life story. To do that, it might be useful to start with some historical information that predates Ted's life but has bearing on it.

When Ted was born at San Xavier, this district of the Papagueria had been a reservation since 1874. Slightly over 71,000 acres were set aside by executive order, about 1,200 under irrigation. Government intervention on the land around the mission established by Father Kino in the 1690s did not immediately change the seasonal migrations of families from permanent villages to summer residence in the flood plains, "where they could take advantage of increased opportunities for farming and food gathering afforded by rains" (Dutton 1975: 222–23).[7] Ted's story about his grandfather and father's experience in the 1888 earthquake attests that his family was still moving to summer quarters well after the reservation had been established, even though they had farmland at San Xavier. However, Ted gives no indication that that practice continued into his own childhood, probably because improved farming and the growing cattle industry had made seasonal migrations unnecessary. Irrigated farmland and the stability of reservation status may also have been what attracted Ted's maternal grandparents to move from Santa Rosa, a part of the Papagueria not designated as reservation until 1912 (Dutton 1975: 223), to the ranch in the Sierra Blanca foothills twelve miles southwest of the San Xavier Mission. Whatever the case, Ted was born into an extended family with established tenure in the San Xavier District. His childhood exposed him to Papago cultural experiences, rituals and practices instituted by the early Catholic missionaries, and events precipitated by proximity to Anglo-American culture. What appears essentially blank in the chronology of Ted's life as it is charted out above is actually a period rich in narrated incidents. As a small child Ted remembers playful episodes both in the village and at the ranch. For instance, he recalls riding burros in the village:

219

We used to ride a lot of burros up there at San Xavier. Because they'd come there—I don't know where they'd come from—some Mexicans brought 'em in—whole bunch. They'd be roaming around, eating paper, rags, whatever they can get a hold of, drinking your water and all that, and when we're at school there, young kids like that, well they kind of like bunch 'em up, get some ropes or whatever, wire or whatever you can get, get a hold of one, start riding it. They're tame, but some of them, they'll buck you off. Used to ride them just like, you know, like to ride 'em when they buck. Most of them, they're tame. Pretty soon, you know, a whole bunch will be in that burro game.

They don't belong to us. We just take care of 'em. And you've got to name certain ones, too, certain names. Whatever their color is. It's when we're kids. Like Blackie or Whitey, or whatever. That's all they do around there at that time—lot of burros, you know—small ones, big one, old ones. Before we round 'em up, we'll say, "Well, I'll take that," and we'll name some of 'em, which one we want. "I'll take this one." Put that wire around the chin like this. Sometimes they get so that they don't want to go, and they just dash right into the mesquite. That's where they can get you off, right in there.

The godfather to my kids, when he was young, he rode on one with his brother. They were going home. They rode that donkey. They said, "Oh, let's take a burro." "Okay, we'll go." He got on, and his brother got on behind him. Started going, and some way, well, they got to the mesquites—the branches going like this, like this [*making tangling motions around his head*], you know, and that donkey don't want to go. Tree there, and it go under there, won't go. So he started to try to hit him, and you know, when he'll hit him on one side and then he'll turn this way. Try to hit him just one like this, you know, and it ran under the branches. And this brother, he got off. He jumped off, grabbed a big piece of board, and he got mad. And this other one, he didn't get off, and instead of hitting the burro from behind, he was hitting his brother there, on the spot. He didn't know—he wasn't looking, and there was too many branches. And his brother was going like this [*like he's swinging a bat*], you know, and trying to get out of there where the burro was going, and this guy was kind of running along— Bam!

When they don't want to go, them burros just go right in those branches. They're mean when they want to. (edited tape 11: 30–31)

This episode connects to his early riding experiences at the ranch and to his eventual recognition as an outstanding cowboy and rodeo competitor, so it might be considered something of a marker in his life story. In terms of Ted's chronology, it is fairly vague, an activity that took place while he was still at the mission school, before he was nine years old and sent to Phoenix. It's an ordinary experience shared with his young playmates, but it is the stuff of life between the watershed dates in his biographical data. It peoples and activates the landscape of his childhood. It establishes the landscape of San Xavier village as rural, which is typical of O'odham villages where houses are usually spaced quite far apart and the desert landscape is relatively little altered (see photo 13). Childhood camaraderie and high jinks and humor are nostalgically remembered and suggest life apart from the institutions of an alien culture. The same tone pervades another recollection from this period in his life. Born into a generation that would make the shift from traditional work—hunting, harvesting desert plants, flood farming, and herding cattle—to wage work in the dominant society, Ted still learns traditional skills as a boy. He remembers,

That godfather of mine, just like I told you, when we were kids, he used to make us bows and arrows out of them trees, and he'd lead us there to the cactus—"Watch for 'em, watch for 'em." I don't know how many times we missed 'em—big ones, you know. And we'd get two. "How we eat 'em?" we'd say. Of course, we don't know. We'd take 'em over—them big ones, you know, take 'em over and build our fire, skin 'em. Used to do it every evening when he was making them bow and arrows. Then he'd say, "Well, let's go" [*points with his chin*]. And we'd follow right along. Lot of cactus where they live—all that trash there. They'll be poking out, pretty soon one of 'em—"There it is." Go like this [*pantomimes drawing a bow*] and miss. Another place—"Over here." This time just miss it again. That's when I used to hit it. And that's the same time I ate that yucca, the stalk. Cut it off, do the same thing. Arrio, my godfather, he done the same thing—roasted it, cut 'em up so many pieces, roast 'em, everyone's—"Here, take it." His father was the neighbor to my grandfather. They do it from olden times. (edited tape 9: 9–10)

In the sequence of Ted's life, roasting cactus rats and yucca are minor events, but they are significant narrative events. They tie him to his Papago identity. The fact that it is his godfather who teaches him to hunt with a bow and to cook traditional foods in the wild points to the extended relationships that bind Tohono O'odhams to a network of families and invest individuals with a strong sense of identity and responsibility within the community. David McCooey supports this view when he says that recollections of childhood are not narrated so much to "suggest what life was like as a child, but in order to figure the extent to which the individual feels connected to the past" (1996: 46). I would expand that to include the connection to the social fabric of the culture. McCooey also argues that early memories "resist emplotment; they are images rather than narratives" (1996: 27). Both observations apply to these incidents. When they occur in the sequence of days and years of Ted's childhood is unimportant. They are vivid images of his childhood world. Cause and effect, position in incremental time? Neither is important. Rather these are narrative images of childhood that define his identity. They set early examples of his lifelong drive to competency.

Even in this early period of his life, Ted is exposed to and open to experiences that introduce him to the non-Papago world. His father, very involved in governmental and business relationships outside the tribe, encourages Ted to embrace change and prepare himself for the influences of white society. As Ted explains, his father wants him to be able to function in a bicultural world. He tells the young Ted, "What's coming on, white man's way, you got to tackle it" (edited tape 10: 7). Frank Rios, according to Ted's narrative, seems to have facilitated interaction with white society for his son at an early age. Besides contact with white teachers at the mission school, Ted talks briefly about popular cultural events that introduce him to the dominant culture — baseball games at San Xavier and in Tucson, about the San Xavier band playing at non-Indian events he attended as a child, and at some length about seeing the circus come to Tucson. Ted seems as much engaged by the spectacle of a circus as he later is with fairs and Indian rodeos or the fiesta in Magdalena. He says,

We went to the circus, the very first — that's when I rode on it [the first truck his father owns]. Took a ride, my uncle and my dad. The circus was in town. We went there. We just took a ride, not really to the circus, but I saw they were there. They used to come by the railroad on Congress Street, by the bridge. I seen a lot of circuses when I was a kid, lot of animals. You know, when the big circus come. They don't do it any more. That's why I was telling all their kids how it is — the animals the circuses used to bring. Now you don't see 'em. You only see 'em in pictures.

Ah, it's a big day — big circus. The train will be at the old cross-road right there that crosses Congress. That's where they used to park. A big train — long train, nothing but animals in there, circus people. Come there and they unload. 'Course, the elephants towing them cars on the ramp, one by one. Them lions, they'll be — you know, when they're bothering 'em they don't like it. They just roar [*nods*]. And they set 'em down on the street in a little harness. They drag 'em up to where the people are, a lot of 'em, putting up tents right in that space. And then the cooks, they're getting ready—putting in bread for the workers, circus people. Lot of cooks—whole bunch. And pretty soon the wagons will be coming in with loads, animals. Elephants will be there, too. Men will be stringing ropes to carry the canvas for the tents. And the tent just goes 'way up there. They got ropes and all, tied in that harness. One elephant will be over here, pulling them wagons— them trailers down off the train, because they're flatcars. Kids watching them while they do it. And then they set up. You see a lot of giraffes. They got a special corral in there. Lead 'em right over.

We used to go to the circus, go in there where the animals are, see all those kinds of animals. Half-ladies and all, the side show. Mm hmm. Kind of surprised me, that lady on the swing— and just sitting like a dummy, statue, but she talks. Forty-nine— an old lady. Just kind of swinging around. There's a lot of them. They bring a lot of freaks [*shakes head*]. Seen 'em all when I was young. When I was young—small, that's when I seen every-thing—clowns and everything. . . .

What interests me is them animals—I never seen them before, you know, like giraffes, lions, bears, whatever. Five-legged ani-mals, two-headed women—everything. And the, at the time, the price wasn't as high as now, I guess. Yeah, yeah, I still remember that because that was something. Maybe once a year—not often. (edited tape 7: 11–12)

As extraordinary as most of his everyday experiences are ordinary, the circus he describes is the epitome of Otherness for Ted as a child. The scene is Tucson, outside the landscape of his cultural experience; it is reached in the first motor vehicle the family owns; the activity is con-centrated and chaotic; the animals are strange and exotic; the circus personnel he describes are extremely alien to his experience. All in all, the memory is vivid and animated, dependent for its impact on a child's naiveté and capacity to be enthralled by the unusual. The level of observation and detail in this episode on the circus is repeated in Ted's narration of several experiences of non-Indian culture during his youth. Though his sense of the strangeness of Anglo culture dissipates in his narrative of his mining and later work experience and his extensive travels, the early episodes of contact with the white world communicate his sense of alterity tempered by interest in the strangeness of the Other. Another episode, which occurs when he is a teenager attending the Phoenix Indian School, illustrates his interest in elements of a culture other than his own, especially those which exhibit extreme elements of white culture. The following is a recollection of trips from Phoenix to San Xavier during his years as an Indian boarding-school student:

> I always come home for part of the summer — by freight. Hopped a lot of freights when I was a kid. Even passenger trains. I've seen a lot of people, ladies and all traveling. Cold — cold at night [*clutches upper arms*]. Used to come home, some big occasion like Christmas, come all the way. Lot of us. We'd get an excuse. 'Course, we got to get excused. Tell 'em we're going. They'll ask us, "You know how to get home?" "Sure, we know how to get home." We never tell 'em how we do it. "Okay" [*nods*]. By the time we get ready — the evening — we know when the freight train leaves Phoenix. Oh, sometimes we'd watch, maybe two or three hours, go to town, wait for the time when the freight started going out, get on it. Got to town about four in the morning, be in Tucson. Then I walk home. Early before the sunrise. Ground is pretty frozen, you know — walks good. It's so cold at the time. Now you don't see any. Be ice all over.
>
> I never felt any cold. 'Course, we're young. Now I won't do it. Going back the same way — vacation over. I've seen a lot of this at the time during the Depression. Seen a lot of them ladies. Coats, blankets, laying on the empty car. It's very sad business. Sometimes the freight will stop along the way. Cold. Some of these guys'll get out and build a fire right around by the freight, be waiting. 'Course, they were old trains. Sometimes they'll stop for maybe an hour before it pulls out again. It's so cold you have to

get out, start building a fire right along the tracks, pull all that old tires up there. Everybody'll start coming out, ladies and all [nods]. When they start going, everybody rushing in there again. Here we go again. 'Course I don't know where they're going; they're going to California maybe. Yet we've got the shortest trip, but sometime we didn't get there when we want to because it stops and stops. . . .

If you're smart enough you don't have to ride that [passenger] train or bus. If you get a chance, you get a freight, go with the freight. Just us boys. 'Course they won't catch us. That's why I say when I was young I'd do this and I'd never tell it to anybody. But my father knew it. He never said nothing. . . .

Well, I did come home on the bus once in a while, if I want to, but I like the freight better. Lot of fun [*smiles*]. I meet a lot of people. I like to see them tramps in the train. Boy. I was very sorry—feel sorry for them and the way they travel—cold and ragged and all that. It wasn't far at the time from Tucson home. Just like I said, it's just open. Be walking and all that. They got a wagon trail right along there. Not like where the roads come in, just straight on, right across straight on, straight as you can get. Shortest. Just go right on there, before everybody was awake, I'd be home. I'd never tell 'em I'm coming. It's a lot of fun [*smiles and raises hands, palms up*].

And the same time we'll know when we're going back. We'll notify each other when we're going to be in town, do the same thing going back, gang up again. Just do the same thing back. That's why I say if you know what you're doing, well—you get along all right [*nods*]. (edited tape 10: 4–8)

For Ted, these trips between San Xavier and Phoenix are adventures. The adults, ladies and all, riding the rails, are described as Others and evoke pity in Ted, who realizes the journey is no lark for them. Youthful, riding the freights by choice, heading for familiar and welcoming places—both of which are homes to him—he feels very different from but sympathetic toward those with far to go and no comfort ahead. These people interest him, as do the circus hands and performers, but he does not identify with them. He uses this episode in his life to make a point: given ability and a willingness to get along, life is manageable, even rewarding; he can go anywhere and adjust to new conditions. The Papagueria is where he is truly at home, but wherever he is, he narrates himself as Papago.

The period of childhood at San Xavier and of his teens in Phoenix are not a blank for Ted. His narrative fills in the years with experiences that are an accumulation of episodic images disconnected from any sequential pattern. Interestingly, the narratives he tells of his childhood—swimming at the river, watching his grandmother make cheese, traveling to Santa Rosa by wagon, watching the men castrate and tag the ears of the cattle at spring and fall roundups, and those above—are all pleasurable and usually connected with his theme of acquiring knowledge and skills that become valuable in his adult life. For Ted and other Papago youngsters, "childhood was a time for doing chores; but mostly it was a time for standing aside or going along and watching how the older ones did it, for what someday would be an inevitable part of life" (Waddell 1969: 88). If there is a linear progression in Ted's narrative, it is not the sequential one I supply above but one of acquiring more and broader competence in the cultures and everyday practices of both Papago and non-Papago cultures.

Nowhere is the drive toward competence more strongly depicted than it is in relation to ranching skills. References to cattle ranching are a consistent thread that runs throughout Ted's chronology. Ranching is, in fact, the most consistent topic in Ted's story of his life, from his early childhood to his opinions about the Papago cattle industry he holds at the time we were taping interviews. Ranching is an employment he returns to again and again throughout his personal history. Why becoming an able cowboy and rancher is so important to Ted and why ranching persists in his thoughts, even though he is no longer physically or financially able to ranch, becomes more comprehensible when his narratives relating to horsemanship and cattle are contextualized in the history of the cattle industry on the Papagueria.

The breeding and raising of cattle introduced by the Spanish missionaries accommodated the traditional migratory life of the Papagos, who moved in relationship to water sources. Practicing horsemanship and animal husbandry introduced by the missionaries in the late 1600s, Papagos had roughly two hundred years to absorb this new means of livelihood into their culture before the coming of large numbers of Europeans into the region. Most of the cattle introduced by the Spanish were probably allowed to remain "semi-wild and formed only a minor part of the substance base of the Papago" (Kelly 1974: 70). But with the drilling of the first wells in the early 1900s, ranching became a substantial factor in the tribal economy, despite the fact that the range was public domain and had been used for grazing by non-Indian ranchers since the Gadsden Purchase in 1853. Moreover, the Papago had created their own livestock economy with no Bureau of Indian Affairs–initiated or supported program, a unique situation in Arizona tribal economic histories (Kelly 1974: 69–71). The old hunting range slowly became cattle range. The longevity and steady production of the Papago livestock economy "proved to be a boon for the Papagos since it is most unlikely that they would have been awarded such a large reservation (2,750,000 acres) had they not been raising cattle on land that required 140 acres per head" (Hanlon 1971: 196). The industry, as it flourished in the early years of the twentieth century, provided Papagos with a food supply and a cash crop. For a few families it became a source of status and relative wealth, at least until the drought of the early 1920s devastated the herds. Ted remembers the drought, though he was only six or seven when it decimated their livestock. He recalls,

> Lot of cattle died off. They didn't sell'em. Lot of them died on account of the drought. I seen part of it. You get 'em on the farm and they try to eat: they bloated out and they die right there.

228

They'll take some water—bloat, die. . . . But I was small when they had to move out of the ranch. They just abandoned everything. They couldn't do much. No rain. So rocky there. Maybe '21 or '22. . . . No water, no feed, no nothing. They died. A lot of cattle died. Well, once that happens, a lot of that disease comes in there, just kills them even if they're not dying. But that disease come in there, kills too, just like that [nods]. That's why I always say, you know, if everything hadn't happened—disease, drought, and everything—I'd be a rich man. (edited tape 11: 16–17)

Ted's protestations, however, do not ring true. As ranchers, his grandfather and father made a recovery from the losses during the drought. In 1925, the recovery was solid enough that Ted and his siblings were given cattle of their own to raise. In fact, it was Ted's father who arranged for the purchase of blooded replacement stock in 1928. Ted also recalls this:

My father and mother brought cattle from Colorado. He went up there to get that cattle from Denver, where they had big meetings. They were given so many head of cattle, people from here. . . . My father arrange for the people to get cattle through the government in Denver, and they paid for it by giving back stock from those they raised. I was too young. I was still going to school [at San Xavier]. (edited tape 8: 9)

Introduction of registered cattle eventually strengthened the herds, which today are still counted as a ready source of cash on the reservation, one that Ted took advantage of to buy his first car in 1935. In a study of Papago culture and economy, Bernard Fontana uses the Rios family to illustrate the effect of ranching and employment patterns over generations. He writes:

The shift in occupational statuses is exemplified in the 43-year-old man whose grandfather was a respected village headman who

farmed and raised cattle; whose father became one of the wealthi-
est Papago cattlemen; and who personally has worked as a mine
laborer, an automobile lubricator, a welder (during World War II),
a rodeo performer, and part-time cowboy, lacking both the material wealth and esteem enjoyed by his forebears. (1960: 151)

Ted, then, is not cheated of his inheritance by the drought of the 1920s;
instead, he sells off his part of the Rios herd and opts for wage work
instead of the risky business of raising cattle and farming in an area
subject to devastating droughts on a fairly regular basis. Because he
is absent so much of the time, his step-brother Jacob falls heir to the
family farming and ranching responsibilities and resources and even
his father's home, leaving Ted, the oldest living son, without assets in
his later years.

Cattle production is, if not as successful for Ted, at least as influential in his life and as dominant in his narrative as mining, which,
especially during his years in Ajo, was both a satisfying and remunera-
tive occupation. As the chronology records, Ted's mining employment
includes work at several mines, one of them at Morenci, where he expands his work experience to include disposing of waste from the ore
separator. Explaining his work in this aspect of copper mining, he says,

Morenci, it's a big one, bigger than Ajo. That's a new one, too —
yeah, I think that's when I left Ajo. I think it was when I left Ajo;
that's when I was over there. It's just like Ajo; people are coming
and going, coming, going. But when I'm back there, well, they
hire me right then [nods]. I worked where they drained that —
what you call leaching field. All that thing that's been ground
up — the mine waste — it comes in slush. Then you got to let it go
into one of the earlier places. Then let it stay. It's simply a mud,
mud, but it's mixed with water. They put it in milky. And then it
stays there for so long, and then it fills up, you know. It's down-
hill, like lot of arroyos. You fill one up — it goes in a pipe, a big

pipe, and you open the pipes. Then you let it run in the ditch, like that. Then it goes for so many days; when it's full, you change. It's a big pipe. It's the main line, and you just open that. Then you go to another ditch. Keep doing that left and right. And then when it gets dry, it settles, just like a cake of slush, and it settles down; maybe it goes down some. Then you've got to change, too, pour some more in here because the — the sludge is coming all the time, because they're grinding the whole thing. It comes in the water. And then they're getting the good ore out, where it's separated. And this is just the waste from the mill. Just like a big river, but it's full of thick mud. We're in a gang. We got to work together. Let it run in there, and then somebody open the pipe. Just keep on going down, you know. It slopes. It's located right in the big mountains, 'way up. So it goes in there and just slush down. They've got big arroyos, big ones, getting deeper, going down that way toward the Gila River that comes through Phoenix.[8] And then they had to dam part of it, so it wouldn't go into the river. And then when one is filled for good, then you keep on moving just further on. There's a lot of those arroyos that could be filled. Nothing grows. Sandy rock. [See photo 14.] In Ajo, well, they just dump it right in a hole, like a big mound.

Same thing. Only they couldn't — they couldn't do any better, because they couldn't run it down because it's a flat ground. Keep on filling, keep on filling. Lot of work. I just done this thing because I didn't get to go in the mine because there's always a lot of men there. I like it out there because we're on top. (edited tape 5: 6–7)

This mining experience is not as dramatic or narrated in as enthusiastic or vivid a fashion as his work in the pit mine at Ajo and in the underground mines. It does not carry the peril or the skill level of the other mining experiences, yet it demonstrates the range of competency Ted achieves and his ability to get some sort of work in the mining industry pretty much at will and in any location in the state.[9] The importance

231

of mining as a source of employment to Papagos of Ted's generation contributes to an understanding that Ted's work in the mines is not an example of unusual work for Papagos. Ted's years of work in the mines is well within the work patterns for male Tohono O'odhams of his generation. His extended narratives about that work connect him to employment shared by many of his peers, thus it also ties him to his Papago identity. Jack O. Waddell notes that work for copper mines is the single most stable off-reservation employment that Papagos engage in from the early 1900s through the 1960s. During the mid-1930s into 1940, about two hundred Papagos were on payroll at the Ajo mine, about 18 percent of the total number of employees. There were lesser numbers at smaller mines, but Papagos were seen as a steady and reliable work force (1969: 51–55). Mining also offered Papagos tangible benefits — year-round work, as opposed to the seasonal work in agriculture, and the pay was substantial. At Phelps Dodge, employees with four month's standing could share the annual distribution of profits (Waddell 1969: 54). Company towns at Ajo and Morenci also offered housing and other social benefits. The employment of men like Ted was expedient for both the mine and the Papago employees. Papagos were local and could stand the hardships of desert labor. They found the mining communities offered a social milieu of Papago families and the opportunity to return to reservation homes frequently.[10] In many cases, the mines accommodated generations of Papago employees. Ted is a good example of this, since his oldest son worked the Ajo pit until he was laid off with a disability, well after Ted had left mining altogether (interview with Kay Patterson, February 18, 1998).[11]

Perhaps the most attractive aspect of working in the copper-mining industry was that it offered structural and social features that made possible "a straddle adjustment to two distinct ways of life" — Anglo industrial organization and reservation kinship systems — possible. Papago miners had access to both good earning potential and to the "reservation's activities and institutions" (Waddell 1969: 58). Had Ted's marriage remained stable, it is very likely that he would have remained at the Ajo mine much longer, but when divorce unsettled his life sufficiently to precipitate his departure from Ajo, he sought employment at another mine despite the fact that he had to take a job lower on the skill hierarchy than at Ajo. He stayed at the Morenci mine only a few months before returning to Ajo, only to leave, but again to find mining work in the tunnels of two underground mines. Warned off by a fortune-teller and nervous about his draft status, he finally opted for a return to residence at San Xavier and a clear-cut defense-industry job building bomber parts. Mining, however, dominates his narrative of work. No other work generates equal volume or specificity. And no other work provides and demands the regularity and attention and the pride that keeps Ted's life productive and centered. The work that follows is all temporary—months, weeks, or days of employment that offer him ready cash and mobility but do not evoke substantive narrative except for his movie experiences, where the glamour of the jobs and the connection of his horsemanship to traditional Papago values seem to generate lively and detailed episodes.

The list of jobs increases after Ted's mine employment, most of them of short duration or intermittent. Ted's narration about them is equally disjunctive and intermittent. Entries in the chronology attest to a decentering of Ted's work; it is diversified and irregular. It fits a pattern that Bernard Fontana terms "sporadic work" of a "week or two to earn enough money to serve whatever some immediate need might be." This, Fontana says, might include work for a Tucson nursery, yard work, temporary construction labor, or agricultural work on truck farms or in groves (1960: 135). Such sporadic work, Jack O. Waddell argues, accommodates chronic use of alcohol (1969: 116). Though Ted does not mention drunkenness in relation to the intermittent pattern of his work after he returns to San Xavier from Los Angeles, his residence part of that time in South Tucson, with its proximity to bars frequented by his friends, is probably a factor in his irregular work and also in his very generalized and brief narrations of episodes in the pecan orchards, hoeing cotton, and picking fruits and vegetables.

233

What is clear in the work episodes Ted narrates about his employment after his years in the mines is that there is little in those experiences to inspire vivid memories and, as a consequence, little to distinguish his off-and-on jobs as compelling narrative. "Just like anything else," is a phrase he uses repeatedly in talking about his agricultural work. The following recollection illustrates the lack of energy in Ted's narration about field jobs:

> After the war sometimes I used to go with cotton choppers, they call it. Lot of people. They got buses, crews. They go from field to different field, you know, like Marana or 'way down there. That's how I know all these farms around here. But that's for anybody if they want to. When they plant, it just goes all the way, and when they grow up they just come in together—too thick. So it's got to be thinned, so they grow faster. Just like corn—same thing. But now they got a machine, machine that plants it. They got it so that it puts 'em just exactly where they're supposed to be. They didn't have it at the time. So you got to do that and—same time you cut the weeds. There's a lot of talking, lot of drinking, and a lot of all that. Ladies and all [*nods*]. Anybody—whites, Mexicans, all of them, colored, Yaquis, girls, ladies, old ladies—hoe. There's nothing to it, but it's tiresome. It's better when there's a lot of weeds. You go slower.
>
> Well, everybody knows that if they want to work the hiring boss tell 'em where to meet the bus. Lot of buses, and you get on the—if you want to. Some guys don't like one of the bosses, well they don't go.
>
> You know, you get paid right there, too, right in the fields. That's how they like it. They got money all the time, right in their pockets. They pay by the hour. . . . Each day. That's why everybody wants to go, because you need cash. (edited tape 8: 1–2)

The work Ted describes is expedient, and the narrative focuses on the motive for work rather than, as in the mining narratives, on the work itself. Ted has little enthusiasm for it; going slower is more desirable that working hard. No skill is required; anybody can do it, unlike the skilled work of the mines. The same is true for his discussion of work as a mason's helper:

> When we're building that block house along in town, east, you know, I learned a lot of that. Some of them they're just crooked. These guys that come around, they want to work. "Well, can you lay block, what?" They'll tell 'em, "Oh, sure, I can do it." Well, if you can they give you a try. I was a helper — hod carrier — bricks, me and another guy. I seen some of these guys come around; they claim they can do it. That old man taught me that fireplace work. He's a funny old man. He's good at everything. (edited tape 10: 9)

That's all Ted has to say about five years of off-and-on work in construction. His temporary jobs do not inspire him to create narrative episodes. Descriptions are generic; the jobs are just items on a list of work that gives him no status and adds nothing to his sense of his own subjectivity. Only when a job is particularly difficult does he engage in detailed narrative, as in the following description of moving cactus for a plant nursery:

> You got to get 'em off the desert, mountains, like saguaro mostly. They like saguaro. Desert, you know. You've got to go to the desert, and you've got to have a permit for the ranch or wherever you're picking. Like ocotillos, all that — everything's under the state law, and you each got to have a license. Then it's got to have tags. You've got to have a tag on 'em, or else they stop you, take it away from you, and they fine you. This fellow has everything, license and everything, from the state, so he can go as far as 'way down there, this side of Benson, big ranch way out in the mountains. We get all that ocotillo, everything, different sizes.
>
> It's those chollas that stick. Get 'em by the root. You got gloves, but still sometimes they stick through that, too. You got to grab

it by where you don't get very many, by the roots and things, and they're heavy like saguaros, them big barrels. If they're certain size that you can lift 'em by yourself, it's better to lift 'em by yourself—grab 'em by the root, just like a watermelon [*hugging motion*]. When they're bigger and heavy, then they get more money. Then it's a lot of trouble. You've got to use ropes—tie around, hang on—but they're heavy. Stand up by the truck, then two men'll get up there and haul it by the rope. And then you got to raise it up. There's a bump, too, and you've got to push 'em in [*wrestling motion*]. You can have ropes and all, clippers. You've got to clean it out, set it up there. You just load 'em up. You've got to know how much to dig. Different plants got certain depth. Lot of work. Lot of weight. I hate the saguaros. But you know the people—like they move to town, like easterners—go for saguaro like bait, and it costs a lot of money, too. Sell 'em a lot. Then we got to haul 'em in. Yucca. They grow deep. They've got a root like a cone, like an ice cream cone. It's got to go deep. Sometimes you have a hard time digging. Plants like cholla, saguaros, you know, the little saguaros, doesn't go deep. Thorns, but you get used to it. There's a lot of them people that we're doing the job for, they're surprised. They don't want to touch them. All right, we're there [*nods*], and we don't care nothing about these. Grab it here [*hugging, wrestling motion*] and just haul it out before the man or the lady of the house, they know somebody's there. Then this man or the lady come out—"Oh, what happened to that? Where's that?" "Oh, it's in the truck." And they'd be surprised, the way—"Oh, I thought it would take you hours and hours to get that many in the truck." "Oh, no, of course not. No, we're experts" [*nods*]. (edited tape 5: 18–19)

Other than his movie stories, this description of harvesting cactus is the only post-mining job narration that exhibits the energy, pace, specificity, and dramatization of a work event. What distinguishes this episode from his brief, flat reports of work in the fields or construction is that, like his mining and movie jobs, this one requires skill and courage; it's difficult, demanding, and dangerous. It marks him as a competent, achieving member of a select group of workers. Aside from this lively, visually explicit episode, the reports of his sporadic work in quick-cash producing jobs, if it is reported at all, is simply that, reportage in the barest terms. This description of loading cacti is the last vividly narrated work episode in the chronological sequence of Ted's life story. Work events that follow this episode are barely mentioned or meagerly narrated. During the last interview, Ted speculates on the work he might yet do. His tone is wistful:

> There's always a lot of things I can do. I won't be idling around. Maybe by this time, I'll be planting that chili, watermelon, cantaloupes, corn — a lot of it, which I done last year. I made it so good on that pumpkins. Yeah, everybody wanted them. And they tell me when I sell — when I sold the pumpkins to them old ladies, you know, and all that — "Oh, they were good." 'Course, they're sweet, you know, by itself. Once you slice 'em and put 'em in the oven, they're sweet, good. Just as yellow as anything [*raises hands from lap*]. That old lady I was talking about — she bought a whole bunch. I gave her some and I told her that's the last bunch of 'em. One lady'd say, "Well, next time you plant plenty of 'em so we can buy." I told 'em, "Well, it takes too much work. I'm too lazy" [*grins*]. "Well, go ahead, they're sweet." And here I am. I could have done it, but I — ah, the things I could do [*sighs*]. (edited tape 12: 9)

At this point in Ted's life, work and the idea of himself as a man who works, who has skills for accomplishing tasks and acquitting himself well among his peers both within and outside Papago culture, is threatened. Given his physical condition, the future is uncertain. Nostalgia for the past, implied here in his regret that his accident has prevented him from planting crops much desired by members of his community, has been a consistent trope throughout his narrative, though perhaps it is most poignantly expressed here at the end of our formal interviews together. Ted's comparisons of past and present in his narrative constitute a structural device that again points to Ted's inclination to narrate in layers rather than in sequence. Among Ted's earliest expressions of nostalgia for the past are his descriptions of the Papagueria of his childhood contrasted unfavorably to the present state of the land. Throughout his narrative there is a whole catalog of contrasts between past and present — farming and ranching better in the old days, Nogales and Magdalena better before the tourists, the land better before the whites came, water more abundant before Anglo corporate farming, traditional foods better than the contemporary diet, community cooperation better in the past than now, etc. At one point he says,

> We had a lot of peaches. The main roads weren't there where they are now. The agency wasn't like it is now. Lots of houses — trees. There's a lot of changes. It's not like it used to be. A lot of farming going on then. They lived up on the farms 'way up to the hills, or mountains. Everybody moved, or gone or whatever. And the people that is related to them, they're not living there any more; they're living out here by the church. Used to be scattered all along there. (edited tape 8: 10–11)

Ted laments the fact that water is scarce and the community is indifferent: "The wells aren't deep enough. And the government came and they tried to dig some wells but they never did get water. And another thing, they never help each other out like the olden people used to. They run out of water, well, they'd go and help 'em, or they'd come around. We made big wells, by hand" (edited tape 8: 11). Like his associative system of telling his life episodes, the past/present trope creates a layered structure. Ted structures not only associations of then and now but a comprehensive system of judgments, an overt expression of values that permeates his narrative. He is not sentimental about the past. He simply posits its superiority to the present. Ted's nostalgia, except in the last statement quoted above, is only secondarily regretful; it is primarily seriously informative. He wants his audience to understand the complexity of change and how his personal experiences relate to the changes his father predicted and prepared Ted to meet. The narrative utility of Ted's contrast between past and present is primarily as a structural element as powerful in developing Ted's life story as his development of his subjectivity as a working man. The two are inextricable; change in Papago culture precipitates Ted's experience of biculturalism. Given his antipathy toward chronological structure, Ted really narrates only two time periods—past and present. Time is of interest to him only in so much as it accommodates his concern with evaluation of the past in terms of a present that offers little promise of pursuing the thematic identifier of his subjectivity—work.

Geography actually dominates over sequence in Ted's narrative. Places, not dates or even the order of episodes, provide the other structural element that operates throughout Ted's oral telling of his life. Place parallels both his concern for the past and his development of his theme of work. Like the associative design of the other two dominant structural systems in his narrative, place is a centering and unifying mechanism. San Xavier is the center place, the point of departure and the point of return, the point of contrast with the non-Papago world. Woven together, place, the value of the past, and the importance of work glue the episodic narrative of Ted's life into an accessible life story. Cultural context and chronological data, while they are helpful in comprehending some of the more obscure or undetailed episodes in Ted's life story, are not part of Ted's narrative design. He tells his life according to his own concept of narrative priorities and dynamics and leaves it up to us to connect his thematic and spatial associations into a comprehensible story. He demands that we participate in and understand his life on his terms, not ours. By resisting—deliberately or not—the conventions of Euro-American biographical narrative, Ted draws us into a mode of narration that is discomforting but, attended to carefully, is ultimately more complex and revealing of Ted's subjectivity than a conventional representation of his life, because his narrative structure exposes not only the experiences of his life but the process of his narrative.

8

THE POETICS AND POLITICS OF

COLLABORATIVE PERSONAL

NARRATIVE

Every field project has an afterlife. *Telling a Good One* has had an exceptionally long prepublication afterlife, some of which has been alluded to in the preceding chapters.[1] But if Native American collaborative personal narrative is to be taken seriously as a process, not simply a vehicle for "amplifying ethnographic questions, examining ethnological questions or providing insight into personality formation" (Blackman 1992b: 3), the afterlife of the collaboration requires thorough and intensive scrutiny. Like all other increments and aspects of the collaboration, the post-field history of the Rios-Sands project offers insight into the text of the personal narrative that is otherwise inaccessible. As a metatext of the collaborative narrative itself, the afterlife of *Telling a Good One* falls into two distinct categories. Some of the afterlife has been personal—a relationship between Ted and me that lasted beyond the informal verification interviews that extended into 1975. Most of the afterlife of this project, however, has been a struggle with the ethical, political, and theoretical issues that have both facilitated and impeded the completion of the project. These aspects of the post-field part of the project have become increasingly complex as it has neared publication. Perhaps, then, it is best to begin with the personal, the sequence of events in the face-to-face relationship Ted and I continued after the twelfth formal interview was completed, and then to take up the more complex elements of the political and ethical aspects of the project.

When Ted and I finished our formal interviews in June of 1974, he expressed concern about what the future would bring. He was eager to be back home at San Xavier and planting crops but worried that he might not be up to the work that he liked and needed to do in order to identify himself as an active member of his community. Nostalgic for the past and anxious about his future, the tone of the last formal interview is ambivalent and tentative. The aftermath of his accident was uncertainty. The flow of his life, erratic as it was after World War II, had been seriously interrupted. The body that had served him so well in all his work was healing, but whether there would be long-term disabling effects, he was unsure.

When we next met in September of 1974 at his home at San Xavier, Ted was more confident and more content. And he seemed vigorous. Our follow-up interviews concentrated on verification and variants, not on his present activities, so I don't know how much work he was able to do as time progressed into 1975. I do remember, however, that in the November of that year, he cut a cord of mesquite firewood for me by hand, hardly a task an infirm man could accomplish.

We stopped all follow-up taping in late fall of 1975. There was no reason to retrace his life over and over, yet Ted seemed willing to go on indefinitely, even though the grant money had all been paid to him by May. Without tape recorder or notepad, I continued to visit Ted sporadically throughout the rest of my graduate studies. When I moved to Phoenix in 1977, I visited him occasionally on trips to Tucson. In 1978 or '79—memory fails me here—he called me from a convalescent and retirement center on the Gila River Reservation near St. John's just southwest of Phoenix, and I went to visit him there several times. He never told me exactly why he was there, and he dearly wanted to go home to San Xavier, which he did after a few months. I saw Ted only one time after that, and we visited only briefly. He was thinner than ever, frail and distracted. I don't remember what we talked about, and I didn't realize at the time that that would be our last contact. There was no more closure to our relationship than there has been to this project.

The afterlife of the project for Ted was relatively minimal — repeating narrative episodes, discussing dates and data for verification, guiding me around to sites of episodes in his life,[2] making the videotape and attending its showing, perhaps some recognition at San Xavier though I have no indication what form it might have taken, and undoubtedly Ted's anticipation of a book and his disappointment that it never was published. Whatever he thought and felt about the collaboration and its lack of tangible outcome is lost. Ted's experience of the post-interview period of collaboration and verification might more accurately be called aftermath — with its connotation of something disastrous — than afterlife. Through absolutely no fault of his own, he didn't reap much benefit for his effort to tell "a good one."

The afterlife of our collaboration for me has been much more enduring though perhaps no less distressing. It has also been much more instructive and rewarding for me than for Ted, because in that time Ted's narrative has drawn me toward new insights into the collaborative process and given me an opportunity to present his narrative publicly.

How to present Ted's life story to a reading audience has been, of course, the ethical, critical, and political crux of the project. Naively optimistic about publishing a conventional collaborative "autobiography" as I was at the beginning of the project, once I had the first twelve tapes completed I knew I didn't want to edit them into a continuous narrative. I didn't know how, and at some level I think I recognized that to put Ted's narrative episodes in sequential order was a violation of his way of telling his life. But the editorial and ethical questions that have dogged my later work on the project were subsurface at this point. I was lazy too. It's a lot of work to edit and sequence episodes. Just listening to the tapes over and over disabused me of any idea that it would be a quick or simple process. I found it easier to abandon the project than wade into the problems it presented. Even when the tapes were fully transcribed, the job seemed overwhelming. In 1984, what I really wanted was for some press to publish the transcripts with me supplying a spiffy introduction. Fat chance. Even now that is a radical idea, though it remains — at least in theory — appealing to me. Not just because I'm lazy, though I still am, and not because I think unedited transcripts are transparent representations of the field events. They aren't. However I do think that uninterrupted, unedited transcripts, reproduced in print and judiciously contextualized, might offer the least colonized and compromised insight into some, and I emphasize *some*, life stories and life-story processes. But not Ted's. Given the poor quality of our interviews, expecting a reading of the full transcripts would be naive. Furthermore, the overall impression they would leave would be a disservice to Ted's narrative skill and style. Wouldn't happen anyhow. The cost and iffy marketability of such a form of publication dictate otherwise. Publishing houses, whether commercial or academic, almost never take the risk such a presentation entails. The "economy of representation," to borrow Ruth Behar's term (1995: 155), makes full reproduction of oral tellings, even concise and sequential ones, extremely rare.

One of the very few is Colville narrator Peter J. Seymour's *The Golden Woman,* translated by Anthony Mattina and Madeline de Sautel and edited by Mattina (1985). This is a traditional oral story reproduced verbatim in print except for what the editor explains is the excising of repetition when the narrator gets "caught in the 'round' " when "the rooster starts telling the story over" (1985: 69). Here Mattina skips the sequence of repetitions and goes directly to the conclusion, so even this volume bows to the "economy of representation" required for publication.[3] The volume also contains contextualizing introductory chapters and a framing glossary. A continuous translation precedes the interlinear text. An introductory chapter establishes Seymour's authority as a storyteller, and a chapter following the continuous translation analyzes the tale, but 225 pages of the 355-page volume are transcription. While the volume is unusual and valuable for its full presentation, it is also limited in that it does not describe in detail the circumstances of the performance of the tale. Whatever its merits and limitations, the risk its publisher took is to be admired but unfortunately was not financially rewarding, confirming, at least for that press, that unconventional presentation of Native American narrative is not a good investment for a publisher.

It's also unrealistic to recommend publication of oral transcripts of collaborative personal narrative based on the viability of traditional-tale transcript publication. Traditional stories are told in community settings in a determined sequence. Framing analyses, therefore, can prepare the reader and interpret the text without requiring internal structuring or management of the presentation. Personal narrative presents a much less tidy body of speech. The dialogic nature of collaborative personal narrative "brings the joint character of this venture to the forefront" (Burns 1995: 77) and begs for interpretation of the dual influences of the participants on the text. Furthermore, analysis of personal narrative also requires more than the folkloric approach Mattina uses—tale type, repetition, formulas, etc.—if the concept of personhood central to collaborative biography is to be adequately interpreted. In Native American personal narrative the teller and the tale are one, performer and performed are inseparable to a degree that does not exist in oral storytelling. And the personal narrator creates his or her story in a way that the performer of traditional stories does not.[4] Framing analyses also "often speak past, rather than to, the native narrative," because they are actually designed to establish the non-Native collaborator's authority on the culture being depicted, not to reveal that the narrative is a version of the self constructed for presentation to the interviewer (Behar 1995: 151).[5]

The politics of publication mitigate against extensive use of "raw" text. Presses decide what to publish and in what form on predictions of reader interest. Economic considerations and a history of publishing and successfully marketing conventional Native American life stories have made experimental presentations, especially such lengthy interview transcript presentations, too risky for presses always under pressure to show a profit.[6] Publishing house editorial boards presume that audiences accustomed to concisely introduced and conventionally structured and edited personal narratives will not invest in a volume that requires readers to work through nonsequential, repetitive, loosely narrated text. Readers may want to participate in Native American experience through personal narrative, but presses believe that their readers don't want to work too hard at it.[7] They are probably right. Readers expect non-Native collaborators to do the structuring, editing, and interpreting for them. They want the intimate experience of personal narrative without the work of putting it together in an accessible form. The process, including the afterlife, and also the shaping influence of tribal ways of narrating in associative rather than linear progression, is of interest only to a very few who focus academic careers on the critical analysis of Native American personal narratives.

The same circumstances that prevent and will probably continue to prevent publication of extensive unedited and unstructured textual representations of collaborative dialogue also, until very recently, have made it very difficult to find publication outlets for collaborative narratives that incorporate extensive analysis of the process of collecting, structuring, and editing Native American life stories. The problem is two-pronged. As Sandra Dolby Stahl states, it is one of either "overloading or underloading the text" (1989: 30). Neither unanalyzed nor intensively analyzed approaches accommodate most projected readers. The latter, intensive analysis of process and interpretation of narrative, also narrows the potential reading audience. Most readers, presses believe, will not tolerate much beyond an introduction to the narrative that sets up the life story with a brief cultural context.[8] A few presses, especially those with a history of critical series on Native American literatures and cultures, have and continue to publish Native American life stories that incorporate substantial interpretive material.[9] *During My Time* (1992) and *Life Lived Like a Story* (1990), discussed in a previous chapter, are good examples. *The Social Life of*

Stories (1998), by Julie Cruikshank, presents both oral traditions and personal narratives in a process framework.[10] But such publications are still rare, which tells us something about the fiscally conservative stance of presses and their power to force Native American life stories to conform to their concepts of marketable presentation. The rarity of such process-oriented publications also reveals something of the academic climate that firmly regulates how both ethnographic and literary presentations of life stories get inscribed.

The publication of the books *Orientalism* (1978), by Edward W. Said, and *Writing Culture: The Poetics and Politics of Ethnography* (1986), edited by James Clifford and George E. Marcus, exposed the power of conservative academic traditions on publication of scholarly research on Native cultures and the careers of those who pursue such work. Subsequent works, like *Culture and Imperialism* (1993) by Said, *The Dialogic Emergence of Culture* (1995), edited by Dennis Tedlock and Bruce Mannheim, and *Women Writing Culture* (1995), edited by Ruth Behar and Deborah A. Gordon, have expanded and reinforced the importance of examining the politics of academe on publication. The observations and arguments of these authors all apply to the inscription and publication of Native American collaborative personal narratives.

Until recently, it has been considered unconventional, especially for literature faculty, to undertake scholarship on Native American texts, even more so for both anthropology and literature faculty to devote attention to Native American personal narrative texts. The history of academic prejudice against such undertakings is a long one. Ruth Underhill's experience in publishing the Maria Chona narrative illustrates the problem. The original publication of the Chona narrative in the *American Anthropologist* in 1936 had a mixed reception. Praise from Clyde Kluckhohn (1945) for its literary quality effectively undermined it as valid social science. Interestingly, Underhill did not hold an academic position until very late in her professional life, and she never did publish the personal narrative of a Walpai man she collected shortly after her work with Chona, both of which she chalked up to academic prejudice against personal narrative in the 1930s (interview, November 3, 1981). Pressures to pursue the conventional have lessened in degree but changed little in form over the years. Still, Native American personal narrative scholarship did not achieve solid legitimacy until the 1960s, when diversity began to impact academic disciplines, ethnic studies programs sprang up, and *Black Elk Speaks* became a regular text on course syllabi. Even then scholarly study of Native American personal narratives was very marginal. They were seen as too anthropological in literary programs and too literary in anthropology departments, and as minor "genres" in both. Collecting and editing such texts also presented problems for faculty inclined to collaborate. Co-authoring was especially problematical for faculty facing tenure and promotion reviews where single authorship and mainstream forms of publication are the standard criteria. Subject matter and methodology were, until recently—and still are in some instances—questioned in the academy. Little encouragement was offered to most faculty who collected, researched, and wrote about Native American personal narratives until the late 1980s and the movement toward interdisciplinary studies that accompanied the questioning of canonicity and narrow definitions of methodology in particular fields. Lamenting the past is not very useful, but understanding the history of scholarship on Native American personal narrative is essential to comprehending the pressures toward conventional topics of study and to understanding why presentation and interpretation of these narratives has been largely published according to disciplinary conventions for other ethnography or literary topics.

A colleague of mine, who I would describe as a literary anthropologist, describes the writing about Native American narratives as "words about other peoples' words."[11] This definition applies to analysis and interpretation of Native American collaborative personal narrative. I like the simplicity of this way of talking about cross-cultural interpretation. That's what we do in both ethnography and literary criticism—

write about other peoples' words. It sounds innocent enough, but as James Clifford points out, "there is no politically innocent methodology for intercultural interpretation" (1997: 19). Any methodology we choose when we write about the Other's words selects, excludes, and emphasizes certain elements of narrative that serve the goals of the research and writing. Often the choices are as much politically expedient as intellectually determined. The politics of the academy and publishing reward the conventional and ignore or even punish the unconventional. As Keya Ganguly succinctly argues, "We have to recognize that, as scholars, our position in the academy is not innocent of motivation — our theories and intellectual productions are inserted into the historical nexus of power-knowledge" (1990: 75). Looking back at my history with the Rios narrative, it is very clear that academic and publishing policies have had an enormous impact on this project from my conception of it, in terms of the conventions of published Native American "autobiographies," to my professional concerns about achieving tenure and promotions.

In 1975, when I over-optimistically thought I could make editing Ted's narrative my dissertation project, I had strong support from my Ph.D. committee chair, but it was a fight to clear the project with the director of graduate studies and the committee members. The subject matter was well outside standard literary dissertation material, and editing was considered a secondary critical methodology. The project was accepted, but only reluctantly.[12] Then, when the opportunity to edit a written autobiography by a Yaqui poet, Refugio Savala, arose, I stopped the work on the Rios transcripts. The English department was also less than enthusiastic about the Savala project until it was accepted for publication some months before my oral defense and was also instrumental in landing me my first faculty position. This personal history is not pointed toward making a case for my dauntless determination to champion Native American personal narrative as a topic for scholarship. Most of what happened with both the Rios and Savala projects amounted to happenstance and considerable good luck. The point is that the academy did and still has considerable influence on both the topic and methodology of scholarly studies, and Native American texts, especially texts that fall somewhere between disciplines, still generate suspicion, collaborative field projects especially so.

I write now from the privileged position of the tenured full professor nearing the end of my academic career. I have enjoyed the academic benefits of tenure, advancement in rank and pay raises that come from research-based teaching and publishing, much of which is based on activity, while not overtly exploitive, accrued from access to Native American narratives.[13] I can afford to experiment. I can afford to talk about failure. I have a publication track record that influences potential publishers. Most of it—except some journal articles on which much less rides—is of a conventional nature. I also have the luxury of writing in an experimental period for both anthropology and literature, "responding to world and intellectual conditions quite different" from those "more consolidated research conventions" of twenty-five years ago (Marcus and Fischer 1986: 42–43). Breaking form at this late date signals no genuine daring on my part. Ted was much more daring from the start than I ever thought of being when he narrated his life in a form and style resistant to the conventional autobiography structure I anticipated and tried to elicit.

Ted's influence on the afterlife of this project has been to determine the poetics of its presentation by how he told his life. His perception and articulation of his life resisted conventional forms and eventually forced me to recognize the integrity of his way of telling.[14] How he narrated has in large measure determined how I have presented that narration. This volume has everything to do with how Ted's narrative shapes not only my presentation of his life story but my interpretation of it. Ted, by telling his life the way he wanted it told, by giving language to his concept of personhood in a recursive, Papago way despite my attempt to force it into conventional autobiographical form, demanded—during and long after the field encounter—that he share at least equally in the authority of his life story not only at the level of content but in terms of directing its interpretation. Being belatedly open to direction from Ted's narrative is surely indebted to the challenges the scholars cited above and others have made to academic and publication conventions. In 1984, Ted's narrative did not direct me as it has in 1998. I was certainly too immature in 1974 and even a decade later to recognize the falsity of my authority to manipulate his text into a composite life story modeled on Western autobiography. The long afterlife of this project has given me the opportunity to reevaluate and to benefit from the aging and maturing process. What seemed significant when I began the project gave way eventually to what Ted narrated into significance. Because our partnership on the project was so limited, and my presumptions about my ability to present and interpret his life story so naive that they precluded eliciting his concepts of life story or his interpretation of his life, my confidence in the appropriateness and validity of the preceding chapters is shaky. Might my interpretation of his narrative be ill-conceived?[15] Very possibly. Might it change in the future? Might there be other ways to present and interpret Ted Rios's life story that would be more effective, more valid, less colonizing? Certainly. What can be learned from narrative differs over time, and "the fixedness of a text is as illusory as the fixedness of an interpretation; neither is final, neither is authorial" (Grigely 1995: 108).[16] There is no final word.[17] Life story "never really reaches a final stasis that can be definitively arbitrated (Watson and Watson-Franke 1985: 45).[18] Louis A. Renza defines experience-based discourse as "endless prelude . . . a purely fragmentary, incomplete literary project, unable to be more than an arbitrary document" (1977: 22). I agree. What seemed to me to be ethical at the time Ted and I worked together seems far less so now. Even the current, more tribally sensitive ethics advocated today seem inadequate,[19] since ethics as we commonly understand them in the academy are academically, not tribally, constructed and therefore still questionable.[20] Even without the overwhelming question of ethical validity, what seems methodologically sound and insightful may appear in the future, and even now, to be inadequate or wrongheaded.[21]

Part of the politics of collecting and interpreting Native American personal narrative that is affected by the academy but is also a very personal issue is the question of the ethics of publishing Native American life stories at all. This is ultimately the most difficult issue that those who work in this area of scholarship must confront and attempt to resolve appropriately. David Moore discusses two elements of work with Native American texts that are relevant to the Rios-Sands project in terms of the abandonment of the project and eventual decision to complete and publish it. They are what he calls "untranslatable difference" and "cultural property" (1997: 3, 10). The former, the difficulty of communicating life experiences across cultural barriers, I've addressed throughout this volume but wish to take up again in regard to how publication of Native American life stories relates to and affects community narrative expression. The latter is directly connected to the colonialism in which " 'free exchange' of knowledge frequently flows in a mercantile direction at the expense of the colonized" (Moore 1997: 3).[22] I've addressed this briefly in an early chapter of this volume, but discussion of the afterlife of the Rios-Sands project demands that I return to it again and tie it into institutional politics and the conventions of publication in this field. Academic institutions reward publication monetarily in the form of faculty promotions, sabbaticals, and pay increases; presses pay publication royalties. The narrators of Native American personal narratives never share in the academic rewards except perhaps through small grant-generated payments during the collection process, as Ted did. Royalties for academic publications are generally modest, so even when narrators share in the profits of book sales, the financial reward is small. In many cases, royalties are not split, let alone turned completely over to the tribal narrator, so the commodification of Native American personal narratives benefits narrators not at all. Moreover, many presses don't support splitting royalties or assigning them to other than the collector-editor; the financial arrangements are thrown back to that individual to be sorted out. Native American communities from which the narrators come almost never share in royalties or other material benefits from the collaboration.[23] Part of the afterlife of the Rios-Sands collaboration has been working out a way to ethically set up distribution of potential royalty payments. Since Ted is deceased, I anticipated that the royalty payments would go to his family, but his son adamantly refused to allow this; as an alternative, all royalties will go to a tribal scholarship in Ted's name.[24] Still, the institutional processes of reward greatly favor the non-Native partner in the collaboration and in the institutions themselves. Cultural property profits the owner little and, equally importantly, usually slips out of the narrator's control once the interviews are completed.[25] The "free exchange," while it may be made freely by the Native American collaborator, is indeed largely one way and largely at the expense of the narrator. There are potential compensations — co-authorship and any recognition it may bring, preservation of one's life story, modest financial rewards — but whether they are enough to create a balanced exchange is very much open to question.

The issue of "untranslatable difference," while less material is no less ethically challenging. Elizabeth Cook-Lynn is adamantly critical of the publication of Native American personal narratives, not only because she sees them as stolen intellectual property but because they undermine the integrity of Native American expression and, she believes, mislead both non-Natives and Natives about Native American identity. She writes, "Though I've referred to the 'informant-based' Indian stories as 'life-story' works, I would like to suggest that they are offshoots of biography, a traditional art form in European literature. Ethnographic biography is not an Indian story at all and does not have significant ties to the interesting bodies of Native literary canons produced culturally and historically" (1998: 121). I agree with her. Indian life stories are cross-cultural collaborative biographies, and, as she says, what they "have to say about what it means to be an American Indian in non-tribal America is not the essential function of art

253

and literature in Native societies" (1998: 124). Native American personal narratives are, in that sense, exploitive. They offer primarily non-Native readers a version of Native American personhood that may lead to a false sense of knowing Indianness. She argues for the view that the "textual model of culture embodies a profound desire to represent other cultures within Western epistemologies" (Worthen 1998: 1098). Cook-Lynn's claim that the difference between Indians and the dominant culture is untranslatable through the medium of collaborative biography is disturbing. She directly challenges the most cited argument for the publication of Native American life stories—the opportunity of non-Native American readers to enter intimately into and understand the life of the Other. Further, she points out that Native American personal narratives support institutions that have histories of exploiting Native Americans (1998: 119-20). This, plus the knowledge that these narratives do not add to or support community-based forms of cultural expression, adds to the ethical dilemma attached to this form of inscription.

None of these issues were on my mind or even in my consciousness when I began working with Ted. Had they been, I doubt that I would have ever met him. But at the time we began our work together, collecting a life story from a Native American individual was not an ethically charged issue in the academy. The assumption was that adding to the knowledge of the Other was sufficient rationale for appropriating and inscribing Native American life stories. It never occurred to me that I was participating in a colonial enterprise when I went into the field. The ethics of respect and care in representation seemed enough at the time. I actually thought I would be performing a service by publishing Ted's narrative; I'd be making public an "authentic" Indian life to counter the stereotypes of popular-culture depictions. I still believe that to be one of the values of Native American personal narrative, but it hardly provides blanket coverage for appropriation of an individual's and a culture's property. At the time, the agreement Ted and I signed seemed all that was necessary to ensure fair and equal treatment in a partnership. I thought the commodification—a term not in currency at the time—of his life was neutralized by split royalties, and I guess I thought that by signing the contract letter Ted's owner-ship of his life story was transferred to me as though the agreement were a deed. As though he could cede ownership of his life story and I could take possession of it. What our agreement did allow me to hold in my possession was the tape recordings, what Barre Toelken calls "sound fossils; important artifacts to be sure but not to be confused with the culture itself" (1998: 386). Tapes and transcripts, at the time, did not seem cultural property, nor did Ted's personal story. They both seemed his, given voluntarily into my safe-keeping for mutu-ally agreed upon use. As for cultural appropriation, I never gave it a thought. It never occurred to me to question what benefits might come to the community, or what negative impact even my presence might have, let alone the ramifications of publication of the "autobiography." I was thinking in terms of how Ted's story would reach a non–Tohono O'odham audience and was told at the time that my commitment to splitting royalties and to co-authorship was unnecessary since I was the one doing the greater share of the work.

The ethical implications of the project, except as described above, didn't set in until I went back to the narrative in 1984. By then I was a little bit more savvy about both academic and tribal politics and engaged with the network of scholars working in the field of Native American literatures discussing ethics in conference forums and journal dialogues. But the full impact of Native American text as intellectual and cultural property really didn't hit me even then; I was too caught up in questions of editing and structuring method-ology and running out of sabbatical time to meditate on ethics be-yond how they affected my immediate editorial decisions. Only as I taught courses, especially graduate courses and worked with doc-toral students in both literature and anthropology, did the complexity of the ethics of collecting, editing, and publishing Native American texts become an issue for almost daily consideration. The weight of the responsibility of training future scholars and guiding field projects made the ethics of research and writing on Native American narratives a predominant concern of my career. In fact, it paralyzed me. I stopped scholarly research and writing and professional activity in Native American studies altogether for six years.[26]

But Ted and his voice and his story wouldn't go away. So I picked up the transcripts again in 1996 — reluctantly — when it came time to propose a sabbatical project. The debt I owed Ted was still there accruing interest. This would be my last sabbatical before retirement. My last chance to find a way to bring our work together to fruition. My last chance to repay in some measure the numerous debts I owed Ted — an article and videotape that helped me get tenure for starters, but also hours of pleasure, training in fieldwork, introduction of my children to Native American individuals and culture, a chance to stretch myself intellectually and test myself ethically. So here I am, far less sure than I was in 1974 that I am doing the right thing, though I'd be dishonest not to admit that I have reasons for still believing in the value of publication of Native American collaborative biography.

Belief in the validity of a project is necessary, or it is never begun (Stahl 1989: 32). My belief in the validity of the Rios-Sands project has evolved over the years into a commitment to a specific way of presenting and interpreting Ted's life story. My belief in the validity of the approach to Ted's narrative that I have taken in this volume and in the value of Native American collaborative biography has been essential to completion of this project. That belief has wavered and disappeared at time, and as the discussion above reveals, contains a large measure of ambivalence. But in the end, I have placed my trust in Ted's life story as substantively and stylistically too good to bury in a file drawer because of my epistemological angst. My promise and debt to Ted have forced me back on my original good intentions and on my acquired intellectual and personal skills to produce a book that simultaneously presents and interprets Ted's narrative and argues for a processual approach to Native American personal narrative. They have led me to produce what I hope is a record of a flawed but ultimately productive relationship that subverts some of the procedures and the structures of the academy and its established "system of authorization" (Worthen 1998: 1099). By foregrounding Ted's actual performance of his narrative, I hope to in some measure help legitimize the value of oral personal narration and point out the "textual bias of Western civilization" (Conquergood 1991: 190). My promise and debt to Ted have also prodded me to attempt to present Ted's story in the context of a multidimensional field of exchange, one which negotiates the binaries of cultural dialectic (Moore 1994: 10) that characterize so much inscription of alterity. Despite all these good intentions, to edit, interpret, and publish Ted's narrative is ethically questionable, but to bury it is unconscionable.[27]

In part, making public Ted's life story is the right course, because narratives of "personal experiences represent one of the most impressive displays of cultural breakthrough. Through them, individuals assert their connection with other people, the social base of even these original accounts of seemingly idiosyncratic experience" (Stahl 1989: 120). Personhood and the connection of the individual to a web of social and cultural systems are at the very core of life story. In Native American collaborative biography, the construction of self is the nexus of cross-cultural dialogue between narrator and audience. As Jay Clayton observes, "narrative creates authority" (1993: 45). Ted speaks — authors — himself into being across cultural boundaries. He defines himself as Other yet makes alterity accessible not only through the experiences of his life but by his way of articulating his memories. His narrative exposes "the ways in which cultures most radically differ from one another" (Marcus and Fischer 1986: 45). I think Ted's story points to exactly the "untranslatable difference" between cultures yet at the same time also reveals ways in which people share experience across cultures. Ted's "conceptions of personhood — the grounds of human capabilities and actions, ideas about the self, and the expression of emotions" (Marcus and Fischer 1986: 45) create a nexus of potential cross-cultural understanding in part because much of his experience was itself cross-cultural. He was conscious of and practiced in cross-cultural communication. In his narrative he selects and tells experiences comprehensible to a non–Tohono O'odham audience while at the same time sustaining a style of telling that is O'odham. Telling his life empowers him to legitimize not only his experiences, and by association similar experiences by his peers, but it allows him to legitimize a way of telling, a complex set of rhetorical norms that add up to a distinctive cultural style. His life story demonstrates an "ability to consolidate subterranean values, to preserve marginal traditions, and to confirm as subjects people who have long been denied that status" (Clayton 1993: 24). Ted's narrative style demands that we acknowledge and pay attention to difference. The complexity and irony of his narrative control both closes and opens distance. As David Moore argues, "if non-Native and Native readers cannot finally read Indian texts to 'know' the other, or even themselves, they can read to trace a path through the text to context, and hence to participation with textual and extratextual concerns of Indian communities" (1994: 19).

Native American personal narrative is interesting in that it defines not only the teller as Other but the audience as Other. Drawing on "counter memory," Native American life stories challenge the "so-called grand narrative of Western civilization and American culture, offering revisions of the past" (Bergland 1994a: 83) by means of insights which are specifically and personally located. At times the audience is a detached, inactive observer conscious of difference, yet at times the audience identifies with the protagonist enough to see and feel as he does. The unfolding personhood and personal relationships of the narrator are dynamic and invite dynamic response that penetrates, in some degree and however briefly, the boundaries constituted by Otherness.

Exposing the collaborative process of oral personal narrative breaks down the binary of difference by creating a dialogic across the barriers of alterity. In Native American collaborative biography, teller, collector, and audience all participate. John Dollard argued fifty years ago that "life history does not speak for itself; the subject is unable to give us the explanatory theoretical paragraphs making sense of the material. He may, on the contrary, and usually does, do the very best he can to disguise it" (1949: 33–34). Dollard seriously underestimates the capacity of a narrator to interpret life experience. Narrative is, we recognize now, an analytical mode, and narrators are unable to interpret their lives only insofar as we prevent them from doing so. Despite the biased attitude he reveals in his statement, Dollard does point toward an analysis of process in presentation of life story that has been advocated in more sophisticated ways in recent scholarship. For instance, Renato Rosaldo argues that in presentation of personal narrative that incorporates the collaborative process, "each viewpoint is arguably incomplete — a mix of insights and blindness, reach and limitation, impartiality and bias." The value of this incompleteness is that "taken together they achieve neither omniscience nor a unified master narrative but complex understanding of ever-changing, multifaceted social realities" (1989: 128). To the effect Rosaldo describes, I would add understanding of narrative strategies. A processual approach also leaves the audience in "a state of provocation" (Marcus and Fisher 1986: 66) rather than numbed by an authoritative text. In the discussion of collaborative process, the provisional and unstable nature of the cross-cultural encounter and the text it produces is available.

Finally, I have go back to the issue of commodity to argue that the collection of life story is not in the same league as appropriating material resources. When Ted told his life story to me, he both gave it and kept it. He had no less of it when I departed with the tapes. Now, his community, most of which would never have access to it without its being published, may put it to use if it chooses. In some measure this volume becomes a repository and resource for Tohono O'odhams as well as for scholars (Feinberg 1994: 22).[28] With publication, Ted's whole community becomes a potential audience for his narrative. Not a narrative told in the way he would have spoken it directly to them, not in their native language, and perhaps not interpreted in the way they would assign meaning to it, but nonetheless the story is accessible, a small part of the counter memory that contributes to the dynamic of cultural survival. That all sounds pretty pompous. I guess what I'm trying to say is that in the end, I hope this volume turns the project Ted and I started a quarter of a century ago into a two-way exchange. Ted's life story rose out of his community and his experiences within and in relationship to it. Now maybe it can go back—not to Ted himself, but to his community. That's the best afterlife I can imagine for Ted's story.

EPILOGUE

The final installment in the afterlife of the Rios-Sands project is one last episode of failure. As usual, my failure. In February of 1998, I went to Tucson for a week to make a number of short trips to places and institutions, which I anticipated could offer information that would answer some nagging questions I had about Ted's narrative and the facts about his life after I last saw him. The trip turned into a frustrating and largely useless field expedition. I was too late in my attempt to do the legwork I should have done during the original fieldwork. Records were missing, doors were closed, agencies were unwilling to open records, and I returned to Phoenix with little more than I had twenty-five years ago.

My first stop was to inquire whether copies of the photographs used with the publication of Ted's magic-egg story in *The South Corner of Time* could be used in this volume. I was informed that they no longer existed and that the printing plates were lost. Since no other still photos of Ted during our interviews existed either, this meant no photos of him telling his life could be included in the book.[1] At the University of Arizona I checked to see if the Southwest Folklore Center had, as I had been informed it did, the original, unedited videotape of Ted telling stories. They did, but in a format that works in no player currently in use.[2] I checked with the on-campus television station, where this disappointing information was confirmed. Carefully archived, the two reels of tape remain permanently inaccessible. At the university library I consulted some unpublished sources on Tohono O'odham culture that have proven useful in contextualizing Ted's experiences. From there I went to the Department of Anthropology to check records at what I thought was still the Bureau of Ethnology.

There I was told that the name had been changed and records dating back to the time I was interested in would be at the Arizona State Museum. So I walked across the campus mall to check whether the Rios family was included in a study of San Xavier that had been done in the 1950s. I was informed that all the records related to this archive were in deep storage while fireproofing was being installed. No telling when the shelves would be restored.[3]

Since it was nearby, I walked over to the Arizona Historical Museum library to check their records on Tohono O'odham history and to find out whether the tapes from the Peter Blaine Sr. life story were available. I checked files, archive boxes, and photograph collections without finding anything pertinent to Ted's narrative. My first break came in confirming that the Blaine tapes and a copy of the book manuscript were available for my use. I scheduled a return to listen to and read them for later in the week.

I began the next day at San Xavier del Bac. I parked by the school and took a long hard look at the house where Ted had lived and at the still-healthy tree under which we did our follow-up interviews. Then I went to the mission office to search the records to verify Rios family marriage, baptism, and funeral information. The staff was most helpful, but records were incomplete. What was available I've used in reconstructing Ted's family tree. The information I was most concerned about finding was when Ted had died. I was embarrassed that I didn't know, but there was no reason why the family should have informed me when he died since my relationship with him was not really a personal friendship and we had not been in contact since 1980. I'd heard he was no longer alive from several people, which was verified by the staff member at the Mission who had known him slightly, but no one I talked to knew the date. Both the staff person and I were puzzled by the lack of funeral information. She checked the records again. She found that Ted's ex-wife Ramona was also deceased, and his sister Lena, but no entry was there for Ted.[4] I left a message for Michael Rios, Ted's son who resides at San Xavier but has no telephone, that I would like to speak to him about his father.

My second stop was at the San Xavier District headquarters, where I hoped to check tribal rolls and records to verify Ted's family history. I was informed that I needed family permission to see the records. This came as no surprise, since I'm well aware that Native American tribes are far more reluctant now than they were twenty years ago to allow outsiders to use their records. Staff personnel were interested in the project, certainly not hostile to my intentions, but firm in their explanation of tribal policy. They suggested that I leave a message for Michael Rios with them since he was in the offices on a regular basis. I did. Then I walked over to the parish school where I hoped to find Ted's enrollment records and, if I were lucky, photographs of him. I wasn't lucky on either count. A school administrator informed me all records older than five years were held at the Tucson Catholic Diocesan offices. No luck there either. The archivist searched thoroughly but found nothing dated before the 1960s. I was more distressed over the general loss to tribal history than my own immediate loss, but the diocesan headquarters were definitely a dead end for any additional information on Ted's early school years. One more potential avenue closed.

I also wanted to check out Ted's employment with Phelps Dodge, so I took the next day to drive to Ajo to check mine records. Along the way I stopped at Sells to refresh my memory about the site of the tribal hospital. That cattle guard was still there. In Ajo, my bad luck held. At the office of the long-closed mine, I was informed that records of all former employees were in deep storage and not accessible to anyone but company staff and former employees and their families. It was a pleasant drive, and I explored the town and old mine site to refresh my sense of these places in relation to Ted's narrative, but I didn't come away with anything tangible.

The next day I returned to the tribal offices at San Xavier. No messages from Michael Rios. I asked for permission to search the cemetery for Ted's grave. Not without family consent.

I headed for the Pima County courthouse Records Division, where I was told no information on a death could be given out without permission of the family. Next stop, the library of the local newspaper, where I was informed that deaths before 1986 were not yet on a computer database, and I would need to have a year and a month for them to do a manual search.

Back to the Arizona Historical Museum library to check their collection of *The Papago Runner* for an obituary. No obituaries or death notices are carried in the newspaper. I photocopied some of the Blaine manuscript and went back to my hotel to read. That's when I received the call from Michael Rios that effectively ended my hope of updating research on Ted's life. At 2:05 P.M., February 19, 1998, I picked up the phone expecting a cordial conversation. When I told Ted's son why I had been trying to contact him, explained who I was, and reminded him that we had met in 1974, he informed me he did not want to be involved in the project in any way. However, he did give me permission for the royalties to go into a tribal scholarship fund. I had not expected his response, but he was clearly firm in his stance, so I gave him information on how to contact me if he changed his mind. There was nothing left to say. The conversation was over at 2:08 P.M. I was so rattled I forgot to ask him when Ted died.

I spent the next day at the historical museum library listening to the Blaine-Adams interview tapes, transcribing one by hand for comparison to the manuscript and the published book.

I came back to Phoenix slightly dazed. Never had I put in so much research time for so little recovery of information. I made one last try, through a roundabout network of friends and friends-of-friends, to crack the security at the Pima County records office — with no results. So here I am confessing what I least want anyone to know about this project. I don't even know when Ted died.

There are, of course, certain ironies in my lack of this final information about Ted's life. Ted never cared much about dates. He might actually find this mystery about his death date humorous. Maybe this is his last act of resistance. It's a timeworn cliché that the collector-editors of a Native American personal narrative say something nostalgic about the passing of the narrator. Ted's left me with nothing to say, so that's another convention he thwarts. Ted narrated the story of his life. That's what he leaves us with, a story that just goes on and on because there is no end. Writing the last two chapters of this volume have also made it clear that it is Ted's story, his voice, that animates this volume. It gets pretty dull when he's not present. That makes it all the clearer that this is Ted's story. It is his words that are memorable, that outlive even the teller.

The endurance of and lack of closure in Ted's narrative doesn't absolve me from finding out when he died. I will, sooner or later. But not knowing when he died, now that I've actually brought this project to a close by writing this volume, not only embarrasses me but, I have to admit, actually amuses the more cynical side of me a little. Begun so ineptly, there seems a measure of justice that it should end ineptly. To quote the sage observation of Marcus Aurelius, "What prevents a work from being completed becomes the work itself" (Lucy 1993: 9). Process and lack of closure, problems and false starts, elusive information and recursive narrative, questions without answers. All so much more intriguing than straightforward narrative and tidy resolution.

Still, if I had known in 1974 what I know now about how the collaboration between Ted Rios and I would work—and end—I'm sure I never would have initiated that meeting in the hospital room in Sells. If I had the opportunity to start it all over again, I wouldn't. But here it is a quarter century later, and I've done what I could to make as good a telling as I can make it. I'm relieved to have keep my commitment to Ted to make his narrative into a book. I'm regretful that I didn't do it sooner and better, and I'm hopeful that *Telling a Good One* will be instructive about the process of Native American collaborative biography.

APPENDIX

Editing Interview Transcripts into Narrative

The purpose of the following material is to provide a substantial demonstration of how the interview transcripts were originally edited. Questions were deleted, references to gestures inserted from field notes, and unclear pronouns replaced with nouns, usually from the preceding interview question. Dashes indicate hesitations, and ellipses indicate points where we overlapped or cut one another off or there is an especially long pause. Material that is unclear or not spoken fluently is either deleted or condensed.

The first section of this transcript has been reproduced photographically to allow readers to view the editing process through my hand-corrected pages. What follows is an electronically edited version of the sample transcript, which reproduces my revision marks typographically. In the electronically edited version, insertions are shown in square brackets, and deletions are shown with strikeout. Changes in capitalization have been marked with either double-underline, to indicate that a lowercase letter should be capitalized, or double-strikethrough, to indicate that an initial cap should be made lowercase. Italicized material in brackets is from fieldnotes I made during the interview.

This transcript taken from the sixth interview, May 23, 1974. The interview was conducted on a patio area of the hospital at Sells, Arizona, which accounts for traffic noise and inaudible words on the tape caused by wind on the microphone. Though the University of Arizona Department of Anthropology supplied me with a high quality reel-to-reel tape recorder for the interviews, the microphone, I discovered when I listened to this tape, was overly sensitive for outdoor recording. Not far from where we sat during our conversation, about a dozen cattle grazed idly. The cattle, with cactus thorns bristling from their muzzles, initiated Ted's taking up the topic of cactus harvesting.

267

Sample of the Pencil-edited Transcript

TR: You know this fruit—red ones, some are yellow—well, they grow in different varieties. It's a certain time. Not all the same—some grow a little bit early or some later—real red ones, dark and kind of yellow. They're sweet.

KS: And what kind of cactus is it?

TR: It's this—what you call it—prickly pear.

KS: Oh.

TR: You have—it grows off the ground in a bunch, I don't know, like well, it's—and on the bottom it's prickly, too. You know, there's a little thorn (inaudible). Every time you load it on the truck, *and you're* if somebody's sitting back in the back of the truck, when you start moving you've got to watch for it.

KS: They jump, huh?

TR: Yeah, they jump [flutters hands], *and* (inaudible) get it right in your eyes. Every time when we load it we have to *put it* way in the back, you know, the cactus, put something over it so it won't *move* (truck noise). It's just like when you're picking them. The ladies used to pick that fruit and the fruit *with* tongs made out of sticks. Well, they brush 'em off first.

KS: How do they do that?

TR: Oh, they got—they make their own brushes, like . . . anything. Brush 'em off, all of 'em, you know—the ones that there's fruit—for fruit, they just brush 'em off and then start plucking 'em (truck noise). Then they get 'em home, whatever they pick 'em (inaudible) *but* then you *they peel* 'em, peel 'em just like that.

KS: With a knife?

TR: No, your hands. It's easy to peel 'em. Why, they just—just like anything else—fruit. Get 'em *the skins* off, and get the—meat to come *s* off, you know, (inaudible), just like any other thing. Same

~~thing.~~ Then they cook it, ~~just like—~~make syrup out of it. But that syrup's too sweet. ~~I can't—~~

I couldn't eat it. It's got too much sugar in it.

KS: ~~Just natural sugar?~~

TR: Natural sugar. And then—~~'course, I hate 'em, too, but~~ it's got a lot of seeds inside, all stuck

~~in that—it's just covered.~~ You've got to eat only ~~the—~~what's good, leave the seeds alone.

They're sweet, too, but yellow, ~~(inaudible)—~~[They] get on your hands or your shirt ~~or—~~ if you're

not careful.

KS: ~~The juice, or the~~ . . .

TR: The juice. And you watch out for your clothes.

KS: ~~Did your mother get these when you were young, or~~ . . .

TR: ~~Yeah, the—~~ the old old old people, ~~you know,~~ they get 'em, ladies and all [nods]. Now

nobody bothers 'em ~~except when you just pluck 'em. Every time you go by one you see that~~

~~it's kind of brushed off, like—the way they do out there. But at a certain time of year, the~~

~~summer, I guess, you can see all them little—you know, the cattle, too.~~

KS: ~~They eat them?~~

TR: ~~They~~ [cattle] eat 'em—deer, anything [nods].

KS: ~~I'm surprised. I would think they would get the thorns in them.~~

TR: I don't think ~~they~~ [the thorns] bother 'em, because they eat—even ~~that ball~~ [the fruit] from the cholla—~~you know~~ [the ones]

~~they hand? It's~~ [that they] got the same kind, only ~~they're~~ smaller—and greener. ~~They~~ [The animals that] like ~~it,~~ too. That's

why you see some cattle ~~get~~ [with] thorns in their faces [points to cows with thorny muzzles],

~~because they eat that—especially when they're hanging down like this [cups right hand].~~

They'll be right around it, no matter if it's [has] any thorns. You watch it.

KS: ~~That's surprising.~~

TR: ~~'Course,~~ they're green, and they ~~just got~~ have a lot of water or salt or something in them. ~~They grow on it.~~

KS: ~~Are there other kinds of desert vegetation that you eat?~~

TR: ~~Yeah, I just got—~~ I was going to say, ~~this—this~~ there's a different kind, too—one ~~is~~ not so thorny. ~~It's kind of—not so much like the other ones.~~ It's just kind of bare. ~~Well, it's not bare,~~ but it's got thorns, but is more soft and ~~it's (inaudible)—~~it won't stick you so much. ~~And that little—see, what the little balls come out like that, too, like (inaudible)~~ and they fall when they drop everything—everything's gone except ~~that,~~ the fruit and you harvest that, too, every one of those little balls—~~harvest that, too,~~ and clean it up—clean 'em up, ~~like anything—cook it,~~ cook them, you know like anything else. When it's done, it's just like you're eating spinach—~~spinach,~~ ~~like—~~tastes like spinach.

KS: ~~Does it grow—is it a cactus?~~

TR: It's a cactus. ~~You can—I used to go out and—she's still living on (inaudible) Navajo lady—she likes it. You know, she lives by that hill where—the other side. Lot's of 'em grow there.~~

KS: ~~Whereabouts is this?~~

TR: ~~On the other side—~~It grows out at the mission—~~I mean~~ on the east side of the mission, by the freeway. There's a lot of 'em~~—same variety.~~ Then they go over there and gather it. ~~Every time I'd come to their house, sometimes they'd have some cooked, and I'd eat it. And~~ they ~~they've got in stores, you know, in bit~~ store them in big jars. ~~Well, I guess she's the only one that's really—you know, she's the big lady, and gets all she wants. And then people come like me—"I'd like to have some of—I'd like to buy some of 'em." And she sells it.~~

KS: ~~Does she store them raw, then?~~

TR: Yeah, just raw, ~~You know, it's just like any~~—like beans or any staple food. ~~It's just like that~~ because ~~it's dry,~~ they're dry. And then you ~~got to~~ cook 'em, like any staple. And then when ~~it's~~ they're cooked in water, ~~in there, well, it~~ they turns out soft, like spinach. Good eating [nods].

KS: ~~What color is it?~~

TR: ~~Oh, it's something like—been in the sun all day.~~ They've ~~It's~~ got no color at all. ~~It's just like a—like a~~ They're like a bare tree, ~~or—it's got no color, just like that tree over in there [points].~~ Just dry, like wood.

KS: ~~Did you ever go out and gather mesquite beans?~~

TR: Oh, yeah. ~~That's a good one—it's~~ Mesquite beans are another thing. Wish I could have some of that, too, right now. ~~It's better than anything I ever—used to—like a lot of—but the way they do it is—of course at the time, everything was better. Now they (inaudible)—oh, as big as those trees.~~ You'd see a whole lot of beans hanging. ~~Then you know when they're ripe—~~when they're real ripe and dry, that's when they're picked. ~~And you've got to taste 'em when~~ they're sweet—got to get the sweet ones. ~~And they're dry. Or so—pick 'em.~~ And you pick 'em dry and then grind 'em, grind 'em in ~~that—like a special grinder. It's like—you know them~~ a metate ~~rocks—the holes, like this dish—something to—or—and then made~~ into a powder, and soak it with water—let it stand. Let it stand for a while and then you ~~kind of~~ stir ~~it~~—all the juice, sweetness gets in there, just like—sweet as anything else, like soda pop, by its own self— nothing mixed.

KS: ~~How is it served?~~

TR: ~~Just like—just like anything, like—any liquid.~~

KS: ~~But it's cold when it's . . .~~

TR: ~~It's cold if you get it in the shade. You know, whatever you want.~~ On the ranch we used to have it—put in big—the beans baskets [makes circle with arms], you know, big round baskets. ~~Put 'em~~

~~in there and~~ then soak ~~it in the~~ them —~~not all of it, not~~—you know, just ~~enough~~ until, The water'll get

~~just like~~—kind of creamy like, ~~not creamy but it's liquid~~ the color of cream. Then drink it with

a cup. Sweet—just like when you get 'em off the tree. See, all the sweetness gets in there. ~~It~~

goes in the water just like—just like the cactus. ~~Same thing. And they do it. But I don't—I~~

~~never did know they could make anything out of it, and syrup (inaudible) far as I know.~~

~~They didn't used to. Used it for the drinks or whatever you want. Something like a~~

~~(inaudible) of soda pop. I liked it. At least I have a lot of it, you know—just gather it, stack~~

~~'em out in sacks or barrels. Every so often (inaudible) soaking.~~

KS: ~~This is your grandmother up on the ranch?~~

TR: Mm hmm. ~~Anybody could do it. Even I could do it right now, if I got a chance to, but~~ Now I'm

too lazy—too lazy to gather it.

KS: ~~What time of year were they ready?~~

TR: ~~When—you know, when they (laundry cart noise).~~ I think it's around autumn, ~~or something,~~

~~you know. When~~ they get ~~so~~ ripe, ~~of course, if it's green, you can pick 'em too, but they're~~

~~green, until~~ they get so ~~that it's~~ dry. They fall on the ground and it's easier—easier to pick

them, ~~you know, instead of—'cause~~ the women go down and they rake ~~it~~ them up ~~at least that's~~

~~the way they do it.~~

KS: ~~Did you go out and get them for your grandmother?~~

TR: ~~No, I was too small. I was—I don't care much about it. Just so I get some of 'em. No, they~~

~~never bother—they know I don't—it's not—the ladies were not like as they are now, so they~~

~~say.~~ Now the ladies are so lazy. They want to be some place in the shade. Olden times, you

never know where the old ladies going to go. They go out there and they get ~~those~~ yucca,

~~you know~~—yucca, ~~we call it~~ for baskets. They get the good ones—green ones or those ripe one[s], white. Gather them—dry 'em up.

KS: ~~The leaves?~~

TR: The leaves. ~~And~~ they got little threads in the sides, ~~you know. They've~~ [so the women] got to clean ~~it~~ [them], clean [them] ~~it~~ very good, and dry them out in the sun. That's when they get real white. And then they use that for baskets. Or if they want green ones, they can always get ~~—you know,~~ the green stalks, cut 'em. But they usually get them long ones, white ones, ~~you know~~—cut in two.

KS: ~~Did your mother make baskets?~~

TR: ~~Oh, yeah.~~ Everybody ~~did,~~ [made baskets] all the old ladies did. Now you never see anybody [lifts hands, palms up], except I['ve] seen some old ones. Some of these ladies now, girls, they know how to make 'em, but they don't want to do it. They're too lazy to gather ~~them~~ [yucca]. ~~They're too lazy to now,~~ they'd rather sit there and turn on the TV. Or be down in ~~the~~ bar or some place. It's not like it used to be.

Electronically Edited Transcript

[¶] ~~TR:~~ You know this fruit—red ones, some are yellow—well, they grow in different varieties. It's a certain time. Not all the same— some grow a little bit early or some later—real red ones, dark and kind of yellow. They're sweet.

~~KS: And what kind of cactus is it?~~

~~TR:~~ It's ~~this~~—what you call ~~it~~—prickly pear.

~~KS: Oh.~~

~~TR: You have~~—it grows off the ground in a bunch[,] ~~I don't know, like well, it's~~—and on the bottom it's prickly, too. ~~You know,~~ there's a little thorn ~~(inaudible)~~. Every time you load it on the truck, [and you're] ~~if somebody's~~ sitting back in the back of the truck, when you start moving you've got to watch for it.

~~KS: They jump, huh?~~

~~TR: Yeah,~~ they jump[,] [*flutters hands*] [and] ~~(inaudible)~~ it might get in your eyes. Every time ~~when~~ we load it we have to [put it]—way in the back, ~~you know, the cactus,~~ put something over it so it won't [move] ~~(truck noise)~~. It's just like when you're picking them. The ladies used to pick that fruit and the fruit [with] —tongs made out of sticks. ~~Well,~~ they brush 'em off first.

~~KS: How do they do that?~~

~~TR: Oh, they got—~~ they make their own brushes[.] ~~like . . . anything. Brush 'em off, all of 'em, you know—the ones that there's fruit—for fruit,~~ they just brush 'em off and then start plucking 'em ~~(truck noise)~~. Then they get 'em home, ~~whatever they pick 'em (inaudible) then you peel 'em,~~ [they] peel 'em just like that.

~~KS: With a knife?~~

~~TR: No,~~ your hands. ~~It's easy to peel 'em. Why, they just—just like anything else—fruit.~~ Get [the skins] 'em off, and ~~get~~ the—meat ~~to~~ come[s] off[.] ~~you know, (inaudible), just like any other thing. Same thing.~~ Then they cook it, ~~just like~~—make syrup out of it. But that syrup's too sweet. ~~I can't—~~I couldn't eat it. It's got to much sugar in it.

275

~~KS: Just natural sugar?~~

TR: Natural sugar. And then—~~'course, I hate 'em, too, but~~ it's got a lot of seeds inside, all stuck ~~in that—it's just covered.~~ You've got to eat only ~~the—~~what's good, leave the seeds alone. They're sweet, too, but yellow[.] ~~(inaudible)—~~ [They] get on your hands or your shirt ~~or—~~if you're not careful.

~~KS: The juice, or the . . .~~

TR: The juice. And you watch out for your clothes.

~~KS: Did your mother get these when you were young, or . . .~~

TR: ~~Yeah, the—~~ t̲he old old old people, ~~you know,~~ they get 'em, ladies and all [*nods*]. Now nobody bothers[.] ~~'em except when you just pluck 'em. Every time you go by one you see that it's kind of brushed off, like—the way they do out there. But at a certain time of year, the summer, I guess, you can see all them little—you know, the cattle, too.~~

~~KS: They eat them?~~

TR: [Cattle] ~~They~~ eat 'em—deer, anything [*nods*].

~~KS: I'm surprised. I would think they would get the thorns in them.~~

TR: I don't think [the thorns] ~~they~~ bother 'em, because they eat—even [the fruit] ~~that ball~~ from the cholla— [the ones that] ~~you know~~ they hang̲? [They] ~~It's~~ got the same kind, only ~~they're~~ smaller— and greener. [The animals] ~~They~~ like [that] ~~it,~~ too. That's why you see some cattle [with] ~~get~~ thorns in their faces [*points to cows with thorny muzzles*], ~~because they eat that—especially when they're hanging down like this [cups right hand].~~ They'll be right around it, no matter if it [has] ~~'s~~ any thorns. ~~You watch it.~~

~~KS: That's surprising.~~

TR: ~~'Course,~~ t̲hey're green, and they ~~just got a~~ lot of water or salt or something [in them]. ~~They grow on it.~~

~~KS: Are there other kinds of desert vegetation that you eat?~~

TR: ~~Yeah, I just got—~~I was going to say, [there's a] ~~this—this~~ different kind, too—one ~~is~~ not so thorny. ~~It's kind of—not so much like the other ones.~~ It's just kind of bare[,] ~~Well, it's not bare,~~ but it's got thorns, but is more soft and ~~it's (inaudible)—~~it won't stick you so much. ~~And that little—see, what the little balls come out like that,~~ ~~too, like (inaudible)~~ and they fall when they drop everything—everything's gone except [the fruit] ~~that~~, and you harvest that, too, every one of those little balls—~~harvest that, too,~~ and clean it up—clean 'em up, ~~like anything—cook it,~~ cook [them] ~~it~~, you know[,] like anything else. When it's done, it's just like you're eating spinach—~~spinach, like~~—tastes like spinach.

~~KS: Does it grow—is it a cactus?~~

TR: It's a cactus. ~~You can—I used to go out and—she's still living on (inaudible) Navajo lady—she likes it. You know, she lives by that hill where—the other side. Lot's of 'em grow there.~~

~~KS: Whereabouts is this?~~

TR: [It grows] ~~On the other side~~—out at the mission—[on] ~~I mean~~ the east side of the mission, by the freeway. There's a lot of 'em—~~same variety~~. Then they go over there and gather it. ~~Every time I'd come to their house, sometimes they'd have some cooked, and I'd eat it. And they've got in stores, you know, in bit jars. Well, I guess she's the only one that's really—you know, she's the big lady, and gets all she wants. And then people come like me—"I'd like to have some of—I'd like to buy some of 'em. And she sells it.~~

~~KS: Does she store them raw, then?~~

TR: ~~Yeah, just~~ [They store them in big jars,] raw[,] ~~You know, it's just like any~~—like beans or any staple food.~~It's just like that~~ because [they're] ~~it's~~ dry, dry. And then you ~~got to~~ cook 'em, like any staple. And ~~then~~ when [they're] ~~it's~~ cooked in water, ~~in there, well,~~ ~~it~~ [they] ~~turns~~ out soft, like spinach. Good eating [*nods*].

~~KS: What color is it?~~

TR: ~~Oh, it's something like—been in the sun all day.~~ [They've] ~~It's~~ got no color at all. [They're] ~~It's~~ just ~~like a~~—like a bare tree, ~~or—it's got no color, just like that tree over in there [points].~~ ~~J~~ust dry, like wood.

[¶] ~~KS: Did you ever go out and gather mesquite beans?~~

TR: ~~Oh, yeah. That's a good one—it's~~ [Mesquite beans are] another thing. Wish I could have some of that, too, right now. ~~It's better~~

~~than anything I ever—used to—like a lot of—but the way they do it is—of course at the time, everything was better. New they (inaudible)—oh, as big as those trees.~~ You'd see a whole lot of beans hanging. ~~Then you know when they're ripe—~~ when they're real ripe and dry, that's when they're picked[,] ~~And you've got to taste 'em when~~ they're sweet—got to get the sweet ones. ~~And they're dry. Or so—pick 'em.~~ And you pick 'em dry and then grind 'em, grind 'em in [a metate] ~~that--like a special grinder. It's like—you know them rocks—the holes, like this dish—something to—or—and then made~~ into a powder, and soak it with water—let it stand. Let it stand for a while and then you ~~kind of~~ stir ~~it~~—all the juice[.] sweetness gets in there, just like—sweet as anything else, like soda pop, by its own self—nothing mixed.

~~KS: How is it served?~~

~~TR: Just like—just like anything, like—any liquid.~~

~~KS: But it's cold when it's . . .~~

~~TR: It's cold if you get it in the shade. You know, whatever you want.~~ On the ranch we used to have it—put [the beans] in big—baskets [*makes circle with arms*], you know, big round baskets. ~~Put 'em in there and~~ then soak [them] ~~it in the—not all of it, not—you know, just enough.~~ [until] ~~T~~he water'll get ~~just like~~—kind of creamy like, ~~not creamy but it's liquid,~~ [the] color of cream. Then drink it with a cup. Sweet—just like when you get 'em off the tree. See, all the sweetness gets in there[.] It goes in the water ~~just like~~—just like the cactus. ~~Same thing. And they do it. But I don't—I never did know they could make anything out of it, and syrup (inaudible) far as I know. They didn't used to. Used it for the drinks or whatever you want. Something like a (inaudible) of soda pop. I liked it. At least I have a lot of it, you know—just gather it, stack 'em out in sacks or barrels. Every so often (inaudible) soaking.~~

~~KS: This is your grandmother up on the ranch?~~

~~TR: Mm hmm. Anybody could do it. Even I could do it right now, if I got a chance to, but~~ [Now] I'm too lazy—~~too lazy~~ to gather it.

~~KS: What time of year were they ready?~~

TR: ~~When—you know, when they (laundry cart noise). I think it's~~ [¶]
around autumn, ~~or something, you know. When~~ they get ~~so~~
ripe ~~—of course, if it's green, you can pick 'em too, but they're~~
~~green, until~~ they get ~~so that it's~~ dry. They fall on the ground and it's
easier—easier to pick them[.] ~~you know, instead of—'cause~~ the
women go down and they rake [them] ~~it~~ up[.] ~~—at least that's the~~
~~way they do it.~~

KS: ~~Did you go out and get them for your grandmother?~~

TR: ~~No, I was too small. I was—I don't care much about it. Just so I get~~
~~some of 'em. No, they never bother—they know I don't—it's~~
~~not—the ladies were not like as they are now, so they say.~~ Now the
ladies are so lazy. They want to be some place in the shade. Olden
times, you never know where the old ladies going to go. They go
out there and they get ~~those~~ yucca, ~~you know—yucca, we call it,~~
for baskets. They get the good ones—green ones or those ripe one,
white. Gather them—dry 'em up.

KS: ~~The leaves?~~

TR: The leaves. ~~And~~ they got little threads in the sides, [so the women]
~~you know. They've~~ got to clean [them] ~~it~~, clean [them] ~~it~~ very
good, and dry them out in the sun. That's when hey get real white.
And then they use that for baskets. Or if they want green ones, they
can always get ~~—you know,~~ the green stalks, cut 'em. But they
usually get ~~them~~ long ones, white ones, ~~you know~~—cut in two.

KS: ~~Did your mother make baskets?~~

TR: ~~Oh, yeah.~~ Everybody [made baskets;] ~~did,~~ all the old ladies did.
Now you never see anybody [*lifts hands, palms up*], except I['ve]
seen some old ones. Some of these ladies now, girls, they know how
to make 'em, but they don't want to do it. They're too lazy to
gather [yucca] ~~them. They're too lazy to—now,~~ they'd rather sit
there and turn on the TV. Or be down in [a] ~~the~~ bar or some place.
It's not like it used to be.

KS: ~~Did you grandmother make pottery, too?~~

[¶] TR: [My grandmother made some pottery] ~~Some. Some,~~ but not
all of it, because ~~—because~~ they [didn't] ~~don't~~ have the clay. [There

was] ~~O~~nly one spot 'way down [south, a] ~~there~~—certain little spot, where they used to go and get the clay. It's small. They need[ed] a lot of clay—good clay, just like [there is] 'way up there ~~in—maybe I told you about it.~~ ~~O~~n this side of the Santa Ritas, where they used to go[,] ~~down there~~— [They went to] Arivaca and down, [to] the old towns[,] ~~—halfway station—~~down [to] Tumacacori's ~~that~~ old mission—where they used to work the fields. And they tell me there's a hill or something 'way back there some place—nothing but clay. Used to go out there and get it, the clay, and then bring it home, bring it to the camp, and they start making pottery, any pottery. And they back 'em—fire, make 'em hard[.] ~~you know how they are.~~ And they haul 'em off to Nogales, ~~w~~[s]ell 'em, get their food. Or either they haul 'em down [to] ~~that way,~~ Tombstone[,] ~~At that time there was (inaudible),~~ [and] sell 'em there. Or else when they have a lot of time, nothing to do, the ladies go over there where that clay is, the mound or whatever it is [and], ~~T~~hey make pottery right there, all on the spot [*nods*].

~~KS: They have to stay there a long time, then?~~

~~TR: Oh, yeah, they can't—there—nothing to it. Water, fire, that's all they need.~~

~~KS: Did you ever go up there with them?~~

TR: ~~No,~~ I didn't [ever] go[.] ~~—I didn't—~~it was done before I was born[.] ~~(inaudible) used to tell him (inaudible).~~ And then ̲they make their potteries right there. ~~By the time they get—nothing,~~ ̲in no time, I guess, because they know how to do it. They just keep on doing it, ~~let 'em get dry—well, they~~ bake 'em, ~~the~~ make 'em hard, and then when they're ready[.] ̲maybe the old men or somebody, they gather 'em up, haul 'em to Tombstone. [See photo 15.]

~~KS: Did you ever watch your grandmother make pottery? Did you ever see her do it?~~

TR: ~~Oh, no.~~ I've seen 'em [make pottery] a lot of times. I never cared much about it. It's none of my business. ~~Tell 'em—they're there learning how to do it (inaudible)—they~~ [The pots] got to be in the fire like ~~anything else—like~~ cooking[,] ~~See, they'll be~~ baking ~~them~~

when they're wet, or ~~you know,~~ when they're half-ready and still wet[.] ~~or maybe . . . I don't know how they do it, but anyway,~~ they put it in the fire so it'll get heated up, just like ~~(jet noise)~~ a blacksmith. He'll get it to a certain temperature, where it gets real hard, ~~or else—they won't get hotter than steel or iron—~~certain temperature.

KS: ~~Did they put it right on the fire?~~

TR: Oh, they put it in the fire—I don't know how—I know they burn it. ~~Put it in the fire and let it—the heat comes from there and I guess it gets so and so and so and so—they know when. Take 'em out.~~

KS: ~~Did they cover the fire up?~~

TR: ~~No. Uh uh, they just . . . what I say, you just pass it around right in there in the flames, see, like this [sweeping motion]. And they know when it's done—it's done, they put it off and get another one. Same thing.~~

KS: ~~They just did one at a time, then?~~

TR: One at a time. ~~See,~~ that' how it works. That's why I say now the younger generation, they don't want to do it[.] ~~'cause—you know how it goes, like~~ they don't want even baskets [*shakes head*].

KS: ~~Were there any kind of other foods from the desert that you ate when you were younger?~~

TR: ~~There must be a lot of them, but they're all gone. One thing—one thing,~~ [¶] you know the yucca tree, the pole—~~I don't know what you call that—anyway—the heart, they call it, too—that comes out of there on top? You know that~~ big stalk? When it grows way up there, ~~I remember when it's still . . . when it's still greet,~~ when it's ripe, ~~I guess, so—~~like a [cane] ~~candy, you know, about so round [thumbs and index fingers in a circle]~~, cut that—cut it in pieces so long [*measures about four inches*], put 'em in the coals—hot coals. Roast 'em, turn 'em over and then [they'd] ~~it'd~~ be ~~just like . . .~~ kind of yellow. [They're] ~~It's~~ like steak. When they're warm, [they're] ~~it's~~ soft, just like meat. Then you eat them. [They're] ~~It's~~ sweet, too.

KS: ~~Did you do that when you were up on the ranch, too?~~

TR: ~~Mm hmm. Old man—~~one old man used to do it. We'd be right around. He said, "You want some? I'll do it." "Yeah" [*nods*]. ~~They'd do it;~~ he'd do it[.] — we['d] just watch him do it. He knows how.

KS: ~~Was this one of the hired men up there?~~]

TR: ~~No,~~ he's just a neighbor, working. You know, he's old[.] ~~and then he's—~~ nothing to do but we'd play around (inaudible) there and then probably he'd, ~~you know,~~ he'd give us Some of it—treat us. And he'd do it for us.

KS: ~~Your brother was with you then?~~

TR: ~~No, it's—the neighbors. But I never seen anybody doing it or—we don't, but . . . but~~ I remember when he used to do it [*nods*]. Another thing—just like when they stew the jack rabbit. I wouldn't even do it myself right now. It was (inaudible) not too long ago when they're rounding up cattle—mostly the riders, were in a bunch and this old man was helping cook around there, you know, cook for the gang of 'em. They were talking ~~something about that~~ and ~~he—~~the old man overheard it[.] ~~while we're talking.~~ Came around and said, "Well, if you want a better one, I'll do it. Just kill me a rabbit—anything—I'll do what you're talking about." The way they do it, they skin that rabbit, or just certain rabbits—they don't bother with certain ones~~, too~~—and then skin it, get everything out of it (inaudible). But he said some way you could just put it in—I think he said just put it in the heat. Dig a hole just about so deep [*measures about two feet*], put rocks in there or coals—~~coals,~~ hot coals, and then put rocks on top of it and heat so hot. Then you dump that rabbit in there and then cover it some way. Then you cook it like so, when it's hot. It's barbecued [*nods*]. And then when, you know, you just pull it by the ears~~,~~ sticking out—pull it by the ears and just undress it like nothing. ~~Skin just—you know,~~ it gets so hot, the skin just rolls right off like a blanket. ~~And there it is, just the way he meant—he said it.~~

KS: ~~Did you watch him do it?~~

TR: ~~No, I never did watch him. I don't even know how to do it. But I've heard so many of that—that this old may was telling about it.~~ He was going to do it, ~~but we tried to catch him do it, you know, we~~ ~~tell him that we're rounding up cattle and~~ we didn't have time to shoot a rabbit[.] ~~or what. Try to tell him each one of us, (inaudible)~~ ~~[*shrugs*]. Yes, will you show us how—~~ <u>y</u>et I want[ed] to see how it's done. ~~But the way he told me to do it that way, I think you just put~~ ~~'em in there and—rabbit as a whole. That—that's why I said that~~ <u>y</u>ou just take it out and pull 'em by the ears, knock his head off, just unfold it. Everything is done.

~~ks: Sounds pretty good.~~

~~tr: Sounds pretty good, but~~ [¶] I know how to skin rabbits. I know that white-tail rabbit; there's always that little green ~~something~~ [*holds finger and thumb about an inch apart*] near the heart. You've got to take that out first, before you ~~ever do anything—~~cook it. ~~He's telling me—~~ <u>i</u>f you don't take that little whatever it is, little green [thing] ~~.... if you don't take it out, (inaudible) I don't~~ ~~know—if you don't take it~~ out when you try to cook it, then ~~all~~ ~~this—it's busted or what—all whatever (inaudible) or whatever it~~ ~~is, just come right through the hole and~~ you can taste it, bitter or something. That's why ~~I always do. I never did—well, he tell me~~ ~~that way.~~ <u>E</u>very time I'm skinning a rabbit I always watch that[,] ~~T~~<u>t</u>ake it out, throw it away [*underhand tossing motion*]. Then I clean it[,] ~~—of course you've got ....~~ intestines and all that, ~~got the legs~~ ~~and everything (inaudible).~~ ~~W~~<u>w</u>ash it, ~~however you want to do~~ ~~it—~~make a stew out of it[.] ~~—~~ <u>i</u>t's better than anything else. It's better than what you get in restaurants. Good [*nods*]. And you cook it slow and it gets ~~so~~ tender[.] ~~...~~ [You] <u>p</u>ut a little something—spices or whatever you want, salt [on it] ~~...~~ and get a fresh tortilla[.] ~~put it down,~~ <u>p</u>ut a piece down there and just kind of roll it, just like they do out in Mexican stands, same thing. You do it. ~~W~~<u>w</u>hile it's hot. Now [we're] ~~you're~~ getting hungry [*grins*].

~~ks: Yeah, you make me hungry. Sounds very good. Did you eat a lot of~~ ~~rabbit and fresh game at the ranch?~~

~~tr: Oh, yes. 'Specially them little cottontails—lot of them around.~~

~~ks: And you grandmother prepared it with ...~~

~~TR: Oh, yeah.~~

~~KS: As a stew?~~

~~TR:~~ [My grandmother made a rabbit stew.] ~~Mm hmm.~~ That's where I learned to skin the rabbit.

~~KS: Did you do that when you were a kid, for your grandmother?~~

~~TR: Mm hmm. I know how to do it.~~ I like to skin the rabbit—it's easy, easy to skin it.

~~KS: Did your grandfather go out and shoot them?~~

~~TR: Oh, yeah. Plenty of times, (inaudible) when they come around.~~ Sometimes we'd eat [rabbit,] ~~something like that and go right out and get one,~~ and at the same time ~~when~~ we had the jerky, from the deer.

~~KS: So you . . .~~

~~TR: Always—~~we always had something like that.

~~KS: So when your grandfather went out deer hunting, then they would dry the mean.~~

~~TR: Oh, yeah.~~ Or else one of us especially during Christmas or something like that, butcher a cow. Lot of steaks. Then we delivered [it to] — the brother for a present. Every so often, you know—not do it all the time, you know. When they want to.

~~KS: They brought it down to San Xavier, then?~~

~~TR: Mm hmm. Oh, yeah,~~ that['s] a lot of fun[.] ~~when we had . . . you know,~~ [¶] they had a lot of—~~lot of~~ ranches and all that. Most of the people, them old people, they live up there, over by that hill, about twelve miles from me. They get around together. ~~'Course,~~ ~~the—~~most of them live on the west side of that hill, with wells and houses, and we live on the south side—east. We would go visiting, Sundays. ~~Well, they go visiting (inaudible)—they do the same, you know.~~ And when they get ready to go on a hunting trip, well, they tell each other—they know. They're ready. 'Course, the deer weren't like now. You could seem 'em down there. Used to be 'way up in the high mountains. So they'd go and kill the antelope or whatever they can get.

~~KS: So many of the men would get together to go?~~

TR: Oh, maybe two three [men] — all depends. Just a few. Maybe three, four, or maybe two. It's better for two or three because ~~they can get~~—they'll have more meat that way, you know. That's why they always have jerky ~~(blank spot on tape)~~ in the coals. Fry 'em up . . . salt 'em . . . there you are [*nods*]. ~~But~~ <u>a</u>t certain times, you know, when they're not drinking too much water, that's when they're fat, especially them antelope. That's when they go and shoot 'em, kill 'em, because they get a lot of [meat on] ~~beef in~~ them. At certain times they don't have ~~(inaudible)~~.

KS: ~~What time of year did they go hunting, then?~~

TR: ~~I don't know—about~~ [They go] when it gets cool, so [the meat] ~~—so it~~ won't spoil.

KS: ~~How did they dry the meat?~~

TR: They hang it, ~~like anything else. Put it on the line, hanging (inaudible), but you got to~~ put a lot of salt on there and ~~have it—~~keep the flies off.

KS: ~~They hung a whole carcass?~~

TR: ~~No, mm, mm [*shakes head*]. No,~~ <u>t</u>hey ~~got to~~ strip it, like they do now. Have some pieces, ~~so~~ long ~~a~~ piece[s] [*measures about a foot*], ~~and—'course, some of the good piece like this [measures about a quarter inch]—that wide , you know—~~just so it will dry. Thin it out just enough~~—put 'em on there and then keep on like that. It'll dry faster. And you got~~ to put a lot of salt on it. It'll dry faster.

KS: ~~Did you help with the mean?~~

TR: ~~(feedback on tape).~~

KS: ~~Did they hang it on racks?~~

TR: ~~No,~~ <u>t</u>hey got a [line] ~~like~~, like a cloth[es]~~ing~~ line. ~~(inaudible)—pull it over here and maybe~~ [with] pole [and] another pole and then string the wire, ~~whatever they've got—wire~~ or rope[,] ~~or something like that.~~ ~~J~~ust like laundry, all the way around. And let [the meat] ~~it~~ stay and dry—good sun—you know the air—sun, dries faster. When they're dry, well, they gather 'em back, and then stack 'em— stack 'em in a container[.] ~~or whatever they got.~~

~~KS: In pottery, or . . .~~

~~TR: Anything, anything you got. They—~~ [Then,] any time, any time during the year, if [they] ~~you~~ want some of it [they] ~~you~~ just get a piece, put on the coals[.] ~~out . . . good.~~ Eat it. Everybody likes it— the ranch people, even the Mexicans—they do the same. If you live on a ranch, grow up on a ranch, you never go hungry. You get everything there. That's why I like it. Everybody likes it, even the Mexicans. ~~They don't have—~~ you don't care about the store, because there's a store right there. ~~Like down by the (inaudible)—~~ [with] whatever you need, like lard or matches or whatever[.] ~~then you want to maybe got to town and get (inaudible).~~

~~KS: There was a store nearby?~~

~~TR: Oh, yeah,~~ there's a store where the mine was, where them hills are[,]

~~KS: There was a mine up in the hills by the ranch?~~

~~TR: Oh, yeah, it's right up~~ where they're mining right now. It's an old place—used to have a lot of crowds up there, celebrations—~~the Mexicans. And there's not on (inaudible)~~ behind ~~there—~~Twin Buttes. ~~It's not too far, but right up there in the—~~ [There were] big [horse] race[s] ~~comes~~ once in a while [with] ~~(inaudible) there—~~lot of fighting and drinking[.] ~~Mexicans.~~ I went up there. [when I was young.]

~~KS: What kind of a race?~~

~~TR: Horse race.~~

~~KS: Was this when you were young, or . . .~~

~~TR: Yeah. Now,~~ there's a schoolhouse [still] there, too[,] ~~Good big—big school up—~~where the kids used to go to school. You can see a lot of those old worn-out buildings. And there's a locomotive there, too[,] ~~—it was,~~ but I don't know if it's still there. ~~It's either a train—train goes up there, or ore.~~ Now it's just a ghost town *[sweeps down]*. And there was a store there not too long ago. ~~And there's another on this side.~~ That's the oldest mines ~~they've got there,~~ before these ones come. They [had] ~~got~~ a store right there, too. I used to go [and it was] —not too far.

KS: ~~Was this when you were really young, or . . .~~

TR: ~~No, when I—well, it was—I guess it was—well, it was—~~everything
was all there when I was—when I wasn't around. But when I grew
up, then I—~~then I~~ went out there to get the horse or ride around,
[and] I'd go up there to that store, buy—~~well, they go up there and
they might ask you for~~ tobacco or whatever. I go over there. It's not
too far ~~(inaudible)~~. Right by that highway—not the main highway,
~~but, you know, that~~ Mission Road that goes ~~. . .~~ right there. I used
to know the people[.] ~~—married to a Spanish lady that (inaudible)
they're grown up.~~

KS: ~~Were they there when you were a child? Was there a store there that
your grandparents . . .~~

TR: I guess [my grandparents] ~~they~~ got everything there before I was
born, because it's a booming town ~~then. I could see it—you could
see it right now, where they used to be—all the—mining town, all
around there's~~ where they used to mine[.] ~~that—~~ well they're
mining it now.

KS: ~~When your folks—when your grandparents needed supplies did
they go to that store there?~~

TR: ~~Oh, sure, they'd go there and get—get whatever—whatever they
need.~~

KS: ~~Did they take the wagon down?~~

TR: ~~(inaudible)~~

KS: ~~Did you go with them?~~

TR: ~~No, I never—no. I didn't—I never didn't (inaudible). I don't get
around. Well, we (inaudible) except then. Because the town—the
towns, they go down this way (inaudible).~~ When I was riding, I
used to go up there, just to look around, to that store [to buy]
~~—but some—~~something. But it's no more. Everybody moved out.

KS: ~~The Mine shut down?~~

TR: ~~And now—mm hmm, it~~ [The mine] shut down. I used to work at
the mine, too, for a while. ~~And right now, they all got this
machinery, see what's happening there now. It's where all the big
mines coming in.~~

~~KS: That's where the Twin Buttes mine is now?~~

TR: It['s] [where the Twin Buttes mine is now] ~~is,~~ and then the other ones, too. That's where all the people come to~~,~~ from town [to] ~~(inaudible)~~ work, every morning. Duval mine and all that—what they call American Smelter. There's about four big mines right along that section. But ~~that—~~at that time, they [had] ~~got~~ a mine[.] ~~but it's different—~~I don't know what company, but anyway[,] — [in] the olden times, it's underground. ~~That's were~~ [A] lot of people living there[,] ~~...~~

~~KS: Mostly Mexicans?~~

~~TR:~~ Mexicans mostly, and whites. It's a booming town, just like ~~any—you know,~~ in the olden days. ~~Just like ... just like that town, like ... good silver ...~~

~~KS: Tombstone?~~

~~TR: No, right behind—~~ [¶] [Just like] Arivaca, where the people own that ranch. I work for them. It's got water ~~around right~~ away up there—cottonwood trees bigger than anything around. Big roots—roots go like this [*spreads his hands*], and there's a little river about so wide ~~as from here as to the~~ [*points to a wall about six feet away*] ~~(inaudible), right around,~~ way out in the desert.

~~KS: When did you work up there?~~

~~TR: Oh,~~ it was just a little time ago.

~~KS: What? When you came back from ...~~

~~TR: No, not from—too long ago,~~ I could go over there right now if I wanted to. I still work with him part-time. ~~Have big—~~ they got a ranch there. I go with them once in a while ~~when—~~during the summer[.] ~~when—see,~~ they got a lot of horses, too. ~~Go over there and just see—fix around.~~ When the water runs down all we've got to do is stock holes. ~~Or so—when you get about so—the gravel, the water comes down.~~ And you keep digging, digging so deep as you can, and big as you can. Then you got a pond right in there—the water comes into it. ~~And~~ during the rainy season, or winter[.] ~~that creek's down around here (inaudible).~~

~~KS: You work as a wrangler for the, then, when you go up there?~~

288

TR: ~~No, I work for them before. No, I—we don't stay there. We just go up there. See,~~ it's a nursery land, too. ~~See, I got a lot of nursery land working for them. It's a nursery land, too. But~~ he's married to a Mexican. And the Mexican lady, I guess her father own[ed]s the place, and they all died and now she takes care of it, and they run the nursery, too. And whenever I want to, I go over there and then we do a lot of nursery [work]. And then the weekends, that's the time when they want me—~~see, if they want me~~ to do something like fixing corrals or anything[.] well, we go on the weekend—sleep over there, do the work, ~~just like I say,~~ come back ~~(inaudible)~~.

KS: ~~His business is in town?~~

TR: His business is in town. Come back in the evening[.] ~~(inaudible)~~—early tomorrow we get another job. ~~'Course, sometime we down (inaudible).~~

KS: ~~You were telling me the first day we started this about making cheese when you were younger. Did your grandmother make it, or did . . .~~

TR: ~~Oh, yeah [*nods*].~~ [¶] All the ladies got to make [cheese.] ~~it—~~ it's not a man's business.

KS: ~~Did the women get together to do it?~~

TR: ~~No, by their self. Any household,~~ they got to ~~do~~—make their own, unless they're in a group, but I never see it. See, the people live across from the other side of the mountain, west side, where they got their own houses[.] ~~so—so distance apart.~~ And they got their own milk, you know, they got their own stock, and they milk so much—~~you know,~~ just enough where they can made the cheese. ~~Well, they do it or else for the milk all the time.~~

KS: ~~Did you have to—did you milk, when you were up there at the ranch, to get . . .~~

TR: ~~Up at the ranch first. Just like I said,~~ you got to get your hands in everything when you're young—you know, as a kid, watch 'em when they do it, and then probably they'll say, "~~(inaudible),~~ try it," and I'd try it, try that. 'Course, they sit on a bucket or something, old bucket—sit down start milking in the bucket [*milking motion with hands*].

KS: ~~Was your grandmother the only woman up there at the ranch?~~

TR: [My grandmother was] ~~T~~he only woman in the family, but some of the neighbors who come, they got ladies staying with them that are too old. Once you get too old, ~~you're~~—you can't get out. But she was—well, she's lively. She's old, but she's lively. She'd do the milking. 'Course she done it in her time. ~~And I'd do something (inaudible).~~ Of course, at the time them old cattle were pretty tame. But once in a while you'd get a new cow in there that'll be just awful~~ly~~—and you've got to ~~get~~—hold it down ~~to get~~—till they get used to it. Just like dairy cows now—I could go up there to the plant and ask for a job—I could get it. Of course, in school, I done a lot of it.

KS: ~~After she got the milk, then what was the process of making the cheese?~~

TR: ~~Well,~~ ~~y~~ou got to wait till when that—the cream come up[,] ~~see, when it gets off the cow,~~ when it's [warm,] ~~war like this, well, you know~~ it~~'~~s start[s]~~ing~~ getting ~~kind of—~~the thickness. ~~Whatever's in there, the cheese, butter, and~~ ~~t~~he fat ~~, you know,~~ is still coming up[.] ~~—you know,~~ ~~i~~t'll start getting heavy, and then you got to work it over some way, and then it'll come out by itself.

KS: ~~The cream comes to the top?~~

TR: Cream will come to the top. And then you've got to stir it every time [*circular motion*]. And then, ~~somewhere, I don't know,~~ some way they just take so much out of it~~, you know,~~ at a certain time, and that's cottage cheese, you know, just like you buy in town. ~~Sometimes it sit there—~~~~i~~f you want cottage cheese, ~~we'll save some. All right, take it out—you know,~~ she knows how. Set it aside and it'll be cottage cheese. All you've got to do is pour salt over it—there you are. Butter, too. Cream butter, you know.

KS: ~~Mm hmm. Did you have to churn it to make it?~~

TR: Churn it—churn it and make about just as good as anything. I like it. ~~And then what's left in there—and then it's—I think boil it, and~~

~~they make something else out of it, it's not the only one.~~ They boil
it, I think they boil it, to make quesadilla, they call it in Mexican—
sell it at the stores, too. ~~Kind of—I like it, too—~~ i̲t's kind of like a
tortilla, only it's cheese. You buy it sometimes in the store. I like
that, too. ~~They make—~~ t̲hey got to cook it[.] ~~and kind of make
it—I don't know how they do it. I never was—but they do it. But~~
i̲t's hard work.

~~KS: Was this the cheese that they took into town to sell?~~

~~TR: Oh, yeah. Make a—they can make a lot of things out of the cheese,
if you know how to do it.~~

~~KS: We were talking about the cheese—when you told me about it
before, you said that they put the intestines from a cow in the
cheese?~~

TR: [They put part of the cow into the milk.] ~~No, the way I—it's not
the intestines. It's something—I couldn't—it's the bladder.~~ It think
it's the bladder. I never get to find out so good about it, but they
call it qual in Mexico. You have to buy it in a slaughterhouse. They
sell it there. It's dried and salted like that. I think either a bladder
or a ~~—you know,~~ piece of it. And they got to dip it in there when
it's ready[.] ~~and I think—I think the whole thing, work it in there
some way.~~

~~KS: when your grandmother made cheese they had to go to the
slaughter-house to get that?~~

TR: ~~Well, they always keep it. You know, when it's dry~~ you've got to
hang it like that and let it dry[,] ~~—you use—~~ we use it over again—
over and over [*pantomimes hanging something up*].

~~KS: Oh, oh.~~

TR: ~~For so long—as long as—you know, when it's no good, like
anything else, get another one.~~ Usually they had a whole row of it
hanging up, ~~you know,~~ for that purpose. It's good all the time,
because it's dry. It's salty—I know it's salty[.] ~~and so on.~~ Just a big
leaf—thinner, too~~, it's not—just like a leaf out of one of those—~~
round [leaf] ~~leave~~, it's just like that, the way it's cut. See, you just
keep it there for the time being. What they do when it gets—when

it gets wet, I guess it's going to fix the ~~whole—whole whatever's in there,~~ fat and all that.
~~ks: So they put it in the pot while they're cooking the cheese?~~
~~tr: No, I don't think so.~~ [Put it in] ~~W~~hile it's not cooking or else the whole thing would cook itself.
~~ks: Oh.~~
~~tr: See,~~ they got to just put it at a certain time, and let it stay for a while, and then it works itself in with the cream or whatever. Then ~~wile it makes so many creamy and~~ the cheese come out, and that's when they start working that. And they have to take it out[.] ~~I guess so—I never did see when they're working.~~ And then they start in—stir [*circular motion*] like anything else. And they take out—take out whatever—whatever they want out, like for cottage cheese or white, and then leave the rest. And then they work it. Then it gets so that it gets ~~so~~ like cheese. ~~And they—you know, let it—you know, they don't work it just right away.~~ They take a while. When it's ready they start over again, doing it some different way. When it gets so in the dough, that's when they put it out in a cloth, on some big white cloth, ~~you know,~~ flour cloth[.] ~~and then its almost (inaudible) never falls off. Then they make it so that—oh, I forgot.~~ They got a wooden ring made for that, about so wide [*ten inch circle*]—like plywood. And it's in a ring, made in a ring. Then you just set that in there and you dump the whole thing. ~~And then you work—work one kind, I guess. Like this—you know they are,~~ round and smooth? ~~Then they got big ones—'course, they got everything.~~ If you're going to make a big one, you've got to have a big one. Smaller one—you know, they got different sizes.
~~ks: They make those themselves, the rings?~~
~~tr: No, they buy it, too. They sell it, too. They used to sell everything. Just like I say, when—before anything like this, you could see the homemade stuff right in the store, tiny store. No you don't see nothing. The machinery's got at it. They used to do it—I seen 'em. Or some—or sometimes somebody makes—they got a special—they know everything.~~ Craftsmen around town, they

292

make those. They could do it. I could do it, too. And then they set
that in there—'course, it's clean, just like anything, all greased up
or something. Set it in there~~, what they call awatche~~—it's made of
wood[.]~~en—like a scrubbing—well, they make food out of it,~~
~~too—grind—it's made out of—out of wood from the ocotillo. So~~
~~much water than this or this—big one—~~ it's got a little spout ~~like~~
~~this,~~ with a handle—set it in there and then ~~just like—see where~~
~~that—whatever comes out, like~~ juice or water—it'll just go right in
there and start draining out.

~~KS: Oh, I see.~~

TR: And then that's when they start—after it's wrapped up in that ring,
getting ready—tight, smoother, smaller. Then they start
weigh[t]ing [it], you know—they got special rocks—smooth ones.
Put one on there, weight it down [*presses down on legs*][,] ~~And the~~
~~next one is—you know, not heavy enough.~~ So all that wet stuff
comes—~~you know,~~ it'll drain out itself. And then it'll be round just
like in a pan.

~~KS: They set something on top of the ring, then that drains off the . . .~~

~~TR: Mm. Hmm, because on account of the weight.~~ See, and it stays
there until the whole thing dries out. ~~And then let it sit, stay all~~
~~day, until they get Everything out of it except for (car noise). And~~
~~then, not only that,~~ they drain the ~~whole—the~~ juice out of the
cheese[.] ~~you know—~~ it's kind of yellow, you know,
~~like—anything—~~green or yellow. And the dogs like it.

~~KS: Oh!~~

~~TR: And it's up to the dogs, whatever they want to do with it.~~ Drink it
like soup. Makes 'em fat, too, because it's got a lot of—lot of fat in
it. And then by that time, ~~I don't know how long—it just all~~
~~depends—may be you can—any time you want to, anytime at~~
~~all—~~it's ready. Just take it out—there it is. Unwrap it—that's the
cheese.

~~KS: And it's hard inside?~~

~~TR:~~ ~~Hard—soft—hard—~~ won't fall apart. ~~And you just~~
~~(inaudible)—put it in—or heat it or whatever, hot . . .~~

~~KS: Did it keep well?~~

TR: ~~Oh, sure.~~ Keeps well, Like any cheese. And then I like fried cheese, you know, fried like potatoes—kind of brownish? I eat a lot of it. Oh, we had cheese all the time. We got it.

~~KS: Did they make a whole lot at one time?~~

TR: ~~No,~~ [They make] one at a time. Next day they'll make another one, and by the time maybe—maybe two or four days, by the weekend, everybody will be heading for town, down the village[.] ~~or maybe—anyplace.~~ Everybody likes it. And you haul it off, sell it to them ~~(inaudible)~~ sell it, peddled it all the way. In no time it's all gone [*nods*].

~~KS: How long did it take—was it made outside, or in . . .~~

TR: ~~Outside, just like anything else. Now you've got the machinery you can just stay inside all you want. You can go out in the fresh air and do it in the shade—you know how they do.~~

~~KS: This was in the spring, when there were calves?~~

TR: ~~Oh, yeah, when there were calves. Just like right now. (Inaudible) used to—even the Mexicans. There's a lot of competition. You got more—more—more cows to milk, like calves—you get bigger milk and you got more help to make these big rounds, like they make in Mexico—I still see them when they come in. You know, that big round—that's how they do it. They got enough milk to cover the whole thing.~~

~~KS: But they didn't have to cook it at all, huh?~~

TR: Well, they cook it some, but just enough to make it spongy. ~~I don't know how they do it. I never did watch 'em. Ah, you've seen 'em—make it kind of spongy, you know.~~ They'll be stirring it just like anything else. But they got to watch it. At a certain point they'll get it off the heat and then separate it from there and then it's—~~it's kind of, you know,~~ dough-like. And then they start in working on it, too. Then you've got to salt it and they do and then you mix it—like dough. ~~And then they got to wait for that—(inaudible), make it work—it's just what I told you about,~~

~~anything like that. These girls around, they know how to do it,~~
~~but—but they're (inaudible). They can go and buy cheese in town.~~
~~KS: Did it take just one day to make the cheese, or many days—to get~~
~~one batch ready?~~
~~TR:~~ As soon as it's dry it's ready. Maybe before evening[.] ~~maybe—and~~
~~keep it as long as you could—take it out—evening or~~
~~[side one of tape runs out].~~

Second edit

What follows demonstrates the second stage of editing. The text shows how the above transcript appeared after the changes were made in the original interview, but some further editing is marked on this sample. Changes were made primarily to facilitate connecting related ideas and condensing repetitious material. Not all the changes that appear in the following sample are indicated by the editing on the transcript. Some were done as the edited version was being typed. Were I to re-edit from the original transcripts now, I would do far less editing and re-arranging, though I would probably still edit out questions and supply nouns where Ted left them out in responding to questions. I would certainly be far more tentative in deleting hesitations, repetitions, and other stylistic characteristics of Ted's oral narrative. This editing, like that shown above, was done in 1984.

You know this fruit—red ones, some are yellow—well, they grow in different varieties at certain times. Not all the same; some grow a little bit early or some later—real red ones, dark, and yellow. They're sweet. It's what you call prickly pear. It grows off the ground in a bunch, and on the bottom it's prickly. There's little thorns. Every time you load it on the truck, and you're sitting back in the back of the truck, when you start moving, you've got to watch for it. They jump [*flutters hands*] and might get in your eyes. Every time when we load it we have to put it way in the back and put something over it so it won't move. It's just like when you're picking them. The ladies used to pick that fruit with fruit tongs made out of sticks. They brushed 'em off first. They made their own brushes, and they just brush 'em off and then start in plucking 'em. Then when they get 'em home, they peel 'em, peel 'em just like that. Get the skin off, the meat comes off. Then they cook it . . . make syrup out of it. But that syrup's too sweet. I couldn't eat it. It's got too much sugar in it. Natural sugar. And then—it's got a lot of seeds inside, all stuck in. You've got to eat only what's good, leave the seeds alone. They're sweet, too, but yellow. They get on your hands or your shirt ~~or~~ if you're not careful. The old, old, old people—they get 'em, ladies and all [*nods*]. Now nobody bothers 'em.

Cattle eat 'em—deer, anything [*nods*]. I don't think the thorns bother 'em, because they eat even the fruit from the cholla[,] — the ones that hang. They got the same kind of fruit, only smaller and greener. The animals like that, too. That's why you see some cattle with thorns in their faces [*points to cows with thorns in their muzzles*]. They'll be right around it, no matter if it has thorns. They're green, and they have a lot of water or salt or something in them. There's a different kind, too—one not so thorny. It's just kind of bare, and it's got thorns, but it's more soft, and it won't stick you so much. During the fall, when they drop everything, the fruit—you harvest that, every one of those little balls — and clean 'em up, and cook 'em. When it's done, it's just like spinach, tastes like spinach [*nods*]. It's a cactus. It grows out at the Mission on the east side by the freeway. There's a lot of 'em. People go over there and gather it. They store them [raw] in big jars ~~raw~~, just like beans or any staple food, because they're dry, dry. And then you cook 'em, like any staple. And when they're cooked in water, they turn out soft, like spinach. Good eating [*nods*]. They've got no color at all. They're just like a bare tree, or just dry, like wood.

You'd see a whole lot of mesquite beans hanging. You know they're ripe when they're real dry. That's when they're picked, when they're sweet—got to get them sweet ones, then grind 'em, grind 'em, soak them in water. Let them stand for a while and then stir all the juice. Sweetness gets in there, by itself—nothing mixed. On the ranch we used to have it. We put the beans in baskets, big round baskets [*makes circle with arms*], then soak them until the water got kind of creamy like, the color of cream. Then we drink it with a cup. Sweet—just like when you get 'em off the tree. See, all the sweetness in there goes in the water—just like the cactus. ~~Now I'm too lazy—too lazy to gather it.~~[1] [no ¶] Around autumn, when they get ripe, they fall on the ground and it's easier—easier to pick them. The women go down and they

---

1. Inserted below.

rake them up. Now the ladies are so lazy. They want to be some place in the shade. [Now I'm too lazy—too lazy to gather it.] [1] Olden times, you never know where the old ladies going to go. They go out there and they get yucca for baskets. They get the good ones—green ones or those ripe ones, white. Gather them—dry 'em up. The leaves got little threads along the sides, so the women have to clean them, clean them very good, and dry them out in the sun. ṯhat's when they get real white. And then they use that for baskets. Or if they want green ones, they can always get the green stalks. But they usually get the long ones, white ones—cut in two. Everybody made baskets—all the old ladies did. Now you never see anybody [*lifts hands, palms up*]. Some of these ladies now, girls, they know how to make 'em, but they don't want to do it. They're too laze to gather the yucca. They'd rather sit there and turn on the TV.—Or be down in a bar some place. It's not like it used to be.

My grandmother made some pottery, too. Only one spot 'way south, a certain little spot, where they used to go and get the clay. It's small. They need a lot of clay—good clay, just like there is 'way up there on the west side of the Santa Ritas; where they used to go. The went to Arivaca and down to the old towns, down to Tumacacori's old mission—where they used to work in the fields. And they tell me there's a hill or something 'way back there some place—nothing but clay. Used to go out there and get it, the clay, and then bring it home, bring it to the camp, and they start making pottery, any pottery. And they bake 'em—fire, make 'em hard. And they haul 'em off to Nogales, sell 'em, get their food. Or either they haul 'em down to Tombstone and sell 'em there. Or else when they had a lot of time and nothing to do, the ladies go over there where that clay is, the mound or whatever it is, and they make the pottery right there, all on the spot [*nods*]. I didn't ever go. It was done before I was born. They'd make their potteries right there—in no time, I guess, because they know how to do it. They'd just keep on doing it, bake 'em, make 'em get hard, and then when they were ready, maybe the old men or somebody would gather 'em up, haul 'em to Tombstone.

I've seen 'em make pottery a lot of times, but I never cared much about it. It's none of my business. The pots have got to be in the fire— like cooking, baking them when they're wet, or when they're half-ready and still wet, they put them in the fire so they'll get heated up, to a certain temperature, where they get real hard—certain temperature. Oh, they put it in the fire—I don't know how—I know they burn it. One at a time. That's how it works. That's why I say now the younger generation, they don't want to do it—they don't want even baskets [*shakes head*].

You know that yucca tree, the pole, when it grows way up there, I remember when it's still green, when it's ripe—like cane, they cut that, cut it in pieces [*measures about four inches*] and put 'em in the coals— hot coals. They roasted 'em, turn 'em over and then they'd be . . . kind of yellow. They're like steak. When they're warm, they're soft, just like meat. Then you eat them. They're sweet, too. One old man used to do it. We'd be right around. He said, "You want some? I'll do it." "Yeah" [*nods*]. He'd do it[;] we'd just watch him do it. He knows how. He's just a neighbor, working. You know, he's old.

We didn't have time to shoot a rabbit. We never did. We were too busy on the cattle and we never did [*shrugs*] —yet I wanted to see how [cooking it is] it's done. And this old man was helping cook around there, you know, cook for the gang. Came around and said, "Well, if you want a better one, I'll do it. Just kill me a rabbit and I'll do what you're talking about." But the way he told me to do it, I think you just put it in there—the whole rabbit. Just put it in the heat. Dig a hole just about so deep [*measures two feet high*], put rocks in there or coals— coals, hot coals, and then put rocks on top of it and heat so hot. Then you dump the rabbit in there and then cover it some way. Then you cook it like so, when it's hot. It's barbecued [*nods*]. Then you just pull it by the ears sticking out and just undress it like nothing. It gets so hot, the skin just rolls right off like a blanket. You just take it out and pull it by the ears, knock his head off, just unfold it. Everything is done.

I know how to skin rabbits. I know that white-tail rabbit; there's always that little green thing near the heart [*holds finger and thumb about an inch apart*]. You've got to take that out first, before you ever cook it. If you don't take that little green thing out when you try to cook it, then you can taste it,[—]bitter. That's why every time I'm skinning a rabbit I always watch that, take it out, throw it away [*tossing motion*]. Then I clean it, intestines and all that, wash it, make a stew out of it. It's better than anything else. It's better than what you get in the restaurants. Good [*nods*]. And you cook it slow and it gets tender . . . you put a little something — spice or whatever you want, salt on it . . . and get a fresh tortilla. Then put a piece down there and just kind of roll it just like they do at Mexican stands, same thing. You do it while it's hot. Now we're getting hungry [*grins*].

My grandmother prepared rabbit stew. That's where I learned to skin the rabbit. I like to skin the rabbit — it's easy, easy to skin it. Sometime we'd eat rabbit, and at the same time we had the jerky from the deer. We always had something like that. My grandfather went out deer hunting[,] then would dry the ~~mean~~ [meat]. Or else one of us, especially during Christmas or something like that, [would] butcher a cow. Lots of steaks. Then we delivered it to the brothers for a present. Every so often, you know — not all the time, you know. When they want to. That's a lot of fun [*nods*].

They had a lot of ranches and all that. Most of the people, them old people, they live up there, over by that hill, about twelve miles from me. They get around together. Most of them live on the west side of that hill, with wells and houses, and we live on the south side — east. We would go visiting, Sundays. And when they get ready to go on a hunting trip, well they tell each other — they know. They're ready. 'Course, the deer weren't like now. You could see 'em down there. Used to be 'way up in the high mountains. [At certain times, you know, when they're not drinking too much water, that's when they're fat, especially them antelopes. That's when they go and shoot 'em, kill 'em, because they got a lot of meat on them. At certain times they don't have.]² So they'd go and kill the antelope or whatever they can get. Oh, maybe two, three men—all depends. Just a few. Maybe three, four, or maybe two. It's better for two or three because they have more meat that way, you know. That's why they always have jerky. Fry 'em up . . . salt 'em . . . there you are [*nods*]. ~~At certain times, you know, when they're not drinking too much water, that's when they're fat, especially them antelopes. That's when they go and shoot 'em, kill 'em, because they got a lot of meat on them. At certain times they don't have.~~ ⁽²⁾ They go when it gets cool, so the meat won't spoil. They hang it up and put a lot of salt on there and keep the flies off. They strip it, like they do now. Have some pieces, long pieces [*measures about a foot*]—just so they'll dry. Thin it out just enough [*measures about a quarter inch*] and put a lot of salt on it. It'll dry faster. They got a line, like a clothes line with a pole and another pole and then string the wire or rope, just like laundry. And let the meat stay and dry—good sun—you know the air—sun, dries faster. When it's dry, well they gather 'em back, and then stack 'em—stack 'em in a container. Then any time during the year, if they want some of it they just get a piece, put on the coals, eat it. Everybody likes it, even the Mexicans.[¶] You don't care about the store because there's a store right there, with whatever you need, like lard or matches or whatever. There's [was] a store where the mine was, where the hills are, right up where they're mining right now. [I guess my grandparents got everything there before I was born, because it's a booming town then.]³ It's an old place—where they used to have a lot of the Mexican celebrations[—]behind Twin Buttes. There were big horse races once in a while with a lot of fighting and drinking. I went up there when I was young. There's a school house still there, too, where the kids used to go to school. You can see a lot of those old worn out buildings. And there's a locomotive there, too. Now it's just a ghost town [*sweeps hand*]. And there was a store there not too long ago. That's the oldest mine there, before these new ones come. They got a store right there, too. I used to go, and it was not too far.

2. Inserted from below.   3. Inserted from below.

Everything was all there[.] ~~when I was—when I wasn't around.~~ But when I grew up, then I went out there to get the horse or ride around, and I'd go up there to that store, buy tobacco or whatever. I'd go over there. It's not too far, right by that highway—not the main highway, but Mission Road. I used to know the people. ~~I guess my grandparents got everything there before I was born, because it's a booming town then.~~ [3] I [can] ~~could~~ see it right now, where the mining town used to be—all around there's where they used to mine. Well, they're mining it now. When I was riding, I used to go up there, just to look around, to that store to buy something. But it's no more. Everybody moved out. It shut down. I used to work at the mine, too, for a while where the Twin Buttes mine is now, and then the other ones, too. That's where all the people come to~~,~~ from town to work, every morning. Duval mine and all that—what they call American Smelter. There's about four big mines right along that section. But at that time, they had a mine—I don't know what company, but anyway in the olden times, it was underground. A lot of ~~the~~ people living there, Mexicans mostly, and whites. It's a booming town, just like in the olden days.

Just like Arivaca, where the people own that ranch. I work for them. it's got water away up there—cottonwood trees bigger than anything around. Big roots—roots go like this [*spreads his hands*], and there a little river way out in the desert. It's was just a little time ago. I could go over there right now if I wanted to. I still work with him part-time. They got a ranch there. I go with them once in a while during the summer. They got a lot of horses, too. When the water runs down, all we've got to do is [dig] stock holes. And you keep digging, digging so deep as you can, and big as you can. Then you got a pond right in there—the water come into it during the rainy season, or winter. It's' a nursery land, too. He's married to a Mexican. And the Mexican lady, I guess her father owned the place, and they all died and now she takes care of it, and they run the nursery, too. And whenever I want to, I go over there, and then we do a lot of nursery work. And then the weekends, that's the time when they want me to do something like fixing corrals or anything[.] <u>w</u>ell I go on the weekend—sleep over there, do the work, come back. His business is in town. Come back in the evening—early tomorrow we get another job.

All the ladies got to make cheese—it's not a man's business. They got to make their own, unless they're in a group, but I never see it. See, the people live across from the other side of the mountain, west side, where they got their own houses. And they got their own milk, you know; they got their own stock, and they milk so [much] ~~must~~—just enough where they can make the cheese. You got to get your hands in everything when you're young[.] ~~—you know,~~ a̲s a kid, watch 'em when they do it, and then probably they'll say, "Try it," and I'd try it, try that. 'Course, they sit on a bucket or something, old bucket—sit down start milking in[to] the bucket [*milking motion with hands*].

My grandmother's the only woman in the family, but some of the neighbors who come, they got ladies staying with them that are old. Once you get too old, you can't get out. But she, she's lively. She's old, but she's lively. She like to do the milking. 'Course, she done it in her time. Of course, at the time them old cattle were pretty tame. But once in a while you'd get a new cow in there that'll be just awful[.] ━ y̲ou've got to hold it down till they get used to it. Just like dairy cows now—I could go up there to the plant and ask for a job—I could get it. Of course, in school I done a lot of it. When it's war[m], [the milk] ~~it~~ starts getting thick. The butter, and all the fat, you know, is still coming up. It'll start getting heavy, and then you've got to work it over some way, and then it'll come out by itself. Cream will come to the top. And then you've got to stir it every time [*circular motion*]. And then some way they just take so much out of it, at a certain time, and that's cottage cheese[.] s̲he knows how. Set it aside, and it'll be cottage cheese. All you've got to do is pour salt over it—there you are. Butter, too. Cream butter, you know. Churn it—churn it and make about as good as anything. I like it.[¶] They boil it, I think they boil it to make this quesidilla, they call it in Mexican—sell it in the stores, too. It's kind of like a tortilla, only, it's cheese. You buy it sometimes in the store. I like that, too. They got to cook it. It's hard work.

[no ¶] You put in part of the cow. [Put it in while it's not cooking or

else the whole thing would cook itself.] [4] I think it's the bladder. I never
get to find out so good about it, but they call it qual in Mexico. You
have to buy it in a slaughter house. They sell it there. It's dried and
salted like that. It think it's either a bladder or a piece of it. And they
got to dip it in there when it's ready, work it in there some way. You've
got to hang it like that [*pantomimes holding up something and hanging
it*] and let it dry—used it over again—over and over. Usually they had
a whole row of it just hanging up, for that purpose. It's good all the
time, because it's dry. It's salty—I know it's salty. Just a big leaf—
thinner, too—round leaf, it's just like that, the way it's cut. See, you
just keep it there for the time being. What they do when it gets—when
it gets we[t], I guess it's going to fix the fat and all that. ~~Put it in while
it's not cooking or else the whole thing would cook itself.~~ [(4)] They got to
just put it [in] at a certain time, and let it stay for a while, and then it
works itself in with the cream or whatever. Then the cheese come out,
and that's when they start working that. And then they have to take
that out. And they start in—stir [*circular motion*], like anything else.
[Well, they cook it some, but just enough to make it spongy. They'll be
stirring it just like anything else. But they got to watch it. At a certain
point they'll get it off the heat and then separate it from there and then
it's dough-like. And then they start in working on it, too. Then you've
got to salt it and then you mix it—like dough.] [5] And then they take
out—take out whatever—whatever they want out, like for cottage
cheese, or white, and then leave the rest. And then they work on it.
Then it gets so that it gets to like cheese. They take a while. When its
ready[,] they start over again, doing it some different way. When it gets
[like] ~~so in the~~ dough, that's when they put it out in a cloth, on some
big white cloth, flour cloth. They got a wooden [ring] ~~right~~ made for
that, about so wide [*ten inch circle*][.] And it's in a ring, made in a ring.
Then you just set that in there and you dump the whole thing, round
and smooth. If you're going to make a big one, you've got to have a big
[ring] ~~one~~. Smaller one—you know, they got different sizes. Craftsmen

4. Inserted from below.   5. Inserted from below.

305

around town, they make those. They could do it. I could do it, too.
And then they set that in there—'course, it's clean, just like anything,
all greased up or something. Set in there, what they call awatche—it's
made of wood—it's got a little spout, with a handle—set it in there and
then juice or water—it'll go right in there and start draining out. And
then that's when they start—after it's wrapped up in that ring—getting
ready—tied smoother, smaller. Then they start weighting it[.] — they
got special rocks—smooth ones. Put one on there, weigh it down
[*presses down on legs*], so all that wet stuff comes—it'll drain out itself.
And then it'll be round just like in a pan. See, and it stays there until
the whole thing dries out. They drain the juice out of the cheese[.] it's
kind of yellow, you know, green or yellow. And the dog like it. Drink it
like soup. Makes 'em fat, too, because it's got a lot of—lot of fat in it.
And then . . . it's ready. Just take it out—there it is. Unwrap it—that's
the cheese. Won't fall apart. Keeps well. Like any cheese. And then I
like fried cheese, you know, fried like potatoes—kind of brownish? I
eat a lot of it. Oh, we had cheese all the time. We got it.

We make one at a time. [As soon as it's dry it's ready. Maybe before
evening.][6] Next day they'll make another one, and by the time
maybe—maybe two or four day, by the weekend, everybody will be
heading for town, down the village. Everybody likes it. And you haul it
off, sell it to them, sell it, peddle it all the way. In no time it's all gone.
~~Well, they cook it some, but just enough to make it spongy. They'll be
stirring it just like anything else. But they got to watch it. At a certain
point they'll get it off the heat and then separate it from there and then
it's dough-like. And then they start in working on it, too. Then you've
got to salt it and then you mix it—like dough.~~ [5] ~~As soon as it's dry it's
ready. Maybe before evening.~~[6]

6. Inserted from below.

306

NOTES

Introduction

1. Tohono O'odham is the official name of the tribe referred to as Papago in most anthropological studies. Many of the sources cited in this volume use the term Papago since they were published before the official name change, and Rios identified himself as Papago. Thus, I use the term Papago more often than Tohono O'odham.

2. He was actually chairman of the San Xavier district, not of the whole O'odham tribe.

3. Archives at the Mission San Xavier del Bac indicate that Ted's maternal grandfather was named William Arnita and that his mother Anselma was married to Francisco Rios under the maiden name Arnita.

4. Ocotillo is a form of cactus that, if the slender branches are cut and stuck in the ground, will grow a living fence.

5. I mean no disrespect in using the shortened form of Theodore Rios's name. I was introduced to him as Ted, and he told me he would prefer that I call him Ted.

6. Substantial samples from transcripts of interviews appear in later chapters.

7. Anthropologist Nancy Oestreich Lurie, in her introduction to *Mountain Wolf Woman,* an autobiography of a Winnebago woman published in 1961, writes: "My interview questions about Winnebago culture helped relieve the tedium of existence in a hospital ward" where Mountain Wolf Woman was a patient being treated for cancer" (xii). So bedside collection of personal narratives is not unprecedented.

8. I use the term Papago here and in other parts of this volume when discussing the period of the Rios-Sands collaboration because it was the tribal name in use at the time. All of these interviews were conducted in English, thus accessible to me as a non-Papago speaker. That Ted was fluent in English, in retrospect, was one criterion for his selection as a potential

narrator. While many Native American autobiographies have been narrated in the tribal individual's native or first language and present the additional difficulty of attempting to trace the process of translation, this project does not. However, as Gerald Vizenor notes, "English, that coercive language of federal boarding schools, has carried some of the best stories of endurance, the shadows of tribal survivance" (1994: 106). It should be recognized though, that had I been able to interview Ted in Papago, the results might have been significantly different. He took pride in his command of his first language and in casual conversations often lamented that the younger generation lacked facility in Papago.

9. In a February 1998 telephone conversation, Fontana told me his acquaintance with Rios was actually based on the fact that Rios had done quite a lot of landscape work for the Fontanas. He recalled particularly Ted removing tamarisk trees from the Fontana residence property, which is near the San Xavier reservation. He commented on how hard Ted worked and that he was successful in wrestling out the toughly rooted trees. He also explained that they were not actually close friends and that he could add nothing to the data I already had on Rios.

10. Nothing in the graduate curriculum of the 1970s addressed editing, and certainly not editing oral narrative into written text. That process was seen as clearly the province of anthropology. Not until the 1980s and the growth of interdisciplinary curricula were literary and ethnographic text-making recognized as intersecting. Another Native American autobiography, this one written by a Yaqui man, became my dissertation. That choice was primarily a matter of expediency since it was already structured.

11. I was taking a course on Papago language and culture in the anthropology department during the spring of 1974.

12. This provision of the contract letter demands that this volume be co-authored; even without this proviso, however, Ted's contribution to the book merits his designation as co-author. Specific discussion of royalty distribution is taken up in chapter eight and the epilogue.

13. Tapes, transcripts, and drafts will be housed at the Arizona State Museum upon publication of this volume. Duplicates will also be given to the Tohono O'odham archives.

14. This volume violates the letter but I hope not the spirit of the contract.

15. George W. Stocking Jr. uses this phrase in discussing the history of how field methods are and are not taught. He says, "For the most part, however, fieldwork training was a matter of learning by doing, and this less in the tradition of apprenticeship than of 'sink or swim' " (1983: 8).

16. A basic key to the punctuation and vocables used in the transcripts follows. The purpose of this system, devised when the tapes were transcribed by Arizona State Secretarial Services and checked and corrected by me while reviewing the audio tapes in the late 1970s, was to preserve as much as possible a sense of voice and pace in the narration. Only two punctuation marks are used in unconventional ways: the dash, which indicates hesitancy before continuing and ellipses, which indicate an overlap in the conversation or an extended pause. The vocable representation "Mm hmm" indicates sounds of assent. Notations of gestures, which appear in brackets, have been added to the text from fieldnotes of the interviews taken as backup to the tape recordings.

17. Jose Rios was a tribal leader in the San Xavier district of the larger O'odham reservation, not tribal chairman for the whole O'odham nation

18. Santa Rosa village is in the central part of the main Tohono O'odham reservation, a site to which Ted traveled with his family occasionally and the locale of a government-run boarding school.

19. A less than successful first interview is something of a pattern in the collection of life stories from Native American individuals. For example, Nancy Oestreich Lurie reports, "The first day's work proved highly disconcerting to me. Mountain Wolf Woman told her entire story on less than half a reel of tape" (1961: xiv).

20. Kevin Dwyer, in an analysis of the asymmetry of the interview situation, quotes from one of his own fieldwork dialogues with an "informant," in which he queries the person regarding the purpose of the project. The man says "As for me, I know that I'm not concerned with a single one of your questions. I know that these questions serve your purposes, not mine. I think about the questions, whether they are small questions or large ones, and I think about them because they serve your purposes, not mine" (1977: 144). Ted might well have expressed the same sentiment about the questions I asked during this first interview, despite the fact that we had agreed on a mutual goal.

21. Also See George E. Marcus's 1997 essay, "The Uses of Complicity in

the Changing Mise-en-Scène of Anthropological Fieldwork," for an extended discussion of the concepts of rapport, collaboration, and complicity in ethnographic fieldwork.

22. Capturing the vulnerability of the encounter is part of the intention of this text, as is revealing the ongoing vulnerability of both partners in the project as a life is made public and the process is analyzed. The balance of the initial encounter shifts as the project moves from the field to the academy. As Ruth Behar argues, the job of the fieldworker is "to bring the ethnographic moment back, to resurrect it, to communicate the distance, which too quickly starts to feel like an abyss, between what we saw and heard and our inability, finally to do justice to it in our representations" (1996: 9).

23. See *Autobiography of a Yaqui Poet*, by Refugio Savala (1980), which I edited from a written text and produced by direct collaboration with the author. Also see "Man Made of Words: The Life and Letters of a Yaqui Poet" (1980: 143–59), which discusses the editing process of the *Yaqui Poet* book. The editing done in 1984 on the Rios transcripts is what appears throughout this book. I seriously considered reediting the transcripts in preparation for producing this volume; however, I abandoned the idea because I determined that further editing would, in fact, preempt the process focus of this study. Furthermore, I am much more reluctant now than I was in 1984 to intrude on Ted's narration.

24. I have not done further editing of Ted's narrative since 1984 because I believe it is important to show the steps in the process as they took place. Each editorial intervention takes the inscribed text further from the interviews; I am very reluctant to increase that distance with additional tampering with Ted's narrative so long after the actual interviews.

25. For a more extended editing sample, please see the appendix to this volume.

1. Theories of Inscribing Collaborative Personal Narrative

1. Lawrence C. Watson and Maria-Barbara Watson Franke make a strong case for revealing the context in which a narrative is collected. They write that it is important to "find out something about the dynamics of the situation, including the motivations, understandings, defenses, and situa-

tional constraints that influenced the data-collecting setting, the results, and the very process of interpretation itself" (1985: 17).

2. James Clifford notes that, anymore, fieldworkers often "don't study in villages, rather in hospitals, labs, urban neighborhoods, tourist hotels, the Getty Center." He also observes that fieldwork may be more a matter of commuting than dwelling (1997: 21, 69).

3. Throughout this volume, I will use the term "informant" in quotation marks because the relationship the term implies is not one I find acceptable in cross-cultural descriptions. Though the term has currency and I would have used it (and did use it) to describe Ted during our fieldwork and for some time after, it is very limiting in that it posits that he is strictly a provider of information. The fact that we agreed to enter into a partnership on a book about his life demands that "collaborator" replace the term "informant," even though the latter term is still widely used in the discipline of ethnography. Edward M. Bruner supports my view of the term when he writes, "They are presented in our ethnographic texts as historically situated persons, with voices, names, and presence. It is hard to call them informants anymore or even by the trendy term 'consultants.' They emerge in these papers as full-fledged personalities, and our new way of dealing with them has changed us." He goes on to note, "To name an informant is to give up some measure of our own power, and paradoxically, to the extent that we yield control we are free to become more creative" (1993: 327).

4. Timothy Dunnigan does not recall having paid Ted (interview, October 21, 1998), but given the fact that the project was grant funded, he may have been paid through the grant.

5. Geyla Frank observes that the life-story project "provides an *occasion* for interaction, an occasion structured by the degree of formality of the interview, its understood purpose, the length of the project and its setting, the respectively perceived role and status of the interviewer and subject, the exchange of money and services, the interviewer's and the subject's motives for undertaking the work, and their conception of the task" (1979: 86). Each of these elements was at work during the interviews Ted and I did.

6. Colonialism as a term and critical approach in ethnography and literary studies postdates the work Ted and I did in the 1970s and the editing work I did in the 1980s.

311

7. What is today called psychological anthropology had its beginnings shortly after the turn of the century and became an increasingly important anthropological subdiscipline from the 1930s onward. The change in terminology is interesting in regard to the change in emphasis it suggests, but examining the history of this area of anthropology is beyond the purview of this study. For a more historical approach and detailed methodology discussion, see Marvin Harris's *The Rise of Anthropological Theory* (1968). Also see James P. Spradley's *Culture and Cognition: Rules, Maps, and Plans,* in which contributor Melford E. Spiro notes, "Personality studies 35 years ago were unsystematic; and cultural studies and their heavy descriptive empirical emphases were self-consciously nontheoretical." He comments further that often this approach to cultural studies, "given the tools available, results in findings that sometimes lack the unqualified conviction characteristic of research in more structured fields" (1972: 101–2). This comment speaks very directly to my own sense of ambiguity and lack of conviction about Ted's narrative as a personality-in-culture document and my resistance to examining it primarily in those terms, even though this approach dominated my original goals for the project.

8. An exception is Michael Hittman, who candidly discusses his rejected attempt of monetary payment to Corbett Mack, a Northern Paiute, whose life story he collected and edited. He discusses alternative payment in the form of tobacco, groceries, and, for a time, liquor (1996: 3, 6–7).

9. The agreement to share royalties also serves this purpose.

10. Steven Webster's view on this matter is somewhat different from mine. He says that "escape from ethnocentrism is our business, but a definitive escape puts us out of business altogether." I disagree with the first part of his statement. The very fact that I have engaged in this project is proof that I choose not to endorse giving up on cross-cultural inscription. I do agree with Webster when he says that "ethnocentrism, like true prejudice, is the only basis upon which we understand at all, and when unavoidable, discriminates good from bad cultural practices (our own and others!)." He recommends anthropological irony as an antidote to ethnocentricity (1982: 101–2).

11. For a critical application of colonial theory to a personal narrative by Papago narrator Maria Chona, see Helen Carr (1996: 237–53). Also see my

response to Carr's analysis of the Underhill's control of the Chona text in "Narrative Resistance: Native American Collaborative Autobiography" (1998a: 4–5).

12. The Santa Cruz River runs north out of Mexico. During Ted's youth on the San Xavier reservation, the Santa Cruz River, which runs through it, ran year round. It no longer runs at all, due to intensive agricultural production by a multistate corporate farm south of the reservation.

13. For a full discussion of these terms see *Mutualities in Dialogue,* ed. Ivana Markova, Carl F. Graumann, and Klaus Foppa (1995).

14. While commonality is not a requirement for narrative performance rather than reportage, as is the case in the interview excerpt, expectation of comprehension and appreciation by the audience are. Ted has no such expectation from me at this point in our relationship and offers only minimal reportage in response to my questions rather than offering narrative anecdotes.

15. David M. Hayano uses the term "auto-ethnography," which he defines as discussion of problems of methodology and theory associated with fieldwork when ethnographers research and write about their "own people" (1979: 99). Because "auto-ethnography," as Hayano defines it, does not apply to cross-cultural collection and presentation, and Barbara Tedlock's use of the term "narrative ethnography" does, I find the latter more accurate in discussing the approach I use in this volume.

16. As early as 1979, Sidney W. Mintz, in an essay entitled "The Anthropological Interview and the Life History," called for what is now termed narrative ethnography. He says that "anthropological life histories are, for the most part, descriptive accounts intended to speak for themselves. But they would be much more useful if the recorder would try to say who he or she is, and why the life history was recorded in the first place." He also recommends that the fieldwork "make an honest effort, at least after the materials have been collected, to address the issue of how the informant and the fieldworker were interacting, why they were drawn together, what developing concerns for (or against) each other influenced the rhythm and nature of the enterprise." And he calls for the ethnographer "to define his or her place between the informant and the reader" (23–24).

17. Whitehead and Conaway point out that "although the fieldworker brings a sense of self to the field, he or she may not be fully conscious of who

that self is. Indeed, most humans seldom go through life pondering why they behave as they do" (1986: 8). Reflexivity, however, demands such pondering. In my case, it is a post-encounter experience.

18. For a discussion of how mediation works in the other dominant form of Native American inscription, see James Ruppert's *Mediation in Contemporary Native American Fiction* (1995).

19. William Schneider cautions the non-Native collaborator: "In oral biographies the issue of explanation is particularly difficult because in working with the narrator's stories, the writer must highlight the description in ways that support rather than overshadow the narrator's telling. It must remain the narrator's book" (Bodfish 1991: 185). This volume attempts to present and elucidate Ted's narrative and his narrative process, but in doing so risks overshadowing the former, which Schneider warns against.

20. For further discussion about "metafictionally self-reflexive inscription," see Linda Hutcheon, "Beginning to Theorize Postmodernism" (1993: 246).

2. Collaborative Life Story as Literary Expression

1. Jeanette Harris uses this term to denote narrative based on "what he or she has experienced or perceived first-hand" as opposed to information-based discourse, which is "at least initially, extraneous to the writer's own experience" (1990: 64).

2. Paul John Eakin notes that intention "becomes the decisive consideration in dealing with both generation and the reception of autobiographical text" (1985: 20). David Murray makes an observation that applies specifically to Native American oral personal narrative as well as written autobiography by Native Americans when he writes, "Given the absence of any contexts within Indian cultures for written autobiography, any accounts we have must be seen as a response to a white initiative, whether at the personal level—being paid to answer questions—or at a cultural level, Indian realization that a vehicle was not otherwise available for the publicizing of certain views" (1991: 68).

3. Opening an autobiography with a genealogy is yet another convention of the genre. Benjamin Franklin's narrative provides a typical example. That tape 1 begins with Ted's ancestry is my incorporation of the convention into the project, not Ted's choice.

4. This may have been due to an internalizing of the Dunnigan-Rios tapes that introduced me to Ted and perhaps became an unconscious model for my questioning. And the experience with Dunnigan may have also influenced Ted's narrative to focus on data rather than personal experience and interpretation of it.

5. Sally McBeth, discussing her collection and editing of Shoshone teacher Esther Burnett Horne, makes the following observations that apply to the Rios-Sands project. She notes that "moving from interview to published account involves countless decisions . . . because the integrated quality of writing contrasts, often dramatically, with the fragmented nature of speaking. . . . Transcripts of conversational data frequently appear to be chaotic and unordered compared to written text" (Horne 1998: xv–xvi).

6. Mary Beth Tierny-Tello notes in her essay "Testimony, Ethics, and the Aesthetic in Diamela Eltit" that literary qualities are subordinate to sincerity, though "aesthetic concerns frequently play a role in such texts" (*PMLA* 1999: 79).

7. What follows is actually the second half of the first interview on May 16, 1974. I've selected it for two reasons: it is relatively brief and it fits with my intention to present throughout this volume the interview transcripts and edited text in roughly the order in which they were narrated. Again, the purpose is to expose, as much as possible, the process as it occurred, which I hope will support the parallel and equally important intention of this volume of analyzing the process of the project.

8. A *charco* is a water catchment for livestock.

9. For a full discussion of theories of illness and curing see *Piman Shamanism and Staying Sickness,* Bahr et al. (1974).

10. Watson and Franke note that life history requires that the narrator "speaks about *his subjective world,* which includes his interpretations of himself and his experience" (1985: 48). Ted's narrative is not self-reflexive.

11. Geyla Frank makes Ted's failure to interpret his experiences somewhat less distressing when she points out that "while life is formed around the meanings an individual develops to connect experiences, the story of a life is not a fait accompli of consciousness but is a form that emerges in discourse with another or with oneself" (1979: 86).

12. This pattern will be more fully examined in chapter 6 as will his performative expression of emotion.

13. Writing about personal narrative, Howard S. Becker says, "To understand why someone behaves as he does you must understand how it looked to him, what he thought he had to contend with, what alternatives he saw open to him" (1966: vi). Discussing his presentation of *Kusiq: An Eskimo Life History from the Arctic Coast of Alaska* by Waldo Bodfish Sr., editor William Schneider describes his desire to gain interpretive as well as behavioral information: "I also wanted to be sure that he [the narrator] discussed the different stages of his life and that he gave explanations for the changes that occurred over his lifetime. Good stories are important, but a life history has to reflect the narrator's life stages and transitions" (1991: 180).

14. Gordon W. Allport, discussing life history as a subjective document, advises, "If we want to know how people feel—what they experience and what they remember and what their emotions and motives are like and the reason for acting as they do—why not ask them?" (1942: 37).

15. Leaving all interpretation to me allowed Ted to recollect his past without too much discomfort over disturbing experiences. This is, of course, a form of narrative control, as is omission and unresponsiveness to specific queries I made regarding certain topics and responses to events.

16. The very fact that Ted's name appears as a co-author of this volume demonstrates the influence of autobiographical convention, though I think it speaks more toward the issue of collaboration than autobiography. Still, it is an "authorizing" strategy as well as a mark of respect for Ted and the contract we made, and for the absolute necessity of his narrative for the existence of this book.

17. While third-person autobiography is not without precedent, Henry Adam's being the most famous in the American literary canon, it is an unconventional approach to the genre.

18. The fact that in the course of our interviews Ted, at my request, narrates multiple variants of several stories he tells makes his narrative less autobiography than ethnography or storytelling, both forms of discourse that seek multiple versions of specific narrative material. Literary autobiography, by contrast, "authorizes" a single version. Variants will be addressed in another chapter.

19. See Daniel Aaron's *Studies in Biography* (1978) for discussion of the characteristics of biography.

20. While I actually prefer "Native American collaborative personal narrative" to the use of "collaborative biography," because the former is such a general term and has no status in any of the disciplinary areas I address in this volume, I have reluctantly given up arguing for its use. Biography is a genre that is firmly established and most nearly accommodates the realities of the Rios-Sands project and many other such projects. It will have to do for now. The search for adequate terminology has been frustrating and confusing in this field of study. For further discussion of the search and debate over terminology see Sands, "Narrative Resistance" (1998a: 16).

3. Native American Collaborative Personal Narrative

1. I do not wish to claim that what I express here necessarily applies to all published collaborative Native American personal narratives. Each collaborative process is culturally, historically, and personally different and needs to be examined in the context of its time, intention, and collaborative relationship.

2. There are exceptions to this. For instance Frank Linderman is overtly a figure in *Pretty-shield: Medicine Woman of the Crows* (1974) and *Plenty-coups: Chief of the Crows* (1962). I have discussed the former in "Collaboration and Colonialism" (1998b). Less obvious presence of the collector-editor in the text occurs in *Papago Woman* (1979), in which Ruth Underhill is directly addressed as "you" by Chona. *Black Elk Speaks* (1979) also exhibits this pattern, as do some other less well-known texts. More currently, Julie Cruikshank's publication of her dialogues with three Yukon women, *Life Lived Like a Story* (1990) and her more recent critical work, *The Social Life of Stories* (1998), offer good examples of a balanced presentation of collaborators in inscribed text. However, while the presence of the collector can be assumed in all collaborative texts, it is usually suppressed.

3. I use the term Native, rather than Native American, here advisedly. Ethnographers have collected narratives from tribal people all over the world, so many narratives are by others than Native Americans. Some of them offer insight into the process of fieldwork and/or inscription. Shostak (1981), Crapanzano (1973, 1980), DuMont (1978), Resaldo (1980), and

317

even Oscar Lewis (1959, 1961, 1963), despite the controversy which surrounds his work, all offer some insight into their methodologies in their published works.

4. I take up the issue of the influence of both academic institutions and publishers in the final chapter of this volume.

5. In a 1981 essay, R. D. Theisz argues a strong case for close examination of introductions, which is a reasonable approach to probing the collaborative process; however, most introductions to Native American collaborative personal narratives are brief and do not provide enough information to make solidly founded inferences about the actual process of bicultural production.

6. Happily, a great deal of very insightful examination of Native American personal narratives is coming into print. Such scholars as — and this list is by no means exhaustive — Arnold Krupat (1985, 1996), David Moore (1994), David Murray (1991), and Greg Sarris (1993) are extrapolating methodological strategies by means of application of new theoretical approaches. To trace the history of the scholarship on Native American "autobiography" by literary critics over the past four decades is beyond the scope of this volume and has been done by the scholars mentioned above and several others, including Arnold Krupat (1985), H. David Brumble (1988), A. LaVonne Ruoff (1990), Gretchen Bataille and Kathleen Sands (1984), and Hertha Wong (1992). Articles on this topic by these and many other scholars often appear in *Studies in American Indian Literatures*.

7. See works by Julie Cruikshank (1990, 1998), Barbara Tedlock (1992), and Dennis Tedlock and Bruce Mannheim (1995), to mention only a few.

8. While David Murray points out that there is a broad range of possible presentations within this "bicultural hybrid form" (1991: 77), most conform to the editor's introduction followed by structured and edited Native American narrative patterns.

9. My intention here is not to discredit theory as a tool for examining Native American personal narrative. It would be foolish to dismiss ethnographic and literary theories that have emerged in the interim between the field collaboration between Ted and me and this volume. Much of my interpretation of the project and the texts it produced is enabled by the new ethnography and postmodern literary theory.

10. These studies generally address both written personal narratives and collaborative ones. My attention in this volume is to oral narratives, not to those actually written by Native Americans, though even these texts are not without instances of elicitation by non-Native Americans—the Simmon-Talesava collaboration that produced *Sun Chief* (1974) being an example—and the mediation by editors that affects all published narratives to some degree.

11. Elsewhere ("Narrative Resistance" 1998a) I have cautioned scholars that too much attention to introductions and too little to Native American personal narrative texts can skew interpretation of the narratives. While I concentrate in the ensuing discussion on collector-editor disclosure of methodology, I want to point out that I do so in order to examine the process of inscription. Several other chapters in this volume focus on the Rios narrative rather than on the experimental nature of its presentation.

12. It may be coincidental that many of the collector-editors discussed in this chapter, myself included, were graduate students when they undertook a collaborative narrative project with a Native American person, but I find it interesting and wonder how the inexperience of the interviewers affected the composition of the narratives. And also how many other collector-editors of Native American personal narratives were also students with little or no experience in the field. The tradition of training by doing and the involvement of amateurs in interviewing personal narrative subjects may have more impact on this form of inscription than heretofore recognized.

13. As a retrospective publication, *The Fifth World* bears similarity to this volume.

14. This is, as Clifford points out in his now famous essay "On Ethnographic Authority," a convention of what he calls confessional ethnography (1983a: 132–35).

15. My contacts with Native Americans before my interviews with Ted were very limited and largely social in nature. I had attended the Pendleton Roundup several times; had several classmates who were Native American when I was an undergraduate, but we had never discussed specifically "Indian" topics; gone to some Yaqui ceremonies as a spectator and visited the San Xavier Mission on the O'odham reservation after arriving

in Tucson in 1969; was acquainted with a Hopi faculty member in the University of Arizona Anthropology Department; and had traveled through reservations and was used to seeing Indians, having lived all my life in the West. But Native Americans were still the exotic Other when Ted and I met. I had never even been to Sells, the O'odham tribal headquarters, until the day I was introduced to Ted.

16. Addressing this aspect of the Bennett-Crapanzano relationship is unique, as far as I know, in a published text of Native American "autobiography," probably only revealed because of the field journal format of the book. Conflict is addressed through hints or as a minor impediment to the collection-editing process in many works—for instance, see David Murray's discussion of Geronimo's autobiography (1991: 69–71)—but is not made an explicit element of the methodological discussion. I suspect that one reason for this is that confrontation is more an Anglo practice than a Native American one and that resistance/conflict in collaboration is expressed by means of narrative rather that in direct verbal exchange as Crapanzano describes in his journal. Greg Sarris's discussion of Elizabeth Colson's inscription of three Pomo women's lives demonstrates this nonconfrontational form of resistance (1993: 79–114). Later discussion of Ted's narration will also directly address this issue.

17. David Murray warns that there is a danger of "textualizing the Indians out of existence" if the presentation of Native American personal narrative is subordinated to a search for signs of "white ideological investment" (1991: 3). That is a danger in the highly self-reflexive form of presentation, one that I am grappling with throughout this volume and that I hope is offset by substantive sections of Ted's narrative in each chapter.

18. I refer in my discussion to the "revised and enlarged edition" published in 1992. The original publication date is 1982.

19. I've written at considerably greater length on both of these works. For discussion of the Davidson narrative, see "Indian Women's Personal Narrative: Voices Past and Present" (1991). For discussion of *Life Lived Like a Story*, see "Collaboration and Colonialism: Native American Women's Autobiography" (1998b).

20. There is a long list of other published Native American personal narratives that could be addressed in this discussion, but none of them offers

potential models for the Rios narrative because they are structured almost identically—methodological introduction, Native American personal narrative, analysis, brief editing sample—as collected and edited autobiographical texts with fairly minimal attention to process. A very recent example of a traditional presentation of a Native American personal narrative is *Essie's Story: The Life and Legacy of a Shoshone Teacher* (1998) by Esther Burnett Horne and Sally McBeth. McBeth's methodological introduction is lengthy, discursive, and up to date theoretically, and a four-page demonstration of the authors' collaborative editing at the end of the volume is informative, but like most other collaborative Native American "autobiographies," this one does not make any significant departures from the standard ethnographic structure and form except for the emphasis on Horne's relationship to Sacajawea and the debate concerning her historical role, and most significantly in that the editing stage of the process was collaborative.

21. This issue is taken up in more detail later in this volume.

22. Returning to a work even several decades after its first publication is not unprecedented in the history of Native American personal narratives. For example, Ruth Underhill added a substantial personal essay about her work with Maria Chona, originally published in 1936, when *Papago Woman* was reissued in 1979.

23. Hittman-Mack (1996); Blackman-Davidson (1992b); and Cruikshank-Sidney, Smith, and Ned (1990) all put much more time into interviews than Ted and I. My formal fieldwork with Ted actually lasted a shorter period than Crapanzano's time with Bennett. Though we did follow-up sessions for several months, the total number of hours is less than fifteen for those.

24. In "Understanding a Life History as a Subjective Document," Lawrence C. Watson notes that in "any life-story document the author is going to tell us, to some extent, what he thinks he is like. Most probably, though, there are aspects of himself that he is either unaware of or consciously conceals from the ethnographer" (1976: 107).

25. I use the term "evoking" here rather than "representing" or "inscribing" in the sense that Stephen Tyler does, as overcoming "the separation of the sensible and the conceivable, of form and content, of self and other,

of language and the world" (1986: 123). He discusses evocation as poly-phonic and as producing a cooperative story in which the "emphasis is on the emergent character of textualization" (1986: 127). These character-istics are all evident in *Life Lived Like a Story.*

26. The influence of Papago narrative style and literary conventions is ad-dressed in a later chapter.

27. See James Clifford's essay "On Ethnographic Allegory" (1986b) for a full discussion of these concepts.

28. I've chosen not to use the transcript partly because this is a long inter-view—forty-eight transcript pages—but also because the interview pat-tern is pretty consistent throughout all the interviews, and transcripts of tapes 1 and 2 used in previous chapters offer substantial examples of inter-view juxtaposed with edited tape, enough to know how much choppier the interview is than the edited piece. How much "raw data" to present even in an experimental volume such as this is still an awkward problem. At what point does two versions of the same material become tedious to the reader, too expensive for the publisher? Both considerations af-fect my decision here. The issue of length and presentation of transcribed interviews are discussed in more detail in the last chapter of this volume.

29. As Arnold Krupat points out, "Native Americans (along with most of the world's people, it would seem) tend to construct themselves not as individuals but as persons, who because of their sensitivity to social 're-straints' may well feel more nearly 'under control,' in Andrew Lock's term, rather than 'in control'" (1991: 175).

30. This was called the "outing program." For a history of the Phoenix Indian School, see Robert Trennert's comprehensive study *The Phoenix Indian School: Forced Assimilation in Arizona 1891–1939* (1988).

31. Phillippe LeJeune notes, "'Identity' is a *constant relationship* between the one and the many" (1989: 34). That seems particularly true of subjects who participate in personal narration who do not posit the individual as the basic unity of society.

32. I strongly believe that the experience of fieldwork is essential for full understanding of the self-narrating process and the published text pro-duced from that process. James Clifford notes that "literary-rhetorical theory or textualist semiotics has no fieldwork component and is at best an anecdotal 'ethnographic' approach to cultural phenomena" (1997: 62).

4. Papago Personal Narratives

1. As William Bloodworth notes, Native American life stories fall into three thematic and temporal categories: "(1) the life story of a once 'wild' Indian whose life began in pre-reservation days but whose educational attainments allowed him to make a transition to civilized life beyond the reservation; (2) the story of a reservation Indian born in pre-reservation times who deliberately sought out sympathetic whites to get his story published; and (3) the autobiography of an Indian who was not born early enough to be a part of pre-reservation life and whose experiences have involved a good deal of exposure to the off-reservation world of the white man" (1978: 71). Chona's narrative fits the second category except for the fact that, like most narratives published from this period, hers was solicited by an outsider, which is actually much more typical than the Native person eliciting help from an outsider. The rest of the narratives cited in this discussion, except for the Dolores text, fall into the third of Bloodworth's categories.

2. Records indicate that Dolores began working for Kroeber as an informant (Kroeber's term) on Papago language in 1911 (misc. Alfred Kroeber papers and correspondence, Bancroft Library, University of California). He later published two monographs in the University of California Publications in American Archaeology and Ethnology series, one on Papago verb stems and another on Papago nouns.

3. There is also a sixteen-page Papago/English narrative collected by Juan Dolores from Antonio Lopez, with whom Dolores was working to collect traditional tribal stories. There is no date on this manuscript, which is in the Dolores archive at the Bancroft Library, and no internal dating. Events and the way of life described suggest that Lopez was born in the nineteenth century, and the first part of his life—up to his marriage in which he follows the Papago tradition of going to his wife's village, much as Chona describes her arranged marriage—was lived in traditional culture. The manuscript ends with his marriage. There is little mention of white society or school; he was sent to go to school at Sacaton on the Pima reservation but ran away before classes started and never actually attended school, being educated by the advice of his elders. He recalls traditional hunting, agriculture, the wine ceremony, travel by horseback, and

running. Because the manuscript is so brief and shares so little with Ted's narrative, I've chosen not to include it in the discussion of this chapter.

4. David McCooey writes, "While many critics consider autobiography as an act only of individual consciousness, the production of autobiography is part of the project of how societies remember, and thus cohere. The act of writing is related to other acts of writing which form a loose, but purposive, system" (1996: 34). Such a system is made apparent in analyzing Papago written and oral narratives in terms of the themes, tropes, and other similarities that relate them.

5. All the other texts are either entirely in English or are translated by the writer himself from Papago into English.

6. See Hertha Dawn Wong's *Sending My Heart Back Across the Years* for further discussion of cross-cultural genre adaptations in what she terms "transitional autobiography" (1992: 116).

7. The original is in the Museum of Anthropology Archive of the Bancroft Library at the University of California at Berkeley, box 134, II.

8. Ted has several anecdotes about horses at his grandfather's ranch, where they had a charco for year-round water. The one referred to on the Antone tape was a time when Ted got the horses riled up enough that one tried to get away and was injured.

9. In the late 1970s I made a thorough search of the Kroeber and Dolores archives at the University of California Bancroft Library, hoping to turn up more of the Dolores autobiography. I was unsuccessful, and subsequent wider searches have convinced me that no full-life narrative exists, though a letter written by his former wife, a woman named Silva Beyer, in December of 1949, eighteen months after Dolores's death, says she is working on Dolores's autobiography. She writes, "I've talked to Dr. Kroeber about the manuscript, and he too would like very much to see it out. He seems to regard the matter as one of blue-penciling, but I see it as something a little more than that—arrangement, and a number of puzzling points to be straightened out. So much has gone into it of Juan, and months and months in which we worked on it together, that it's got to be right. Others beside me think it has both scientific and literary value" (box 134). Beyer is also deceased, and no copy of her text has been located. While searching for more of the autobiography, I perused enough correspondence and other material to piece together a skeleton of a biography

on Dolores. He attended Hampton Agricultural Institute in Virginia from 1898 to 1901. After graduation he came west to do construction work, primarily in California, according to a letter in the Kroeber correspondence files at the Bancroft Library. Little is known about his life from then until 1912, when he went to work for the Department of Anthropology, serving in various capacities from guard to research fellow to preparator to janitor until his retirement in June of 1948, only a short time before his death on July 19 in Tucson. For further information on Dolores's life see his obituary published in *American Anthropologist* 51 (1): 1949.

10. A 1937 attempt by Albert Kroeber (Kroeber correspondence archive, Bancroft Library) to ascertain when Dolores attended the mission school was unsuccessful. The school is no longer in existence.

11. The unidiomatic English throughout the autobiography occurs because it is a literal, interlinear translation of Papago that has not been edited for either clarity (some passages are obscure) or style.

12. In Papago this is *Tuc Con,* the name of a mountain which gives the city of Tucson its name.

13. While I hesitate to characterize Ruth Underhill as a feminist in the current sense of the term, her selection of a female narrator was a fairly daring act in the 1930s, when very little attention was being given to female experience by anthropologists. The fact that Underhill characterizes Chona as an "executive woman" in her introduction to Chona's narrative is indicative, as are many other interpretive comments, that she saw Chona standing for the independence and accomplishment possible for Papagos and, one suspects by extension, all Native American women. While Underhill's approach is appealing to postmodern feminists, it should be noted that it is Underhill's, not explicitly Chona's. In her narrative Chona never interprets any of her actions as challenging Papago gender norms. In fact, she says, "I wanted to be a good woman! And I have been" (59). She does characterize herself as someone who knows her culture thoroughly and has achieved much in her lifetime.

14. This narrative, under the title "Autobiography of a Papago Woman" was first published in the *American Anthropologist* in 1936, for an obviously academic audience, and reissued, with the addition of an interpretive introduction by Ruth Underhill, as a separate volume in 1979 for more general readership.

15. Julie Cruikshank supports my view that the Native language has a significant influence on how location in space is articulated when she notes, "The English language pays particular attention to time, space, and quantity: speakers of Athapaskan and Tlingit languages may choose to pay attention to form and shape, and to other characteristics. . . . Athapaskan languages also express directions, distance and the relative position of things differently from English" (1991: 19).

16. Writing about orally narrated autobiography, William Bloodworth supports a view that relating information may "violate Native American cultural conventions or the ordinary narrative patterns of the informant" (1978: 69).

17. For more detailed discussions of Chona text, see Bataille and Sands (1984: 47–68), Brumble (1988: 13, 77–82, 120, 223), Carr (242–53), and Sands (1989: 53–67).

18. Copies of interview tapes and photocopies of the edited manuscript are available at the Arizona Historical Society Museum Library in Tucson. Unfortunately, no fieldnotes or tape transcripts are archived, only edited material, with all interview questions deleted.

19. For detailed discussion of godparenting as practiced by Papagos, see William S. King (1954: 97–107).

20. Though transcripts of the Blaine-Adams tapes are not available, I was able to listen to the interviews and wrote out a transcription of the first tape so that I could get a sense of Adams's editing technique. I did not make transcripts of the numerous other tapes but did listen to several. Adams was a less intrusive interviewer than I, but Blaine was also a more self-directed narrator. His intention becomes clear both in the interviews and as the published text continues; he wants to discuss changes in Papago government and economics and his role in those changes, particularly from 1932 to 1943, when he served in government tribal positions of influence.

21. David McCooey observes a pattern in personal narrative openings; he writes: "The adult prefaces the autobiography with regional and family history, not in order to suggest what life was like as a child, but in order to figure the extent to which the individual feels connected with the past" (1996: 46). That observation may be applied to both Blaine and Rios but would not apply to Dolores or Chona, who dwell much more fully—and in Dolores's case exclusively—on childhood experience. In all Papago

personal narratives, however, linkage to the past is provided by recollection of family and childhood places and events.

22. Hermosillo is the capital of the state of Sonora, Mexico. Many Tohono O'odhams lived, and still live, in Sonora, the international border being, from their point of view, an artificial barrier across traditional tribal territory.

23. This was a Catholic boarding school run by the Franciscan order, which also served and still serves the San Xavier Mission.

24. Tape transcript 7: 21–22.

25. It would be interesting to know who made the decision to leave this negative comment from the manuscript out of the published text.

26. It is fairly typical that name changes occur when individuals in a bureaucratic position anglicize Native American names or misunderstand them and record them incorrectly. The Lolorias-Dolores name change is a good example of school officials changing names.

27. Ted does slight jobs he doesn't like. This narrative strategy is discussed in chapter 7.

28. I return to Ted's narration on his motion-picture work in the next chapter, since one of the stories he tells about his motion-picture experience is also one he narrates at length to Timothy Dunnigan.

29. Writing about ethnic American autobiographies, William Boelhower says that "many ethnics become quickly deterritorialized" (1991: 135). This claim is generally not true of Native American autobiographers and definitely does not apply to Ted Rios, who consistently throughout his life identifies San Xavier as home.

Ted is also not atypical in identifying strongly with the Papagueria as home. According to a U.S. government report, "In view of the employment possibilities on and off the reservation many individuals leave the reservation to find employment and remain off the reservation while they are employed. When they retire, lose jobs, or for various reasons find employment opportunities dwindling, many return to the reservation. Most Papagos have a family living on the reservation, relatives to whom they can turn in times of need ("Demographic and Socio-Cultural Characteristics: Off-Reservation Service Population, Sells Service Unit, Arizona" 1968: 66).

30. Ted does not make an issue of avoiding the draft, but on tape 12 explains

that he was in the second classification and doing defense work, so he was pretty sure he wouldn't get called up. Then he says, "The friends I got, they're all killed in the war" (transcript 12: 5), which suggests his reluctance to serve in the military might be more a matter of hindsight than a strong view at the time of the conflict.

31. Discussing dualism in life-story narratives, David McCooey notes the "double nature of those who leave their home" (1996: 128). Those Papago narrators for whom travel is a central motif do exhibit bicultural capacities and a dualism in narrated identity that is both grounded in the Papago landscape and as travelers in non-Native American settings and cultures.

32. They both form what Eric Wolf says should be thought of as "multiple external connections" (1982: 387). James Clifford sees the traveling subject as an intercultural figure (1997: 25).

33. Capistran John Hanlon writes that Papagos are "noted for their residential stability. . . . Papagoes do not like to be away from 'home' for a long time. 'Home' for a Papago is the desert. It is the place of one's birth and origin surrounded by familiar landmarks. It is the place where one hears the sounds of the Papago language on the lips of one's friends and relatives" (1971: 270). James Clifford notes, "Home is not, in any event, a site of immobility" (1997: 85), which is certainly true in Ted's case since he works at sites across the southern part of Arizona after his return to San Xavier.

34. Citations to the Rios-Dunnigan tapes throughout this volume are by page number, not tape or date because the transcripts are inconsistent in recording tapes by either number or date. They are also inconsistent in patterns of punctuation. Based on these inconsistencies, I infer that several different people transcribed the tapes, which is not surprising given the magnitude of the Duke project. The tapes of my interviews were all transcribed by the same person with my guidance as to a consistent system of punctuation and tape identification.

35. The taping with Antone could also be classified as a failed project, but in this case the project was discontinued by Ella for reasons that had nothing to do with the quality of the cross-cultural endeavor. She was suffering from diabetes and had many family obligations. After two trips to Santa Rosa to find her gone and numerous unsatisfactory phone messages left

at the village store, I realized Ella was not really interested in pursuing the project but was reluctant to tell me personally, avoidance of conflict being a preferred politeness system for most O'odhams, at least of her generation.

36. See Bataille and Sands 1984: 47–68.

37. For a discussion of Antone's work with Chona and Underhill, see Bataille and Sands 1984: 56–57, 62–63.

38. The Rios family home was the one his father built at their farm near the dry riverbed of the Santa Cruz, where he lived until his death in 1947. When I worked with Ted, his younger stepbrother was living in the house, and it is now occupied by Ted's son Michael Rios.

39. I don't want to make too much of the quantity of taped time focused on food. At the time I suspected that Ted was sick of hospital food and longing for good things to eat. Also, he tended to talk more about food the closer it got to lunchtime.

5. More Than One Way to Tell "A Good One"

1. During these tapings that were primarily to verify the material collected at Sells, I brought my two children with me to play with Ted's three grandchildren, whom he was keeping an eye on at his place at San Xavier. His son Michael and his wife were living in the house that had once been Ted's grandmother's, and Ted occupied a separate one-room building next to it. Our taping, in the shade of a tree, attracted some attention. Ted told me people wanted to know whether I was a social worker or if I was there about mine leases on the reservation. He never told me who he told them I was.

2. While I would just as soon totally ignore Ted's drinking, the evidence from both interview series and from my observations and "off the record" conversations with Ted attest to the pervasive effects of alcohol use in his life and contribute motives to many of his actions. To leave this aspect of his life undisclosed or unanalyzed would distort the narrative that he told during our taped interviews and create a biographical depiction of him that was inaccurate and dishonest. Alcoholism is such a sensitive issue among Native Americans, and an element in Native American life that contributes to many negative stereotypes, that including this aspect of

Ted's life is troublesome to me. However, Ted's portrayal of his drinking is presented in such an unameliorated way that I think his honesty about it is of value. This is also a theme that is addressed in many written autobiographies by Native Americans, so perhaps this section on Ted's drinking might be viewed in that context.

3. In a telephone conversation, October 21, 1998, Timothy Dunnigan, when queried about the circumstance of his interviews with Ted, also noted that they never drank together, though unlike me, he had observed Ted when he had been drinking, perhaps because the Rios-Dunnigan interviews were conducted in the evening whereas my interviews with Ted were always in the morning.

4. The traditional homeland of the Yaquis is along the banks of the Río Yaqui in Sonora, Mexico, not the Río Mayo, which is the home of the Mayo Indians. Whether Ted is mixed up here and the dancers were Mayos, who perform some dances similar to the Yaquis, or whether they actually were Yaquis who were living near the Río Mayo, or his geography is simply inaccurate is unclear. At the time I did not know enough about either tribe to notice the confusion and query him for clarification.

5. Studies of Papago drinking behavior support this interpretation. See Jack O. Waddell (1969: 111–17).

6. This videotape, filmed as a test run for on-location taping for the *Words and Place* series produced by Larry Evers, is not a life-story narration. Rather, it is a series of traditional, family, and personal stories that I cued him to relate. My questions and cues are edited out of the final tape.

7. Conversations about Ted with other people at San Xavier almost always alluded to his drinking. He asked me for lifts to South Tucson several times after interviews and always had me drop him off at a bar frequented by Indians. And during our interviews, he was recovering from injuries and surgery caused by an accident outside this bar.

8. David McCooey points out that "autobiographers tidy themselves up, misremember, and downright lie" because it is a form of testimony. He explains that "some suspicion is a healthy attitude to take toward texts," but that trust too is necessary, though not blind trust. Testimony, he says, must be tested against "the witness's competence, the consistency of the testimony, how it relates to that told by other, and so on" (1996: 189).

9. For a discussion of my initial views on Ted's narration as it relates to his sense of himself, see Sands 1983: 55–65.

10. Interview, Dr. Bernard Fontana, July 2, 1998. Dr. Fontana coordinated the program at the University of Arizona but does not recall how narrators were selected. In a telephone conversation with Timothy Dunnigan, October 21, 1998, he recalled that it was Dr. Fontana who directed him to Ted and to the other men and women with whom he conducted interviews.

11. Jack O. Waddell (1969) uses numerous case histories of male Papagos in *Papago Indians at Work,* but they are focused on employment and work-related behaviors, not comprehensive life histories, and they are not nearly as lengthy as the Duke collection materials.

12. Ted's interviews with Dunnigan, because they are more specific about dates, are very useful in establishing a chronology of narrated events; the interviews I did were less clear on the sequence of events and especially on dates. A chronology of Ted's life based on evidence from both sets of interviews appears in chapter 7.

13. Another topic Ted refused to discuss with me is related to his family's status as cattle ranchers and his role in the decline of the family fortune after his father's death in 1947. Bernard Fontana had told me, even before I met Ted, that before the reservation had been fenced off, Ted's father had run a large herd of cattle in partnership with the prominent Ronstadt family in Tucson, and by Papago standards the family was very prosperous. Ted later confirmed his father's status in the southern Arizona ranching community. What he never admitted to was what Fontana described as his role in the decline of the family fortunes in the 1950s. Ted, as the oldest surviving son, had taken over management of the still-successful cattle business, but over a period of time, he sold off the herd. Ted greatly admired his father—though when I asked him about their relationship, he informed me Papagos do not talk about such private things—so he probably avoided the topic of his failure to keep the cattle business thriving because he felt considerable guilt.

14. This is true of several narrative episodes and stories that I collected in multiple versions. However it should be noted, as Erving Goffman explains, that "listeners can appreciate that the speaker has told the same tale several times before, without this discrediting the teller's spontaneous involvement in his task, his savoring the unfolding of his own storytelling" (1974: 507). What is lost in multiple tellings to the same audience is ignorance of the outcome.

15. The interview on this topic with Dunnigan makes it clear that he is referring to Mexican riders here (1969: 117), not Yuma Indians. By Yumas, he means riders hired in the Yuma area.

16. Bear Canyon is located in the mountains immediately north of Tucson.

17. Benson is an agricultural community about an hour southeast of Tucson.

18. Tubac, the historic site of a Spanish presidio, in recent years has become an artist colony. It is on the highway between Tucson and Nogales, about halfway to the Mexican border.

19. Old Tucson is a tourist site west of Tucson where many motion pictures and television westerns have been filmed, and shoot-out reenactments are staged for paying customers.

20. None of the narratives that I categorize as storytelling appear in the tapes Ted recorded with Dunnigan.

6. Personal-Narrative Performance, Storytelling, and Audience

1. Paul Smith prefers the term "individual" to indicate the determining narrator, the agent who inscribes his or her own narrative (1988: xxxiv–xxxv).

2. In his essay on speech genres, M. M. Bakhtin notes that when the speaker constructs an utterance, he or she actively tries to determine a response. Among the things the speaker considers are the extent to which the audience is familiar with the situation and whether it has "special knowledge of the given cultural area of communication" (1986: 95).

3. Gerald Vizenor notes that "autobiographies must arise from memories and shadows of heard stories" (99), both of which this story of the dangers of mining incorporate.

4. Harold Scheub (1977) offers an informative discussion of the relationship of narration and nonverbal elements of performance.

5. It took me awhile to catch on to the source of Ted's omission of nouns as a culture-based speech pattern. At first, reluctant to expose my confusion, I did not press him for clarification, but I soon realized that establishing topics clearly was part of my role in the collaboration. Interestingly, the more we talked, and the more we repeated topics previously covered, the fewer nouns Ted used. That often left me thoroughly muddled, and I learned to ask him to be more specific even when I was reluctant to interrupt the flow of the narrative. I did not, however, harp on this issue, so

there are many places where I did not interrupt, hoping that the narrative would eventually supply the identifiers, and frequently it did, as the reader can trace in the fortune-teller/mine episodes.

6. For a discussion of stories as emergent from context, see John A. Lucy 1993.

7. For instance, see Ventura Jose's telling of "I'itoi and Ho'ok'oks" (1981).

8. By this time I had training in and was doing scholarly articles on folklore.

9. I make no claim to expertise at lining out a story. While I am familiar with Dennis Tedlock's method and with the one Dell Hymes uses on traditional storytelling performances, my editing here is not based on any single theory. Rather, it is dependent on my familiarity with Ted's speech rhythms, word emphasis, etc. and on several reviews of the audio tape. This edited version was published in *The South Corner of Time* (1981). Anthony Mattina points out that "a transcript of a narrative has no more sound than a musical score. The understanding which readers gain from the script is in direct proportion to what they know about the tradition and the context of the text" (1985: 143). While I agree with his statement, numerous techniques, such as those used by Tedlock and Hymes, facilitate greater insight into the meaning and performance of oral narratives.

10. Lining out personal narrative might also expose the stylistics, themes, etc. of the life story better than either interview or prose format. What's worked so well on prose versions of myths and tales might be a way to preserve performance in personal narrative, though it would be a labor intensive process for a full life story.

11. For a full discussion of the importance of framing to storytelling, see Fine (1984), Bauman (1989), and Scheub (1977).

12. For a discussion of how story performance links the teller to the past, see Richard Bauman (1989).

13. The videotape with Ted is not part of the *Words and Place* series. It was filmed in black and white as an experiment in on-location taping. Technicians had to tap into overhead power lines, and setting up reflectors and seating caused considerable commotion that drew some attention. Once set up, the taping went smoothly and Ted enjoyed it enough to say at the end, "I could go on talking all day." The edited tape was shown at the University of Arizona, with Ted present and thoroughly enjoying the appreciation of the audience. In October of 1975 part of the videotape was

shown on *Rocky Mountain Mix,* a regional PBS television series. Unfortunately, when I checked on the original in February of 1998, I discovered that it is in a videotape format for which there is no longer viewing equipment available. However, KUAT-TV at the University of Arizona does have the edited tape in a viewable format.

14. Avrom Fleishman supports this view, stating, "The need to shape a story will lead the writer to the story types that prevail in his culture; similarly, the desire to conceive a protagonist will be abetted by the character types that have predominated in those stories" (1983: 43). Paul John Eakin concurs, saying that "the ostensibly autonomous practice of autobiography is necessarily embedded in a preexisting context of discursive practice" (1992: 93). W. S. Penn comments specifically on Native American autobiography and stories, saying, "Stories — all stories handed down or made anew — like people get their meaning from reflection on the past, the connection with tradition, and in Native America that tradition remains oral" (1995: 109).

15. He's referring here to the Gulf of California area, the site of traditional Papago salt treks.

16. See Dell Hymes for a detailed discussion of the range of performances, from desultory or perfunctory to authoritative or authentic (1981).

17. For a full rendering of the traditional Children's Shrine story and discussion of the shrine's present-day significance, see James S. Griffith (1992: 22–28).

18. See Roger Abrahams (1972), Beverly J. Stoeltje and Richard Bauman (1988), Dell Hymes (1981), Dennis Tedlock (1983), and William M. Clements (1996) for comprehensive discussions of the role and status of the storyteller within a cultural community and of storytelling as performance.

19. As Roland Barthes notes, "The unity of a text is not in its origin but in its destination," confirming that the multiplicity of what is collected is ultimately sited in the reader (1989: 54).

7. Life-Story Structure and Context

1. Arnold Krupat, in *The Turn to the Native,* cites Wolfgang Hochbruck's term "fabricated orality" (1996: 82 n.15). This concept seems a particu-

larly applicable to my attempt to sustain some sense of Ted's orality in presenting printed representations of his narration.

2. I have deliberately incorporated materials that overlap in content or are variants of the same incidents in order to roughly, indeed very roughly, replicate the repetitious quality of Ted's oral narration.

3. Julie Cruikshank points out that "narrative is fluid, transformative, and intersubjective," and it is "situated in process and performance" (1998: 162). Repetition relates to all of these factors, each of which points to the continuous revision and reinterpretation of events (1998: 155). Cruikshank notes that "events are always made into a story by suppressing some aspects and highlighting others" and "based on a selective reading of the past, especially when they are retold to make meaningful connections to the present" (1998: 4), so it should not be surprising that repetitions are never exact but, instead, variants that change to suit the narrator's purposes. See Moses Cruikshank's *The Life I've Been Living* for editor William Schneider's discussion of the uses of repetition in Native American life story (1986: 122–23). Also see Nora Marks Dauenhauer and Richard Dauenhauer's introduction to *Haa Shuka, Our Ancestors: Tlingit Oral Narratives* for discussion of repetition in published texts (1987: 15–16).

4. David McCooey observes that "there is no given or inevitable starting point or end point for self-consciously narrating one's life" (1996: 15).

5. Mike Crang, in his essay "Spacing Times, Telling Times and Narrating the Past," argues for Ricoeur's concept that the "the world is basically chaotic, that events do not occur in ready-made *intelligible* order." He says, rather, that "events have an order imposed on them by their *emplotment* into a narrative: their significance is determined by their placement in a story" (1994: 31). Ted's narrative is "emplotted" three ways in this volume: associatively by Ted, as evidenced in the transcripts and edited episodes; analytically, in my interpretation of his narrative; and chronologically, in the sequenced list of his life events in this chapter. Each form of emplotment tells a different story.

6. Where there is conflict on dates, I have generally deferred to the interviews with Dunnigan because they are more specific and detailed, and internal evidence supports the chronology he gives to Dunnigan.

7. An extensive history of the Papagueria is beyond the purview of this vol-

ume. For a comprehensive cultural history of the Papagos and their relations to neighboring tribes, see Edward H. Spicer's *Cycles of Conquest*
(1962) and Ruth M. Underhill's *The Papago Indians of Arizona and their
Relatives the Pimas* (1940), *The Social Organization of the Papago Indians* (1939), *Papago Indian Religions* (1946), and *Children of the Crimson
Evening* (1951).

8. The Salt River runs through Phoenix. The Gila River runs about thirty
miles south of Phoenix.

9. Jack O. Waddell, in a chart enumerating the skill levels of Papago mining
employees, lists the jobs Ted describes in his narratives as semi-skilled
(1969: 61)

10. A 1960 survey indicates there were 143 American Indian households in
what was know as the Indian Village in Ajo and a total of 703 Indians
(Waddell 1969: 55).

11. Phelps Dodge records indicate Theodore Rios Jr. worked at the Ajo Mine
from 1961 to 1964 and again from 1968 to 1969, when he went on disability
pay. No records are available for Ted because his employment at the mine
ended so long ago (interview, Kay Patterson, Cornelia Branch of Phelps
Dodge, Ajo Arizona, February 18, 1998).

8. The Poetics and Politics of Collaborative Personal Narrative

1. For full discussion of this concept, see David King Dunaway's "Telling
Lives: The Aftermath" (11–18), Margaret B. Blackman's "Introduction:
The Afterlife of the Life History" (1–9), and other essays on the topic in a
special issue of the *Journal of Narrative and Life History* 2 (1): 1992. In her
introduction, Blackman observes, "Although one associates afterlife with
postpublication, the afterlife of the life history really begins long before
the life story is published" (5).

2. We rode around the reservation several times, mostly on back roads to
his grandfather's ranch, but also off-reservation to places he had worked.
These trips always put him in good humor and led to more narration,
none of which I recorded, unfortunately. On one trip, to the house his
father had built near the Santa Cruz River, my old Rambler station wagon
slid off the muddy road and mired in a ditch, scaring my six-year-old
daughter, though none of us was hurt. Ted tramped up the road and came

336

back with the reservation farm agent, who pulled it out with his tractor. Nothing much ever rattled Ted, not even the clatter when the fan went into the radiator on another trip. That one took a bit more complex arrangements to solve.

3. Mattina speaks to this issue when he says that he tried to publish a linguistic-focused collection of Colville stories without success because it was rejected for lack of contextualizing materials required for interpretation or interest except from grammarians (1985: 1).

4. While some tellers of traditional Native American lore own the stories they tell by virtue of community authorization of the particular teller and story, traditional tellers do not make the story in the sense of drawing on lived experience to form the narrative substance; rather, they create a new "edition" of an established story with each performance.

5. Another sort of framing device also works to establish the authority of the collector-editor rather than the narrator. Acknowledgments, endnotes, and bibliographies all establish the collector-editor's position in the academic community. As Edward M. Bruner points out, "A bibliographic citation is very much a part of the text but is not just an objective reference: it is also a political statement that stakes the author's claim to a position within a particular scholarly tradition" (1993: 330).

6. Lest I seem too sympathetic toward presses, be assured I realize how powerful they are in dictating what does and does not get published and how conservative most are in their decisions to invest in Native American literatures and anthropology texts at all. The impact of their power, of course, is directly connected to academic politics and the need for scholars to publish, which puts scholars at a great disadvantage in negotiating changes in press publication policies. Added to that is the fact that most presses hold copyright on the books they put under contract, which means writers have little legal leverage in the production or postpublication of their work.

7. Contrary to this view, Roland Barthes argues that it is the responsibility of the reader to integrate a text. He writes that the multiplicity of the text is collected in, "not the author, as has hitherto been claimed, but the reader; the reader is the very space in which are inscribed, without any of them being lost, all the citations out of which a writing is made; the unity of a text is not in its origin but in its destination" (1989: 54).

Presses, unfortunately are not willing to bank on the validity of Barthes's statement.

8. I've had personal experience with this attitude. When I edited the written autobiography by Refugio Savala, a Yaqui Indian (1980), the methodological introduction I wrote was excised from the manuscript by the press that accepted it for publication. As a graduate student with no track record of book publication, I felt I had no recourse but to accede to their decision. I was actively seeking an academic position, and a book under contract was too important to jeopardize. I regret that I didn't take the risk and place it with a more enlightened press. *Autobiography of a Yaqui Poet* is now out of print and the press that controls the copyright has refused to let another press that would publish a methodological introduction re-issue it. Presses have a great deal of power to determine not only what but how Native American personal narratives get into print.

9. Books by authors such as Renato Rosaldo (1980), Marjorie Shostak (1981), Jean-Paul Dumont (1978), Vincent Crapanzano (1980), Michael Taussig (1984), et al. also use unconventional approaches and incorporate substantial interpretive material, but they are not on Native American subjects so I have not included them as examples of publication of unconventional or experimental studies.

10. I do not cite Raymond DeMallie's *The Sixth Grandfather: Black Elk's Teachings Given to John Neihardt* (1984) here because this study does not integrate Black Elk's narrative with DeMallie's analysis of process, and DeMallie is not a collaborator in the original project.

11. I'm not sure he would agree with this appellation, but his work on Native American myth consistently crosses disciplinary lines, and he has made significant contributions to Native American oral traditions courses and scholarship.

12. Had the job market not been so bad at the time, I doubt that the committee would have taken the risk of letting me pursue the Rios project. Also, because I was older than most of the graduate students by about ten years, I think my potential for a job was not taken very seriously at the time. In other words, I was not seen as a particularly promising doctoral student, so my unconventional request was of less concern that it otherwise might have been.

13. Barre Toelken supports the view that even where collaboration by Native

Americans is voluntary, the benefits realized from the "partnership" accrue largely to the collector, not the narrator (1998: 389).

14. Keya Ganguly points out that "it is useful to remember that it is a standard colonialist tactic to cast the other as a regressive image of the self, as if the colonized have no discursive subjectivity of their own" (1990: 74).

15. Barre Toelken asks a similar question in his recent article about his work with Navajo traditional storyteller Hugh Yellowman and his disposition of the tape recordings they made thirty years ago. He writes, "What could I have done differently to have brought about another resolution?" (1998: 388). He also regrets not having made a plan with Yellowman for the long-term life and completion of their project.

16. Julie Cruikshank writes that "work conducted during one period, within one set of guidelines, will inevitably be evaluated differently a generation later. . . . The theoretical perspectives that animate one generation of scholars are frequently reinterpreted by the next as the dead hand of history" (1998: 161).

17. As Jeanette Harris notes, "There is really no such thing as a completed text if, by that term, we mean a piece of discourse that cannot be revised or rewritten or used as an impetus for another text" (1990: 66).

18. Graham Watson argues that it is also necessary that "readers should learn to tolerate unending ambiguity" (1987: 36).

19. Perhaps any inscription of subaltern narrative is by its very nature limited and ethically questionable. Gayatri Spivak notes that "ethics is the experience of the impossible," even when extensive fieldwork is undertaken to establish "ethical singularity" with the other ("Preface" 1995: xxx, xxiv).

20. Tribal research and publication policies like those enacted by the Hopi and Yaqui nations are beginning to have a balancing effect on the heretofore unrestricted freedom of academics to collect, interpret, and publish tribal materials.

21. As long as the original documents — tapes, transcripts — are available, reinterpretation potential is endless. That's why it is so important that all materials from a field and writing project be archived.

22. A good deal has been written on this topic, from Vine Deloria's *Custer Died for Your Sins* (1988); to a special issue of *The American Indian Quarterly* (20 [1]: 1996), edited by Devon A. Mihesuah; to *Indians and Anthropologists* (1997), edited by Thomas Biolsi and Larry J. Zimmerman,

though little has been published directly on the ethics of Native American personal narrative appropriation.

23. A notable exception to this is the American Indian Lives series from the University of Nebraska Press, which has a policy of book revenues being shared with designated community organizations.

24. I was seriously taken aback when I contacted Michael Rios regarding publication of this volume. Though I knew Ted did not have a warm relationship with his son, I was unprepared for the response I got. When I informed him that I was completing the book started in 1974—I had met him then and he knew about the project—and I wanted to make arrangements for royalty payments to the family and ask some questions about his father, he was terse and firm in his response. He wanted nothing to do with anything related to his father, including book royalties, and I could do whatever I chose with them.

25. Don Handelman notes that the products of cross-cultural discourses "are the commodities of the ethnographer's career; in varying degrees, he or she claims proprietary rights over them for professional purposes. . . . Without the commodities, identified with his or her name, the ethnographer would be largely anonymous, and so unable to pursue a career" (1993: 146). The demand for professional individuation and production is an institutional one that maintains the subordination of the field to the academy through the appropriation of Native discourse.

26. I continued to teach courses and still do teach Native American literatures to graduate students and direct dissertation projects, though no field projects. Courses are a venue for discussion of the question of cultural property and academic politics as well as Native American texts. During the six-year hiatus in my scholarly work on Native American literatures, I have gone into the field only to assist Allison Sekaquaptewa Lewis, a Hopi, in collecting material for tribal use. I will not take on any other scholarly projects in Native American cultural or literary inscription as I finish out my professional career, though I will continue to teach Native American students how to collect and work with Native American texts, work with Allison toward finishing her project, and encourage non-Native American students to study and bring current theoretical and ethical sensibilities to Native American texts.

27. Phyllis Morrow argues in her essay "On Shaky Ground" that in collabo-

rative narratives "we are caught between the author and narrative functions, between saying too much and too little. That cultural contexts require explication is no news to folklorists, nor is the dilemma of just how much contextual information is necessary." She goes on to ask, "Is this a legitimate enterprise? It seems that collaboration creates a working space for the recognition of cultural difference, but it is merely a staging area for a more honest and self-aware interaction than that represented by the old research/informant dichotomy, not a solution." She admits, "We satisfy our consciences as best we can and leave the rest of meaning making to you." But finally she argues that collaboration "tends to entangle, untangle, unravel, and enrich dialogue between native and non-Native collaborators, tradition-bearers, listeners, and readers — and it shows us that these apparently contrasting categories of people overlap and intertwine, especially in these media-shared times" (1995: 43, 46–47). While I am inclined to agree with her conclusions, I'm somewhat less optimistic that what she suggests can actually be achieved.

28. Numerous scholars have written on the topic of increasingly active participation by tribal communities in field projects and also on the interest Native American communities have in the work that is published about them. My experience of talking with Tohono O'odham people at San Xavier about Ted Rios and the book project in February of 1998 verifies the interest Native American people take in what is written about them. At San Xavier people expressed eagerness to read about one of their own and also wanted to know about other life stories by tribal members and other literature related to their tribal history and culture.

Epilogue

1. The two photos of Ted in *The South Corner of Time* were among several taken by my former husband at the time of the fieldwork. When our marriage dissolved, I did not think to ask him for the negatives, and they have long since disappeared.

2. I checked out possible video companies that might have the necessary equipment when I returned to Phoenix and was informed that I would have to go to either Los Angeles or New York to find such outdated technology. Since I knew that all the narratives Ted told during the tapings were repeats of ones I had audiotaped, I decided not to pursue the matter.

3. My last check on the state of the archive was in July of 1998. Still unavailable.

4. The fact that there is no record of a funeral is puzzling and suggests that Ted may not have been at San Xavier when he died, which makes the search for records of his death all the more difficult.

BIBLIOGRAPHY

Aaron, Daniel. 1978. *Studies in Biography.* Cambridge: Harvard University Press.

Abrahams, Roger D. 1972. "Folklore and Literature as Performance." *Journal of the Folklore Institute* 9 (2–3): 75–94.

Allport, Gordon. 1942. *The Use of Personal Documents in Psychological Science.* New York: Social Science Council.

Antone, Ella. 1981–82. Interview with the author. Audio tapes. Arizona State Museum, Tucson.

————. 1981–82. Interview with the author. Transcripts. Arizona State Museum, Tucson.

Babcock, Barbara A. 1980. "Reflexivity: Definitions and Discriminations." *Semiotica* 30 (1–2): 1–14.

Bahr, Donald, J. Gregorio, D. I. Lopez, and A. Alvarez. 1974. *Piman Shamanism and Staying Sickness.* Tucson: University of Arizona Press.

Bakhtin, M. M. 1986. *Speech Genres and Other Late Essays.* Austin: University of Texas Press.

Barthes, Roland. 1989. *The Rustle of Language.* Berkeley: University of California Press.

Bataille, Gretchen, and Kathleen M. Sands. 1984. *American Indian Women Telling Their Lives.* Lincoln: University of Nebraska Press.

Bauman, Richard. 1989. "American Folklore Studies and Social Transformation: A Performance-Centered Perspective." *Text and Performance Quarterly* 9 (3): 175–84.

Becker, Howard S. 1966. Introduction to *The Jack-Roller: A Delinquent Boy's Own Story,* by Clifford R. Shaw. Chicago: University of Chicago Press. v–xviii.

Behar, Ruth. 1995. "Rage and Redemption: Reading the Life Story of a Mexican Marketing Woman." In *The Dialogic Emergence of Culture.* Ed. Dennis Tedlock and Bruce Mannheim. Urbana: University of Illinois Press. 148–78.

343

————. 1996. *The Vulnerable Observer: Anthropology That Breaks Your Heart.* Boston: Beacon Press.

Behar, Ruth, and Deborah A. Gordon. 1995. *Women Writing Culture.* Berkeley: University of California Press.

Benstock, Shari. 1988. "Authorizing the Autobiographical." In *The Private Self: Theory and Practice of Women's Autobiographical Writings.* Ed. Shari Benstock. Chapel Hill: University of North Carolina Press. 10–33.

Bergland, Betty. 1994a. "Rereading Photographs and Narratives in Ethnic Autobiography: Memory and Subjectivity." In *Memory, Narrative, and Identity: New Essays in Ethnic American Literatures.* Ed. Amritjit Singh, Joseph T. Skerret Jr., and Robert E. Hogan. Boston: Northeastern University Press. 45–87.

————. 1994b. "Postmodernism and the Autobiographical Subject: Reconstructing the 'Other.'" In *Autobiography and Postmodernism.* Ed. Kathleen Ashley, Leigh Gilmore, Gerald Peters. Amherst: University of Massachusetts Press. 130–66.

Bernstein, Richard J. 1996. "The Hermeneutics of Cross-Cultural Understanding." *Cross-Cultural Conversation: (Initiation).* Ed. Anindita Niyogi Balslev. Atlanta: Scholars Press. 29–42.

Blackman, Margaret B. 1992a. "Introduction: The Afterlife of the Life History." *Journal of Narrative and Life History* 1:1–9.

————. 1992b. *During My Time: Florence Edenshaw Davidson, a Haida Woman.* Seattle: University of Washington Press.

Blaine, Peter, Sr. 1981. *Papagos and Politics.* Tucson: Arizona Historical Society.

Blaine, Peter, Sr., and Michael S. Adams. 1978. Interview audio tape, May 25. Arizona Historical Museum, Tucson.

————. Undated interview transcripts. Arizona Historical Museum, Tucson.

Bloodworth, William. 1978. "Varieties of American Indian Autobiography." *MELUS* 5 (3):67–81.

Bodfish, Waldo, Sr. 1991. *Kusiq: An Eskimo Life History from the Arctic Coast of Alaska.* Ed. William Schneider. Fairbanks: University of Alaska Press.

Boelhower, William. 1991. "The Making of Ethnic Autobiography in the United States." In *American Autobiography: Retrospect and Prospect.* Ed. Paul John Eakin. Madison: University of Wisconsin Press. 123–41.

Brumble, H. David, III. 1988. *American Indian Autobiography.* Los Angeles: University of California Press.

Bruner, Edward M. 1993. "Epilogue: Creative Persona and the Problem of Authenticity." *Creativity/Anthropology.* Ed. Smadar Lavie, Kirink Narayan, and Renato Rosaldo. Ithaca: Cornell University Press. 321–34.

Bruss, Elizabeth W. 1976. *Autobiographical Acts: The Changing Situation of a Literary Genre.* Baltimore: Johns Hopkins University Press.

Burns, Allan. 1995. "Video Production as a Dialogue: The Story of Lynch Hammock." In *The Dialogic Emergence of Culture.* Ed. Dennis Tedlock and Bruce Mannheim. Urbana: University of Illinois Press. 75–95.

Carr, Helen. 1996. *Inventing the American Primitive: Politics, Gender and the Representation of Native American Literary Traditions, 1789–1936.* New York: New York University Press.

Clayton, Jay. 1993. *The Pleasures of Babel: Contemporary American Literature and Theory.* New York: Oxford University Press.

Clements, William M. 1996. *Native American Verbal Art: Texts and Contexts.* Tucson: University of Arizona Press.

Clifford, James. 1983a. "On Ethnographic Authority." *Representations* 1 (2): 118–46.

———. 1983b. "Power and Dialogue in Ethnography." In *Observers Observed: Essays on Ethnographic Fieldwork.* Ed. George W. Stocking Jr. University of Wisconsin Press. 121–55.

———. 1986a. "Introduction: Partial Truths." In *Writing Culture: The Poetics and Politics of Ethnography.* Ed. James Clifford and George E. Marcus. Berkeley: University of California Press. 1–26.

———. 1986b. "On Ethnographic Allegory." In *Writing Culture: The Poetics and Politics of Ethnography.* Ed. James Clifford and George E. Marcus. Berkeley: University of California Press. 98–121.

———. 1990. "Notes on (Field)notes." In *Fieldnotes: The Makings of Anthropology.* Ed. Roger Sanjek. Ithaca: Cornell University Press.

———. 1997. *Routes: Travel and Translation in the Late Twentieth Century.* Cambridge: Harvard University Press.

Cohen, Anthony P. 1992. "Self-Conscious Anthropology." In *Anthropology and Autobiography.* Ed. Judith Okely and Helen Callaway. London: Routledge. 221–41.

Conquergood, Dwight. 1991. "Rethinking Ethnography: Towards a Critical Cultural Politics." *Cultural Monographs* 58 (2): 179–94.

Cook-Lynn, Elizabeth. 1998. "American Indian Intellectualism and the New

Indian Story." In *Natives and Academics: Research and Writing about American Indians.* Ed. Devon A. Mihesuah. Lincoln: University of Nebraska Press. 111–38.

Crang, Mike. 1994. "Spacing Times, Telling Times and Narrating the Past." *Time and Society* 3 (1): 29–45.

Crapanzano, Vincent. 1972. *The Fifth World of Forster Bennett: Portrait of a Navajo.* New York: Viking.

———. 1973. *The Hamadshai: A Study in Moroccan Ethnopsychiatry.* Berkeley: University of California Press.

———. 1980. *Tuhami: Portrait of a Moroccan.* Chicago: University of Chicago Press.

Crick, Malcolm. 1992. "Ali and Me: An Essay in Street-Corner Anthropology." In *Anthropology and Autobiography.* Ed. Judith Okely and Helen Callaway. London: Routledge. 175–92.

Cruikshank, Julie. 1990. *Life Lived Like a Story: Life Stories of Three Yukon Native Elders.* Lincoln: University of Nebraska Press.

———. 1991. *Reading Voices/Dan Dha Ts'edenintthe'e: Oral and Written Interpretations of the Yukon's Past.* Vancouver: Douglas and McIntyre.

———. 1998. *The Social Life of Stories: Narrative and Knowledge in the Yukon Territory.* Lincoln: University of Nebraska Press.

Cruikshank, Moses. 1986. *The Life I've Been Living.* Ed. William Schneider. Fairbanks: University of Alaska Press.

Dauenhauer, Nora Marks, and Richard Dauenhauer, eds. 1987. *Haa Shuka, Our Ancestors: Tlingit Oral Narratives.* Seattle: University of Washington Press.

Davis, Robert Con, and Ronald Schleifer. 1991. *Criticism and Culture: The Role of Critique in Modern Literary Theory.* New York: Longman.

———. 1994. *Contemporary Literary Criticism: Literary and Cultural Studies.* New York: Longman.

Deconcini, Barbara. 1990. *Narrative Remembering.* New York: University Press of America.

Degh, Linda. 1975. *People in the Tobacco Belt: Four Lives.* Ottawa: National Museum of Canada.

Deloria, Vine, Jr. 1988. *Custer Died for Your Sins: An Indian Manifesto.* Norman: University of Oklahoma Press.

———. 1997. Conclusion to *Indians and Anthropologists: Vine Deloria Jr. and the Critique of Anthropology,* ed. Thomas Biolsi and Larry J. Zimmerman. Tucson: University of Arizona Press. 210–21.

DeMallie, Raymond, ed. 1984. *The Sixth Grandfather: Black Elk's Teaching Given to John G. Neihardt.* Lincoln: University of Nebraska Press.

"Demographic and Socio-Cultural Characteristics: Off-Reservation Service Population, Sells Service Unit, Arizona." 1968. Tucson: Health Program Systems Center, Indian Health Service.

Dollard, John. 1949. *The Criteria for the Life History: With Analysis of Six Notable Documents.* New York: Peter Smith.

Dolores, Juan. Undated. "Autobiography." 56-page MS. Bancroft Library, Berkeley.

Dumont, Jean-Paul. 1978. *The Head Man and I: Ambiguity and Ambivalence in the Fieldworking Experience.* Austin: University of Texas Press.

Dunaway, David King. 1992. "Telling Lives: The Aftermath." *Journal of Narrative and Life History* 2 (1): 11–18.

Dunnigan, Timothy. 1998. Telephone conversation with the author, October 21.

Dutton, Bertha P. 1975. *Indians of the American Southwest.* Englewood Cliffs NJ: Prentice-Hall.

Dwyer, Levin. 1977. "Case Study: On the Dialogic of Field Work." *Dialectical Anthropology* 2 (2): 143–51.

Eakin, Paul John. 1985. *Fictions in Autobiography: Studies in the Art of Self-Invention.* Princeton: Princeton University Press.

———. 1989. Foreword to *On Autobiography,* by Philippe Lejeune. Minneapolis: University of Minnesota Press. vii–xxi.

———. 1991. *American Autobiography: Retrospect and Prospect.* Madison: University of Wisconsin Press.

———. 1992. *Touching the World: Reference in Autobiography.* Princeton: Princeton University Press.

Evers, Larry. *Words and Place: Native Literature from the American Southwest.* Videotape series. New York: Clearwater Publishing.

Fabian, Johannes. 1983. *Time and the Other: How Anthropology Makes Its Object.* New York: Columbia University Press.

Feinberg, Richard. 1994. "Contested Worlds: The Politics of Culture and the Politics of Anthropology." *Anthropology and Humanism* 19 (1): 20–35.

Fine, Elizabeth C. 1984. *The Folklore Text from Performance to Print.* Bloomington: Indiana University Press.

Fleishman, Avrom. 1983. *Figures of Autobiography: The Language of Self-Writing in Victorian and Modern England.* Los Angeles: University of California Press.

Fontana, Bernard L. 1960. "Assimilative change: A Papago Indian Case Study." Ph.D. diss., University of Arizona.

———— 1998. Telephone conversation with the author, February 19.

Frank, Gelya. 1979. "Finding the Common Denominator: A Phenomenological Critique of Life History Method." *Ethos* 7 (1): 68–94.

Friedman, Susan Stanford. 1988. "Women's Autobiographical Selves: Theory and Practice." In *The Private Self: Theory and Practice of Women's Autobiographical Writings.* Ed. Shari Benstock. Chapel Hill: University of North Carolina Press. 35–62.

Ganguly, Keya. 1990. "Ethnography, Representation, and the Production of Colonialist Discourse." *Studies in Symbolic Interaction* 11:69–79.

Goffman, Erving. 1974. *Frame Analysis: An Essay on the Organization of Experience.* Cambridge: Harvard University Press.

Graumann, Carl F. 1995. "Commonality, Mutuality, Reciprocity: A Conceptual Introduction." *Mutualities in Dialogue.* Ed. Ivana Markova, Carl F. Graumann, and Klaus Foppa. Cambridge: Cambridge University Press. 1–7.

Griffith, James S. 1992. *Beliefs and Holy Places: A Spiritual Geography of the Pimeria Alta.* Tucson: University of Arizona Press.

Grigely, Joseph. 1995. *Textualterity: Art, Theory, and Textual Criticism.* Ann Arbor: University of Michigan Press.

Gusdorf, Georges. 1980. "Conditions and Limits of Autobiography." In *Autobiography: Essays Theoretical and Critical.* Ed. James Olney. Princeton: Princeton University Press. 28–48.

Handelman, Don. 1993. "The Absence of Others, the Presence of Texts." In *Creativity/Anthropology.* Ed. Smadar Lavie, Kirin Narayan, and Renato Rosaldo. Ithaca: Cornell University Press. 133–52.

Hanlon, Capistran John. 1971. "Acculturation at San Xavier: Changing Boundaries of a Southwest Indian Community." Ph.D. diss., University of Colorado.

Harris, Jeanette. 1990. *Expressive Discourse.* Dallas: Southern Methodist University Press.

Harris, Marvin. 1968. *The Rise of Anthropological Theory: A History of Theories of Culture.* New York: Thomas Y. Crowell.

Hayano, David M. 1979. "Auto-Ethnography: Paradigms, Problems and Prospects." *Human Organization* 38 (1): 99–104.

Horne, Esther Burnett, and Sally McBeth. 1998. *Essie's Story: The Life and Legacy of a Shoshone Teacher.* Lincoln: University of Nebraska Press.

Hutcheon, Linda. 1993. "Beginning to Theorize Postmodernism." In *A Postmodern Reader.* Ed. Joseph Natoli and Linda Hutcheon. Albany: State University of New York Press. 243–72.

Hymes, Dell. 1981. *"In Vain I Tried to Tell You": Essays in Native American Ethnopoetics.* Philadelphia: University of Pennsylvania Press.

Jameson, Fredric. 1981. *The Political Unconscious: Narrative as a Socially Symbolic Act.* Ithaca: Cornell University Press.

Jose, Venture. 1981. "I'Itoi and Ho'ok'oks." *The South Corner of Time: Hopi, Navaho, Papago, Yaqui Tribal Literature.* Ed. Larry Evers. Tucson: University of Arizona Press. 110–21.

Kaiser, Rudolf. 1984. "Chief Seattle's Speech(es): American Origin and European Reception." In *Recovering the Word: Essays on Native American Literature.* Ed. Brian Swann and Arnold Krupat. Los Angeles: University of California Press. 497–536.

Kelly, William H. 1974. "The Papago Indians of Arizona." *Papago Indians III.* New York: Garland Publishing.

King, William S. 1954. "The Folk Catholicism of the Tucson Papagos. M.A. thesis, University of Arizona.

Kluckhohn, Clyde. 1945. "The Personal Document in Anthropological Science." In *The Use of Personal Documents in History, Anthropology and Sociology.* Ed. L. Gottshalk, Clyde Kluckhohn, and R. Angell. New York: Social Science Research Council. 78–193.

Krupat, Arnold. 1981. "American Autobiography: The Western Tradition." *Georgia Review* 35 (2): 307–17.

———. 1985. *For Those Who Come After: A Study of Native American Autobiography.* Los Angeles: University of California Press.

———. 1991. "Native American Autobiography and the Synecdochic Self." In *American Autobiography: Retrospect and Prospect.* Ed. Paul John Eakin. Madison: University of Wisconsin Press. 171–94.

———. 1992. *Ethnocentrism: Ethnography, History, Literature.* Berkeley: University of California Press.

———. 1996. *The Turn to the Native: Studies in Criticism and Culture.* Lincoln: University of Nebraska Press.

Langness, L. L., and Gelya Frank. 1981. *Lives: An Anthropological Approach to Biography.* Novato CA: Chandler and Sharp Publishers.

LeJeune, Philippe. 1971. *L'Autobiographie en France.* Paris: A. Colin.

———. 1989. *On Autobiography.* Minneapolis: University of Minnesota Press.

Leo, John Robert. 1978. "Riding Geronimo's Cadillac: *His Own Story* and the Circumstancing of Text." *Journal of American Culture* 1 (4): 819–37.

Lewis, Oscar. 1959. *Five Families: Mexican Case Studies in the Culture of Poverty.* New York. Basic Books.

———. 1961. *The Children of Sanchez: Autobiography of a Mexican Family.* New York: Random House.

———. 1963. *Life in a Mexican Village: Tepoztlan Restudies.* Urbana: University of Illinois Press.

Linderman, Frank. 1962. *Plenty-coups: Chief of the Crows.* Lincoln: University of Nebraska Press.

———. 1974. *Pretty-shield: Medicine Woman of the Crows.* Lincoln. University of Nebraska Press.

Lucy, John A. 1993. "Reflexive Language and the Human Disciplines." In *Reflexive Language: Reported Speech and Metapragmatics.* Ed. John A. Lucy. Cambridge: Cambridge University Press. 9–23.

Lurie, Nancy Oestreich. 1961. *Mountain Wolf Woman, Sister of Crashing Thunder: The Autobiography of a Winnebago Indian.* Ann Arbor: University of Michigan Press.

Mack, Corbett. 1996. *The Life of a Northern Paiute as told by Michael Hittman.* Lincoln: University of Nebraska Press.

Marcus, George E. 1997. "The Uses of Complicity in The Changing Mise-en-Scène of Anthropological Fieldwork." *Representations* 59 (2): 85–108.

Marcus, George E., and Michael M. J. Fischer. 1986. *Anthropology as Cultural Critique: An Experimental Moment in the Human Sciences.* Chicago: University of Chicago Press.

Markova, Ivana, Carl F. Graumann, and Klaus Foppa. 1995. *Mutualities in Dialogue.* Cambridge: Cambridge University Press.

Mattina, Anthony. 1985. *The Golden Woman: The Narrative of Peter J. Seymour.* Tucson: University of Arizona Press.

McCarthy, James. 1985. *A Papago Traveler: The Memories of James McCarthy.* Tucson: University of Arizona Press.

McCooey, David. 1996. *Artful Histories: Modern Australian Autobiography.* Cambridge: Cambridge University Press.

Mihesuah, Devon A., ed. 1996. "Writing About American Indians." Special issue of *American Indian Quarterly* 20 (1): 1–108.

Mintz, Sidney W. 1979. "The Anthropological Interview and the Life History." *The Oral History Review* 7: 18–26.

Moore, David. 1994. "Decolonializing Criticism: Reading Dialectics and Dialogics in Native American Literatures." *Studies in American Indian Literatures* 6 (4): 7–35.

————. 1997. "Sensitive Material: Cultural Representation as Cultural Property." Unpublished MS. 1–27.

Morrow, Phyllis. 1995. "On Shaky Ground: Folklore, Collaboration, and Problematic Outcomes." In *When Our Words Return: Writing, Hearing, and Remembering Oral Traditions of Alaska and the Yukon*. Ed. Phyllis Morrow and William Schneider. Logan: Utah State University Press. 27–51.

Murray, David. 1991. *Forked Tongues: Speech, Writing and Representation in North American Indian Texts*. Bloomington: Indiana University Press.

Neihardt, John G. 1979. *Black Elk Speaks*. Lincoln: University of Nebraska Press.

Patterson, Kay. 1998. Interview with the author, February 18. Cornelia Branch, Phelps Dodge, Ajo, Arizona.

Penn, W. S. 1995. *All My Sins Are Relatives*. Lincoln: University of Nebraska Press.

Renza, Louis A. 1977. "The Veto of the Imagination: A Theory of Autobiography." *New Literary History* 9: 1–26.

Ricoeur, Paul. 1976. *Interpretation Theory: Discourse and the Surplus of Meaning*. Fort Worth: Texas Christian University Press.

Rios, Theodore. 1969. "Autobiography of Theodore Rios, a Papago Indian as Told to Timothy Dunnigan." Arizona State Museum, Tucson.

————. 1975. *Papago Storyteller*. KUAT videotape. Produced by Larry Evers. Tucson: Southwest Folklore Center, University of Arizona.

————. 1981. "The Egg." In *The South Corner of Time: Hopi, Navajo, Papago, Yaqui Tribal Literature*. Ed. Larry Evers. Tucson: University of Arizona Press. 151–54.

Rios, Theodore, and Kathleen Mullen Sands. 1974–75. Interview audio tapes. Arizona State Museum, Tucson.

————. 1984. Interview transcripts. Arizona State Museum, Tucson.

Robinson, John A. 1981. "Personal Narratives Reconsidered." *Journal of American Folklore* 94 (371): 58–85.

Rosaldo, Renato. 1980. *Ilongot Head Hunting 1883–1974: A Study in Society and History.* Stanford: Stanford University Press.

———. 1989. *Culture and Truth: The Remaking of Social Analysis.* Boston: Beacon Press.

Ruoff, A. LaVonne. 1990. *American Indian Literatures.* New York: Modern Language Association.

Ruppert, James. 1995. *Mediation in Contemporary Native American Fiction.* Norman: University of Oklahoma Press.

Said, Edward. 1978. *Orientalism.* New York: Pantheon.

———. 1983. *The World, the Text, and the Critic.* Cambridge: Harvard University Press.

———. 1993. *Culture and Imperialism.* New York: Knopf.

Sands, Kathleen Mullen. 1974. Rios interview fieldnotes. Arizona State Museum, Tucson.

———. 1980. "A Man Made of Words: The Life and Letters of a Yaqui Poet." *American Indian Culture and Research Journal* 4 (1–2): 143–59.

———. 1983. "Telling 'A Good One': Creating a Papago Autobiography." *MELUS* 10 (3): 55–65.

———. 1989. "Ethnography, Autobiography, and Fiction: Narrative Strategies in Cultural Analysis." In *Forum I: American Indian Literatures.* Ed. Laura Coltelli. Pisa: Servizio Editoriale Universitario. 53–67.

———. 1991. "Indian Women's Voices Past and Present." *American Women's Autobiography: Fea(s)ts of Memory.* Ed. Margo Culley. Madison: University of Wisconsin Press. 268–94.

———. 1998a. "Narrative Resistance: Native American Collaborative Autobiography." *Studies in American Indian Literatures* 10 (1): 1–19.

———. 1998b. "Collaboration and Colonialism: Native American Women's Autobiography. *MELUS* 22 (4): 39–59.

Sanjek, Roger. 1990. "A Vocabulary for Fieldnotes." In *Fieldnotes: The Makings of Anthropology.* Ed. Roger Sanjek. Ithaca: Cornell University Press. 92–118.

Sarris, Greg. 1993. *Keeping Slug Woman Alive: A Holistic Approach to American Indian Texts.* Los Angeles: University of California Press.

Savala, Refugio. 1980. *Autobiography of a Yaqui Poet.* Tucson: University of Arizona Press.

Scheub, Harold. 1977. "Body and Image in Oral Narrative Performance." *New Literary History* 8 (3): 345–67.

Shapiro, Stephen A. 1968. "The Dark Continent of Literature: Autobiography." *Comparative Literature Studies* 5 (4): 421–54.

Shostak, Marjorie. 1981. *Nisa: The Life and Words of a !Kung Woman.* Cambridge: Harvard University Press.

Simmons, Leo W. 1974. *Sun Chief: The Autobiography of a Hopi Indian.* New Haven: Yale University Press.

Smith, Paul. 1988. *Discerning the Subject.* Minneapolis: University of Minnesota Press.

Smith, William, Jr. 1975. "American Indian Autobiographies." *American Indian Quarterly* 2 (3): 237–45.

Spicer, Edward H. 1962. *Cycles of Conquest: The Impact of Spain, Mexico and the United States on the Indians of the Southwest.* Tucson: University of Arizona Press.

Spiro, Melford E. 1972. "Cognition in Culture-and-Personality." In *Culture and Cognition: Rules, Maps, and Plans.* Ed. James P. Spradley. San Francisco: Chandler Publishing. 100–109.

Spivak, Gayatri. 1995. Preface to *Imaginary Maps,* by Mahasweta Devi. Trans. and ed. Gayatri Spivak. New York: Routledge. xxiii–xxxix.

Stahl, Sandra Dolby. 1989. *Literary Folkloristics and the Personal Narrative.* Bloomington: Indiana University Press.

Stocking, George W., Jr. 1983. *Observers Observed: Essays on Ethnographic Fieldwork.* Madison: University of Wisconsin Press.

Stoeltje, Beverly J., and Richard Bauman. 1988. "The Semiotics of Folklore Performance." In *The Semiotic Web.* Ed. Thomas A. Sebeok and Jean Umiker Sebeok. New York: Mouton de Gruyter. 585–95.

Streefkerk, Hein. 1993. *On the Production of Knowledge: Fieldwork in South Gujarat, 1971–1991.* Amsterdam: VU University Press.

Taussig, Michael. 1980. *The Devil and Commodity Fetishism in South America.* Chapel Hill: University of North Carolina Press.

———. 1987. *Shamanism, Colonialism, and the Wild Man: A Study in Terror and Healing.* Chicago: University of Chicago Press.

Tedlock, Barbara. 1991. "From Participant Observation to the Observation of Participation: The Emergence of Narrative Ethnography." *Journal of Anthropological Research* 47 (1): 69–94.

———. 1992. *The Beautiful and the Dangerous: Encounters with the Zuni Indians.* New York: Viking.

Tedlock, Dennis. 1983. *The Spoken Word and the Work of Interpretation.* Philadelphia: University of Pennsylvania Press.

Tedlock, Dennis, and Bruce Mannheim. 1995. *Dialogic Emergence of Culture.* Urbana: University of Illinois Press.

Theisz, R. D. 1981. "The Critical Collaboration: Introductions as a Gateway to the Study of Native American Bi-Autobiography." *American Indian Culture and Research Journal* 5 (1): 65–80.

Tierney-Tello, Mary Beth. 1999. "Testimony, Ethics and the Aesthetic in Diamela Eltit." PMLA 114 (1): 78–96.

Titon, Jeff Todd. 1980. "The Life Story." *Journal of American Folklore* 95 (369): 276–92.

Todorov, Tzvetan. 1984. *The Conquest of America: The Question of the Other.* New York: Harper and Row.

Toelken, Barre. 1998. "The Yellowman Tapes, 1966–1997." *Journal of American Folklore* 111 (442): 381–91.

Trennert, Robert A., Jr. 1988. *The Phoenix Indian School: Forced Assimilation in Arizona 1891–1930.* Norman: University of Oklahoma Press.

Tyler, Stephen A. 1986. "Post-Modern Ethnography: From Document of the Occult to Occult Document. In *Writing Culture: The Poetics and Politics of Ethnography.* Ed. James Clifford and George E. Marcus. Berkeley: University of California Press. 122–40.

Underhill, Ruth M. 1938. *Singing for Power: The Song Magic of the Papago Indians of Southern Arizona.* Berkeley: University of California Press.

———. 1939. *Social Organization of the Papago Indians.* New York: Columbia University Press.

———. 1940. *Papago Indians of Arizona and Their Relatives the Pima.* Washington DC: Education Division, U.S. Office of Indian Affairs.

———. 1951. *People of the Crimson Evening.* Washington DC: Education Division, U.S. Office of Indian Affairs.

———. 1979. *Papago Woman.* New York: Holt, Rinehart and Winston.

———. 1981. Interview with the author, November 2. Denver, Colorado.

Vizenor, Gerald. 1994. *Manifest Manners: Postindian Warriors of Survivance.* Hanover: Wesleyan University Press.

Waddell, Jack O. 1969. *Papago Indians at Work.* Tucson: University of Arizona Press.

Watson, Graham. 1987. "Make Me Reflexive—But Not Yet: Strategies for Managing Essential Reflexivity in Ethnographic Discourse." *Journal of Anthropological Research* 43 (1): 29–42.

Watson, Lawrence C. 1976. "Understanding a Life History as a Subjective Document: Hermeneutical and Phenomenological Perspectives." *Ethos* 4 (1): 95–131.

Watson, Lawrence C., and Maria-Barbara Watson Franke. 1985. *Interpreting Life Histories: An Anthropological Inquiry.* New Brunswick: Rutgers University Press.

Webster, Steven. 1982. "Dialogue and Fiction in Ethnography." *Dialectical Anthropology* 7 (2): 91–114.

West, Rebecca. 1994. *Black Lamb and Grey Falcon: A Journey through Yugoslavia.* New York: Penguin.

Whitehead, Tony Larry, and Mary Ellen Conaway, eds. 1986. Introduction to *Self, Sex and Gender in Cross-Cultural Fieldwork.* Urbana: University of Illinois Press. 1–15.

Wiget, Andrew. 1985. *Native American Literature.* Boston: Twayne Publishers.

Wolf, Eric. 1982. *Europe and the People without History.* Berkeley: University of California Press.

Wong, Hertha Dawn. 1992. *Sending My Heart Back Across the Years: Tradition and Innovation in Native American Autobiography.* New York: Oxford University Press.

Worthen, W. B. 1998. "Drama, Performativity, and Performance." PMLA 113 (5): 1093–1107.

Xie, Shaobo. 1997. "Rethinking the Problem of Postcolonialism." *New Literary History* 28: 7–19.

INDEX

Adam, Henry, 316 n.17
Adams, Michael S., 111, 122, 124, 128
Agnes (grandmother), 1, 13, 21
Ajo, 106, 108, 136; mine at (*see* Phelps
  Dodge Copper mine)
alcohol: among Native Americans, 329–30
  n.2; and Papagos, 330 n.5; and Ted Rios,
  148–50, 153–55, 157, 233, 329–30 n.2, 330
  n.3 n.7
Allport, Gordon W., 316 n.14
Anselma (mother), 2, 15, 23, 162, 307 n.3
"The Anthropological Interview and the
  Life History" (Mintz), 313 n.16
anthropology, 30, 312 n.7, 313 n.16
Antone, Ella Lopez, 111, 120, 142–45,
  328–29 n.35
Apaches, 95, 116, 167, 178, 204
Arizona Historical Museum, 262, 264
Arizona State Museum, 5, 10, 308 n.13
Arnita, William, 1, 307 n.3
asymmetry, of interactants, 39
Aurelius, Marcus, 265
autobiography: (*see also* personal narrative), 314 n.1; agency in, 69; chronology
  in, 335 n.4; collaborative (*see* collaborative autobiography); defined, 67;
  and discourse, 315 n.11; dualism in, 328
  n.31; dual signature in, 69–70; ethnic
  American, 327 n.29; Euro-American
  understanding of, 3–4, 16, 51, 67, 69,
  71, 77, 211; and genealogy, 314 n.3; and
  intention, 314 n.2; literary, 71, 77; as
  literary genre, 51, 316 n.18; meaning and
  identity in, 67; motivation revealed in,
  69; Native American (*see* autobiography, Native American; autobiography,
  Papago; collaborative autobiography,

Native American; personal narrative,
  Native American); partiality of, 321 n.24;
  pattern in openings of, 326–27 n.21;
  repetition in, 211, 335 n.2; subjectivity in,
  315 n.10, 316 n.14; third-person, 316 n.17;
  transitional, 324 n.6; truthfulness in, 330
  n.8; unending ambiguity of, 251, 339 n.17
  n.18
autobiography, Native American: (*see also*
  autobiography, Papago; collaborative
  autobiography, Native American; personal narrative, Native American), 77,
  78; alcoholism in, 329–30 n.2; categories
  of, 323 n.1; critical studies of, xiv–xv,
  78, 81, 319 n.10; and cultural conventions, 326 n.16; danger of self-reflexivity
  in, 320 n.17; and ethics, xii, xiv; and
  ethnography, 85; Euro-American understanding of, 80; historical and cultural
  background in, 214; and literary genre,
  30–31, 80, 85, 318 n.6; methodology in,
  79–80, 317–18 n.3, 318 n.5 n.6 n.8, 320–21
  n.20; and oral tradition, 181, 210; personality and culture form of, xv; place
  in, 327 n.29; present compared to past
  in, 100; as response to white initiative,
  314 n.2; stories in, 334 n.14
autobiography, non-Western, 71
autobiography, Papago, 111; dualism in,
  328 n.31; and the past, 326–27 n.21; and
  the Rios-Sands project, 111–12, 142–
  45; themes and cultural values in, 112,
  141–42, 145, 324 n.4
"Autobiography of a Papago Woman"
  (Underhill), 325 n.14
Autobiography of a Yaqui Poet (Savala), 310
  n.23, 338 n.8

357

ethnographic biography of, 24–26; contract with Kathleen M. Sands signed by, 10–11, 30, 308 n.12, 308–9 n.13; cultural origins of narrative of, 70, 112, 210–11, 212, 213–14; death of, xv, 34, 262, 264–65, 264–65, 342 n.4; depersonalization by, 70–71, 98; divorce of, 157, 216, 233; early life of, 219–24, 227; family home of, 329 n.38; family of, 1–2, 160–62, 164, 165, 166; fluency in English of, 307–8 n.8; identity of, 104–5, 108, 129, 328 n.31; interviews with Dunnigan, 6, 7, 9, 11–12, 17, 29–30, 311 n.4, 315 n.4; Kathleen M. Sands's first encounter with, 4–10; Kathleen M. Sands resisted by, 48–49, 121, 155–56, 210, 211, 250, 331 n.13; marriage of, 105, 157, 216, 217; and meaning, 68–69, 316 n.15; mining work of, 106–8, 127, 132–38, 140, 165, 169, 182, 216–17, 230–33, 232–33, 327 n.27, 336 n.9; money given to, 31–34, 312 n.9; movie work of, 101, 108, 132, 139–40, 169–79, 177–79, 211, 217, 233, 327 n.28, 332 n.15; narration controlled by, 155–56, 157, 164–65, 182, 211, 258; narrative development of subjectivity by, 181, 182, 188–89, 190, 212, 240, 332 n.2; narrative embellished by, 95–96; narrative style of, xiii, 5, 70, 92–93, 115, 120–21, 209–12, 214, 238, 239–40, 250, 258, 334–35 n.1, 335 n.2; and the non-Papago world, xii, 128–29, 197, 222–27, 239; photographs of, 261, 341 n.1 n.2; place in narrative of, 239; present compared to past by, 99–100, 118, 127, 131, 145, 237–39; and public life, 123–24; relationship with Fontana, 5, 308 n.9; relationship with Kathleen M. Sands, 147, 157–58, 241–43, 262, 336–37 n.2; and San Xavier, 141, 327 n.29, 328 n.33; shortened form of name of, 307 n.5; storytelling by, 92, 182–208, 190–91; temporary work of, 217–18, 233–36, 237; traditional skills learned by, 221–22, 227; travels of, 140–41, 140–41, 157, 217, 328 n.31; voice of, 18–19

Rios, Theodore Jr. (son), 105, 216, 232, 336 n.11
Rios-Dunnigan project, 147–48, 156, 179, 330 n.3; chronology in, 218, 331 n.13, 335 n.6; transcripts of, 158–64
Rios-Sands project, xi, xii–xiii, 315 n.5; alternate presentation of, 109–10; as bicultural work, 111–12; chronology in, 52–53, 209, 210, 212–19, 239, 315 n.6, 335 n.5; colonialism in, 33–35; dual signature in, 69–70, 316 n.16; editing of, 19–24, 310 n.24; in English language, 307–8 n.8; and ethnography, 29, 52, 77–78, 110; historical and cultural background in, 219; inscription of, 28; interviews in, 89, 321 n.23; Kathleen M. Sands's criticism of, 19, 77–78, 92; lack of closure of, 261–65; as literary genre, 51, 110; methodology of, xvi, 30, 52; models lacking for, 79, 80, 80–81, 110, 317 n.1, 318 n.9, 320–21 n.20; original intention of, xiii–xiv, 44, 51; and Papago culture, 142, 257–58; political and ethical aspects of, 241, 243–44, 249–53, 254–60, 338 n.12, 339 n.15 n.17 n.19, 340 n.24; precedents for, 81–82, 87; prepublication afterlife of, 241, 243, 250–51, 261–65, 336 n.1, 342 n.3; and San Xavier, 259–60, 341 n.28; subjectivity in, xii–xiii, 76–77, 257–58; taping circumstances of, 147, 329 n.1; Ted Rios's intentions concerning, 1, 3, 34, 79, 156–57, 179, 182, 189, 208; transcripts of, 328 n.34; validity of, 256; voices in, xv–xvi; what ifs of, 91–92
Rio Yaqui, 330 n.4
Robinson, John A., 187, 188
Rocky Mountain Mix, 333–34 n.13
rodeos, 167
Rosaldo, Renato, 259, 338 n.9
Rosanna (half sister), 2
roundups, 101

saguaros, 2, 93–95, 117–18, 154; harvesting, 235, 236
Said, Edward, 141–42, 247

In the series AMERICAN INDIAN LIVES

I Stand in the Center of the Good
Interviews with Contemporary Native American Artists
Edited by Lawrence Abbott

Authentic Alaska
Voices of Its Native Writers
Edited by Susan B. Andrews and John Creed

Dreaming the Dawn
Conversations with Native Artists and Activists
By E. K. Caldwell
Introduction by Elizabeth Woody

Chief
The Life History of Eugene Delorme, Imprisoned Santee Sioux
Edited by Inéz Cardozo-Freeman

Winged Words
American Indian Writers Speak
Edited by Laura Coltelli

Life, Letters and Speeches
By George Copway (Kahgegagahbowh)
Edited by A. LaVonne Brown Ruoff and Donald B. Smith

Life Lived Like a Story
Life Stories of Three Yukon Native Elders
By Julie Cruikshank in collaboration with Angela Sidney,
Kitty Smith, and Annie Ned

LaDonna Harris
A Comanche Life
By LaDonna Harris
Edited by H. Henrietta Stockel

Essie's Story
The Life and Legacy of a Shoshone Teacher
By Esther Burnett Horne and Sally McBeth

Song of Rita Joe
Autobiography of a Mi'kmaq Poet
By Rita Joe

Catch Colt
By Sidner J. Larson

Alex Posey
Creek Poet, Journalist, and Humorist
By Daniel F. Littlefield Jr.

Mourning Dove
A Salishan Autobiography
Edited by Jay Miller

John Rollin Ridge
His Life and Works
By James W. Parins

Singing an Indian Song
A Biography of D'Arcy McNickle
By Dorothy R. Parker

Crashing Thunder
The Autobiography of an American Indian
Edited by Paul Radin

Telling a Good One
*The Process of a Native American
Collaborative Biography*
By Theodore Rios and Kathleen Mullen Sands

Sacred Feathers
*The Reverend Peter Jones (Kahkewaquonaby)
and the Mississauga Indians*
By Donald B. Smith

Grandmother's Grandchild
My Crow Indian Life
By Alma Hogan Snell
Edited by Becky Matthews
Foreword by Peter Nabokov

Blue Jacket
Warrior of the Shawnees
By John Sugden

I Tell You Now
Autobiographical Essays by Native American Writers
Edited by Brian Swann and Arnold Krupat

Postindian Conversations
By Gerald Vizenor and A. Robert Lee

Chainbreaker
The Revolutionary War Memoirs of Governor Blacksnake
As told to Benjamin Williams
Edited by Thomas S. Abler

Standing in the Light
A Lakota Way of Seeing
By Severt Young Bear and R. D. Theisz